Evaluative Perception

MIND ASSOCIATION OCCASIONAL SERIES

This series consists of carefully selected volumes of significant original papers on predefined themes, normally growing out of a conference supported by a Mind Association Major Conference Grant. The Association nominates an editor or editors for each collection, and may cooperate with other bodies in promoting conferences or other scholarly activities in connection with the preparation of particular volumes.

Director, Mind Association: Julian Dodd
Publications Officer: Sarah Sawyer

RECENTLY PUBLISHED IN THE SERIES:

In the Light of Experience
Edited by Johan Gersel, Rasmus Thybo Jensen, Morten S. Thaning, and Søren Overgaard

Perceptual Ephemera
Edited by Thomas Crowther and Clare Mac Cumhaill

Common Sense in the Scottish Enlightenment
Edited by Charles Bradford Bow

Art and Belief
Edited by Ema Sullivan-Bissett, Helen Bradley, and Paul Noordhof

The Actual and the Possible
Edited by Mark Sinclair

Thinking about the Emotions
Edited by Alix Cohen and Robert Stern

Art, Mind, and Narrative
Edited by Julian Dodd

The Social and Political Philosophy of Mary Wollstonecraft
Edited by Sandrine Bergès and Alan Coffee

The Epistemic Life of Groups
Edited by Michael S. Brady and Miranda Fricker

Reality Making
Edited by Mark Jago

Evaluative Perception

EDITED BY
Anna Bergqvist
and Robert Cowan

OXFORD
UNIVERSITY PRESS

OXFORD
UNIVERSITY PRESS

Great Clarendon Street, Oxford, OX2 6DP,
United Kingdom

Oxford University Press is a department of the University of Oxford.
It furthers the University's objective of excellence in research, scholarship,
and education by publishing worldwide. Oxford is a registered trade mark of
Oxford University Press in the UK and in certain other countries

© the several contributors 2018

The moral rights of the authors have been asserted

First Edition published in 2018

Impression: 1

All rights reserved. No part of this publication may be reproduced, stored in
a retrieval system, or transmitted, in any form or by any means, without the
prior permission in writing of Oxford University Press, or as expressly permitted
by law, by licence or under terms agreed with the appropriate reprographics
rights organization. Enquiries concerning reproduction outside the scope of the
above should be sent to the Rights Department, Oxford University Press, at the
address above

You must not circulate this work in any other form
and you must impose this same condition on any acquirer

Published in the United States of America by Oxford University Press
198 Madison Avenue, New York, NY 10016, United States of America

British Library Cataloguing in Publication Data
Data available

Library of Congress Control Number: 2017961513

ISBN 978-0-19-878605-4

Printed and bound by
CPI Group (UK) Ltd, Croydon, CR0 4YY

Links to third party websites are provided by Oxford in good faith and
for information only. Oxford disclaims any responsibility for the materials
contained in any third party website referenced in this work.

Contents

List of Contributors — vii

Introduction — 1
Anna Bergqvist and Robert Cowan

Part I. The Existence and Nature of Evaluative Perception

1. Rich Perceptual Content and Aesthetic Properties — 19
   Dustin Stokes

2. Can We Visually Experience Aesthetic Properties? — 42
   Heather Logue

3. Moral Perception Defended — 58
   Robert Audi

4. Evaluative Perception as Response-Dependent Representation — 80
   Paul Noordhof

5. Doubts about Moral Perception — 109
   Pekka Väyrynen

6. Seeing Depicted Space (Or Not) — 129
   Mikael Pettersson

7. Perception of Absence as Value-Driven Perception — 143
   Anya Farennikova

Part II. The Epistemology of Evaluative Perception

8. Moral Perception and Its Rivals — 161
   Sarah McGrath

9. Perception and Intuition of Evaluative Properties — 183
   Jack C. Lyons

10. On the Epistemological Significance of Value Perception — 200
    Michael Milona

11. Epistemic Sentimentalism and Epistemic Reason-Responsiveness — 219
    Robert Cowan

Part III. Evaluative Perception and Value Theory

12. Value Perception, Properties, and the Primary Bearers of Value — 239
    Graham Oddie

13. Moral Perception, Thick Concepts, and Perspectivalism 258
    Anna Bergqvist
14. The Primacy of the Passions 282
    James Lenman
15. Sexual Objectification, Objectifying Images, and 'Mind-Insensitive Seeing-As' 295
    Kathleen Stock

Bibliography 311
Index 331

List of Contributors

ROBERT AUDI is John A. O'Brien Professor of Philosophy at the University of Notre Dame. He has research interests in wide range of areas: epistemology, ethics, philosophy of action, philosophy of mind, philosophy of religion, and political philosophy. He is the author of several books, including *The Good in The Right* (2004), *Rationality and Religious Commitment* (2011), and *Moral Perception* (2013), as well as a wide range of journal articles.

ANNA BERGQVIST is Lecturer in Philosophy at Manchester Metropolitan University. Her principal research interests are aesthetics and moral philosophy. She is co-editor of *Philosophy and Museums: Ethics, Aesthetics and Ontology* (CUP, 2016) to which she has contributed a thematic piece on objectivity in interpretation. She has also published on aesthetic particularism, thick evaluative concepts, and selected issues in philosophy of language (semantic contextualism). She also works on the intersection between metaethics, philosophy of perception, and philosophy of psychiatry, and is currently preparing a monograph on particularism and personalized medicine.

ROBERT COWAN is Lecturer in Philosophy at the University of Glasgow. His research is focused on ethics, epistemology, and the philosophy of mind. In particular he is interested in the nature and epistemology of intuition, perception, and emotion, as well as the connections between these and accounts of ethical knowledge. He has recently published papers on these topics in *Canadian Journal of Philosophy*, *Ethics*, and *Philosophy and Phenomenological Research*.

ANYA FARENNIKOVA is Lecturer in Philosophy at the University of Bristol. Her research interests lie in philosophy of mind and cognitive science. She has recently published on the perception of absence in *Philosophical Studies*.

JAMES LENMAN is Professor of Philosophy at the University of Sheffield. His research focuses on ethics, especially metaethics. His recent work has dealt with issues relating to moral realism, moral expressivism, moral psychology, moral epistemology, and moral responsibility, compatibilism, consequentialism, contractualism, constructivism, and contingency.

HEATHER LOGUE is Lecturer in Philosophy at the University of Leeds. Her research focuses on issues in metaphysics and epistemology, and particularly on issues concerning perceptual experience. She has published and forthcoming papers on Naïve Realism, disjunctivism, scepticism about the external world, experience of high-level properties, and the metaphysics of colour. Recent publications include 'Good News for the Disjunctivist about (one of) the Bad Cases' (*Philosophy and Phenomenological Research*, 2013), and 'Experiential Content and Naïve Realism: A Reconciliation' (*Does Perception Have Content?* ed. Berit Brogaard, OUP, 2014).

JACK C. LYONS is Professor of Philosophy at the University of Arkansas. His research is mainly in epistemology, cognitive science, and philosophy of mind. He has recently published a book entitled *Perception and Basic Beliefs* (OUP, 2011), and is the editor for the journal *Philosophical Topics*.

SARAH MCGRATH is Assistant Professor of Philosophy at Princeton University. Her primary areas of interest are metaphysics and ethics; key recent publications include 'Skepticism About Moral Expertise as a Puzzle for Moral Realism' (*Journal of Philosophy*, 2011) and 'Moral Knowledge and Experience' (*Oxford Studies in Metaethics*, 2011).

MICHAEL MILONA completed his dissertation on the role of emotions in moral epistemology in August 2016 at the University of Southern California. For the 2016–17 academic year, he is a postdoctoral researcher at Cornell University working on the nature and value of hope.

PAUL NOORDHOF is Anniversary Professor in Philosophy at the University of York. His main research interests are in philosophy of mind, action theory, and metaphysics. He has published extensively in these areas, and is currently writing a book which presents a counterfactual theory of causation, and another book on the nature and explanatory character of consciousness.

GRAHAM ODDIE is Professor of Philosophy of the University of Colorado at Boulder. His main research areas are metaphysics, value theory, metaethics, formal epistemology, philosophical logic, and aesthetics. He is author of two monographs, *Value, Reality, and Desire* (OUP, 2005) and *Likeness to Truth* (Reidel, 1986), and co-editor of two other books *What's Wrong* (OUP, 2004) and *Justice, Ethics, and New Zealand Society* (OUP, 1992).

MIKAEL PETTERSSON is Assistant Professor in Philosophy at the Lingnan University, Hong Kong. His area of specialization lies within aesthetics (broadly construed), in particular its intersection with philosophy of mind (perception and imagination) and metaphysics (causation). He has published on the phenomenology of photography, about the role of causation in photography, and an oft-neglected phenomenon in pictorial representation, namely that of pictorial occlusion.

KATHLEEN STOCK is Reader in Philosophy at the University of Sussex. Her main research interests are aesthetics and philosophy of mind, especially the imagination She has published extensively in these areas, and on fiction and definitions of art. She is editor of *Philosophers on Music* (OUP, 2007) and co-editor of *New Waves in Aesthetics* (Palgrave, 2008).

DUSTIN STOKES is Assistant Professor in Philosophy at the University of Utah. He works primarily in philosophy of mind and cognitive science. His research includes work on perception, imagination, and creative thought and behaviour. He is currently co-writing a book on *Imagination* and his paper 'Cognitive Penetration and the Perception of Art' was the winner of the 2012 *Dialectica* Essay Prize.

PEKKA VÄYRYNEN is Professor of Moral Philosophy at the University of Leeds. He is the author of *The Lewd, the Rude and the Nasty: A Study of Thick Concepts in Ethics* (OUP, 2013) and articles on a wide range of topics in metaethics.

Introduction

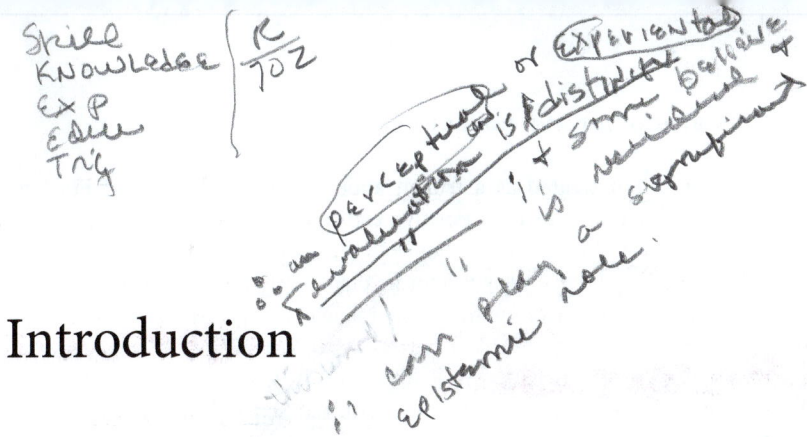

Anna Bergqvist and Robert Cowan

Evaluation is ubiquitous. It isn't an exaggeration to say that we assess actions, character, events, and objects as *good*, *bad*, *cruel*, *kind*, *beautiful*, *ugly*, etc., almost every day of our lives. A paradigm of evaluation is evaluative judgement. For example, Jen makes the judgement that the north-west Scottish Highlands are *beautiful*, while Phil judges that the rise of religious intolerance is a *bad* thing. Indeed, if we are liberal about how we classify the 'evaluative'[1] such that it includes the *deontic—rightness*, *wrongness*, *obligation*, *blameworthiness*, etc.—then the pervasiveness of evaluative judgement is even more striking.

So far, so uncontroversial. A more contentious set of issues arise when we consider whether evaluative judgements are expressions of cognitive or non-cognitive states, whether they deploy distinctively evaluative concepts, whether they are ever true, or can be epistemically justified, etc. Note, however, that recent developments in metaethics, in particular the emergence of versions of Quasi-Realism,[2] somewhat complicate debates about these questions.[3] For example, if we adopt a deflationary view of truth, then even Non-Cognitivists can agree that some evaluative judgements are true. Given this, assuming that evaluations can be true, etc., is perhaps not as controversial as it might first seem. In what follows we will speak as if evaluative judgements can indeed be true and epistemically justified.

Historically, it has been thought that a distinctive kind of evaluation is *perceptual* or *experiential*. Further, some have also believed that this sort of evaluation can be veridical, and can play significant roles, e.g. epistemic.[4] To illustrate: in aesthetics, many philosophers have claimed that adequate aesthetic judgement must be grounded in the appreciator's first-hand experience of the item judged. Thus, Frank Sibley asserts that

we have to read the poem, hear the music, or see the picture (not merely have it described in non-merit and even determinate terms if that were possible) and then *judge* or *decide* whether an aesthetic merit term applies to it or not.[5]

---

[1] We won't attempt to provide some set of necessary and sufficient conditions for what gets to count as 'evaluative'. Suffice to say that we are assuming a broad notion.

[2] See e.g. Blackburn (2006).   [3] See e.g. Drier (2004).

[4] Note, that as was the case with value judgements, notions of veridicality, etc., can presumably be understood in a deflationary sense too.

[5] Sibley (2001), 99.

This claim is often treated as a truism about aesthetic discourse.[6] Further, some philosophers[7] have also made a positive claim about what critical debate involves: that its purpose is to bring one's audience to see the object in a certain way. Some also think that criticism does not depend for its plausibility on general aesthetic criteria, if that means deductive reasoning from general aesthetic claims, for no such claims are available.[8] In any case, the point of critical discussion is not the formation of belief, but the engendering of perception. Related to this, within the tradition from Hume through to Sibley in analytic aesthetics, acquired sensibilities of taste (and similar conditions such as a sense of humour) are seen as cognitively necessary in the appreciation of aesthetic merit qualities.[9] This is suggestive of an important role for experience in the normative standing of aesthetic beliefs.

In ethics, Aristotle and modern-day Virtue Ethicists such as John McDowell[10] characterize practical wisdom in terms of a perceptual ability. Along somewhat similar lines, other philosophers[11] have emphasized the importance of ethical 'vision' as a matter of seeing things *aright*, particularly with respect to its ability to lead us to revise our preconceptions about particular objects, persons, and events. As Iris Murdoch puts it, goodness is

a refined and honest perception of what is really the case, a patient and just discernment and exploration of what confronts one, which is the result not simply of opening one's eyes but of a certain perfectly familiar kind of moral discipline.[12]

Elsewhere, Moral Sense Theorists like Frances Hutcheson[13] seemed to think that an affective experience of moral (dis)approbation constituted our primary awareness of moral qualities.

Contemporarily, there has been continued and renewed interest in the connection between the evaluative and the perceptual. We here note five examples.

Firstly, in aesthetics there has been growing discussion of the idea—introduced by Richard Wollheim[14]—that the phenomenon of Seeing-In, which is often claimed to be typical of pictorial experience, marks out a sui generis kind of perception.[15] Second, a relatively substantial literature on the existence and nature of ethical perception has sprung up over the last decade.[16] Much of this has been informed by recent work in the philosophy and epistemology of perception. Specifically, (and this is our third example) it has been influenced by the emergence of High-Level views[17] about the contents of perceptual experience, i.e., roughly, views which allow

---

[6] But see Livingston (2003).
[7] See e.g. Hampshire (1967); Sibley (1959/2001), (1965/2001), and (1983/2001); Strawson (1966).
[8] See e.g. Bergqvist (2010); Isenberg (1967); Mothersill (1984).
[9] For further discussion of this point, see e.g. Hopkins (2006) and (2011).
[10] McDowell (1998).
[11] See e.g. Blum (1994); DePaul (1993); McNaughton (1988); Murdoch (1970); Sherman (1989).
[12] Murdoch (1997), 330. For in-depth analysis of the implications of Murdoch's account of moral perception for the possibility objectivity in ethics, see Bergqvist, Ch. 13 in this volume. For its importance to the history of moral philosophy in the twenty-first century, see Bergqvist (2015).
[13] See e.g. Hutcheson (1728/1991).   [14] See e.g. Wollheim (1980).
[15] See e.g. Lopes (1996) and (2005); Hopkins (1998); Pettersson (2011).
[16] See e.g. Audi (2013) and (2015); McBrayer (2010a); Väyrynen (2008a); Werner (2016).
[17] See e.g. Bayne (2009); S. Siegel (2010a).

that we can perceive (in the canonical modalities) complex properties such as natural kinds and other categorical properties. Interest in ethical perception has also been informed by recent work on the view that perception in the canonical sensory modalities is Cognitively Penetrable, i.e., roughly, perception is susceptible to non-trivial influence from cognitive states like beliefs and desires (more on this later).[18] Fourth, there has been much recent interest in the development or further refinement of perceptual views of desires,[19] emotions,[20] and pains[21] according to which they are experiences of value. Fifthly, and finally, there has been some recent work[22] on the connection between the existence of evaluative perception and views in value theory, e.g., whether perceptual theories of the emotions are compatible with particular kinds of Sentimentalism about value concepts and properties.

Despite this history and recent developments, there has only been limited interaction between philosophers working on these various topics. This volume aims to remedy this by bringing together philosophers in aesthetics, epistemology, ethics, philosophy of mind, and value theory, to contribute in novel ways to debates about what we call 'Evaluative Perception'. Specifically, they contribute to answering the following questions:

Questions about Existence and Nature: Are there perceptual experiences of values? If so, what is their nature? Are experiences of values sui generis? Are values necessary for certain kinds of experience?

Questions about Epistemology: Can evaluative experiences ever justify evaluative judgements? Are experiences of values necessary for certain kinds of justified evaluative judgements?

Questions about Value Theory: Is the existence of evaluative experience supported or undermined by particular views in value theory? Are particular views in value theory supported or undermined by the existence of value experience?

In the following three sections we provide an introduction to some of the main topics of discussion, and to the volume papers.

Before doing so, the reader should note the following. As shall become clear, the fifteen papers in this volume are all concerned with answering one or more of these questions, and often cross-cut different areas, e.g., epistemology and value theory. For that reason, it is somewhat artificial to divide them into discrete subgroups. However, to aid the reader in seeing the connections between the papers, and to contribute to the thematic unity of the volume, we have placed the papers into three subgroups. The first is primarily concerned with the *Existence and Nature of Evaluative Perception*. Here we have placed contributions by Dustin Stokes, Heather Logue, Robert Audi, Paul Noordhof, Pekka Väyrynen, Mikael Pettersson, and Anya Farennikova. The second group is mostly addressed to questions about *Evaluative Perception and Epistemology*. Here we have contributions from Sarah McGrath, Jack C. Lyons, Michael Milona, and Robert Cowan. Finally, the third subgroup is focused

---

[18] See e.g. Firestone and Scholl (2014); Macpherson (2012); S. Siegel (2012).
[19] See e.g. Oddie (2005).   [20] See e.g. Döring (2003).   [21] See e.g. Bain (2013).
[22] See e.g. Brady (2013); Cowan (2016); Tappolet (2011).

on the connections between *Evaluative Perception and Value Theory*. Here can be found the contributions by Graham Oddie, Anna Bergqvist, James Lenman, and Kathleen Stock.

1. Existence and Nature of Evaluative Perception

Many of the papers in the volume are concerned with the existence and nature of Evaluative Perception. As we are characterizing it, this involves the experiential representation[23] of value properties, i.e., there are some perceptual experiences with evaluative content.

Before clarifying this and different kinds of evaluative perceptual experience, the phenomenon should be distinguished from two others.

Firstly, there is what we call 'De Re Perception of Values'.[24] That is, we perceive objects, persons, events, states of affairs that as a matter of fact instantiate evaluative properties, e.g., *moral rightness*, *beauty*. Everyone but the value Error Theorist can assent to the claim that there is De Re Perception of Values. For our purposes, the crucial difference between this and Evaluative Perception is that the De Re Perception of some F by a subject is compatible with the subject not having a perceptual 'experience' of F, i.e., an experience with evaluative content.

Second, there is what we call 'Evaluative Seeing-That'. This involves making an evaluative judgement in response to a perceptual experience (often it is assumed that the evaluative judgement has some positive epistemic status, e.g., constitutes knowledge). One way in which some restrict the notion of Evaluative Seeing-That is by insisting that it must be both psychologically and epistemically non-inferential, i.e., the relevant judgements mustn't be the result of, nor be epistemically dependent upon, inference.[25] Given this restriction, there is scope for philosophical debate as to whether all putative instances of Evaluative Seeing-That involve some sort of inferential epistemic dependence (for more discussion see Section 2 of this Introduction). For our purposes, the important difference between this and Evaluative Perception is that Evaluative Seeing-That is consistent with the perceptual experience only representing non-evaluative properties, e.g., the properties upon which the evaluative property supervenes or is consequential.

Now to clarify Evaluative Perception. Although there is an important distinction between non-factive perceptual experience, and perception which is factive, we will mainly focus on the former and for ease of expression simply refer to it as 'Evaluative Perception'. If there is Evaluative Perception, in this central sense, then subjects can have perceptual experiences that represent the instantiation of evaluative properties

---

[23] In characterizing things this way, we are using the language of an Intentionalist or Representational theory of perception. On a Relational view of perception, by contrast, veridical experiences do not have representational content, but instead involve the obtaining of a perceptual relation between the perceiver and worldly objects, such that the relevant objects can be said to literally constitute one's experience. See e.g. M. G. F. Martin (2006). For brevity we will speak of perceptual representation (partly because most of the papers in the volume assume it) but the Relational view ought to be kept in mind.

[24] Or 'non-epistemic seeing'. See Dretske (1969), esp. ch. 2. See also Dretske (1993).

[25] One might go further and provide a positive characterization of the aetiology of Seeing-That, e.g., they have their source in modular perceptual systems; see Jack Lyons (Ch. 9 in this volume).

of the sort described above, i.e., some perceptual experiences are accurate only if they represent evaluative properties. Later we will introduce some other phenomena which, although they don't fall under this category, are worthwhile considering alongside discussion of Evaluative Perception proper.

There are at least three different kinds of Evaluative Perception that are worth distinguishing.

The first of these is what we call 'Canonical Evaluative Perception'. This involves a commitment to the representation of evaluative properties in one or more of the five canonical sensory modalities. Some version of this view is defended or endorsed in this volume by Robert Audi (at least on one interpretation), Paul Noordhof, and Dustin Stokes.

The second kind of Evaluative Perception is what we refer to as 'Affective Evaluative Perception'. This involves the representation of evaluative properties in an affective or conative state, such as desire, emotion, or pain. On each of these views, the relevant mental state apparently shares important features with ordinary perceptual experience, e.g., they have phenomenal character, representational content, can be recalcitrant to doxastic changes, exemplify some covariance with the subject's environment, and can play a non-inferential epistemic role. The point of interest for our purposes is that if such experiences could have an evaluative content—and proponents all seem to think that they can, e.g., Oddie[26] conceives of desires as experiences of *goodness*, Döring[27] thinks that moral emotions such as guilt represent *moral* properties, Bain[28] thinks that pain experiences represent bodily damage as *bad for the subject*—then there could be perceptual experiences with evaluative content, albeit 'non-traditional' ones. Versions of this view are discussed or defended by Robert Cowan, Graham Oddie, Michael Milona, and Paul Noordhof in this volume.

The third kind of Evaluative Perception is what we call 'Sui Generis Evaluative Perception'. This involves the representation of evaluative properties in a sui generis kind of experience (by 'sui generis' we simply mean that it doesn't reduce to familiar sensory or affective phenomena). One example of this, which is discussed or defended in this volume by Robert Audi, Michael Milona, and Pekka Väyrynen, is the view that Evaluative Perceptions are 'integrated' experiences, which are an amalgam of sensory, emotional, and imaginative components. This is distinct from, e.g., Canonical Evaluative Perception in part because the sensory component of an integrated experience need not have an evaluative content. Another example of Sui Generis Evaluative Perception, which is discussed by Jack Lyons in this volume, is the view that, although evaluative properties aren't represented in sensory experience proper, they can be represented in perceptual seeming states. Roughly, these are propositional non-doxastic states that are the causal upshot of sensory experience or a sensory system.[29]

Due to space constraints, our discussion will be focused on the prospects for Canonical Evaluative Perception. However, this will still allow us to make extensive

---

[26] Oddie (2005) and Ch. 12 in this volume. [27] Döring (2003). [28] Bain (2013).
[29] For extensive discussion of seemings, see C. Tucker (2013).

reference to other kinds of Evaluative Perception in this section and throughout the Introduction.

It is first worth noting that Canonical Evaluative Perception runs counter to the mainstream view according to which canonical perceptual experience, e.g., vision, only represents what are called 'Low-Level' properties such as colour, shape, and motion. If there is Canonical Evaluative Perception then 'High-Level' properties, e.g., aesthetic and ethical, must also be represented in perceptual experience.

Why would anyone think that there is Canonical Evaluative Perception? One kind of evidence—already noted in this Introduction and highlighted in chapters by Audi, Logue, Noordhof, Stokes, Väyrynen—is that we often use perceptual language when talking about the evaluative. For example, it would not be unusual to hear someone say 'the Botticelli looks incredible close up', or, 'I could hear her demeaning tone'. However, this sort of evidence is quite weak. Even if we accept that such cases are psychologically (or perhaps even epistemically) non-inferential, this doesn't clearly support the truth of Canonical Evaluative Perception, as opposed to some other kind of Evaluative Perception. Indeed, it doesn't obviously support any kind of Evaluative Perception, if such cases can be explained as cases of Evaluative Seeing-That on the basis of non-evaluative perceptual experience.

A more promising strategy is perhaps to appeal to what have come to be known as 'Contrast Arguments'. This sort of argument has been presented by some philosophers of perception, notably Tim Bayne[30] and Susanna Siegel,[31] in support of the High-Level (or 'rich' or 'liberal') view of perception, with a focus on natural kind properties, e.g., being a pine tree, and causal relations. Very roughly, Contrast Arguments involve conceiving of two experiences with very similar or identical low-level content, but where there is plausibly a difference in the phenomenology between them, e.g., the contrast between the experiences of looking at pine trees before and then after acquiring a familiarity with what their characteristic look is. The crucial move in Contrast Arguments is to say that the best explanation of the phenomenological difference is a difference in the representational contents of perception as opposed to, e.g., attentional differences.

Put very simply:

P1: There is a phenomenological difference between target experiences e and e*.

P2: The best explanation of the phenomenological difference between target experiences e and e* requires positing some high-level content, c, in experience.

C: (Probably) some experiences have some high-level, c, content.

Most are willing to accept P1. Thus the central task for proponents of Contrast Arguments is to show that positing high-level perception is indeed the best explanation of the relevant cases.

Is this kind of argument more or less promising in the evaluative case? In this volume Dustin Stokes provides a Contrast Argument in favour of the conclusion that at least some aesthetic properties, e.g., gracefulness, are represented in canonical experience. Interestingly he thinks that this sort of argument is more promising in

---

[30] See Bayne (2009).   [31] See S. Siegel (2010a).

the aesthetic case than for other high-level properties such as natural kinds. Stokes argues that there is no way to account for the phenomenology of aesthetic cases without admitting perceptual representation of some organizational gestalt, e.g., an organizational gestalt typical of impressionist works. Crucially, to experience organizational aesthetic gestalts just is to experience the relevant aesthetic properties. Interestingly, this feature is lacking in cases of natural kind or even colour properties (a similar view is defended in Bergqvist's discussion of value theory in this volume).

Against this kind of optimism and the general line of thought, Heather Logue in Chapter 2 casts doubt on aesthetic Contrast Arguments. She thinks that there is another plausible explanation (which is just as parsimonious as positing Canonical Evaluative Perception) for the difference in phenomenology: appeal to emotional states (Affective Evaluative Perception). Notably, this alternative explanation may be absent in the case of other high-level properties like natural kinds. Logue also considers and rejects arguments in favour of Canonical Evaluative Perception of aesthetic properties which appeal to the putative 'observationality' of some aesthetic properties—roughly, for an aesthetic property, F, in ideal viewing conditions, if something visually appears to be F, it is F—or to their allegedly 'superficial' metaphysical nature. Regarding the latter, Logue draws attention to the idea that aesthetic properties are plausibly response-dependent (a feature that might complicate Stokes's argument).

In Chapter 5 Pekka Väyrynen considers a Contrast Argument for moral perception,[32] but finds that the phenomenological difference can be explained just as well by a model which posits that a non-perceptual moral representation results from 'an implicit habitual inference or some other type of transition in thought which can be reliably prompted by the non-moral perceptual inputs jointly with the relevant background moral beliefs'.[33] The representations involved may be affective in nature (hence Väyrynen may be interpreted as countenancing the existence of Affective Evaluative Perception or Sui Generis Evaluative Perception). Further, he thinks that this alternative model possesses theoretical virtues of simplicity and unity that give it an advantage. Positing Canonical Moral Perception adds no explanatory power. Thus P2 of a moral Contrast Argument should be rejected.[34]

Another kind of argument that could be offered in favour of Canonical Evaluative Perception is epistemological:

P1: There could be a certain kind of justified belief, J, only if there were Canonical Evaluative Perception.

P2: There is justified belief J.

C: There is Canonical Evaluative Perception.

P1 claims that Canonical Evaluative Perception is a necessary condition for a particular kind of epistemic justification (a similar argument could be constructed

---

[32] Note that Werner (2016) presents a contrast argument in favour of moral perception.
[33] Pekka Väyrynen (Ch. 5 in this volume).
[34] Väyrynen thinks that whether a Contrast Argument is likely to succeed depends on the properties in question, and his view is that it is a good deal less promising in the moral case as compared with other high-level properties (as Logue argues with regard to aesthetic properties).

for knowledge and other positive epistemic properties). We will postpone discussion of this idea until Section 2 of the Introduction. For now note that Logue discusses and rejects this sort of epistemic argument in her chapter.[35]

Even if one is somewhat sympathetic to arguments in favour of Canonical Evaluative Perception, there remains, inter alia, the question of how value properties could be represented in experience. For example, it might seem highly implausible that value properties are represented in a similar way to that in which low-level properties like colours and shapes are represented in vision. This point is not only noted by opponents of Canonical Evaluative Perception—see Jack Lyons's paper in this volume—but also by proponents of the view, such as Audi and Noordhof (both in this volume). Whether or not this is fatal for the view depends upon whether we allow that there are different kinds of representation in perceptual experience. For example, Audi distinguishes, inter alia, between what he calls the 'perceptual', associated with 'cartographic', 'pictorial' and 'basic' representation (the sort allegedly involved in the representation of colours and shapes), and the 'perceptible', which involves non-cartographic, non-pictorial, and non-basic representation. Crucially, he seems to think that some perception (in the canonical modalities) is of the perceptible. Noordhof also distinguishes between 'sensory' and 'non-sensory' representation in canonical perception.[36] If we admit that there can be different kinds of perceptual representation, then Canonical Evaluative Perception may be a good deal more plausible.

One thing that makes it difficult to determine whether there really is Canonical Evaluative Perception is that it is hard to see how we can satisfactorily resolve disputes between those who, like Audi and Noordhof, think that there is something like non-sensory representation, and those, like Lyons, who think that what is being referred to as non-sensory perceptual representation is actually something post-perceptual, e.g., a perceptual seeming state which has phenomenal character (though perhaps it is *bland* character) and conceptual content. Note, however, that Noordhof provides arguments in favour of admitting non-sensory representation (one which appeals to the phenomenology of chicken sexers and speech perception, the other which appeals to epistemic considerations), as well as reasons for doubting the existence of perceptual seemings in his chapter. Also, in this context it is worth noting Heather Logue's view that there may not be a fact of the matter regarding the question of whether aesthetic properties are represented in canonical perceptual experience.

Even if one allows that there can be non-cartographic or non-sensory perceptual representation, e.g., perhaps this is what all high-level representation involves, some still might think that there are specific problems for Canonical *Evaluative* Perception.

---

[35] Robert Audi (Ch. 3 in this volume) also suggests the following sort of argument for moral perception: *if* there is perception of emotion, e.g., anger, then there is little reason to doubt the existence of moral perception. Of course, one might doubt that the antecedent is true, and in any case might doubt the truth of the conditional. As Pekka Väyrynen argues, admission of perceptual contents should proceed on a case-by-case basis.

[36] Although some aspects of Noordhof's distinction appear to be similar to Audi's, Noordhof places emphasis on discriminability of properties in order to flesh out the difference.

INTRODUCTION 9

In his chapter, Noordhof thinks that there may be some resistance to the idea of Canonical Evaluative Perception even among those who countenance non-sensory representation because of the common thought that value properties are in some way response-dependent (also highlighted by Logue).[37] In order to address this, Noordhof presents an account of intrinsic response-dependent representation—i.e., representation of a property that has nothing to do with the representation standing in relation to something independently characterized in the world. He illustrates this with reference to the perception of badness in pain and moral perception.

Suppose that a plausible argument can be made for thinking that there is Canonical Evaluative Perception. To support this, proponents will need to identify psychological mechanisms by which this could take place. This is, of course, an empirical matter that can't plausibly be settled from the armchair. One candidate model that has received attention in the recent literature on moral perception is that Canonical Evaluative Perception could be brought about by a process of Cognitive Penetration.[38] Roughly, Cognitive Penetration of sensory experience is possible if and only if it's possible for two subjects to have experiences which differ in content and/or phenomenal character, where this difference is the result of a causal process that traces more or less directly to states in the subjects' cognitive system, and where we hold fixed the perceptual stimuli, the condition of the subjects' sensory organs, the environmental conditions, and the attentional focus of the subjects.[39]

Potential cognitive penetrators include: moods, beliefs, desires, emotions, and character traits. Such a model might help to explain how there can be expertise with respect to values, e.g., in aesthetics. What the expert has, and the novice lacks, is a set of background commitments that cognitively penetrate their sensory experience such that it comes to have an evaluative content.

Although there is growing evidence for the Cognitive Penetrability thesis,[40] it is still highly controversial. It is therefore worth noting that adopting the Cognitive Penetrability model requires proponents of Canonical Evaluative Perception to undertake substantial empirical commitments regarding the capacities of ordinary perception and its relation to cognition. In this volume, Bergqvist, Cowan, Lyons, Pettersson, Stokes, and Väyrynen discuss Cognitive Penetration.

Another model appeals to Perceptual Learning, which involves a repeated associative process that takes place within the perceptual system. For example, after repeated exposure to a particular kind of artwork (and top-down processing within the visual system) perhaps one's visual system may come to encode information about aesthetic properties. Stokes discusses this possibility in Chapter 1 in this volume. If we think that there is such a thing as aesthetic expertise, one might think that one feature that distinguishes the expert from the novice is that they have been repeatedly exposed to artworks. Note, however, that a similar sort of

---

[37] Noordhof also thinks that there is a lack of 'phenomenal presence' in the case of aesthetic and moral representation, though not in the case of the representation of badness in pain experience.
[38] Cowan (2015b).   [39] See e.g. Vance (2014).
[40] See e.g. Bruner and Goodman (1947); Delk and Fillenbaum (1965); Hansen et al. (2006). See also D. Stokes (2013).

repeated exposure may be less common in the moral case (although this might be overstating things).

A final model for Canonical Evaluative Perception is that our perceptual systems are hard-wired for evaluative representation (in the way that representation of colours and shapes seems to be). One might think that a necessary condition for perceptual hard-wiring is that possessing the relevant representational powers will be of use to subjects who possess them in almost any environment in which they might be placed.[41] Notice that, while it is not implausible that moral properties meet the necessary condition, it is perhaps a good deal less so for kind properties, e.g., being a pine tree, and aesthetic properties.

In Chapter 3 in this volume, Robert Audi may be interpreted as defending a sort of hard-wired view about Evaluative Perception; however, it is not entirely clear whether he is willing to countenance this for Canonical Evaluative Perception or only for a kind of Sui Generis Evaluative Perception (integrated experiences). Finally, it is worth noting that in the case of Affective Evaluative Perception—regarding emotion and pain in particular—philosophers seem to be more sanguine about the claim that evaluative representation is hard-wired.

Although the majority of the papers in the volume are engaged in debates about Evaluative Perception (as we have defined it), two of the volume papers—those by Mikael Pettersson and Anya Farennikova—discuss distinct kinds of phenomena which we think are usefully grouped with these other papers.

Firstly, there is the phenomenon of Seeing-In, typical of pictorial representation, which—as noted earlier—some have thought marks out a distinctive form of perception. For instance, it is often said that an important part of our experience of pictures, such as looking at a wedding photograph in the family album, is that we see its subject matter 'in' its surface, in a way that is different from watching the world (its pictorial content) face-to-face.

In Chapter 6 in this volume, Mikael Pettersson problematizes extant accounts—*resemblance*[42] and *recognitional*[43]—of Seeing-In by considering how they fare with respect to the phenomenon of seeing *empty space* in pictures. Although seeing empty space in a picture (and seeing-in more generally) isn't a form of Evaluative Perception (as we have defined it), the alleged distinctiveness of this form of perception, and its apparent significance for aesthetics, e.g., the aesthetic appreciation of some pictures will depend on our experience of empty space or void in the picture, make inclusion of discussion of this topic in this collection important. Pettersson rejects cognitive accounts of seeing empty space in pictures (what we earlier referred to as Seeing-That) and goes on to sketch an *imagination* theory, which according to one model involves the cognitive penetration of perceptual experience by imagination.

The second phenomenon is that of perceptual experiences which, though not themselves Evaluative Perceptions, are nevertheless allegedly causally dependent for their occurrence upon subjects having certain sorts of evaluative commitments. For example, perhaps possessing certain aesthetic beliefs makes one more perceptually

---

[41] See e.g. Macpherson (2012).   [42] See Hopkins (1998).   [43] See Currie (1995).

INTRODUCTION 11

attentive to particular low-level features of artworks, e.g., colour and shape arrays, even if such experiences don't represent the instantiation of evaluative properties. In addition, we might include *affordances*, as a related kind of evaluative perceptual experience that represents not an evaluative property as such but rather features of the perceived lived environment that bear intimately on action in reasonable perceptual agents—such as giving up one's seat on the bus upon seeing a visibly tired person.[44] Rather than an Evaluative Perception, these are perhaps better called 'Value-Enabled Perceptions'.

In Chapter 7 in this volume, Anya Farennikova argues that perceptual experiences of *absences*, e.g., seeing that Pierre is not in the café, or noticing the absence of a ring on someone's fourth finger, are dependent upon the subject's desires or values. Roughly, the idea is that desiring and valuing more generally can make one perceptually sensitive to the existence of the absence of certain things in one's environment. Without those values, one wouldn't recognize what isn't there. Thus, Farennikova thinks that one's desires *enable* the perception of absences: they are value-driven experiences.

2. Epistemology and Evaluative Perception

As was noted in Section 1, one kind of argument that is sometimes offered in favour of Canonical Evaluative Perception is epistemological. What is perhaps the crucial premise in that argument claims that Canonical Evaluative Perception is necessary for the existence of some kind of justified evaluative belief or knowledge. One candidate might be the existence of justified evaluative beliefs about concrete particular cases, e.g., John's judgement that the hoodlums were wrong to set fire to the cat, or Lucy's belief that the lead ballerina's movements in the final act were graceful.

In this volume there are several papers that argue against this sort of view. In Chapter 2, Logue at one stage suggests that an Inferentialist picture could perhaps accommodate justified beliefs in aesthetic cases, e.g., Lucy's justified belief about the gracefulness of the ballerina might be the result of her justified background belief that features F, G, H are usually sufficient for movements to be graceful, and the belief or perceptual registering that the ballerina possesses those features.

In Chapter 8, Sarah McGrath—focusing primarily on moral perceptual knowledge—argues at length against versions of Inferentialism (albeit focused on moral cases): deductive, inductive, and abductive. These models allegedly fail to adequately explain moral knowledge in particular cases. She also considers and rejects a more sophisticated Inferentialist model found in the work of Kieran Setiya,[45] according to which the relevant moral 'perceptual' knowledge is actually inferred from non-moral evidence. However, McGrath doesn't think that Canonical Evaluative Perception is necessary for justified belief or knowledge in the relevant cases. Instead, she argues that non-inferential Evaluative Seeing-That is sufficient. Interestingly, McGrath argues that such non-inferential 'perceptual' judgements about particular concrete cases—as

---

[44] This example is from Bengson (2016). [45] Setiya (2012).

opposed to judgements about hypothetical cases which are implicitly general[46]—can play an important and hitherto unrecognized role in the process of arriving at reflective equilibrium.

Jack Lyons, in Chapter 9, also argues—from an epistemological Reliabilist perspective—that the sort of justification that one might have thought could only be gained by Canonical Evaluative Perception, can also be delivered by Sui Generis Evaluative Perception (perceptual seemings), or what he calls 'value intuitions', i.e., cognitive seemings with evaluative content.

Finally, a more extreme version of the view that Canonical Evaluative Perception plays some epistemically essential role would claim that it is required for the existence of any justified (substantive) evaluative belief. In Chapter 10, Michael Milona argues against this,[47] concluding that for any substantive justification gained from Canonical Evaluative Perception, subjects could gain similar justification by imaginatively considering the relevant cases and having some sort of affective, e.g., emotional, response to it. Indeed, Milona goes further and claims that the question of whether there is Canonical Evaluative Perception is not important *at all* for debates about evaluative epistemology (but recall McGrath's point about the epistemic significance of perceptual evaluative judgements). Note, however, that Milona seems to think that Affective Evaluative Perception—desires or emotions—is a necessary condition for justified substantive evaluative beliefs. We'll return to this view shortly.

Even if Canonical Evaluative Perception isn't necessary for evaluative justification (and thus epistemological arguments for its existence are likely unsound), we can ask whether it could be sufficient for justified evaluative beliefs. Further, if it turns out that Canonical Evaluative Perception were sufficient for basic or non-inferential justification then it could still have epistemological significance, i.e., it could be a source of regress-stopping justification. Is it?

On one view of non-inferential experiential justification, in order for an experience to immediately justify a belief that p, this requires that the experience has distinctively *presentational* content with respect to p. Being presented with p is meant to differ in important respects from representing p (contrast seeing a red ball with simply thinking about one). In Chapter 4, Noordhof claims that moral perception lacks presentational character in a way that other sorts of Evaluative Perceptions, e.g., pain experiences, do not. He suggests that this impacts on the former's capacity to confer justification. On the other hand, Audi (Chapter 3) has no problem with the idea that moral perceptions could be presentational. One explanation for the difference in views is that there are competing views of what presentational content is.[48] Which is the correct view arguably needs to be settled on independent grounds.

If one thinks that non-inferential epistemic justification or knowledge require *reliability*, then one needs to give an account of how Canonical Evaluative Perception could be reliable. Robert Audi's considered view—in the moral case—is that this has something to do with the possession of moral concepts.

---

[46] See Kagan (2001).

[47] Note that Michael Milona (Ch. 10) interprets Audi's Integration model as a form of Canonical Evaluative Perception. Others, e.g. Väyrynen (Ch. 5 in this volume), do not.

[48] For a particular conception, see Chudnoff (2013).

However, one might wonder how concept possession could make one reliable in this way, and whether this renders the relevant knowledge/justified belief non-empirical. An alternative view is that reliability will depend upon the background beliefs or value commitments that one has. However, one might worry—as Väyrynen does in Chapter 5—that this introduces an epistemic dependence that is antithetical to non-inferential justification. In this context it is worth noting Lyons's argument (Chapter 9) against the view that causal cognitive influence (penetration) on some mental item should lead us to posit an epistemic dependence relation. Instead, what matters is whether the cognitive influence is such that the mental item can be said to be *based* upon the influencing cognition. So even if Canonical Evaluative Perception is brought about by cognitive penetration by background beliefs, if this doesn't involve basing then this would be consistent with Canonical Evaluative Perceptions being sources of immediate justification or knowledge (so long as they are reliable).

As was noted earlier, Michael Milona suggests that Affective Evaluative Perceptions could be sources of immediate justification for evaluative beliefs (indeed, he appears to suggest that they may be necessary for such justification). However, one might wonder whether emotions, e.g., could be sources of immediate justification, if they are always grounded in 'cognitive bases',[49] e.g., beliefs, perceptions, imaginative episodes concerning non-evaluative objects and events. For example, David's guilt is based upon his belief that he lied to his partner. One might think that for his guilt to justify an evaluative belief, e.g., that he has done something wrong, his belief about having lied must be justified. But then it looks like his emotion isn't a source of immediate justification. Further, this sort of basing/epistemic dependence might make us doubt that emotions really are Affective Evaluative Perceptions (similar points could be made about desires). In Chapter 11, Robert Cowan argues that even if all emotions have cognitive bases, and even if this entails an epistemic dependence of the emotion upon the cognitive base, this is compatible with emotions playing an epistemically fundamental role with respect to evaluative propositions.

3. Value Theory and Evaluative Perception

If we define Evaluative Perception in terms of a non-factive representational state, then it might seem as though there are little or no connections between its existence and questions in value theory about, e.g., the metaphysics of values.

However, that's a bit quick (see also Noordhof (Chapter 4) and Stokes (Chapter 1)). To illustrate, consider a simple Sentimentalist view of value properties (a similar view could be developed about concepts), according to which X possesses value property, F, iff X elicits emotional response, E, from all who consider X. One way to understand this view would be as a *reductive* analysis of value properties, i.e., the right-hand side has explanatory priority. However, if emotional responses have evaluative content, e.g., guilt represents wrongness, that might problematize a reductive version of this view (since the right-hand side will make reference to value properties, albeit the

[49] See Deonna and Teroni (2012), 5.

representation of such properties). This might push us in the direction of some other kind of account, e.g., a no-priority view.

Even if one has doubts about the previous line of thought, if we assume that at least some Evaluative Perceptions are veridical, and that they can play some epistemic role, e.g., justify evaluative beliefs, then there are arguably clearer connections between the existence of Evaluative Perception and Value Theory. For example, it has recently been argued[50] that a view according to which emotions are Affective Evaluative Perceptions, which can non-inferentially justify evaluative beliefs,[51] is incompatible with Neo-Sentimentalism about value concepts—according to which X possesses value property, F, iff X merits or justifies an emotional response from those who contemplate X, E, e.g., X is admirable iff X merits admiration. This is because the combination would appear to have the counter-intuitive consequence that emotions can confer justification for themselves.[52]

In Chapter 12 Graham Oddie defends the view that desires are Affective Evaluative Perceptions, i.e., they are experiences of the *goodness* of things that can confer prima facie justification for evaluative beliefs about *goodness*. However, Oddie argues that if we think *states of affairs* are the primary bearers of value, then the view that desires are value perceptions faces an isomorphism problem. On the one hand, if there is Affective Evaluative Perception then it might seem that it ought to be reflective of the evaluative facts. Certainly, it seems that our evaluative beliefs ought to be this way. But on the other hand, it seems that at least some kinds of value experience—in particular desire and emotion experiences—are legitimately perspectival, e.g., it seems legitimate for me to prefer that my mother be saved rather than someone else's in a scenario where only one can be saved. After suggesting a somewhat metaphorical way of addressing this (which appeals, inter alia, to value distance), Oddie suggests that the isomorphism problem can be dealt with if we adopt the view that *properties/states of being*, e.g., *being happy*, are the primary bearers of value and objects of desire. This is because Oddie thinks properties, in particular, 'local' properties (a property that can be borne by one thing without everything possessing it), have their own 'built-in' perspective.

In Chapter 13, Anna Bergqvist also considers the perspectival nature of evaluative perception. On Bergqvist's reading of Iris Murdoch, moral perception involves not only being attuned to one's environment thanks to cognitive penetration through the concepts that we deploy, but also the claim that one's conceptions of these concepts decisively influence what we see. Bergqvist argues that we can nonetheless make good on the robust realist claim that the salient concepts of an individual's life-world can be revelatory of value without appeal either to Platonism or value constitutivism. Bergqvist distinguishes two readings on the concept of 'non-perspectival value'—an epistemic reading and a non-epistemic one—and argues that commitment to the thesis that value is in some sense always value for us does not as such rule out value's being non-perspectival in the sense of existing independently of any actual world views or perspectives in the non-epistemic sense. Bergqvist

---

[50] See Brady (2013).   [51] Defended by e.g. Döring (2003); Pelser (2014).
[52] But see Cowan (2016) for a response.

considers the possible objection as to how to account for the notion of structure and unity of moral thought if we follow through on Murdoch's suggestion and take the central target notion of world view to be an unruly holistic admixture of evaluative and non-evaluative concepts: are there any limits as to what might plausibly be counted as 'value for us'? In her estimation, what is needed is a separate argument that speaks to the practicality of thick moral concepts as action-guiding concepts, and the notion of action-oriented perception more generally.

By contrast with Bergqvist's perspective-neutral view about the nature of value, in Chapter 14 James Lenman explores the topic of Evaluative Perception within the context of a broadly Expressivist (or Quasi-Realist) metaethical framework. According to this metaethical view, our reasons for action (including moral reasons) emerge out of a relatively stable network of desire-like attitudes and commitments, arrived at via some process of reflection and deliberation. Despite a sort of ultimate dependence of reasons on desire, it can apparently still make sense to speak—from within our web of commitments—of desire-independent moral reasons and moral truth. With this view on the table, Lenman rejects the idea that Canonical Moral Perception takes place: this sort of position would only seem to make sense if we assumed some sort of naturalist realism. Even then, Lenman thinks that the real epistemic work would be done by moral theorizing about the relation between natural and moral properties, not sensory perception. Instead, he affords a limited role to Affective Evaluative Perception (emotions and desire) in disclosing value to us, where the latter process is understood more as self-interpretation rather than some sort of perceptual-like engagement with an external evaluative reality. However, it is clear that Lenman is more favourable to a picture of ethical thought as reflective and interpretative, rather than immediate and perceptual.

Finally, in Chapter 15, Kathleen Stock appeals to a kind of perception in order to illuminate a particular kind of practice with evaluative and normative significance: *objectifying* behaviour, i.e., treating people like objects. Specifically she argues that a mediating role between objectifying images (e.g., those found in pornography) and objectifying behaviour is played by a distinctive kind of perception: what she calls 'mind-insensitive seeing-as'. This amounts to a mode of perceiving people on a par with looking at mindless inanimate objects, and involves a sort of gestalt which can come in various types, e.g., *seeing-as body*, *seeing-as fungible*. Positing this phenomenon explains some important kinds of objectifying behaviours, e.g., the attentional and cognitive habits towards members of objectified groups. Although the sorts of experiences that Stock appeals to may not themselves have an evaluative content (strictly speaking), they may be said to be evaluative perceptions in a broader sense, due to the morally significant way they involve presenting their intentional objects (persons). Even if it were objected that the phenomena that Stock points to is not a class of Evaluative Perception, one significant feature is worth noting. The experiences that Stock describes would themselves seem to be the appropriate *object* of evaluation, whether or not they represent value properties, i.e., they nevertheless constitute *Morally Evaluable Perceptions*.

PART I

The Existence and Nature of Evaluative Perception

1

Rich Perceptual Content and Aesthetic Properties

Dustin Stokes

Both common sense and dominant traditions in art criticism and philosophical aesthetics have it that aesthetic features or properties are *perceived*. It is commonplace to hear someone in a gallery say something like 'Look how balanced this piece is' or at a symphony performance 'Can you hear how unified the string section is?' or at an electronic music show 'Can you feel the power of the bass?' These remarks are posed in such a way so as to direct *perceptual* attention to some aspect of the object or performance. The same is true of criticism. Critical language is rife with examples of aesthetic features being discussed in sensory and phenomenal terms. And one finds the same in philosophical aesthetics, from Baumgarten to Hume to Kant and to more contemporary figures like Budd and Levinson and Lopes. Here is Frank Sibley,

[A]esthetics deals with a kind of perception. People have to *see* the grace or unity of a work, *hear* the plaintiveness or frenzy in the music, *notice* the gaudiness of colour scheme... They may be struck by these qualities at once, or they may come to perceive them only after repeated viewings, hearings, readings, and with the help of critics.[1]

One's own phenomenological introspection should suggest the same: *if* one identifies the sombreness of a Wyeth painting or of certain movements of a Mahler symphony, or the frenzy of the Pollock action painting or the Bad Brains punk rock number, does it not seem obvious that these features characterize one's sensory experience? One is most naturally inclined to describe the identified features as part of the phenomenology of one's conscious perceptual experiences. Taken alone, none of these observations are conclusive. But together, the convergence is strongly suggestive: 'the aesthetic' is something experienced. Here is a simple thesis that captures the unified thought concerning *aesthetic perception*:

    AP: Aesthetic properties are sometimes represented by perceptual experience.

---

[1] Sibley (1965/2001), 34. See Budd (1995); Levinson (1984) and (1994); Lopes (2005).

The 'sometimes' indicates that aesthetic properties need not be categorically perceptually represented, while it is plausible that they are very often perceptually represented. For all that (AP) has going for it, it turns out there is quite a cast of reasons to be sceptical of the thesis. Here are three.

First, the traditional representationalist model of perception supposes that perceptual experience represents only low-level properties. In the context of art appreciation, one visually perceives the colours and shapes of the painting on the gallery wall, but aesthetic properties like 'being graceful' or 'being vivid', like 'being a mountain' or 'being a dancer' (as represented by the painting), are post-perceptual, represented by a judgement or a belief. So this is a general view about perception and cognitive architecture:

S_c: Perception represents only low-level properties.

S_c implies that AP is false: aesthetic properties are high-level properties, and so are cognized at the level of judgement or evaluation or belief.

The second reason for scepticism regarding AP is ontological. On almost all theories of perception, perceptual experience is descriptive: perception functions to accurately describe or report features of one's environment. Accordingly, if one wants to claim that one sees some aesthetic property F, then one thereby commits to the objective, mind-independent reality of Fness. Barring instances of illusion and hallucination, if one is seeing F in some object o, then o must really possess feature F. And there is a long tradition of worrying about objective aesthetic and moral properties both. So we have:

S_o: There are no mind-independent aesthetic properties.

The revision is to say that although one may claim that one sees aesthetic property F in o, the 'sees' here should be interpreted cognitively or epistemically: one only judges that o is F.

The third reason is often coupled with this last one. But it centres not on the ontology but the normativity of aesthetic attributions. Aesthetic responses may vary dramatically from subject to subject. Although not the most illuminating characterization, responses to artworks are, as we say, highly subjective. Thus,

S_h: Aesthetic responses are purely subjective.

This claim is often couched in hedonistic terms: different subjects take pleasure (or not) in different things and experiences. Accordingly, an aesthetic response is something more like a report of how one is struck, pleasurably or not, by an artwork. This implies that matters of taste are not matters of fact. Now, if perception is largely descriptive and veridical, then perceiving aesthetic properties would require representing objective features of the world. But this looks incompatible with the subjective variability of aesthetic response. So, AP must be false and aesthetic assessment a matter of something non-perceptual.

Taken together, these three propositions provide a substantial hurdle for the proponent of AP, and from a variety of theoretical angles: mental architecture, ontology, normativity. They are, however, separable and so AP can largely be defended against each one independently. A substantial amount of work has been done on the second and third reasons for doubt.[2] Comparatively less has been written on the first challenge, S_c. For this reason, and in the context of this particular volume of research, the following discussion offers an attempted defence of AP against S_c. If successful, this contributes to vindicating an intuition common to appreciator and theorist alike, namely, that the aesthetic is a perceptual phenomenon.

1. For and Against the Sceptical Challenge from S_c

1.1. Sparse versus rich perceptual content

From a lay perspective, we do not often distinguish the features that 'just appear' to us from those that require some interpretation or judgement. But cognitive science has made a tradition of attempting to do just that, and one dominant view is conservative with respect to those features that simply appear (to all normal perceivers), while a lot more is admitted into the contents of interpretation, judgement, and belief. So as you look out your window, vision carries information about the colours and shapes of the afternoon sky. You see blues, yellows, whites, and greys, and the outlines of the clouds and distant mountain range. But representation that an object is of a natural or artefactual kind is done at the level of cognition. So you judge the presence of the mountain range or of the clouds. These properties—being a mountain, being a cloud—while mentally represented by you, are not represented by vision.

It is worth taking a brief moment to clarify some motivation for the traditional, sparse view. Although it takes some time to develop beyond the Jamesian blooming, buzzing confusion of sensory stimuli, the vast majority of human beings develop normal perceptual capacities, essential for making sense of (literally) and acting upon objects and events in the immediate environment. And for each sense modality, there is a dominant set of norms, a convergence on colour discrimination, tone discrimination, and so on. Add to this the apparent fact that once developed, perceptual systems work extremely quickly, with no person-level effort (once proprietary input has been received by the relevant receptors), and in a way that most typically accurately represents the immediate environment. This has encouraged many theorists to think that perceptual systems must be biologically hard-wired, and must process limited, modality-specific classes of information. Put one way, input from other non-sensory parts of the cognitive system (what one knows, one's goals, and so on)

---

[2] There is too much literature to list, so here is just one defence of AP for each of the other two sceptical worries. On the second, ontological, reason for doubt, Frank Sibley (in Sibley and Tanner 1968) argues by analogy that aesthetic attribution meets (enough of) the same standards as colour property attribution. And insofar as meeting these standards suffices for some kind of objectivity (not necessarily 'purely' mind-independent objectivity), then aesthetic qualities may be properly understood as perceivable, genuine properties. Regarding the third, hedonic, reason for doubt, David Hume's (1757/1874–5) solution to the problem of taste remains one of the best. Aesthetic experience is, for Hume, grounded in perceptual experience. And although different subjects respond differently to the same work, there are a number of ways that perception can be deficient. Objectivity in this context is thus revealed by identification of an ideal judge who enjoys unhindered perceptual experience of works. So although subjective, one's aesthetic responses are more or less appropriate in a way that depends upon how well one's perceptual experience of works approximates that of the ideal judge.

would undermine the observed cross-perceiver convergence on discrimination, speed, and objectivity and so, by inference to the best explanation, perceptual systems must function largely independently of those cognitive systems, processing only basic, context-neutral features of the environment.

Generalizing, we have the claim that grounds the relevant sceptical challenge to AP:

S_c: Perception represents only low-level properties.

The incompatibility approaches logical contrariness: If perception represents only low-level properties, and all theorists agree that aesthetic properties are not low-level properties (if 'real' properties at all), then AP is false: aesthetic properties are never represented by perceptual experience.[3]

1.2. Two aesthetic cases and two categories of explanation

Being dynamic and being serene are standard examples of aesthetic properties.[4] They also typically oppose one another: it is rare that one finds an object to be both dynamic and serene. Now consider the following thought experiment, modelled on a famous example given by Kendall Walton. First, suppose you are in Madrid and you visit the Museo Nacional Centro de Arte Reina Sofía, which houses Picasso's *Guernica*. As most readers would agree, experience of *Guernica*, in this context, is well described as dynamic, violent, disturbing, vital. Now imagine that, on a different occasion, you visit the Gallery of Guernicas. This is the gallery of Walton's hypothetical society of artmakers who produce works of art in the category of *guernicas*. Works in this category are

like versions of Picasso's *Guernica* done in various bas-relief dimensions. All of them surfaces with colors and shapes of Picasso's *Guernica*, but the surfaces molded to protrude from the wall like relief maps of different kinds of terrain. Some *guernicas* have rolling surfaces, others are sharp and jagged, still others contain several relatively flat planes at various angles to each other, and so forth.[5]

Now there is no actual category of *guernicas* for reference, so the reader must simply imagine the perceptible contrast between *guernica*-makers' *guernicas* and Picasso's *Guernica*. And then imagine that in the Gallery of Guernicas, after many viewings of the *guernica*-makers' works, you turn the corner and encounter Picasso's *Guernica*. It is very likely that in this rather different viewing situation you would describe your

---

[3] There is no standard *definition* of 'low-level' or 'high-level' as pertains to perceived properties, but instead a standard contrast. Susanna Siegel characterizes high-level properties negatively, where high-level properties for vision are those 'other than color, shape, illumination, motion, and their co-instantiation in objects' (S. Siegel (2006), 481). The discussion here will just follow this convention. Likewise 'sparse content' will characterize experiences, as theorized, that involve representation of only those low-level properties; 'rich content' will characterize experiences, as theorized, that involve representation of something more than those basic, or low-level properties.

[4] 'Standard' at least according to one common picture given in analytic aesthetics. See Sibley (1959/2001). There is of course substantial debate regarding what makes a property (or feature or concept or term) aesthetic vs. non-aesthetic. See Sibley (1965); Cohen (1973); Kivy (1975). Here it is just assumed that there is some, perhaps loosely delineated, set of paradigm aesthetic properties.

[5] Walton (1970), 347.

experience of Picasso's work as cold, or lifeless, or serene, or 'perhaps bland, dull, boring—but in any case *not* violent, dynamic, and vital'.[6] To select a property each from Walton's lists, in the first case one attributes being dynamic to *Guernica*; in the second case, one attributes being serene to the same work, *Guernica*. Take this as our first case of a contrast in aesthetic reaction.

Consider a second case. Most of us are familiar with impressionist paintings. But of course each of us had to learn about this particular movement (and learn by viewing, either in person or through reproductions). Once learned, it is plausible that one thereby learns to identify, by sight, impressionist paintings as such (with varying levels of precision and reliability of course). So at one point, perhaps as a child, one did not have the capacity to attribute 'impressionist' to paintings with any reliability and, at a later point, one acquired this capacity and then readily and accurately identifies paintings in just this way. A natural description of the latter says that some paintings just strike one as impressionist. Furthermore, it is natural to describe impressionism in terms of a gestalt, even if that gestalt cannot be defined in rigorous terms. Impressionist paintings are typified by a number of perceptible features: highlighting of natural light and reflection; a regular (but not categorical) use of lighter colours; identifiable quick, short strokes of paint; an emphasis on a scene rather than any one figure or group of figures; use of angles and composition creating a candid rather than posed depiction of people and events. To know impressionism, is to know and respond to some cluster of these features. And this is an important difference in the aesthetic reaction of the naïve vs. experienced viewer.[7]

Summarizing, these are both cases of contrast: one where one subject responds to an artwork (or category of artwork) in one way, and a distinct subject (or the same subject in a different context) responds to the same artwork in a clearly different way. This difference in aesthetic reaction entails a difference in the overall mental experience of the two types of subjects. Plausibly, this difference will involve a difference in the overall feel or phenomenology of the contextually distinct viewings (in the first case) and the naïve viewing vs. the informed viewing (in the second case).[8] And by hypothesis, this difference depends upon some difference in learning, experience, or knowledge. The question is how this difference should be further explained and whether the most plausible explanation favours S_c or AP?

Two categories of explanation are relevant. The first explanation says that the *aesthetic* difference is explained post-perceptually: the informed viewer makes different judgements or evaluations, premised on the knowledge she has and the naïve lack. But this is not, and does not depend upon, a perceptual difference.[9] Put in its

---

[6] Walton (1970), 347.

[7] One might maintain that 'being impressionist' is an artistic property, but not an aesthetic property, perhaps because it seems to be a property instantiated only by artworks, by contrast to more broadly-instantiated properties like 'being dynamic' or 'being balanced'. Granting this distinction makes no difference to the argument that follows.

[8] This is not meant to be question-begging in the current dialectical context: the overall phenomenology of one's mental experience may include more than just sensory phenomenology. See S. Siegel (2006).

[9] A great deal more could be said about candidate cognitive states or processes here. For example, is there a difference between a judgement and an evaluation? What is the role of (occurrent) belief? These questions should be analysed, but not here. All that matters here is that there are a number of cognitive

strongest form, the perceptual experiences of the distinct subjects are the same (in phenomenal character and representational content). If pressed, this theorist could concede a sensory phenomenal difference, but this difference would be explained in terms of sparse content only.

The motivation is this: if aesthetic properties like 'being dynamic' and 'being impressionist' are high-level properties, then they are not represented by experience. Again, perception is fast, hard-wired, and objective across perceivers and cultures, and so plausibly only represents basic properties of the environment. An explanation of this kind is further motivated by acknowledgement of the (hypothesized) fact that the naïve versus informed subjects differ in what they have learned about artworks and aesthetic features. So, the reasoning would go, the resultant (aesthetic) differences will be at the level of post-perceptual cognition. One learns some typifying features of impressionism and is then able to judge and report which paintings are impressionist. And note finally how these two points work in tandem: if one is already committed to the claim that perception represents only low-level properties, and the difference (between naïve and informed subjects) involves high-level properties the identification of which depends on background learning, then it must follow that those properties will (post-learning) be represented in later cognitive (non-perceptual) processes.

Now for the second category of explanation. Consider once more our two examples. In each case, there is a difference in the aesthetic reaction of the two subjects that depends upon some background learning or cognition. And plausibly, the overall experience between naïve and informed subject will differ in broad phenomenology. How can the proponent of AP explain these differences?

The general type of explanation says that the phenomenal contrast is best explained as a difference in rich perceptual representation. There is a line of argument now standard in the literature on admissible contents that appeals to phenomenology. Susanna Siegel argues that the overall phenomenal difference before and after one learns to recognize pine trees is a perceptual difference. For the pine-tree spotter, vision represents pine trees; and for the pine-tree naïve, it does not.[10] This position has been buttressed with some empirical support. For example, Tim Bayne argues that the difference between the visual associative agnosic and a normal human perceiver is that while the former possesses intact low-level perceptual capacities, she lacks intact high-level perceptual capacities.[11] So the agnosic sees the telephone (its spatial and colour properties) but does not visually recognize the telephone. Bayne thus draws an inference on the basis of what's missing for the agnosic: normal human perception represents high-level properties like 'being a telephone'. One can see how this line of argument provides a template for thinking about rich perceptual representation of aesthetic properties.[12]

---

states typically theorized and, their possible differences notwithstanding, they are all supposed to be non-sensory, post-perceptual states. Accordingly, this is a category of explanation unified by its distinction from the second category involving perceptual explanation.

[10] See S. Siegel (2006) and (2010a).

[11] See Bayne (2009). One can find similar arguments, or at least suggestions, in Van Gulick (1994) and Siewert (1998).

[12] For a discussion of this sort, see D. Stokes (2014).

In the discussion that follows, a new argument for rich perceptual representation is offered. This argument employs Siegel's contrast method, as well as some of her original analysis, but focuses on how to best understand mental occurrences described as 'seeing-as', with an emphasis on the phenomenology of visual perception of ambiguous figures. It takes inspiration from related discussions in Wittgenstein and N. R. Hanson.[13] The results of this argument are then applied to the cases of aesthetic contrast, where the aesthetic cases are specially illuminating. This general explanation can then be extended by appeal to three different kinds of mental mechanism. This abundance of explanatory options for the proponent of AP shifts the burden of proof to the critic of AP.

2. Ambiguous Figures and the Argument from Seeing-As

2.1. *The argument*

Figure 1.1 includes two famous examples of ambiguous figures: the duck/rabbit and the Rubin goblet.[14] Consider the duck/rabbit. First see it as a duck. Then see it as a rabbit. The term 'seeing-as' comes naturally here.[15] The same goes for the Rubin goblet. First see it as a goblet. Then see it as a pair of faces directed at one another. Here again, you *see as* a goblet or *see as* a pair of faces (and cannot do both simultaneously). Plausibly, the overall experiences of seeing the image as a duck versus seeing the image as a rabbit differ in phenomenology: what it's like to see something as a duck is broadly different from what it's like to see it as a rabbit. The most natural explanation of these observations is that the switch from seeing-as a duck to seeing-as a rabbit involves a change in visual representation. The difference is

Figure 1.1

---

[13] See Wittgenstein (1953/2009); Hanson (1958) and (1969).
[14] The reader should note the particular duck/rabbit image used. The choice of this image over the also common, mere two-dimensional outline shape image is deliberate, since the latter may not work for the line of reasoning that follows, and for reasons that hopefully become clear.
[15] Indeed, for whatever it is worth, it is incredibly difficult to write these instructions in some non-'seeing' or 'perceiving'-involving way. 'Judge it to be a duck', 'Interpret it as a duck', 'Cognize it as a duck', 'Believe it is a duck'... are all forced at best.

a genuine perceptual difference. Same goes for the Rubin goblet and many other ambiguous figures.

How might a proponent of S_c explain these switches while denying any rich perceptual difference? Here the low-level theorist will encounter a challenge in the form of a trilemma. First, a low-level theorist could claim that there is no phenomenal difference between seeing-as a duck and seeing-as a rabbit. Second, one could grant that difference but claim that it is an entirely cognitive phenomenal difference. Third, one could claim that there is a difference in judgement accompanied by a change in low-level perception only. Each of these explanations is either less plausible than the opposing high-level perceptual explanation, or collapses into that very explanation.

The first horn has the low-level theorist rejecting the claim that there is a difference in the phenomenology of seeing-as a duck versus seeing-as a rabbit. There is no difference in what it's like to have these two experiences. This position is implausible. A theory that denies that it feels different to see an image as a duck versus see it as a rabbit is almost entirely lacking in intuitive force, looking instead like an unfortunate theoretical consequence. Intuition and introspection are fallible, but both strongly favour phenomenal differences between the two experiences.[16]

Second horn: a low-level theorist may grant the difference in phenomenology, but explain it as deriving from a difference in the non-perceptual cognizing of the two images. This claim is also problematic. First, cognitive phenomenology (by contrast to sensory phenomenology) is controversial. Many have argued that there is nothing it is like to have a belief or make a judgement.[17] More substantively and less theory-committal, examples where judgement and phenomenology come apart are easy to come by. First, there are cases where a change in judgement causes no change in phenomenology; visual illusions illustrate this point. Most are familiar with the Muller-Lyer illusion (Figure 1.2), but of course each of us learned at some point that it is an illusion. It is commonly accepted that as one's beliefs (or judgements) about the lengths of the lines change (one learns that the two lines are in fact of the same length), one's phenomenology stays the same. The illusion persists and there is no obvious difference in what it is like across the pairs of experience.[18] Second, there are many cases where phenomenology changes while judgement remains the same. Consider colour constancy. Imagine a pink book on your desk, illuminated by the setting sun, moving from bright sunlight at t_1 to the last sunlight of the day at t_2. Across this entire window of time, your belief that the book is pink is stable. And, in one sense, you still perceive the book as pink (per constancy mechanisms) and would

---

[16] This does not seem to be the sort of claim for which further argument is appropriate, since it flatly appeals to intuition. That said, and for what it's worth, a number of disparate theorists share the intuition, as discussed in Macpherson (2006). See Goldstone (1988); Millar (1991); Tye (1995).

[17] One classic critic of cognitive phenomenology is Dennett (1988). See also Kim (2005). For arguments that cognitive states enjoy distinctive phenomenology, see Siewert (1998); Flanagan (1991); Horgan and Tienson (2002); Loar (2003). For a recent volume of papers on this topic, see Bayne and Montague (2011b).

[18] Macpherson (2006) makes this point, partly in service of a challenge to non-conceptual intentionalist theories of perception which, she argues, struggle to explain experiences of ambiguous figures, once it is granted that the gestalt shifts involve shifts in phenomenal character. The discussion of ambiguous figures in the present paper is indebted to Macpherson's analysis.

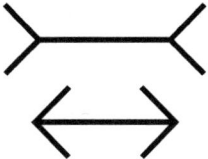

Figure 1.2

judge it accordingly. However, it is undeniable that there is a difference in what it's like to see the book at t_1 versus what it's like to see the book at t_2.[19] So, phenomenology comes apart from cognition (judgement) in both directions. The theorist under consideration would have to claim, implausibly, that all cases of seeing-as are somehow different, where changes in relevant judgement (*that* is a duck) always come with changes in non-sensory phenomenology.

The intermediate conclusion to this point is that seeing-as is most plausibly understood as a sensory perceptual phenomenon. For some object *o*, seeing *o as* an *F* is a distinct perceptual experience from seeing *o as* a *G*.[20] The final step is to extend the argument to defend a rich perceptual content thesis. This third horn of the trilemma requires more lengthy discussion.

First consider the ambiguous figures just discussed. It is eminently plausible that (assuming a non-naïve viewer), when one sees the duck/rabbit figure, say, as a duck, some of a cluster of properties—'being a duck' or 'being a duck appearance' or 'being an image of a duck' or 'being like a duck'—are thereby mentally represented as instantiated.[21] And note that each of the properties in this disjunction is a clear example of a high-level property. If this is correct, and the first two horns of the trilemma are successfully challenging, then there remains one way for the low-level theorist to maintain her position. What this theorist must say is that the phenomenal difference (from switch to switch) is at the level of low-level property representation,

---

[19] Some will note that constancy phenomena may, for reasons intimated here, be taken as a challenge to intentionalist theories of perception, since it appears that we have an instance where representational content is the same across phenomenal changes. An early example of this challenge can be found in Peacocke (1983). More recently, see B. Millar (2013). For a representationalist defence, see Dretske (2003). And for alleged explanations of constancy phenomena in terms of Fregean content, see Chalmers (2006); Thompson (2009). For general discussion, see S. Siegel (2010b).

[20] This should be qualified with 'sometimes' or 'for many *F*s and many *G*s', since this is not intended as, nor need it be, a categorical claim about all instances of seeing-as. For example, in cases of indiscernibles—say a pair of identical twins—there may be no perceptual, phenomenal difference between seeing the same object as being one or the other of the indiscernible pair (for instance, seeing an individual as being one or the other twin). The argument here only needs to be plausible for many, but not all, uses of 'seeing-as'. And furthermore, there may be deviation in, or different uses of, 'seeing-as'.

[21] This qualification is made for a pair of reasons. First, there are extra complications introduced since, strictly speaking, the duck/rabbit figure is a mere depiction and so one does not take there to be (in any sense of mental representation) a real, living, breathing duck in one's visual field (when viewing the duck/rabbit figure). Second, there is an open question, not sufficiently discussed in the literature, about whether the rich content theorist needs to claim that kind properties (e.g. the natural kind property 'being a duck') are themselves part of the content of perceptual experience. It is plausible, as discussed momentarily, that a much weaker claim is sufficient for rich perceptual content.

while 'being a duck' and the other relevant high-level properties are cognitive contents (e.g. one interprets the image as a duck, or as a duck representation, or as being a duck appearance, and so on). The question is what the former difference in perceptual content amounts to. It is both introspectively and psychologically implausible that each time the switch occurs, perception represents distinct colours or distinct edges (with the same duck/rabbit figure in view throughout). Moreover, as again introspection should reveal, it isn't just (or even) the outline shape that changes. Instead, such a change would have to be in something like an overall gestalt, some organization of low-level properties. A familiar way to put this is that the duck (or the rabbit) 'pops out'. So, for the duck/rabbit image, when one sees it as a duck, call the candidate, pop-out feature of content 'being organized like a duck'. Is it correct to insist that this kind of perceptual representation of an organization of low-level features involves only low-level content?

This is a fine line to walk. Note that the switches in question are reliable, in the sense that (with these and most ambiguous figures) one switches between only two things: now it's a duck, now it's a rabbit, now it's a duck, etc., and one will tend to have the organized-like-a-duck experience only when appropriate stimuli are available (one will not have that kind of experience when viewing, say, the Rubin goblet or a sunset). Furthermore, the phenomenology is, all else being equal, relatively stable across these switches: it isn't as if the figure strikes the perceiver, across a range of switches, with a wide variety of duck-appearances.[22] All of this is supposed to be explained by the low-level theorist under consideration as a switch in interpretation (between 'that's a duck' and 'that's a rabbit') and an accordant shift between visual experience representing the world as containing the relevant organizational gestalt (as containing an overall organization of edge, colour, and shape typical of a duck, then of a rabbit, etc.). These considerations in hand, what reason is left to deny that this content is rich content of visual experience?

One way to put things is in terms of discriminatory capacities. The low-level theorist in question says that one's visual experience characterizes some cluster of low-level properties (colours, edge, shapes) as being 'organized like a duck', where this is the (or at least *a*) appearance—a coherent organization of looks—typical of a duck. And she must grant further that tokens of this visual experience type reliably co-vary with ducks or duck images or duck appearing objects. This implies a visual capacity for discriminating a kind of thing: things whose basic features are organized so as to appear like a duck. And this is just another way to say that vision

---

[22] In this way, at least when applied to ambiguous figures, this proposal is distinct from the one criticized in S. Siegel (2006), in her defence of perceptual representation of kinds. One rejoinder from the low-level theorist she considers is that, in the case of pine-tree spotting, one perceptually represents a general pine-tree gestalt that is invariant across differences between individual pine trees. Siegel argues, plausibly, that this is phenomenologically implausible, considering at least a series of viewing distinct pine trees. But the suggestion here is that two distinct overall organizational gestalts, and fairly stable ones, are likely to correspond, phenomenologically, to the switch between seeing-as a duck and seeing-as a rabbit. And in this case, unlike the pine-tree case, there is not a variety of distinct stimuli (since one is just viewing the same duck/rabbit figure). Generalizing, the suggestion here is not that, when seeing-as, we token some stored, individual-invariant gestalt representation. This is what Siegel seems to have in mind, but surely this is not the only way to think about perceptual organization vis-à-vis 'gestalts'.

discriminates—that is, represents—*more than* just colours, shapes, edges, motion, and location. It represents objects in the world as organized, where those organizational gestalts correspond in some systematic way to the kinds of objects that populate one's environment. This perceptual discrimination manifests in instances where we recognize an object (or image) *as* being of this kind or that kind, or at least, recognize an object as appearing as being of this kind or that kind. We see the image as a duck and then as a rabbit.[23]

Now recall the two aesthetic cases. In the first case, a perceiver, in two importantly distinct contexts of appreciation, ascribes first 'dynamic' and then 'serene' to Picasso's *Guernica*. The second case contrasts a subject with the capacity for attributing 'impressionist' to works with a subject who lacks this capacity. In both cases, there is a contrast in aesthetic reaction. Here again, it is natural to describe the contrast as a perceptual one: one sees the *Guernica* as dynamic or sees it as serene. One sees a work as impressionist or not. An opponent of AP who wants to maintain that this is either a purely cognitive difference or a difference only in low-level perception encounters the same trilemma.

The first and second horns of the trilemma are applied here as they were to ambiguous figures. First, a claim that there is no phenomenological difference between aesthetic reactions is implausible. What it is like to react to an artwork as being dynamic is phenomenally distinct from what it is like to react to the work as serene. Second, the claim that all phenomenal differences are purely cognitive is implausible, saddling the objector with rich cognitive phenomenology, and contrary to common instances where judgement (or other cognitive states) and phenomenally characterized experience come apart. These two horns are sharpened in the aesthetics cases. Both ordinary opinion and ordinary language suggest that aesthetic reactions to artworks are sensory in character. Anyone unversed in sophisticated philosophical debate about these topics would default to a sensory-phenomenal characterization of recognizing the dynamism or impressionism in a work. Same goes for both artists and art critics. Visual artists, for example, create works with intentions of establishing certain aesthetic 'looks' or 'appearances', and assume that their uptake is visual. And critical discourse is full of aesthetic description couched in sensory terms.[24]

The final horn challenges the theorist who grants a phenomenal change, but maintains that it is a feature only of low-level perception. So, the difference between the impressionist spotter and the impressionist naïve is that the first, and not the second, judges of a work 'that is impressionist', and this is accompanied by some difference in low-level perceptual representation. At least in this type of case, it is implausible that there is a difference in basic colour or shape or edge perception. More plausibly, there is some difference in the way these basic features are perceptually organized. The impressionist spotter enjoys perceptual experience as of an

---

[23] Bear in mind that the point is not one about linguistic representation. Figuring in the content of perception does not require some tokening of a linguistic symbol. This is equally true for the property 'being red' as it is for the property 'being a duck'; it is not a condition on perceptual content that 'red' or 'duck' is mentally represented.

[24] See also D. Stokes (2014) for discussion of these matters, and in relation to the cognitive penetrability of perception.

impressionist gestalt. And here, as with ambiguous figures, the most plausible way to understand this option is in a way that concedes rich perceptual representation. And with the aesthetic case, once again, things can be sharpened. Unlike natural and artefactual kind properties, which on many accounts have a non-perceptible essence or kind-determining underlying structure, many aesthetic properties are exhausted by appearance features.[25] There is nothing to the property of 'being dynamic' or 'being impressionist' (at least when in the context of aesthetics and artworks) beyond an organization or gestalt of basic features.[26] Accordingly, if a work is recognized as 'being impressionist', and perceptually recognized as an overall organization, then 'being impressionist' is perceptually represented. Therefore, in the aesthetic case, if the low-level theorist (or other sceptic of AP) grants a sensory difference in terms of the perceptual organization of features, this is equivalent to granting that aesthetic properties are perceived. And to grant this is to grant that some high-level properties figure in the content of experience.

A clarification of the argument at this stage will be useful. The argument is not, simply, that because (many) aesthetic properties are appearance properties, they must be perceptually represented (if mentally represented at all). Instead, considering pairs of contrasting aesthetic reactions, attempts to explain the contrast in strictly non-phenomenal ways (Horn 1) or strictly cognitive ways (Horn 2) are implausible. The opponent of AP is then left with a hybrid explanation, where a contrast in judgement is accompanied by distinctive sensory phenomenology (Horn 3). The latter perceptual differences are not sufficiently explained in terms of only colour or shape or edge perception, but instead require some appeal to an overall organization of those basic features. But, to perceptually experience that kind of organization—an impressionist gestalt—*just is* to perceptually experience the relevant aesthetic property. Therefore, aesthetic reaction sometimes involves perceptual representation of high-level properties. It involves rich perceptual content.[27]

2.2. A rejoinder and some general lessons

The low-level theorist might reply to the above argument by taking on Horn 3, as follows. Grant that these instances of seeing-as involve *some* rich content, while maintaining that genuine kind properties are not themselves perceptual contents. One way to articulate this rejoinder is in familiar terms of accuracy conditions. If perceptual experience is representational then, in a rather intuitive sense, it says to

---

[25] The 'many' qualification here is deliberate. As already noted, just what is and is not an aesthetic property (or quality, term, or concept) is controversial. And one point of debate is whether aesthetic properties are, or are exhausted by, appearance properties. For example, it is plausible that literary works have aesthetic qualities, but at least some of those qualities have nothing to do with the visual or auditory appearance of the words as they appear on the page or as they are spoken. This general debate can be reasonably avoided, since the case being made here for rich perceptual content of aesthetic properties only requires that some aesthetic properties are exhausted by appearance. The discussion will assume this qualification, even if it is not always made explicit with 'some' or 'many'.

[26] Note that the question about the relation between aesthetic properties and basic properties is important, but orthogonal to the present line of reasoning. Note also that this is not to suggest that there is no objectivity to aesthetic properties or that there are no correctness conditions for aesthetic responses and attributions.

[27] This discussion owes much to Siewert's (1998) discussion of perceptual recognition and organization.

the perceiver how the world is here and now.[28] Representations can be more or less accurate with respect to how they represent; perceptual experiences can be more or less accurate in what they say about how the world is here and now. Accordingly, for any experience token *e*, one can identify the way(s) *w* the world would need to be (here and now) for *e* to be accurate (setting to one side difficulties about degree of accuracy). If the world is way *w*, then *e* is accurate (and if not, then not). To specify these accuracy conditions is to specify what any experience *e* is about; it is to specify the content of *e*. The debate about admissible contents concerns the types of properties that are *needed* in order to specify accuracy conditions and, thereby, to adequately capture the content of perceptual experience. Here two questions should be distinguished: (1) Are basic properties sufficient (so, for vision: colour, edges, shape, motion, location)? (2) Are natural or artefactual kind properties needed? It is often assumed that if one answers 'no' to question (1) then one answers 'yes' (perhaps *must* answer 'yes') to question (2). Working through this final rejoinder reveals that this may be an unnecessarily coarse way to think about the richness of perceptual representation.

Consider once more the ambiguous figures. The option being considered (Horn 3) is that seeing-as a duck in the presence of the duck/rabbit image involves a judgement that 'that's a duck' plus a perceptual experience that is best characterized as 'being organized like a duck'. The low-level theorist might attempt to maintain that the content of this perceptual experience is low-level by reasoning as follows. Plausibly, one will have this experience in a variety of circumstances, only some of which involve the instantiation of the property 'being a duck'. Thus, one will token this (broadly individuated) experience type in the presence of living, breathing ducks, or in the presence of plastic duck decoys, or certain landscape paintings or, as in the case in question, in the presence of the duck/rabbit image in Figure 1.1. Furthermore, it seems plausible that the experience is accurate if one is in the presence of any of these stimuli. And notice that the natural kind property 'being a duck' is instantiated only in the first circumstance listed here. So it cannot be the case that the kind property 'being a duck' is part of the content of the relevant experience, since it only figures (and *need* only figure) as one factor in a disjunctive set of accuracy conditions. In other words, there is an array of circumstances, any one of which would render the experience accurate but only one of which involves instantiation of the relevant kind property. By contrast, the various low-level properties are part of the content of the experience. So, if part of the character of the experience involves a vertical line or edge (say part of the duck-outline), then this experience (or sub-experience, if one prefers) is accurate only if there is a vertical line or edge in one's presence. The basic, low-level property 'being a line (with such-and-such orientation)' must be instantiated here and now. Accordingly, this low-level property is part of the content of the experience. Notice further how this will be part of the content no matter which of the listed circumstances obtain (real duck, duck decoy, duck/rabbit image, etc.). So the low-level theorist argues by disanalogy, and concludes that while the relevant

---

[28] S. Siegel (2010) argues that a rich content thesis could be suitably adjusted even if a content thesis fails, for example, if one favours some direct realist theory of perception.

experience involves the 'being organized like a duck' character, that character is sufficiently captured by appeal to basic properties only. In particular, the property 'being a duck' is unnecessary in specifying the representational content of the experience. And the disanalogy generalizes, low-level properties are necessary to specify perceptual content (as accuracy conditions) while kind properties are not necessary to specify content.

There is an important insight in this rejoinder, but it will not service the low-level theorist's defence. The argument was that kind properties are unnecessary for specification of content (as accuracy conditions), and by an alleged disanalogy with perceptual representation of basic features like colours and edges. The theorist is right about kind properties, but wrong about the disanalogy: the same is plausibly true for low-level properties as well. Consider colour. Suppose one has a properly functioning visual system, and has an experience as of a red globe. One might employ the same technique as above and claim that this experience is accurate just in case there is some object, here and now, that instantiates the property 'being red'. There must *really be*, as we sometimes say, some red globe in one's visual field. So, the property REDNESS is part of the content of one's experience. But brief reflection reveals that this is too strong. First, notice how it depends upon *some form* of colour realism being true. If all forms of colour realism should turn out false, then colour perception is systematically inaccurate: there isn't *really* a red thing in one's visual field, ever. Perhaps this is unsurprising to some philosophers of colour (perhaps it is even the makings of a transcendental argument that some realists might employ). But it suggests that something has gone wrong with the theory if accuracy of basic forms of perception is beholden to accuracy of ontological theorizing. Second, ontological theories to one side, this specification of content still renders much of experience inaccurate. Suppose in having the experience as of a red globe, with the content specified as per above, one in fact is not in the presence of a red globe. Instead, one is in the presence of a white globe, perfectly illuminated by hidden red lighting so as to have the appearance as of a red globe. In this circumstance, the object of perception (the globe) does *not* instantiate the property 'being red' but only appears red (to any normal perceiver). Indeed, as described, no single object here and now instantiates 'being red'. But as specified, the experience represents the object (the globe) as instantiating the property 'being red'. Accordingly, the experience is inaccurate. This is an odd result. Situations like these are entirely ordinary and one has, by hypothesis, a normally functioning visual system. Extended, this would render a great deal of perfectly normal, appearance-tracking perception, inaccurate.

The conclusion should be that perceptual representation of high-level or kind properties and perceptual representation of low-level properties are analogous (instead of disanalogous) with respect to how properties figure into content. In both cases, there is a risk concerning the fineness of grain in identifying accuracy conditions (and thus content). Whether an experience has a reddish character or a duck-ish character, if for accuracy of the experience it is required that the properties ('being red' or 'being a duck') be, strictly speaking, instantiated here and now, then inaccuracy among normal perceivers is rampant. In other words, by parity of reasoning, if the low-level theorist maintains that the property 'being a duck' is unnecessary to adequately capture the content of the experience type with the 'being organized like a duck' character (since it would render inaccurate many relevant experiences, including the experience of the duck/rabbit), then one should maintain the same for standard low-level experiences, including colour experiences. Comparing the results of this line of reasoning to the case of aesthetic properties suggests some more surprising conclusions.

Suppose for the moment that some objectivism about all three 'types' of property is true—basic properties like colour, kind properties like 'being a duck', aesthetic properties like 'being dynamic' are all real in at least the minimal sense that ascription of each type is truth-evaluable. Consideration of aesthetic properties is instructive in this context. Supposing an expert perceiver (perhaps a visual artist), perception provides full access to aesthetic properties. Aesthetic properties (or again, at least many of them) are something approaching pure appearance properties.[29] And so a suitably trained perceiver can ascribe and identify aesthetic properties with high frequency *just on the basis of her experiences*. This is because there is no hidden nature or essence to a property like 'being graceful' or 'being impressionist', and this contrasts with both kind properties and basic colour properties. Glossing over a vast amount of theoretical detail and controversy, what makes something an instance of the natural kind DUCK is some underlying structure, not detectable by perception alone. And so there are many circumstances where uncertainty or mistakes about duck-identification will not be correctable by perception alone.[30] Put in terms of expertise, there is no relevant expert perceiver (say an ornithologist) who, knowing all there is to know about ducks, will not have the organized-like-a-duck experience in the presence of, say, some hereto unencountered duck-looking non-duck creature from a faraway land. Correcting misascription in this case requires more than what even expert perception can provide. And note, crucially, that this correction will correct judgement but will not correct perception: the expert still has an experience (of the non-duck) characterized as 'being organized like a duck'. A similar story would be told for artefactual kinds, where here the essence might involve some conventional function or role. And finally, the same is true for colour properties. Assuming again some expert perceiver (perhaps an expert colourist), there are many

---

[29] Note that this is compatible with variation in capacity for recognizing these appearances. So, we can train ourselves, and sometimes may need to. We can better recognize appearances by repeated experience or learning of some kind. As discussed in Section 3, this could be achieved by a variety of cognitive mechanisms.

[30] For simplicity, this discussion (like all of the discussion of perception of kind properties) proceeds on the assumption that some kind of realism about kinds is true and, moreover, that we are liberal in our kind taxonomy. Thus, ducks and pine trees are natural kinds. However, the discussion could be adjusted in various ways without undermining the argument. For example, if one is a conventionalist about kinds, then the conventions (rather than some underlying microstructure) are what cannot be perceived. Or, perhaps one does not think that things like ducks or pines are kinds, but instead are species (understood as individuals or classes or sets). Here again, there will be criteria for being a member of a species that exhaust the perceptible, macrostructural features of any perceived biological thing, for example, the capacity to successfully interbreed or the sharing of a common ancestry. Indeed, this was a point anticipated even by Darwin in *The Origin of Species*, 'adaptive characters, although of the utmost importance to the welfare of the being, are almost valueless to the systematist. For animals belonging to two most distinct lines of descent, may readily become adapted to similar conditions, and thus assume a close external resemblance; but such resemblances will not reveal—will rather tend to conceal their blood-relationship to their proper lines of descent.'

perceptual circumstances where vision will present the world as containing an object with some coloured appearance, but where that object in fact lacks whatever underlying (non-perceptible) features are required for an object to *really* be that colour. One can, at the cognitive level, correct any such misidentification by further investigation (perhaps manipulating the environment by checking the light, or asking about the light, etc.), but this does nothing to correct, in any relevant sense, the experience. The white globe in red light will still appear red to the expert, even after she knows it is not *really* red.

The important difference between aesthetic properties vs. kind and colour properties is that sensory perception can (often) provide full access to the first but to neither of the second. Again, put somewhat crudely, aesthetic properties are something approaching pure appearance properties (exhausted by organizational gestalts); kind and colour properties are not (for reasons given just above). One might then reason that it follows that *perception* of the second will just more often be in error, while *perception* of the first is rarely in error. But this locates the difference in the wrong place, and saddles both low-level and putative high-level perception with too much inaccuracy. Instead, one should locate the difference in the world: in the way that these various properties are, or at least are theorized by our best methods of taxonomy. Accordingly, there will be differences in cognition of or judgement about or empirical investigation of these broad types of properties (i.e. how they are ascribed and identified), but there need be no general difference in how *accurately* they are *perceptually* experienced.

Here then is a radical lesson, cautiously drawn from the attempted disanalogy in the rejoinder above. Perhaps properties the natures of which are not exhausted by appearance should never figure in the contents of experience. This is clearest with kind properties. Natural kinds have essential structures hidden to perception. Sensory perception alone cannot provide access to kind properties. And so kinds are not contents of perception, because they do not figure in the accuracy conditions for experience. But what is true for kind representation is true for colour perception: if instantiation of the property 'being red' is a condition for the accuracy of perception, then many normal visual perceivers in ordinary circumstances, will suffer inaccurate experiences. Here again there are aspects to colour properties that go beyond appearances, that go beyond what perception is able to access. We are left with the awkward result that because my experience of the red-illuminated white globe says 'that is red', it is impugned as inaccurate. This holds a well-functioning visual system accountable to something that it cannot access *because of* the nature (or theorized nature) of the relevant properties.[31]

Instead, we should include in the content of perceptual experience only those properties or aspects of properties that are accessible *to perception*. Both kind and colour properties have characteristic appearances. That is, for most kinds and most

---

[31] As an anonymous referee notes, this line of reasoning would seem to commit to a claim (of some strength) that phenomenal content (or character) determines perceptual content, and claims of this kind are controversial. This is another way in which the radical lesson drawn is a cautious one. To fully support the lesson (which is simply not the central aim or intention of this paper), then, one would need to provide a thorough analysis of the relation between sensory phenomenology and perceptual content.

basic properties, there is a typical feature or aspect (or cluster of aspects) that, by normal subjects, is detectable by perception alone. The aspect 'being organized like a duck' is such an example. These aspects of the relevant properties are more appropriate candidates for contents qua accuracy conditions. Note what follows. In one respect, perception of aesthetic properties, kind properties, and colour properties are on a par, since in all cases those experiences are about the typical appearance aspects of said properties. In another related respect, only perception of an aesthetic property is perception *of* the property, since there is nothing to an aesthetic property beyond some complex organizational gestalt. But one never, strictly speaking, perceptually represents kind or colour properties.

All of this is to think of the accuracy of perception as *appearance-aptness* but not as *truth-aptness*. The latter is often assumed, but this may smuggle in considerations better reserved for doxastic cognitive states. To count as knowledge, beliefs must be true and justified. And so, because truth is the aim of belief (getting all of the facts we might say), it is appropriate that accuracy of belief *qua representation* is understood accordingly. A belief of the white globe illuminated in red light *that* it is red fails at its aim, and is accordingly inaccurate. What is different is that belief can, in this circumstance, still achieve its aim. Investigation may be required, but belief can be corrected according to its aim. So when it fails, it is not impugned for something it cannot do. This contrasts with (visual) perception. Vision cannot do any better than it does in this circumstance: even upon receipt of information about the lighting in the room, one will still experience the white globe as red. And so it shouldn't, in this case, be impugned as inaccurate. Including the property 'being red' in the accuracy conditions, and therefore content, of the perceptual experience delivers this very verdict of inaccuracy. So, properties of this kind, as well as kind properties, by contrast with aesthetic properties, should not be included in the specification of perceptual contents.[32]

2.3. Concluding the argument: rich perceptual content of aesthetic properties

There are less revisionary (or at least different) ways to conclude from this analysis. So one might grant that kind properties are not (or are rarely) contents of experience, while colours and more basic properties are. One possible motivation here is the defensible view that colours *just are* appearance properties, by contrast to most kind properties.[33] Or, one might maintain that inclusion of a property in the accuracy conditions of experience does not entail that the properties *actually* be instantiated in the perceiver's environment. It is only required that some member of a cluster of relevant properties (some of them perhaps gerrymandered) is instantiated, where the cluster involves the range of stimuli that typically cause the relevant broadly typed

---

[32] Siewert (2012) suggests worries about inclusion of kind properties as such in perceptual contents. Another worry looming in the vicinity here, in response to the hypothetical rejoinder, is to conclude that there is a problem not with inclusion of properties in contents but, more fundamentally, with specifying perceptual contents by specifying accuracy conditions.

[33] At least with respect to perceptual representation of basic properties like colour, a related proposal is found in Shoemaker (1994).

experience in normal perceivers. Thus the experience with the character 'being organized like a duck' is accurate just in case the perceiver is in the presence of a living, breathing duck or a duck decoy or a duck depiction or... This kind of proposal might be further defended if coupled with a liberal, but surely revisionary, theory of kind properties, where any instance of one of the disjuncts from the list just given *is* an instantiation of 'being a duck'. The important point for the proponent of AP is that, no matter one's choice about these more general matters, the work has already been done to defend the claim that aesthetic properties *are* admissible contents of experience.

The argument from seeing-as, briefly applied to the aesthetic contrast cases once more, ran as follows. Explanations of the contrast in strictly non-phenomenal ways or in strictly cognitive-phenomenal ways are both (comparatively) implausible. The best move for the critic of AP then is to grant the phenomenal difference, but explain it in terms of differing judgements accompanied by a sensory-phenomenal difference. The sensory-phenomenal difference is not plausibly one in perceived colours or edges or other basic features; it is most plausibly a difference in the overall perceptual organization of those basic features. The impressionist spotter enjoys an experience of an organizational gestalt typical of impressionist works. And finally, to come this far is to grant rich perceptual content. An experience of this type represents more than basic colours and edges and shapes; it represents a kind of organization of features, distinctive of impressionism.

A return to the questions posed in Section 2.2 helps to further show that this all implies rich perceptual content, and motivation for AP. Those questions concerned what is needed to specify accuracy conditions (and so content) for perceptual experience. They were, (1) Are basic properties sufficient (so, for vision: colour, edges, shape, motion, location)? (2) Are natural or artefactual kind properties needed? The argument from seeing-as suggests a clear 'no' to question (1). The relevant part of the argument implies that specification of the contents of the contrasting aesthetic experiences (or the contrasting seeing-as a duck and seeing-as a rabbit experiences) just in terms of colours, shapes, and edges, would indicate no contrast, and so clearly not explain the apparent contrast. What is needed is specification of relevant organizational gestalts. But note also that, when the emphasis is on the aesthetic cases, the answer to (2) doesn't matter. Put most strongly, suppose one accepts one version of the radical lesson provided in Section 2.2, that kind properties are not contents of perceptual experience. Then, trivially, one would have to answer 'no' to question (2). In effect, one can have rich perceptual content without perceptual representation of kind properties. Perception of aesthetic properties involves rich perceptual content.

3. Further Motivating AP: Mechanisms for Explanation

Additional support for AP can be adduced by noting the various cognitive mechanisms or processes that might underlie, and therefore explain, apparent instances of rich perceptual experience of aesthetic properties. Here, the proponent of AP enjoys a great deal of explanatory freedom.

Candidate mechanism 1 is cognitive penetration of perception. A number of theorists have argued that cognitive states may influence, in a relatively direct way, perceptual experience. As it is often put in the literature, two perceivers with similarly well-functioning sensory organs and attending to the same object and in the same viewing conditions, may have phenomenally distinct sensory experiences as a consequence of differences in their background beliefs. Theorists who argue that perception can be cognitively affected in this way appeal to a variety of empirical research.[34] Much of the research suggests a cognitive effect on some *low-level* feature of conscious experience. In this respect, one might worry that the putative empirical evidence for cognitive penetration is of no direct import to the high-level content debate, or to the possibility of aesthetic perception. Nonetheless, the cases made for cognitive penetration, if successful, illustrate one way that background cognitive states could influence perceptual experience and should encourage new experimental investigation into the possibility of similar effects on (possible) perception of aesthetic properties and/or other high-level properties.

From a less experimental perspective, apparent cases of cognitive penetration of rich perceptual experience have been suggested and discussed in the context of the theory-ladenness of scientific observation and theorizing. For example, N. R. Hanson often described images like Figure 1.3 in such a way. A trained physicist, by contrast to a layperson, would experience the image distinctly, as an X-ray tube viewed from the cathode. (The reader might imagine her own, more updated, examples involving scientific imaging technologies.) Much of Hanson's discussion focuses on seeing-as

Figure 1.3

[34] Some examples of empirical research recently discussed include Bruner and Goodman (1947); Bruner and Postman (1948); Delk and Fillenbaum (1965); Hansen et al. (2006); Olkkonen, Hansen, and Gegenfurtner (2008); van Ulzen et al. (2008); Witzel et al. (2011). Examples of recent philosophical discussion include S. Siegel (2012) and (2013); Macpherson (2012); D. Stokes (2012) and (2013); Wu (2013). For a volume of new papers devoted to the topic, see Raftopoulos and Zeimbekis (2015).

and Wittgenstein's discussion thereof. In the example given, Hanson urges, it seems undeniable that the expert sees the object *as* an X-ray tube. And Hanson argues further, like the arguments given above, that 'seeing-as' denotes a genuine sensory phenomenon, rather than some adjunct to seeing, or some post-sensory interpretation of what has been seen.[35] What's special about these alleged cases is that they involve a kind of improvement of perception, where some expertise is penetrating perceptual experience (for example, so that the technical apparatus is seen for what it is or how it can be used). The aesthetic cases might appeal to a similar mechanism, where knowledge about art penetrates perceptual experience. The expert thus sees the impressionism or gracefulness in a work that the naïve can only accept by testimony.[36]

Candidate mechanism 2 is attention. Attentional mechanisms may be crucially involved in some instances of perception of aesthetic properties. So, with the duck/rabbit, one might think that the switch from seeing as a duck to seeing as a rabbit is enabled by attending to certain parts of the image, whereby the overall perceived organization of the image switches in the ways described in Section 2.1. Similarly, one might think that a perceiver with some degree of knowledge of art attends differently to the Monet or Sisley or Pissarro and, accordingly, sees the works as impressionist. The contrast in overall perceptual organization (in the impressionist spotter vs. impressionist naïve) thus depends upon an attentional mechanism, driven by background cognitive processes. It is important to note that this could involve an intentional act of attention, but it is not obvious that it must involve this. Individuals versed in art may sometimes deliberately invoke learned methods of attending to works; but it is also probable that they have internalized some such methods. So while they know how to look they need not always think about how to look. There is a variety of research that supports this hypothesis. For example, a number of studies have suggested that saccadic eye-movement patterns vary between artistically trained versus artistically untrained perceivers. In one study, artists attend more to structural and formal features, while the untrained subjects attend more to human faces and individual objects. Artists also perform better in recall of those same pictorial features.[37] And there is general evidence that attentional selection mechanisms *not intentionally used by the agent* affect perceptual performance. Moores et al.[38] found that object representations and associated cognitive representations strongly influence attentional selection and, in turn, perception in visual search tasks. For example, in an explicit visual search task for a MOTORBIKE image, subjects would more quickly recognize (and better recall post-stimulus presentation) an associated (but

---

[35] See Hanson (1958); Wittgenstein (1953). See also Kuhn (1962).

[36] A reader familiar with these literatures might recognize a potential difference between apparent cases of cognitive penetration of basic perception (e.g. of colour or shape perception) and the cases discussed in the theory-ladenness literature, namely, that the former effects appear to be relatively synchronic, while the latter are more plausibly diachronic (e.g. where experience of a scientific image changes as one's expertise or theory changes over time). And it has often been assumed that cognitive penetration requires a relatively synchronic effect on perception. See Churchland (1988); Fodor (1988); D. Stokes (2015). However, this is a debate that is orthogonal to present concerns. What matters here is that perception of high-level properties is explained, and in this case by some cognitive effect (say, knowledge about art). It makes no matter to this point whether any such cases 'count as'—depending upon timing of the relevant effect—cognitive penetration.

[37] Vogt and Magnussen (2007).   [38] Moores, Laiti, and Chelazzi (2003).

non-visually resembling) item like HELMET, with weakened recognition of unrelated distractors like LOCK or KETTLE. And in an additional experiment, the data suggests modulation of low-level (non-intentional) processing: saccadic eye movements were typically directed at images of objects associated with the explicit target in a search array.[39,40]

Candidate mechanism 3 is perceptual learning. One standard way to characterize perceptual learning is as involving some sensory change to one's uptake of a stimulus type by virtue of repeated exposure to tokens of that type. The phenomenon involves *learning* insofar as the sensory change is typically performance-enhancing, for example, involving an improved capacity for discriminating instances of that stimulus type.[41] Some theorists take this to be a perceptual achievement that can occur in the absence of semantic or cognitive learning. Thus one might learn to more reliably distinguish closely resembling shades of red without any sophisticated concepts for those same shades. Understood this way, perceptual learning is not the kind of mechanism that will factor into any relevant explanation which alleges a *cognitive* effect on perception. But here again the proponent of AP enjoys more flexibility in explanation. It is no doubt true that some alleged instances of perception of aesthetic properties are better explained by some kind of cognitive learning (perhaps in terms of cognitive penetration and/or attention as per above). But it is plausible, given that some aesthetic properties are exhausted just by appearance, that perceptual recognition thereof could involve *just* perceptual learning. So, one can imagine a perceiver who repeatedly views ballet performances, while remaining ignorant of any relevant theories, terms, or sophisticated concepts about the art form (or, to strengthen the case, *any* art form or theory). It is still plausible that, as exposure is increased, the perceiver may acquire a capacity for discriminating graceful performance from non-graceful performance. She would have thereby acquired a capacity for seeing certain actions as graceful, as organized in the ways typical of 'being graceful', but without possessing the relevant terms. This would be rich perceptual experience of an aesthetic property, enabled by perceptual learning.

Finally, if used in the service of explaining AP, and the arguments given above, these three types of mechanism are non-exclusive. Some instances of rich perception

---

[39] Moores, Laiti, and Chelazzi (2003). See also M. G. Stokes et al. (2012); Gazzaley and Nobre (2012).

[40] Those familiar with the cognitive penetration literature may recognize this as a point of debate. Attention-mediated cognitive effects on perception have often been interpreted as non-instances of cognitive penetration. Indeed, Jerry Fodor invokes this rejoinder with respect to the duck/rabbit and other ambiguous figures, arguing that perception in these cases simply involves an agent knowing how to act (attentively) so as to effect a distinct experience (say, seeing the image as a duck). Fodor may be right about this but, again, it is important to note that attention plausibly does not always take the form of an agent-driven act, and so the question is whether non-agential selection mechanisms can be caused by cognitive processes and in turn affect perception. In any case, here again the debate about (attention and) cognitive penetration is irrelevant. If seeing-as and recognizing aesthetic properties are (sometimes) to be understood as argued above, then cognitive penetration or not, perception sometimes enjoys rich content. And in the case of seeing a work as dynamic or impressionist, this rich perceptual experience may be the causal result of attentional mechanisms. The artist, for example, looks (intentionally or not) differently and so sees differently. See Fodor (1988). See also D. Stokes (2014) and (forthcoming); Wu (2013); Mole (2015).

[41] Two classic discussions of perceptual learning are J. J. Gibson and E. J. Gibson (1955) and E. J. Gibson (1969). For a more recent empirical review, see Goldstone (1988).

of aesthetic properties may involve cognitive penetration; others may involve perceptual learning. There is no feature of AP, nor the arguments given for it here, that implies or requires a singular underlying mechanism for each instance of the phenomenon. Moreover, the three types are in some cases complementary. Instances of perceptual learning, for example, very probably involve changes in attentional behaviours as the subject is repeatedly exposed to similar stimulus patterns. Accordingly, a full theory of aesthetic perception would best explore each of these cognitive mechanisms, which could in turn be used to further buttress the case for AP.

4. A Conclusion and a Speculation

The argument from seeing-as was first applied to ambiguous figures. When one sees the duck/rabbit figure as a duck, one enjoys an experience best phenomenally characterized as 'being organized like a duck'. The argument concluded that there is no way to explain the contrast between this experience and the seeing-as a rabbit experience without admitting perceptual discrimination of an overall organization, namely, that typical of a duck. That content is not specified just in terms of low-level properties. But it also need not, and perhaps should not, be specified in terms of the natural kind 'being a duck'. The argument is even more compelling when applied to aesthetic properties. There the claim was that in cases of aesthetic reaction, explaining phenomenal differences requires invoking an organizational gestalt: when one sees a work as impressionist, one perceives some overall impressionist gestalt. But, with aesthetic properties like these, to perceptually experience the relevant gestalt *just is* to perceptually experience the property. Therefore, aesthetic properties can figure in the contents of perceptual experience.

At the very least this argument—coupled with the rich array of cognitive mechanisms that might (non-exclusively) explain contrasts in aesthetic reaction—shifts the burden of proof to the sceptic of AP. And if AP can be defended against the other two worries—ontological and hedonic—then a traditional intuition will be vindicated: the aesthetic is a perceptual phenomenon.[42]

Finally, to end on a speculative note. Consideration of aesthetic cases—both in terms of aesthetic properties and ambiguous pictorial representation—sheds novel light on general philosophy of perception. If the analysis in this chapter is successful, aesthetic properties are sometimes perceptually represented. And seeing-as, at least when viewing pictorial representations, often involves perceptual recognition of the organizational gestalts typical of kinds of things. This is rich perceptual experience. And it is rich perceptual experience without perceptual representation of kind properties. The general proposal, only partly defended in Section 2.2, was that kind properties may be inappropriate contents for experience, not because sensory perception *fails* in any sense to represent them but because kinds, being what they are (or are theorized to be), are not the sorts of things to which perception *can* be sensitive. What it can represent, and more or less accurately, is the way basic features of an object are organized. This is the phenomenal character that pops out when one

---

[42] At least some of the time, the unexciting qualification should be.

shifts from seeing-as a duck to seeing-as a rabbit, and perhaps it is what pops out when one learns to recognize pine trees.

This would be neither a retreat for the rich content theorist, nor a trivial revision of the thesis. These experiences are rich not just in the mere contrastive sense that they represent 'more than' the basic features of colour, shape, and so on. They are rich in ways that matter to various theoretical agendas traceable to the first explicit discussions of rich content and kinds: to theories of cognitive architecture, psychopathology, epistemology. Focusing just on epistemology, there are two sides to the coin. First, if experience is potentially rich, then we can acquire more information by perceiving the world, and so some sceptical worries may be less motivated. Second, if an experience is rich, it will serve as a justificatory basis for fewer belief contents.[43] Specifying rich contents as involving organizational gestalts typical of kinds, but not kind properties themselves, still implies both consequences. Take Siegel's relevant example: Suppose I know what peaches are, and I am in the visual presence of a peach. Generalizing the suggestion given in this paper, this experience gives me more than mere colours, shapes, and location, but also a phenomenally salient organization of these features typical of a kind of thing. If the kind 'being a peach' is not included in the content of the experience, I don't get immediate justification from my experience for the belief that 'that is a peach'. Instead what I get, at most, is some link between perceptual content involving the organized-like-a-peach gestalt and the resultant belief, where this link involves various beliefs and perceptual memories about instances of the kind and their typical appearances. The beliefs that this experience can justify are accordingly restricted, given the learned link between gestalt and kind. By contrast with the peach naïve, I'd be justified in a belief about the presence of a peach but not about the presence of, say, an orange, bouncy ball. On this view, perception does not do everything for me, but it does do what it can.[44]

---

[43] See S. Siegel (2006).
[44] Special thanks to Anna Bergqvist and Robert Cowan, and an anonymous referee, for helpful feedback and suggestions. Versions of this paper were given at the Conference on Perception and the Arts, Institute of Philosophy, London, and at the Impure Perception Conference at the Berlin School of Mind and Brain, Berlin. Special thanks to the organizers of these events: Bence Nanay and Joerg Fingerhut, Lara Pourabdolrahim and Jesse Prinz, and to the participants at these events for critical feedback.

2

Can We Visually Experience Aesthetic Properties?

Heather Logue

Which properties can we visually experience?[1] This question has been the subject of much debate in recent philosophy of perception. There are some properties that pretty much everyone agrees we can visually experience: for example, colour, shape, and size. These are typically called 'low-level' properties. There are others that everyone agrees that we cannot visually experience: for example, pitches, tastes, and the property of being composed of carbon, hydrogen, and oxygen atoms. The disagreement is about so-called 'high-level' properties, which are neither obvious nor implausible candidates for properties that we can visually experience. These include biological kind properties (e.g., being a pine tree), artefactual kind properties (e.g., being a table), semantic properties of words,[2] causal properties,[3] dispositional properties (e.g., being edible),[4] others' mental states (e.g., being sad),[5] moral properties (e.g., being morally wrong, being kind), and aesthetic properties (e.g., being graceful).[6]

Those who think that we *can't* visually experience high-level properties don't deny that we can *see that* something is a banana, or that a movement is graceful. They simply deny that we can see (or, for that matter, visually experience) something's property of being a banana, or a movement's property of being graceful.[7] There is a distinction between seeing an object and its properties, on the one hand, and seeing *that* an object has a given property, on the other. To borrow an example from

---

[1] Of course, analogous questions could be raised with respect to experiences in other sense modalities. I will restrict the focus to visual experience in order to keep it clear that the issue here is *not* whether we experience aesthetic properties via a sui generis modality (as opposed to the five traditional sense modalities). More on this shortly.

[2] See e.g. S. Siegel (2006). In the literature on experience of high-level properties, what I'm calling 'biological kind properties' are usually called 'natural kind properties'. However, one might think that *colours* are natural kind properties, in which case the claim that we experience at least some natural kind properties would be uncontroversial. (Thanks to Nico Silins for raising this point.) So I think the controversy at issue is best captured by the question of whether we experience *biological* kind properties.

[3] e.g., S. Siegel (2009).   [4] e.g., Nanay (2011) and (2012).   [5] e.g., McDowell (1982).

[6] I don't know of anyone who argues for the claim that moral or aesthetic properties can be specifically *visually* experienced (as opposed to experienced in a sui generis sense-modality; see n. 1 and the discussion below). However, these claims are often not distinguished.

[7] The distinction between seeing and visually experiencing will be discussed in Section 4.

Susanna Siegel, I can see that my neighbour is on holiday, in the sense that I have *visual evidence* affording me knowledge that she is (the dark interior of her house, the mail spilling out of her mailbox). But this doesn't involve seeing my neighbour or her property of being on holiday.[8] Roughly, those who deny that we can visually experience high-level properties think that seeing that something is a banana, or that a movement is graceful, is more like seeing that my neighbour is on holiday, and unlike seeing that the banana before me is yellow and crescent-shaped.

More precisely, what's at issue in this paper is whether (a certain family of) high-level properties are experienced *via the modality of vision*. A related yet distinct issue is whether they are experienced in some more *general* sense of 'experience' that *isn't* solely a matter of experiencing via one or more of the five traditional sense modalities. For example, one might think that there is a sui generis mode of experiencing aesthetic properties, which is an amalgam of (e.g.) sensory, imaginative, and emotional capacities.[9] We can distinguish three kinds of theses:

1. High-level properties can be visually (or auditorily, or gustatorily... etc.) experienced.
2. High-level properties can be experienced via sui generis perceptual modalities.
3. Awareness of high-level properties is an entirely post-perceptual affair (i.e., it manifests in judgement, belief, and so forth).

The focus of this paper is on arguments for and against the visual version of (1).

Note that what exactly visually experiencing a property amounts to depends upon your theory of perceptual experience. For example, according to Intentionalism, it amounts to visually representing the property as instantiated.[10] According to Naïve Realism, it amounts to perceiving either an instance of the property, or whatever is going on in cases of non-veridical experience (e.g., according to Martin, having an experience that is subjectively indiscriminable from one in which you perceive an instance of the property).[11] We will return to this issue in Section 4.

The general debate about whether we can visually experience high-level properties can be broken down into more specific debates concerning each type of high-level property at issue. So, for example, one might focus on more specific theses such as the following:

(K) We can visually experience biological kind properties.
(A) We can visually experience aesthetic properties.[12]

The focus of this paper is potential arguments for and against (A). Some working in aesthetics seem to take it for granted that we can visually experience aesthetic properties, but as I implied above, some philosophers of perception would regard that claim as one in need of argument. Nevertheless, the debate amongst philosophers of perception tends to focus on other high-level properties. In this paper,

---

[8] S. Siegel (2009), 481.   [9] Cf. Audi (2013).   [10] e.g., Tye (2000).
[11] e.g., M. G. F. Martin (2004).
[12] I confess uncertainty about precisely what makes a property an *aesthetic* one. I will assume that we have a good enough grip on the notion by way of paradigm examples (e.g., gracefulness, delicacy, gaudiness).

I will explore whether arguments for and against (K) can be adapted to apply to (A). Then, I will consider whether a certain feature specific to at least some aesthetic properties yields a unique kind of argument for (A).

1. Arguments for (A) from Phenomenological and Epistemic Considerations

There are at least two broad ways of constructing a case for (K) or (A). First, one could argue that such a claim is required to adequately account for the *phenomenal character* of experience. Second, one could argue that such a claim is required to adequately account for the *epistemological role* of perceptual experience.

Let us begin with a paradigm example of the first strategy—Susanna Siegel's 'phenomenal contrast' argument for (K). It begins with the claim that there is intuitively a difference between having a visual experience prior to developing a certain recognitional capacity (e.g., the capacity to recognize pine trees), and having a visual experience of something with exactly the same colour, shape, size, and so forth after developing the capacity. Siegel then argues that this difference is best explained in terms of a phenomenological difference between the experiences, and one which stems from the fact that only one of them involves experiencing a high-level property—for example, the property of being a pine tree.[13]

This style of argument could be used to support (A) as follows.[14] Suppose you start out knowing nothing about ballet, and then at some point you start going to the ballet regularly. Over time, you acquire a capacity to recognize graceful pirouettes. Let E1 be a visual experience of a graceful pirouette you have before you develop this capacity, and E2 be an experience of a graceful pirouette you have afterward. We can argue for (A) as follows:

0. The overall experience of which E1 is a part differs from the overall experience of which E2 is a part.
1. If the overall experience of which E1 is a part differs from the overall experience of which E2 is a part, then there is a phenomenological difference between the visual experiences E1 and E2.
2. If there is a phenomenological difference between the visual experiences E1 and E2, then there is a difference in the properties experienced in the course of having E1 and E2.
3. If there is a difference in the properties experienced in the course of having E1 and E2, it is that in E2 you experience the property of gracefulness but in E1 you don't.
4. In E2 you experience the property of gracefulness but in E1 you don't.

Premise 1 claims that the difference between your overall mental state is a difference between E1 and E2 (as opposed to, say, a difference in belief, desire, or

---

[13] S. Siegel (2009), 491.

[14] I should note that the argument to come is an extension of Siegel's strategy, not an argument she gives herself (although presumably she would be sympathetic to it).

emotional state). Premise 2 claims that the difference between E1 and E2 is a difference between the *properties* you experience (as opposed to, say, a difference in a non-representational 'raw feel'). Premise 3 claims that if there is a difference in the properties you experience, it is a difference in which *aesthetic* properties you experience (rather than a difference in which low-level properties you experience). Premise (0) is accorded the status of an intuition which we are invited to share, and Siegel argues for the others by arguing against alternative explanations of the differences at issue.

I share the intuition underlying (0). However, I'm sceptical of premises (1), (2), and (3). My scepticism about premises (2) and (3) stems from the plausibility of explaining the phenomenal difference in terms of a difference in how you distribute your *attention* over visual scenes involving dancers. (This suggestion is inspired by an analogous one made by Richard Price with respect to (K).[15]) Plausibly, one who has developed a capacity to recognize graceful pirouettes attends differently to the details of dancers' movements than one did before developing it. This point can be developed into an objection to either (2) or (3). If differences in attention can make a phenomenal difference all on their own, without making for a difference in the properties one experiences (as suggested by, e.g., David Chalmers[16]), then we have an alternative explanation of the phenomenal contrast to the one given by premise (2). Alternatively, if the difference in how you attend to dancers' movements makes for a difference in which low-level properties you experience (e.g., highly determinate arrangements of dancers' limbs), then we have an alternative explanation of the phenomenal contrast to the one given in premise (3). I won't pursue the question of which is the better way to develop the point about attention here. For present purposes, it's sufficient to note that the point is plausible, and would undermine the phenomenal contrast argument one way or the other.

The type of objection just outlined can also be raised against Siegel's argument for (K).[17] My reason for scepticism about premise (1), on the other hand, is specific to the argument for (A). In defending the analogous premise (1) in her argument for (K), Siegel argues against the alternative hypothesis that the phenomenal contrast consists in the expert enjoying a feeling of familiarity, which may or may not be realized in terms of a difference in *doxastic* states (e.g., a difference in occurrent judgements).[18] Let us suppose that Siegel's arguments against such an alternative hypothesis also work in the case of the argument for (A). Nevertheless, there is *another* alternative hypothesis available in this case that isn't plausible in the case of the argument for (K)—namely, that the phenomenal contrast consists in a difference in *emotional* states. It is likely that, in a typical subject, seeing a pirouette that she takes to be graceful is reliably connected with a broad sort of emotional response (presumably some form of pleasure). If that's right, then we could account for the phenomenal contrast by saying that the experience you have after you acquire

---

[15] Price (2009).   [16] Chalmers (2004).   [17] See Price (2009); Logue (2013), 5.
[18] S. Siegel (2009), 492–7. Another possibility is that the phenomenal contrast could be explained by a difference in 'seemings' that are neither experiential nor doxastic (see e.g. Reiland 2014). It's not clear to me that seemings are really distinct from what Siegel takes perceptual representation to be; but elaborating this worry would take us too far afield.

the capacity to recognize pirouettes as graceful engenders an emotional response with its own phenomenal character, whereas the experience you have before acquiring this capacity does not.[19]

Now, one might object that a subject can *recognize* gracefulness without being *moved* by it (i.e., without feeling any associated emotions). That seems plausible, but also irrelevant to the dialectic—for it's far from clear that there would be a phenomenal contrast in such a case. To attend to the dancers' movements in each case in a robotic, emotionless manner (to control for the phenomenal contributions made by emotions) would be to engage with dance in a rather peculiar way. Typically, dance, and art more generally, is supposed to prompt emotional engagement (among other things). As a result, I find it impossible to clearly imagine the cases at issue; and I doubt I'm alone in encountering this imaginative resistance. Given that verdicts about phenomenal contrasts stem from imagination of putative contrast cases, we have no way of even getting a verdict on the cases at issue. In short, all that matters is that whenever we have the phenomenal contrast, we also have the emotional difference. Although it seems possible to recognize gracefulness without emotional engagement, it is not clear how one could establish that there is a phenomenal contrast between this case and one in which the subject lacks the recognitional capacity.

So it appears that the phenomenal contrast strategy doesn't yield a decisive case for (A).[20] Let us see whether an appeal to epistemic considerations fares any better. Perceptual experiences are supposed *justify beliefs* about, and thereby afford *knowledge* of, one's environment. Accordingly, a proponent of (A) might suggest that an experience could justify your belief that a dancer's movement is graceful, and thereby afford knowledge of this fact, only if it involves your literally visually experiencing the movement's property of being graceful.[21]

As with the phenomenal contrast strategy, this method of arguing for (A) requires dispensing with alternative explanations. And here's an alternative explanation of how your experience justifies your belief and affords knowledge: you literally visually experience low-level properties only (e.g., certain size, shape, and motion properties), but you're *also* in a non-experiential mental state with the content that a movement with these low-level properties is graceful. These two states *together* justify the belief and afford knowledge that the dancer's movement is graceful.[22]

---

[19] This alternative hypothesis isn't plausible in the case of the argument for (K)—we don't usually get emotional about pine trees (or biological kind properties in general).

[20] Of course, the alternative explanations of the phenomenal contrast that I've offered undermine the argument for (A) only if they are at least as parsimonious as the explanation in terms of perceptual experience of gracefulness. (Thanks to Dustin Stokes for pressing this point.) It would take us too far afield to flesh out all the explanations in enough detail in order to compare them on this score conclusively; for now it must suffice to say that I see no reason to suspect that the alternatives I've proposed will turn out to be less parsimonious.

[21] First, note that this argument for (A) is precarious in light of the possibility that we experience gracefulness via a sui generis sense-modality (see above). However, one might argue that the explanation in terms of *visual* experience of gracefulness is to be preferred on grounds of parsimony. Second, at least as far as I'm aware, no one actually defends an analogous argument for (K). Presumably, this is because the alternative explanation analogous to the one I'm about to propose is even *more* plausible in that case.

[22] One might worry that this explanation commits us to the view that 'thick' aesthetic properties (such as gracefulness) can be analysed in terms of descriptive properties (i.e., visible low-level properties) plus an

There are two broad ways of developing this alternative. On the first (which I'll label 'accessibilism'), the non-experiential mental state is an introspectively accessible justified belief. On the second (which I'll label 'reliabilism'), the non-experiential mental state is an introspectively inaccessible component of a reliable belief-forming process that takes you from experiences of low-level properties to judgements about gracefulness.[23] I won't pursue the question of which is the better way to develop the alternative here. However, it is worth noting that if principles linking low-level properties to aesthetic properties are difficult to articulate (which is plausible in many cases), and states with contents that the subject cannot easily articulate are disqualified from being beliefs (which isn't so obvious), then the reliabilist way of developing the alternative is superior.

Either way, one might worry that the *contents* of the states that the alternatives posit (i.e., the principles linking low-level properties and aesthetic properties) are *false*. For although

aesthetic words apply ultimately because of, and aesthetic qualities ultimately depend upon, the presence of features which, like curving or angular lines, color contrasts, placing of masses, or speed of movement, are visible, audible, or otherwise discernible without any exercise of taste or sensibility... there are no non-aesthetic features which serve as *conditions* for applying aesthetic terms.[24]

That is: there's no true proposition of the form if x is F, G, and H, then x is A (where F, G, and H are low-level properties and A is an aesthetic property). So, for example, we cannot make *any* general statement of the form 'If the vase is pale pink, somewhat curving, lightly mottled, and so forth, it will be delicate, cannot but be delicate'.[25] If there are no true propositions of this form, then one might object that the non-experiential states may not be fit to do the epistemological work I'm asking of them: either they are false beliefs (in which case they would be questionable foundations for knowledge), or it's not clear that the belief-forming processes of which they are components would be reliable (further work would be required to show that the process is reliable *in spite of* involving a state with a false content).

However, this worry is misguided. First, we need not hold that the contents of the states at issue are conditionals of this form. Rather, we can say that the contents are claims that admit of *exceptions*, e.g. the claim that pale pink, slightly curving, and lightly mottled vases are *usually* delicate (i.e., such vases are delicate much more often than not). On the face of it, a belief with this content, in conjunction with an experience of a vase as being pale pink, slightly curving, and lightly mottled, would be sufficient to justify the belief and afford knowledge that the vase is delicate. And a belief-forming process involving a state with *this* content doesn't face the worry

---

evaluative component. (For a helpful discussion of thick aesthetic concepts, see Bergqvist (forthcoming).) However, the epistemology of thick aesthetic properties doesn't dictate their metaphysics. It could be that we come to *know* that thick aesthetic properties are instantiated by relying upon generalizations mentioning specific descriptive properties, even though they cannot be *analysed* in terms of these descriptive properties. Indeed, the fact (discussed below) that there aren't any visible low-level properties that are necessary for gracefulness precludes such an analysis.

[23] Cf. Silins (2013), 29–30.   [24] Sibley (1959/2001), 424.   [25] Sibley (1959/2001), 426 n. 25.

about reliability just outlined (provided that it *is* generally the case that pale pink, slightly curving, and lightly mottled vases are delicate). Second, reliabilism is in the clear as long as the unqualified claim is *usually* true. If the unqualified claim is false in general but true in most cases, there's no cause for concern about how a state with that content can figure in a process that produces true beliefs most of the time.[26]

In summary, it appears that the arguments for (A) from the phenomenal character of experience and its epistemological role are on shaky ground at best.[27] Let us now turn to a potential argument against (A).

2. An Argument Against (A) from Illusion

One main source of resistance to (K) is the worry that it misclassifies some veridical experiences as illusions.[28] An experience is illusory if the subject sees something as having a property it doesn't really have. For example, if one can experience the biological kind property of being a banana, then an experience of a yellow, crescent-shaped *plastic* thing as being yellow, crescent-shaped, and a *banana* is illusory. But one might insist that there's nothing illusory about this experience—intuitively, the error rests in the beliefs one is likely to form on the basis of this misleading experience, rather than in the experience itself.[29] So given that the experience under discussion shouldn't be classified as illusory, then one cannot experience the property of being a banana after all. In order to adapt this argument to the case of (A) and the property of gracefulness, we need a claim of the following form: if one can experience the property of gracefulness, then an experience of an F, G, H movement as being F, G, and *graceful* is illusory. As with the analogous claim in the argument against (K), H should be a property that disqualifies the movement from being graceful. Now, I see no reason to think there isn't such a claim (although I don't know enough about gracefulness to formulate it myself). But an interesting disanalogy between the arguments against (K) and (A) emerges at this point.

The argument against (K) trades on the fact that being a banana (and in general, having a certain biological kind property) requires having a particular biological constitution. Since whether or not something has such a constitution isn't something that can be seen by the naked eye, it's possible that a thing could have visible low-level properties typically associated with being a banana (e.g., yellowness, crescent-shapedness) and not be a banana. By contrast, being graceful is more *superficial* than being a banana. Plausibly, the only properties of a movement that play a role in

---

[26] Thanks to Jack Lyons and Jennifer Corns for this suggestion.

[27] The situation with the epistemological argument is more complicated than I've let on. My considered view is that the rival explanation recommended above doesn't quite work as it stands—it needs to be supplemented by according an epistemological role to relevant emotional responses. However, exploring this issue would take us too far afield for present purposes (although I take it up in a work in progress). Suffice it to say that if we were to go through this epicycle, it would still turn out that there is a perfectly adequate and arguably simpler explanation of our aesthetic knowledge in terms of experiencing low-level properties.

[28] Something along the lines of this objection can be found in Byrne (2009), 449.

[29] Perhaps some readers don't share this intuition (thanks to an anonymous referee for encouraging me to mention this). I'm very sympathetic to this reaction; as I will go on to argue below, such intuitions aren't to be trusted in this dialectical context anyway.

determining whether or not it is graceful are visible low-level properties.[30] Hence, whatever we fill in for H would be a visible low-level property that disqualifies the movement from being graceful. Of course, just because the disqualifying property is *visible* doesn't mean that it's actually *seen*—for example, unfavourable viewing conditions may prevent perception of a disqualifying low-level shape property.[31]

In any case, this disanalogy doesn't block the formulation of the argument against (A). One could argue as follows: if one can experience the aesthetic property of gracefulness, then an experience of an F, G, and H thing as being F, G, and *graceful* is *illusory*. But arguably, there's nothing illusory about this experience—intuitively, the error rests in the beliefs one is likely to form on the basis of this misleading experience, rather than in the experience itself.

Of course, the plausibility of this argument turns partly on how we fill in the placeholder letters (which, as I've admitted above, requires an aesthetic expertise that I lack). But we don't need to fill them in to see that the argument is deeply problematic. For it seems likely that our intuitions about whether the experiences are illusory stem from our *prior beliefs* about which properties we can visually experience. And if that's right, both the argument against (K) and the one against (A) are ultimately question-begging—the intuitions would depend upon the assumption that the high-level properties cannot be visually experienced, which is precisely what is at issue. So it seems that intuitions about which experiences count as illusory cannot be regarded as non-negotiable starting points in this dialectical context; at least, not as long as the possibility that the intuitions come from prior question-begging beliefs hasn't been ruled out.[32]

In summary, it seems that the (K)-inspired arguments for and against (A) are not very promising. However, the disanalogy between the arguments against (K) and (A) suggests other forms of argument *for* (A)—ones that appeal to features that seem to be unique to aesthetic properties (among the high-level properties). In Sections 3 and 4, I will outline and evaluate arguments of this sort.

3. An Argument for (A) from 'Observationality'

As noted above, one's visual evidence can suggest that a movement is graceful when it really isn't—as in a case where unfavourable viewing conditions prevent one from seeing a feature that renders a movement ungraceful. But what if the viewing conditions are favourable, and (what's better) one's visual system is functioning properly, and one has the chance to view the movement from all angles? Given that such conditions are satisfied, it's very hard to imagine how a movement could *seem* to be graceful on the basis of visual evidence without actually *being* graceful. This seems to be a feature that gracefulness shares with uncontroversial cases of

---

[30] Note that this claim is compatible with Sibley's observation that no set of visible low-level properties is sufficient for any aesthetic property (see Section 1). For it could be that an aesthetic property supervenes on visible low-level properties in an *anomalous* manner; cf. Davidson (1970). Also, see Section 4 for a discussion about how to modify this claim in order to accommodate the idea that aesthetic properties are response-dependent.
[31] Thanks to John Kulvicki for this observation. [32] Cf. Logue (2013), 6.

low-level properties—and one which is *lacked* by properties we can't visually experience, as well as by other high-level properties. One might suggest that this feature marks the divide between the properties we can visually experience and those that we can't. In this section, I will flesh out this line of thought into an argument for (A), one which is inspired by Christopher Peacocke's discussion of *observational* concepts.[33]

Consider the low-level property of *being a square*. It is not possible that someone has the capacity to visually recognize squareness, *and*:

- from all the different angles from which an object may be seen,
- [on the basis of visual evidence, it appears to be] square,
- his perceptual mechanisms are operating properly,
- the circumstances of perception (the environment in which the causal processes take place) are normal,
- the object is constant in shape, and yet
- that presented object [is not] square.[34]

Given that these conditions obtain, we cannot even begin to fathom how the object could fail to be square after all. How on earth could it *not* be? Try as we might, we couldn't conjure up an explanation of how it could appear to be square in such conditions, but nevertheless not be square. For the only kinds of explanations we could appeal to have been ruled out by the conditions stated (e.g., 'one's perceptual system isn't working properly', 'the lighting is weird', 'the subject is looking at the thing from a weird angle').

Strictly speaking, I suppose it's possible that there could be a brute, *inexplicable* failure of the subject's recognitional capacity. That is, perhaps there is a bizarre possible world in which the object appears to be square on the basis of visual evidence and yet isn't, and there is simply no explanation for the mismatch to be had. For our purposes, we can set this kind of case aside; what is of interest is that, by and large, something's appearing to be square on the basis of visual evidence in 'ideal' perceptual conditions (whatever those amount to, exactly) goes hand in hand with its being square.[35]

By contrast, consider the high-level property of *being a banana*. In a sense, it is easier to go wrong about whether something is a banana just on the basis of vision. In

---

[33] Peacocke (1983). Thanks to Keith Allen for suggesting an argument along these lines.

[34] Peacocke (1983), 99 (bullets mine). While it is handy to quote Peacocke's conditions at length, it should be noted that the notion he is after differs from the one I'm in the process of delineating here. His notion concerns concepts, i.e., ways of thinking about properties (Peacocke (1983), 89), rather than properties themselves; and what's epistemically possible for one who possesses a given concept, rather than what's metaphysically possible. It would take us too far afield to discuss the relationship between the notions here. Moreover, note that, in light of the dialectic under discussion in this paper, it's crucial that we understand the appearance mentioned as merely *epistemic* (i.e., something's seeming to be the case on the basis of evidence). For when it comes to the case of gracefulness, understanding the appearance as specifically *visual* would amount to begging the question in favour of (A) (insofar as visual appearances of F-ness are visual experiences of F-ness). Peacocke's concerns are different; in the chapter cited, he assumes that high-level properties can be visually experienced (Peacocke (1983), 88).

[35] Of course, spelling out the notion of *ideal* perceptual conditions is a non-trivial endeavour: what are *normal* circumstances? And what qualifies as *proper* operation of one's perceptual mechanisms? But let us grant that this can be done for the sake of argument.

particular, a subject with a properly functioning visual system who has the capacity to visually recognize bananas could see one from every possible angle in normal viewing conditions, such that it appears to be a banana on the basis of visual evidence; nevertheless, it is possible that it isn't a banana. It is easy to fathom how the thing could fail to be a banana, in spite of all of the specified conditions being met: to borrow an example from Section 2, it could simply be a *plastic* thing that happens to have all the low-level properties typical of bananas. There is a straightforward explanation of how the thing could appear to be a banana on the basis of visual evidence, and yet fail to be one, namely: as noted in Section 2, we simply *can't see* what disqualifies it from being a banana, no matter how closely we look at it (well, without a microscope).

Let us take stock. The property of being a square has a certain feature that the property of being a banana lacks. Specifically, in ideal visual conditions, if something appears to be F on the basis of vision, it is F (brute failures aside). Let us call this feature *observationality*, in recognition of the power it accords to perceptual observation: perceptual observation of a property with this feature *rules out* all the situations in which the thing observed *doesn't* have the property, except for those resulting from fallibility of perceptual observation itself (i.e., situations in which the observation is non-ideal in some respect).

Observationality seems to be a hallmark of low-level properties—for example, it seems to hold for colour and location.[36] So, in our attempt to figure out whether (A) is true, it is natural to ask whether any aesthetic properties are observational in this sense.[37]

As I hinted above, it seems that gracefulness is. On the face of it, it doesn't seem possible that someone has the capacity to visually recognize graceful pirouettes, and:

- from all the different angles from which a movement may be seen,
- it appears to be graceful on the basis of visual evidence,
- her perceptual mechanisms are operating properly,
- the circumstances of perception are normal,
- the movement is constant in aesthetic quality, and yet
- the movement isn't graceful.

Just as in the case of squareness, given that these conditions obtain, we cannot even begin to fathom how the movement might actually fail to be graceful after all. For how on earth could it *not* be? Try as we might, we couldn't conjure up an explanation of how it could appear to be graceful in such conditions, but nevertheless not be. For the only kinds of explanations we could appeal to have been ruled out by the conditions stated (e.g., 'one's perceptual system isn't working properly', 'the subject is looking at the movement from a bad angle').

---

[36] Of course, we must recognize that things have different *subject-relative* locations from different points of view; so we can't use Peacocke's specification of the relevant conditions exactly as stated.

[37] I should note that Peacocke wouldn't use observationality (in his sense, as a feature of concepts) to sort the properties we can perceptually experience from those that we can't. On his view, it isn't the case that all and only concepts of properties that can be perceptually experienced are observational. For example, he thinks that we can visually experience the property of being a tomato, but also that the concept *tomato* is non-observational (Peacocke (1983), 92–4). So on his view, there are some properties that can be visually experienced such that our concepts of them are non-observational.

Now, as in the case of squareness, we must allow for the possibility of *brute failures* of the capacity to recognize gracefulness. But one might wonder whether such a situation is as bizarre as a brute failure of the capacity to recognize squareness. After all, the capacity to recognize gracefulness requires rather more specialized training than the capacity to recognize squareness. One has to be sensitive to fine-grained low-level properties, as well as evaluative interactions between them (e.g., a certain low-level property might disqualify a movement from being graceful only when co-instantiated with certain other low-level properties). As a result, there seems to be more room for occasional anomalies, thanks to minor 'glitches' or imperfections in the subject's grasp of the complicated connection between low-level properties and gracefulness. (If the anomalies aren't just occasional, then the subject wouldn't count as having the capacity.) So the idea of an inexplicable failure in this case seems somewhat less bizarre—recognizing gracefulness when one sees it is no mean feat, and so it seems more plausible that attempts to do so might just inexplicably go wrong once in a while.

However, it's not clear whether a situation involving glitches in one's capacity to recognize gracefulness is one in which one's perceptual mechanisms are operating *properly*. Whatever 'ideal' conditions amount to, they include such a 'proper functioning' condition. And while it's not entirely clear what *that* condition amounts to, a situation in which there's a *glitch* in one's capacity isn't obviously one in which it's functioning *properly*. (Note that it can't be assumed in this dialectical context that the capacity to recognize gracefulness isn't a *perceptual* capacity—that's part of what's up for debate.) But more importantly, even if there can be relatively ordinary inexplicable failures of the capacity to recognize gracefulness, this fact doesn't undermine the claim that gracefulness is observational. Plausibly, it's still the case that *by and large*, in ideal conditions, you don't get appearances of gracefulness on the basis of vision in the absence of gracefulness—it doesn't really matter how bizarre the exceptions are, provided that they're few and far between.

We've just seen a case for the claim that gracefulness, like squareness, is an observational property. One might hope to parlay this similarity into an argument for (A). In particular, as hinted above, one might suggest that observationality marks the line between the properties we can visually experience and those we can't. So given that gracefulness is observational, then (A) is true—there is at least one aesthetic property we can visually experience.

However, it's not clear that observationality has this significance. For the claim that we cannot visually experience gracefulness is *compatible* with the claim that it is observational. For example, we noted that gracefulness seems to be superficial, in that the only properties that determine whether or not a movement is graceful are visible low-level properties. Now, it could be that while we don't literally visually experience gracefulness, it nevertheless counts as observational simply in virtue of the fact that its instances are determined by instances of properties that are themselves observational. It stands to reason that if one can't easily go wrong in ideal conditions about the instances of low-level visible properties on which gracefulness depends, then one can't easily go wrong in ideal conditions about gracefulness, either (provided that one has the capacity to recognize it in the first place, of course). In other words, gracefulness is observational because it is superficial, but a property's superficiality (i.e., the mere fact that its instantiation is determined by the instantiation of visible low-level properties) doesn't obviously entail that it can be visually experienced.

In short, I cannot quite see how to support the move from a property's observationality to the claim that it can be visually experienced. So the argument for (A) from observationality is inconclusive as it stands.

4. An Argument for (A) from the Metaphysics of Aesthetic Properties

In Sections 2 and 3, we've encountered the idea that at least some aesthetic properties (like our test case, gracefulness) are *superficial*—more precisely, that whether or not something has the property at issue is determined by which visible low-level properties it instantiates. But what is the metaphysical 'cash value' of this claim? And, more to the point, might the metaphysics of superficial aesthetic properties bear on the truth of (A)? In this section, I will sketch such a metaphysics, and discuss an argument for (A) based upon it.

The selection of metaphysical options will be familiar from discussions of the metaphysics of mind and colour. The rough idea is that such properties supervene on more 'basic' properties—in these cases, properties characterized in scientific terms, and ultimately, in the language of fundamental physics. In the case of aesthetic properties, we're not drilling down quite so deep: the idea is simply that at least some aesthetic properties supervene on colour, shape, location, and/or motion properties.

Note that I am not suggesting that *all* aesthetic properties supervene on such visible low-level properties. For example, some aesthetic properties have a historical dimension to them. Whether or not a painting counts as inventive presumably depends partly on its relation to paintings that have come before it. If that's right, there is no subset of a painting's low-level properties that determines whether it is inventive. The suggestion is simply that at least *some* aesthetic properties are superficial, in the sense that whether they are instantiated is determined by the instantiation of visible low-level properties.

In short, the type of question we're asking is familiar from other domains: how exactly are superficial aesthetic properties related to the more 'basic' properties that determine them? Let us call the more basic properties 'base properties', and the properties supervening upon them 'target properties'. With that terminological convention in place, here is our familiar menu of options:

- *Type-identity*: the target properties are identical to base properties (cf. pain is identical to C-fibre firing; redness is identical to a specific surface spectral reflectance profile).
- *Token-identity*: instances of the target properties are identical to instances of the base properties (cf. instances of pain are identical to instances of C-fibres firing, or instances of other base properties; instances of redness are identical to instances of various kinds of surface spectral reflectances), and the properties themselves are disjunctions of the various base properties.

- *Role-based accounts*: the target properties are characterized in terms of a specific role that is realized by the base properties.
  - *Role-identity*: the target properties are identical to the role (cf. pain is identical to the role of being caused by bodily damage... etc.; redness is identical to the role of being disposed to cause a certain kind of experience in a certain kind of perceiver)
  - *Realizer-identity*: the target properties are identical to the realizers of the role (cf. pain is identical to whatever realizes the role of being caused by bodily damage... etc.; redness is identical to whatever realizes the role of being disposed to cause a certain kind of experience in a certain kind of perceiver)
- *Brute supervenience*: the target properties supervene on the base properties, but not in virtue of any further relationship between them (such as the identity claims just mentioned)[38]

Now, in the case of gracefulness (and, plausibly, superficial aesthetic properties in general), the type-identity option is off the table—obviously, we can't give an analysis of gracefulness in terms of visible low-level properties, for gracefulness is *multiply realizable* by a wide variety of combinations of such base properties. For example, the property of gracefulness can be realized by one complex of shape, location, and motion property instances in one case, and a completely different complex of low-level property instances in another.

This fact can be accommodated by any of the other options. But arguably, the role-identity option is the front runner; for it is the only one that can accommodate the plausible idea that aesthetic properties are *response-dependent*.[39] The property of gracefulness would be identical with the role of being disposed to cause a certain kind of aesthetic response in certain kinds of viewers, and its instances would be identical with instances of specific complexes of low-level visible properties. (By contrast, on the token-identity and realizer-identity options, gracefulness is a rather motley disjunction of various visible low-level property complexes.)

I should note that accommodating the claim that aesthetic properties are response-dependent requires qualifying the characterization of superficial aesthetic properties. We need to allow for possibilities in which the connections between complexes of visible low-level properties and dispositions to cause aesthetic responses are different—e.g., the possibility that a certain kind of aesthetic response is typically caused by different complexes of visible low-level properties than it actually is. This possibility means that (e.g.) whether a movement instantiates gracefulness isn't *entirely* determined by which visible low-level properties it instantiates—it's also determined by the contingent connections between complexes of visible low-level properties and dispositions to cause the relevant aesthetic response. But there is still a sense in which gracefulness is superficial: if we *hold fixed* the connections between complexes of visible low-level properties and dispositions to cause aesthetic

---

[38] There is, of course, a dualist/emergentist option, but our interest here is restricted to metaphysics on which the instantiation of an aesthetic property is *determined* by the instantiation of visible low-level properties.

[39] Thanks to Dan Cavendon-Taylor for raising this issue.

responses, *then* whether a movement instantiates gracefulness is just a matter of which visible low-level properties it instantiates.

In any case, nothing in the argument for (A) I have in mind depends on which of the options outlined above (besides brute supervenience) is correct. All that matters for the argument is that there are at least some aesthetic properties such that their instances are token-identical to instances of low-level property complexes. Given this sort of metaphysics, there is a straightforward route to the conclusion that we can see instances of aesthetic properties: if one sees an instance of a low-level property complex, and this instance is *identical* to an instance of an aesthetic property, then one sees the instance of the aesthetic property.

However, it's not obvious that perception of a property instance is sufficient for perceptual *experience* of that property.[40] We must distinguish perception, which is a relation between a subject and mind-independent entities, from perceptual experience, which is a state a subject can be in even when she doesn't bear this relation to any mind-independent entities (as in total hallucination). The precise connection between perception and perceptual experience is a subject of dispute. Naïve Realism is naturally interpreted as claiming that at least some experiences that involve the obtaining of the perceptual relation (i.e., veridical experiences and illusions) are simply *identical* to that very state of affairs. So, for example, my veridical experience of the banana on my desk just is my perceiving the banana on my desk.[41] By contrast, others think that the connection isn't quite this tight. For example, intentionalists think that all kinds of perceptual experience consist in *representing* one's environment as being a certain way (e.g., as containing a yellow, crescent-shaped thing). Of course, representing one's environment as being a certain way is something one can do even if one isn't perceiving anything in it (as in a case of total hallucination). So on this view, perceptual experience, including veridical experience, is distinct from the obtaining of the perceptual relation.

Now, *if* veridically experiencing F-ness *just is* perceiving an instance of F-ness, then veridically perceiving an instance of F-ness is sufficient for visually experiencing it. *If* that's right, then we have an argument for (A)—at least from the Naïve Realist perspective. Given that an instance of gracefulness is identical to an instance of a low-level property complex, and that one sees the instance of the low-level property complex, then one sees the instance of gracefulness. And given that seeing an instance of gracefulness amounts to visually experiencing it, then we can visually experience an aesthetic property.

However, if the metaphysics of aesthetic properties described above is true of any aesthetic property at all, a Naïve Realist *shouldn't* claim that seeing an instance of a property is sufficient for visually experiencing it. For seeing an instance of a low-level property complex that is in fact an instance of gracefulness *before* one learns anything about ballet would be sufficient for *visually experiencing* gracefulness. I take it that no

---

[40] Thanks to Nico Silins and Fiona Macpherson for pressing this point (in different ways).
[41] As for hallucinations, these must consist in something else—this is why Naïve Realism goes naturally with *disjunctivism* about perceptual experience, which is roughly the view that veridical experiences and at least hallucinations are fundamentally different. For a detailed characterization of disjunctivism, see (e.g.) Logue (2014).

party to the debate over experience of high-level properties would want to claim that a ballet appreciation *novice* visually experiences gracefulness in the case described. This claim entails that visual experience of gracefulness can be phenomenologically and epistemically *inert*. It's agreed on all sides that the novice isn't in a position to recognize graceful pirouettes, and that she doesn't enjoy any phenomenology associated with gracefulness—this is (part of) what makes her a ballet appreciation novice.[42] So if a novice *does* visually experience gracefulness in virtue of perceiving what is in fact an instance of it, this doesn't make any distinctive contribution to the novice's epistemic position or the phenomenal character of her overall mental state. In short, the fact that one visually experiences gracefulness would have no phenomenal or epistemic upshot whatsoever.

One might reasonably suggest that a visual experience with no phenomenal or epistemic upshot whatsoever is no visual experience *at all*—for part of what it is to be a visual experience is to have such an upshot. I won't insist on this claim; this isn't the place to get tangled up in claims about the essence of visual experience. At the very least, the sense in which the novice visually experiences gracefulness is rather *uninteresting*.[43] The fact that she visually experiences gracefulness doesn't do any explanatory work; it just drops out as a consequence of a certain kind of metaphysics of aesthetic properties and a particular metaphysics of perceptual experience. This seems like a rather hollow victory for a proponent of (A).

To summarize: the argument for (A) and the Naïve Realist account of veridical experience in terms of perception don't mesh well—the former is built upon a metaphysics of aesthetic properties that, in conjunction with the latter, yields the implausible result that aesthetic *novices* perceptually experience aesthetic properties. So the Naïve Realist argument for (A) cannot get off the ground. And without Naïve Realism, the proposed metaphysics can get us *perception* of aesthetic properties; but it cannot get us all the way to *perceptual experience* of them. For that, we'd need to appeal to phenomenological or epistemological considerations—but as we've seen, the arguments that do that are inconclusive at best.

5. Conclusion

In previous work, I have argued that we should take seriously the possibility that there is no fact of the matter as to whether we can visually experience biological kind properties.[44] My worry is that the arguments for and against (K) are inconclusive as they stand, and I can't see a clear path towards settling the matter one way or the other. Thus, I suspect that the line between perceptual and post-perceptual states is not as sharp as we tend to assume. It may well be that it's simply *indeterminate*

---

[42] I suppose that one could say that the novice does enjoy such phenomenology, but lacks the training required to exploit it in order to recognize gracefulness when she sees it. But it's not clear how one could support this claim—a novice wouldn't be able to recognize the phenomenology by introspection, and it strikes me as dubious that experts could distinguish between learning to recognize phenomenology they've always had, on the one hand, and acquiring the capacity to enjoy new phenomenology, on the other.
[43] Thanks to David Chalmers for this thought.   [44] Logue (2013).

whether we visually experience biological kind properties, given that we can account for the relevant phenomenological and epistemological data either way.

This paper was born out of the hope that the matters are different when it comes to aesthetic properties. Although I think that the arguments for and against (A) analogous to the ones pertaining to (K) are also inconclusive, we can formulate arguments for (A) that trade on a feature that seems to be unique to aesthetic properties among high-level properties (what I've been calling their *superficiality*). Alas, it seems that these arguments are also inconclusive. I think that the argument from observationality deserves further elaboration and consideration, but at present I find myself drawn towards the conclusion that there's no fact of the matter with respect to (A), either.[45]

---

[45] Thanks to audiences at the Centre for Aesthetics at the University of Leeds, the Conference on Philosophy of Perception and Aesthetics at the University of Antwerp, the Conference on Evaluative Perception at the University of Glasgow, the University of London Institute of Philosophy Lunchtime Seminar, the University of York Mind and Reason seminar, and a symposium on Perception of Aesthetic Qualities at the 2014 Pacific APA for helpful questions and comments. Thanks also to the editors of this volume and an anonymous referee for their useful suggestions.

3

Moral Perception Defended

Robert Audi

The topic of perception is crucial for many fields of philosophy. Epistemology, philosophy of mind, and aesthetics are obvious cases, but metaphysics, too, concerns the nature of perceived objects and, of course, what it implies about the constitution of perceivers. In ethics, by contrast, most major writers have taken for granted that there is perceptual knowledge and have considered any moral knowledge we possess to be largely dependent on perceptual knowledge but quite different in kind. In recent years, however, philosophers have been exploring the analogy between singular moral cognitions and non-moral perceptions, and some have argued—as I have in considerable detail—that moral phenomena are genuinely perceptible and that moral perception can ground perceptual moral knowledge of its objects.[1] This paper will both summarize some essentials of my account and extend it by responding to some problems that have not yet been given the scrutiny they deserve.

1. Outline of a Theory of Moral Perception

Moral philosophers have not doubted that we can perceive—say, see or hear—phenomena that are moral in nature, such as a bombing of non-combatants or a brutal stabbing. But it is essential to distinguish between *moral perception* and mere *perception of a moral phenomenon*. The latter may be simply perception of a deed that has moral properties—something possible for a dog. Seeing a deed that has a moral property—for example the property of being wrong—does not entail seeing its wrongness, any more than seeing a beautiful painting entails seeing its beauty. We can hear a lie, as where, just after we see A receive change for a 100-dollar bill, A tells B (who needs a small loan) that A has no more cash. Can we, however, also morally perceive the lie—thereby perceiving *the wrong* that such a lie implies?

1.1. The perceptible and the observable

I have argued in detail that such moral perception is possible and apparently not uncommon. If so, we may take literally discourse that represents moral properties—or apparent moral properties—as perceptible. One objection to taking such discourse

---

[1] The most detailed statement of my theory of moral perception is presented in Audi (2013), which, in Section 1 of this paper and in a few later passages, I draw on heavily, though with some revisions.

literally is that we do not see or in any sense perceive moral properties, but only non-moral properties or non-moral events that evidence their presence. Skeptics and noncognitivists may go further: they might say that, at best, we perceive natural properties that cause us to tend to ascribe moral properties (or apply moral predicates) to their possessors or to express moral judgments about the acts, persons, or other things that are objects of moral appraisal. I grant that much of what I say about moral perception does not preclude a certain skepticism about achieving moral knowledge and also leaves open the possibility of noncognitivist or other anti-realist reinterpretations on which there are no moral properties but instead moral attitudes and moral language appropriate to them. In *Moral Perception* (especially chapters 1–3) my response to this view and to skepticism is indirect, and it will be here: I simply aim to present a more plausible alternative.

Suppose the causal hypothesis just mentioned is true and that it is because we perceive certain non-moral properties that we tend to ascribe moral properties—and we tend to say that we see, for instance, wrongdoing. Philosophers should still ask what relations hold between the two sorts of properties[2] and, correspondingly, between non-moral cognitions and moral ones, such as moral judgments. Second, we should ask whether these relations differ importantly from relations common outside the moral realm. Third, if the two kinds of relation do differ importantly, does the difference show that we do not acquire moral knowledge or moral justification through moral perceptions of the kinds I have illustrated?

To begin with, we should set aside certain unwarranted assumptions that may seem plausible. Above all, we should not expect moral perception to be exactly like physical perception, at least exactly like perceiving everyday visible objects seen in normal light (I take vision as paradigmatic for perception, as is common in philosophy). First, moral properties are not easily conceived as *observable*, in what seems the most elementary way: no sensory phenomenal representation is possible for them, as opposed to intellective representation, though sensory representations, especially of actions, may be integrated with phenomenal elements, including certain moral emotions, that are distinctive of moral experience. Second, even the perceptible properties on which the possession of certain moral properties is based may not be strictly speaking observable, at least in this elementary way. On my view, you can see one person do a wrong to another by, for example, seeing the first slashing the tires of the other's car. The slashing is uncontroversially observable. It is an 'observable fact'. But what we may be properly said to observe here may be not just a matter of what we visually perceive; it may also reflect what we already know, such as that the car belongs to the second person, not the first. We must grant, however, that even though you can visually observe the basis of the wrongdoing, your seeing the wrongdoing depends on your understanding, to at least some degree, the normative significance of the destruction of someone else's property. Moral perception presupposes both non-moral perception and a certain background understanding of interpersonal

---

[2] As suggested in the text, I assume here that there are moral properties. If my position on moral perception is plausible, that in itself provides reason to favor cognitivism in ethics. For one thing, perceptual beliefs are paradigms of cognition.

relations that, even if quite unsophisticated, enables the moral character of what is perceived to affect the perceiver's sensibility.

1.2. The analogy between perception and action

At this point we can learn much from considering the analogy between perception and action. Conceived in terms of what might be called success conditions action and perception have different 'directions of fit' to the world. Action succeeds (at least in an agent-relative sense appropriate to intentional action) when it changes the world to fit the relevant aim(s) of the agent; perception succeeds when it represents a change (or state) in a perceived object, where the perception fits—i.e., in some sense correctly represents—the world. There is a sense in which action goes from the inside out, and perception goes from the outside in. These are rough formulations; but they are a good starting point, and good theories of action and perception should enable us to refine them in illuminating ways.[3]

A second aspect of the analogy between perception and action is important for understanding moral perception. Just as we do not do anything at all without doing something *basically*, i.e., by doing it other than *by* doing something else, and, in that way, 'at will', we do not perceive anything at all other than by perceiving something basically, say by simply seeing its colors and shapes, as with visual perception of a tree. Now consider a counterpart case of action: my greeting you. I cannot do this without, for instance, raising my hand. I greet you *by* raising my hand. But for me, as for most people, that is a basic act: I do not do it by doing anything else. *Someone* might be able to move the relevant muscles at will; I cannot: I can move them only by moving my hand. This shows that there is a difference between a movement I make as an action and a movement of or in my body necessary for the action. Similarly, I see a tree by seeing its colored foliage and its shape, but I do not see these by seeing anything else. Granted, I cannot in fact see them without their conveying light to my visual system, but *that* set of events is not my basic perception. Moreover, neither the visual system's reception of the light nor my seeing the colors and shapes is a kind of doing, conceived as a volitional phenomenon, much as neither my raising my arm nor my muscle movements underlying that action are perceptual phenomena. The structural parallels between action and perception do not undermine the ontological differences between them.

We can now see how basic perceptions reveal *the perceptible*, something we can be perceptually aware of *by* (say) seeing. Some perceptible entities are not perceived basically but only by perceiving something else—in the sense of something distinct from it even if intimately connected with it in the way that raising a hand can be intimately connected with greeting. We can see this point more clearly by considering whether the kind of perceptibility in question is a matter of being, for us, *observable*, where the object is constituted roughly by what is, for us, perceivable basically. The 'for us' reveals a species-relativity, but not the subjectivism implied by taking the 'for' to be doxastic, say entailing that what we observe depends on what we

---

[3] A recent example of theorizing that focuses significantly on parallels between perception and action is Sosa (2015).

believe in the situation. The relativity view here is that a given species or subspecies tends to have a characteristic basic level of perception; it is not that the concept of perception requires positing an absolutely basic level across all species capable of perception. More generally, for any perceiving being and any time, there is a perceptually basic level for that perceiver at that time; but it does not follow, and I believe is not true, that there is some 'ultimate' perceptual level that is basic for every perceiver at every time.

Now consider injustice as a major moral phenomenon. Is it ever observable, in the most basic sense, which apparently goes with perceptual properties, roughly the kind basic for us? Is seeing injustice, for example, observational in the sense corresponding to the perceptual properties of color, shape, and motion? Or is such moral perception equivalent to seeing—in a distinctive way that is at least not narrowly observational—a set of 'base properties' for injustice, such as a patently unequal distribution of needed food to starving children, where these properties are seen in a way that makes it obvious, upon seeing them, that an injustice is done? The second alternative points in the right direction, and the remainder of this section will clarify the distinctive way in which moral perception may be visual and thereby a case of seeing. We should begin with some further points about the consequentiality of moral properties.

In asking about the relation between moral perception and seeing the relevant base properties, i.e., properties on which injustice is *consequential*, I assume something widely held: that actions and other bearers of moral properties do not have those properties *brutely*, but on the *basis* of (consequentially on) having 'descriptive' properties. Consequential properties may also be called *grounded* or *resultant*, terms that also indicate that a thing possesses the consequential (grounded) properties *because* it possesses the base properties. An act is not simply wrong, in the way in which an act can be simply a moving of one's hand (though in certain underlying ways even such basic acts are not simple). It is essential to the wrongness of an act that is wrong that it be wrong *on the basis of* being a lie, or *because* it is a promise-breaking, or *as* a stabbing, and so forth. Similarly, a person is not simply good, but good *on the basis of*, or *because of*, or *as*, having good governing motives together with beliefs appropriate to guide one toward constructive ends.[4]

If, however, we see moral properties on the basis of seeing non-moral properties, the question arises—or at any rate philosophers will ask—whether one ever really sees a moral phenomenon, such as an injustice. Recall the distinction between seeing an action that is wrong and seeing its wrongness. It is not controversial that one can see a deed that *is* wrong (unjust, a violation of a moral right, and so forth); this requires simply seeing the deed and its in fact being wrong. We can also see *that* a wrong is done. But do we even in the former case literally see such properties as wrongness or injustice? Consider seeing a babysitter consuming the last piece of chocolate cake and then later accusing a child of eating it. Do we not, given what we

---

[4] That moral properties are consequential is a view articulated in G. E. Moore (1903) and Ross (1930), esp. ch. 2. It is developed further in Audi (2004), ch. 2. I here presuppose that certain properties, such as, on the negative side, killing and, on the positive side, promising are a priori grounds of moral properties, but my theory of the nature of moral properties does not require a particular list of such grounds or indeed a particular list of moral properties.

know, see and hear wrongdoing in the accusation? We do, but the moral perception this illustrates is not the elementary kind of perception illustrated by seeing the shape of a tree.

It would be a mistake, then, to think that the phenomenal elements in perception properly so called must be sensory in the representational way that characterizes paradigms of seeing and some of the exercises of the other senses among the five ordinary senses. But why should we expect perception of injustice, which is not a basic perception for us and has a normative, non-sensory phenomenon as object, to be just like perceptions of color, shape, motion, flavor, or sound, which are physical or in any case sensory, non-normative, and, in typical cases, basic for us? Why should there not be, for instance, a phenomenal sense of injustice that is—appropriately, on my view—not 'pictorial' in the way exemplified by the visual impression of a tree or a painting? Here it is well worth considering non-visual perception. Where a moral perception is auditory, as with hearing a lie, or tactual, as with feeling a stab in the back, we are not tempted to expect it to be pictorial, at least in the way visual experience of many kinds of things may be taken to be.

One might still think that genuine perceptual experience must be cartographic, having content that provides a 'mapping' from phenomenal properties, such as a tactual impression of a shape one can feel in darkness, to physical properties causing the impression. From sensations of touch one can 'map' the shape and size of a box felt in the dark. But wrongdoing and, on the positive side, justice, do not admit of mapping, even when they can be seen in a mappable distribution of boxes, as where a supply of food from the United Nations is placed symmetrically on the ground for equal distribution to needy families waiting for help. What we see must be perceptible; but even if *perceptible properties*, such as being wrong or unjust,[5] must be seen by seeing *perceptual properties* (often called observable or considered to be expressed by 'observations terms') such as bodily movements, not all perceptible properties are perceptual. The senses can yield the base by which we see certain perceptible properties without their being on the same level as the perceptual properties pictured or mapped by the senses. To make the relevant notion of perceptibility clearer, we must explore the sense which moral perception is representational.

2. The Representational Character of Moral Perception

Given what we have seen so far, we should distinguish two kinds of demands one might make on a theory of moral perception. One demand requires the theory to provide a phenomenal—and especially, a cartographic—representation of, say, injustice. The second, more plausible demand centers on a phenomenal representation constituted by a (richer) perceptual *response* to injustice. The sense of injustice, then, a kind of impression of it, *as* based on, and as phenomenally integrated with, a

---

[5] Perceptibility here is relative to circumstances: the perceptibility (for us) of wrongness does not entail that every kind of wrongness is perceptible (say plagiarism); but the same holds for heat, which is perceptible (for us) only within a certain range.

suitable ordinary perception of the properties on which injustice is consequential—on which it is *grounded*, in a main use of that term—might serve as the experiential element in moral perception. Let me develop this view—call it an *integration theory of moral perception*.

2.1. Sensing physically versus sensing morally

An important constituent in this phenomenal integration is the perceiver's felt sense of connection between, on the one hand, the impression of, say, injustice or (on the positive side) beneficence and, on the other hand, the properties that ground the moral phenomena. This felt connection is at least akin to what some have called the sense of fittingness. The sense of connection I am describing normally produces, moreover, a non-inferential disposition to attribute the moral property of the action (or other phenomenon in question) on the basis of the property or set of properties (of that action) on which the moral property is grounded. Suppose, for instance, that I see injustice in a distribution, say, a larger box of food for a family smaller than the other families standing in line for the distribution of one per family. My sense of injustice normally yields a disposition to believe that distribution to be wrong *because* it is (on the ground that it is), say, giving more to one family in the same needy position. My awareness of injustice, however, if perceptual, is non-inferential.[6] It is not based on any premise but is a direct response to what I see. The directness is, of course, epistemic and not causal—philosophical analysis places no restrictions on what causal processes may occur in the brain. A related point is that the perception is not and certainly need not be tied to the term 'injustice' or any synonym. Any of a range of terms may be appropriate, and we may indeed leave open the extent to which the property-attribution depends of the perceiver's use of language at all.

Any kind of perception, on my view, is experiential in having *some* appearance in consciousness—though (apart from self-perception) not entailing *self*-consciousness or any internally directed attitude. *Moral* perception in some way embodies a phenomenal sense—which may (but need not) be in some way emotional—of the moral character of the act. This sense may, for instance, be felt disapproval, or even a kind of revulsion, as where we see a man deliberately spill hot tea on his wife's hand in retaliation for her embarrassing him. The sense need not be highly specific; it may, for instance, be a felt *unfittingness* between the deed and the context, as where we see male and female children treated unequally in a distribution of medical supplies for patients with the same infectious disease. Similarly, but on the positive, approbative side, a felt *fittingness* may play a positive phenomenal role in moral perception. Think of the sense of moral rebalancing if one sees the unequal distribution of medicine rectified by a health professional who takes over the case. The equality of treatment befits the equality of need.

In each instance of moral perception, the moral sense of wrongness, injustice or, in the positive case, of welcome rebalancing is essentially connected to perception of non-moral properties on which the moral properties are grounded. In cases like these, we might be said to *sense morally*, rather as someone who hears a melody in a

---

[6] More is said later to explain why many moral attributions can be non-inferential.

howling wind blowing through open drainpipes might be said to sense musically. This is not because moral properties (or comparable aesthetic ones) are sensory—they are not—nor because there is a special moral faculty dedicated to the ethical realm, but because there is a kind of perceptual experience that manifests moral sensibility and appropriately incorporates a response to the properties that ground the moral property that we sense.[7] Perceptibility through our moral sensibility is wider than, though it depends on, perceptuality at the level of observable properties accessible to the five senses.

Consider the vivid description we find in the parable of the Good Samaritan:

A priest happened to be going down the same road, and when he saw the [injured] man, he passed by on the other side. So too, a Levite...passed by on the other side. A Samaritan... came where the man was; and when he saw him, he took pity on him. He went to him and bandaged his wounds, pouring on oil and wine. Then he put the man on his own donkey, brought him to an inn and took care of him. The next day he took out two denarii and gave them to the innkeeper. 'Look after him,' he said[8]

The wounded man is a pitiful sight to which even a child might respond with a kind of distress. We are to see the priest and Levite as either lacking moral perception or, if not, responding instead to contrary motivation, whereas the Samaritan has a strong sense of what he ought to do. Granted, pity alone could yield the action, but the continuation of the story suggests a perception of the kind manifesting a sensitivity to the obligation of beneficence. Phenomenologically, seeing the wounded man as wronged or seeing what one ought to do, or both, may have experiential elements blended with pity. Indeed, the moral perception here may be *bimodal*, with sounds of pain emanating from the wounded man combining with the visual spectacle. Perception is not limited to receptivity by only once sense at a time. Just as the sense of harmony in music or of gracefulness in dance depends on both one's aesthetic sensibility and what is directly perceived through both sight and hearing, moral perceptions depend on both one's moral sensibility and what one perceives. Moral perception achieves an integration of elements that come from the constitution of one's sensibility with elements perceived on the occasion of its stimulation.[9]

2.2. The multileveled character of perception

One way to view the theory of perception I have outlined is to consider it *layered*. We can accommodate moral perception by incorporating into our theory of perception a distinction between perceptual representations of an ordinary sensory kind that are low-level and perceptual representations that are of a richer kind and are higher-level, being based in part on ordinary sensory representations. Can this layered,

---

[7] This is not to say that 'Moral perception is a form of pattern recognition', as does Max Harris Siegel in setting out my view in his generally clear and quite informative review of my *Moral Perception*. See M. H. Siegel (2014), 239. Some moral perceptions may be cases of pattern recognition, but not all are—even if each case *has* some pattern—since the grounding relations essential for moral perceptions need not yield a familiar pattern. But I do cite pattern recognition, e.g., with faces, as an example in which perception may require information-processing, yet need not entail inference.

[8] Luke 10: 31–5 (New International Version).

[9] Here one might recall the element of felt demand cited by Mandelbaum (1955); see e.g. pp. 48–9, where he speaks of situations of acute human need as 'extorting' action from us.

multilevel theory of perception, however, explain how moral perception can have a causal character? It can. To see how in a familiar kind of non-moral case, consider recognizing a person in an airport. The property of being Rosaria (construed as including at least her essential characteristics) does not cause my recognition of her; the causal work is done mainly by the properties of color and shape (or their instances) that identify her to me as Rosaria. Similarly, moral perception should not—and I think need not—be taken to be causal by treating (moral) perceptual property instances, such as seeing injustice, as causally produced or sustained by instances of moral properties. The causal work is done mainly by the base properties.

The theory of moral perception developed here is neutral regarding the possibility that moral properties themselves are causal. It does, however, construe seeing certain subsets of base properties for, say, injustice as—at least given appropriate understanding of their connection to moral properties—a kind of perception of a moral property; and this kind includes, as elements, such ordinary perceptions as seeing a violent seizure of woman's purse and hearing a loud catcall aimed at preventing a priest from saying a prayer. Depending on our psychological constitution, we may be unable to witness these things without a phenomenal sense of wrongdoing integrated with our perceptual representation of the wrong-making facts.[10] For many people, certain perceptible wrongs perpetrated in their presence are morally salient and unignorable. For many of us, then, moral perceptions of certain salient moral wrongs committed in our field of vision or hearing are virtually unavoidable.

So far, the relation between moral perception and moral knowledge has been left implicit. More must be said about this. It is one thing to hold that there are genuine moral perceptions and another to take them to ground *knowledge* or justification regarding the moral phenomenon perceived. I defend both views but do not take the epistemic power of moral perception to depend, in a way it might seem to, on the perceiver's possessing a priori knowledge. One might think

> [T]hat the epistemic credentials of moral phenomenal responses are derivative of subject's grasping ostensibly synthetic a priori entailments between moral properties and their non-moral grounds, which will presumably be a non-empirical matter. Hence, moral 'perceptual' knowledge looks to be crucially dependent upon substantive non-empirical knowledge.[11]

Four points are crucial here. First, a sensitivity to the properties on which moral properties are grounded does not require believing the conceptually high-level propositions that link the former properties to the latter or grasping the relations that provide this link. Second, even if it did, my view of moral perception allows that these linking propositions and relations be empirical. Thirdly, regarding moral judgments, the ability of moral perception to justify these judgments does not depend on the modality of the underlying process by which the perception arises: the important thing is that the process be sufficiently justificatory or adequately evidential (say, reliable) and that the perceptual content (understood in terms of properties one is perceptually aware of) be relevant to that of the judgment. Fourth, sufficiency of justification or evidence here need not be taken to imply that the relevant grounds

---

[10] For related work developing a partial phenomenology of moral perception, see Horgan and Timmons (2008). They also explore phenomenological aspects of fittingness.

[11] Cowan (2014), 1169.

are 'conclusive' evidence for the moral properties they indicate. The notion of moral perception leaves open just how tight a connection is required, though a merely accidental connection is ruled out. Viewing a stabbing may give even a child a basis for taking the assailant to be doing wrong, even if the child does not yet have the general belief that stabbings are wrong and even if their wrongness should be only empirically implied by their harmful character and the relevant probability is below 1.

2.3. Moral perception as a basis for moral knowledge

We have seen the difference between a moral perception of wrongdoing and a perception that is merely of an act that *is* wrong. We have also seen that moral perception does not entail the formation of moral belief or moral judgment. Still, although moral perception is not belief-entailing, it remains true that given how—if we understand moral phenomena—we see certain base properties that are sufficient for injustice, we sometimes perceptually know, and are perceptually justified in believing, that, for instance, one person is doing an injustice to another. We are thus justified in seeing the deed *as* an injustice. When we have such perceptual knowledge or perceptual warrant, we are often properly describable as *seeing that* the first is doing an injustice to the second and, indeed, as knowing this.

This point does not imply that seeing *an injustice* is intrinsically conceptual, even for someone who has the relevant concepts. But seeing *that* an injustice is done *is* conceptual. By contrast, merely seeing a deed that constitutes an injustice is possible for a dog or a prelingual child lacking moral concepts. Once the child acquires moral concepts, of course, the same physical perception might immediately yield a moral conceptualization of the act or indeed moral knowledge thereof. Even before developing of moral concepts, however, the child may be disturbed at seeing an injustice in the kind of act in question, say giving medicine to a fevered shivering male but not to a female in the same condition.

It seems quite possible and, from a developmental point of view, important that the sense of unfittingness in such unjust action may occur prior to conceptualization: the disparity in treatment might, in the relevant way, disturb the child. This sense of unfittingness might be a factor in moral development (a speculation I cannot pursue here). It is certainly possible that in many children there is a perception of disparity that, together with the sense of its unfittingness, reflects a discriminative sensitivity to differential treatment of persons—especially when it is, in Aristotelian terms, dissimilar treatment of similars—and this sense of unfittingness puts such children in a good position to develop the concept of injustice. If this picture is correct, moral perception may precede moral concept-formation and indeed may lie on a normal developmental route to it.

Where there is perception, one would think it should make sense to speak of possible misperception and even hallucination. Nothing said here implies that what perceptually seems to have a property actually has it, nor need every perceptual or intuitive seeming regarding a proposition—a (conscious) perceptual or intuitive impression of its truth—yield belief of the proposition it supports. A preplanned vigorous exchange between friends could be misperceived as intimidation. This might lead to a false moral belief. One might also hallucinate a brutal stabbing and thereby have a moral experience that is quasi-perceptual.

Moreover, even where one sees a wrong, such as a lie, and so might believe the perceptually knowable proposition that A lied to B, one might not initially have a sense that the action is wrong or, especially, see *that* it is wrong. Here seeing a wrong done may not even be a moral perception and certainly need not yield a propositional perception that the deed is wrong. Consider a different example. We might see a man we view as domineering shake the hand of another, smaller man of lower social status before a meeting and notice a hard squeeze, with the result of redness in the other's hand. It might not seem to us until later that we have witnessed an intimidation, though we could have been more alert and seen at the time that the former was wrongfully intimidating the latter. Moral perceptual seemings, moreover, may or may not be partly emotional, as where indignation is an element in them.

One way to explain such phenomena is to say that initially, one does not see the squeezing of the hand *as* domineering. If we take seeing *as* to be essential for moral perception, it is essential to distinguish at least three cases. First, one may see the act (or other thing) as having a property, where this is *ascriptive* and not conceptual: roughly taking the thing to have the property in a way that reflects the information that it has that property but does not require conceptualizing that property as such (if at all). Perhaps seeing an approaching dog as dangerous can be like this for a very young child, yielding perceptually guided avoidance behavior but not depending on any conceptualization of danger as implying possible harm. Second, there is conceptual seeing *as*; this would be illustrated by viewing the hand-squeezing under a description such as 'intimidating' (though no verbalization is required). Third, seeing *as* may be doxastic, as where I say, to someone who took the hand squeezing to be intimidation, that I saw it as—roughly, viewed it as—intended to express enthusiasm. Doxastic seeing *as* is of course not factive, and even seeing an actual, inexcusable wrong is compatible with mistakenly seeing it as, say, justified self-defense. If moral perception entails seeing *as* at all (say, a kind of taking *as*), then in the simplest cases it requires only ascriptive seeing *as* and neither conceptual nor doxastic seeing *as*. Perhaps one way to describe sensing morally is to call it a special case of ascriptive seeing *as*.

To recapitulate what has been said so far, on my view of perception, it is a kind of experiential information-bearing relation between the object perceived (which may be an action or other event) and the perceiver. I have not offered a full analysis of this perceptual relation but have said enough to indicate how, even if moral properties are not themselves causal, they can be perceptible. We perceive them by perceiving properties that ground them, which, in turn, may or may not be perceived in the basic way in which we perceive some properties other than by perceiving still others. But the dependence of moral perception on non-moral perception does not imply an inferential dependence of all moral belief or moral judgment on non-moral belief or non-moral judgment (a counterpart point also applies in the aesthetic domain). Indeed, although perceiving moral properties, as where we see an injustice, commonly evokes belief, it need not. When it does, it may do so in a way that grounds that belief in perception of the properties of (say) the unjust act in virtue of which it *is* unjust. This kind of grounding explains how a moral belief arising in perception can constitute perceptual knowledge and can do so on grounds that are publicly accessible and, though not a guarantee of ethical agreement, a basis for it.

3. The Phenomenological Problem

The phenomenology of perception poses challenges for even the simplest cases of moral perception. One concern is representationality. I have stressed that the sense in which a moral perception represents, say, wrongdoing, is not cartographic. But 'represent' can still mislead. Consider this worry: 'What we are trying to achieve here is a conception of a state that is genuinely perceptual, but has a moral content. The phenomenal properties of outrage [say, outrage upon viewing a brutal stabbing], even when added to a perception of the base properties, don't seem to generate a content of that sort.'[12] A crucial issue here is what counts as 'content'. In one sense, the percept represents the wrongdoing by virtue of representing the properties on which it is grounded: their presence a priori entails, by a kind of constitutive relation, the wrongdoing. But suppose content must be propositional. Then, on the natural assumption that one is acquainted with the content of one's perception, some may take this propositional view of content to imply that the content must be believed or at least conceptualized by the perceiver. The demand for moral content taken to have this doxastic or conceptualistic implication is unreasonable: one can have a moral perception yet fail to believe or otherwise conceptualize a proposition that is the (or a) content appropriate to what is perceived, such as that an act like the discriminatory delivery of injections to children is unjust.

3.1. The presentational aspect of perception

The idea I have proposed to account for the representative element in moral perception is not the view that, in moral perception, a proposition is believed or even conceptualized by the perceiver. Rather, (morally) perceiving (say) an injustice yields an experiential sense of it that is integrated with—not merely added to, as Dancy apparently imagines—perception of the base properties for this injustice. The integration may or may not involve emotion, but it must go beyond the phenomenology of merely perceiving the moral phenomenon or of that merely conjoined with a moral belief concerning that phenomenon. The integration must also appropriately reflect a relation between the felt moral element, such as injustice, and the properties grounding that element, such as patently unequal treatment.

A moral perception has its own phenomenology. It is not 'neutral' for the perceiver. As I have stressed, a *moral perception* is not merely a *perception of a moral phenomenon*, such as injustice. I have even left open what (if any) conceptual sophistication—as opposed to discriminative sensitivity—is needed for moral perception, but even if, for normal moral agents, forming a belief is typical in seeing such a blatant case of wrongdoing as the brutal stabbing, conceptualization is not required for every case of moral perception. (I will return to this matter in Sections 6 and 7.)

As to the question of how my account reflects the presentational element in perception,[13] I have answered this concern in part by noting that representation need be neither cartographic nor doxastic nor even conceptual. This is not to deny

---

[12] Dancy (2010), 102.
[13] Terence Cuneo has raised this problem (for both me and for Thomas Reid) in his critical commentary on *Moral Perception* (Cuneo 2014).

that *having* moral concepts might be needed for the discriminative phenomenal responses crucial in moral perception or indeed for the moral sensibility required for having moral perceptions. But even if, as I leave open, a measure of moral *conceptuality* is needed *to be* a moral perceiver, it does not follow that moral *conceptualization* is needed for every instance of moral perception. A necessary condition for achieving an ability need not be present on every occasion of its exercise. In any case, it is not at all obvious that experiencing a *presentation* of a moral phenomenon entails having a cartographic or, especially, a conceptual *representation* of it, and I do not think that it does.

3.2. Perception of emotion as an analogous case

Perceptions of emotions in others are a good analogy to moral perception. Here it is helpful to compare moral perception with seeing an angry outburst that warrants comments like 'He's furious!' Shall we say that the anger is not really perceived because it is seen through perceiving constitutive manifestations of it, such as redness of countenance, screaming, and puffing? Granted, these can be mimicked by a good actor; but a well-made manikin may similarly mimic a living clothes model in a static pose. We should not conclude that living clothes models are never seen, or never seen directly. Why, then, may some injustices not be as perceptible as anger?

It is true that whereas anger is seen by its manifestations, moral wrongs are seen by seeing their grounds. But why should moral perception be conceived as limited to responses to effects rather than causes or grounds? More broadly, why should perception not be possible as a phenomenologically realized, often rich response to a variety of other reliable indicators or determinants of the perceived phenomenon? Let me explain.

Suppose we think of perception as—in part—a kind of reception and processing of information that reaches one by a causal path from an information source to the mind, where the processing, as distinct from its resulting perceptual product in the mind, need not imply events in consciousness.[14] This conception certainly comports well with the role perception plays in providing everyday empirical knowledge of the natural world. On this conception, it should not matter whether the information impinging on the senses is determined by what is perceived, such as a flash of light, or, instead, by determiners or evidences of that. We can know a thing either by its effects that mark it or by its causes that guarantee it. Perceptual knowledge, like much other non-inferential knowledge, is latitudinarian regarding the variety of routes by which the truth of its object is guaranteed.

4. Perception and Inference

I have taken the perception of emotion to illustrate how perception is possible when its object is perceived not by directly seeing it but by perceiving properties reliably related to it. Such cases also bear on the objection that moral perception is at least

---

[14] For discussion of the sense in which perception is information processing, Dretske (1981) is a good source. Processing information is more than its mere reception; see Burge (2010), e.g. 299–301, for discussion of both notions and points concerning Dretske's view.

tacitly inferential, an objection posed to my view (if with qualifications) by Pekka Väyrynen.[15] Imagine a context in which someone receives news of a setback due to someone else's surprising incompetence in their joint project. Then recall the example of seeing an angry outburst, which might be a response to such news. I have suggested that some moral phenomena, such as injustices, can be as perceptible as anger. More broadly, why should perception not be possible as a noninferential response to a variety of other reliable indicators or determinants of the perceived phenomenon? The 'function' of perception, one might plausibly suppose, is to enable us to navigate the world safely and skillfully.[16] Fulfilling that function leaves open many ways in which information needed for such navigation can reach the mind and guide the agent.

A further concern of some philosophers is how much we represent, and can thereby know, perceptually. Väyrynen refers, for instance, to a debate concerning whether natural kind properties, such as water, can be 'perceptually represented' and, apparently thinking that moral perceptual kinds would be similar, writes:

> By Audi's own lights, for my response to what Harman's hoodlums [who are seen burning a cat] are doing to count as a *moral* perception, it should be appropriately causally grounded in *both* perceiving the hoodlums setting the cat on fire *and* suitable background beliefs relating those properties to moral wrongness. So the relevant responses should be construed as 'theory-laden,' in that what background beliefs one holds can causally affect what experiences one has.[17]

I have three points here. First, granting that 'background beliefs' may be essential for *possessing* at least certain of the moral concepts that may be needed to *have* the moral perceptions in question, it does not follow that either a moral perception or a belief it elicits need be 'causally grounded in' or—especially, *justificationally* based on, such beliefs. I doubt both claims. Second, I grant that the beliefs one holds can 'causally affect' what experiences one has, but this is consistent with my first point. Third, supposing that in some way perception, including certain instances of moral perception, can be *conceptually* laden, this does not entail that perception is specifically 'theory-laden' if that term implies either that it *inferentially* depends on some belief or conception or that perception is distorted (or even biased) as a result of a theory or view accepted by the perceiver.

One might now wonder whether my case 'relies on a fairly narrow notion of inference, on which a belief counts as being based on inference only if it is consciously drawn from premises that are explicitly noted as premises or evidence'.[18] That notion is too narrow, and I do not rely on it. I have long held that a belief can be inferential, in the epistemic sense that it is *based on* another belief, even if the person does not episodically infer the propositional object of the former from that of the

---

[15] In Cuneo (2014).

[16] For a view of perception that has some similarities to mine but is more 'practically' oriented and provides a conception of the navigation metaphor, see Bengson (2016). He conceives perception as 'fundamentally practical' in the sense that it renders perceivers '*poised* for action'.

[17] Pekka Väyrynen, commentary on a draft of my 'Moral Perception and Moral Knowledge'; Väyrynen (2009), 4.

[18] Väyrynen (2009), 4.

latter. A belief held *for* a reason, hence inferential in its basis, need not be a reasoned belief—one arrived at by reasoning. Moreover, my view is not that perceptual beliefs are non-inferential because they are not *elicited* by other beliefs, such as background beliefs, or by an episode of inference. Nor do I hold that perceptual beliefs must be *uninfluenced* by other beliefs. These are causal possibilities. My point is epistemic: perceptual beliefs are neither inferentially nor justificationally *based* on other beliefs and hence their *justification* does not rest on that of other beliefs.[19] This is important for understanding their normative status. It is also part of what supports their role in grounding the objectivity of ethics. Perceptual beliefs are in a sense ground-level. Some grounds are firmer than others, and some people find solid grounds more readily than others do, say in constructing a justification of their views. But perceptual grounds are normally at least objective in being intersubjectively available.

It is also essential to see here that a belief, and especially a perceptual one, need not arise from inference just because the believer *has* premises for it among the person's beliefs. When we do infer a proposition or engage in reasoning that leads to our inferring something from one or more premises, the inference takes us mentally along a path from what is represented by one or more psychological elements to what is represented by another such element.[20] It is true that we can traverse such a path without noticing it, but the mind also has its shortcuts. The territory may be familiar; our destination may be in plain view; and through the power of the imagination or some other informationally sensitive faculty we can sometimes go directly to places we would ordinarily have to reach by many steps. Perception is often like imagination in this and, without bypassing consciousness entirely, can take us from information acquired directly by vision to a belief that might, under studied conditions—or less favorable conditions—also have been reached by inference.

One source, then, of a tendency to posit inferences underlying the formation of perceptual belief is assimilating information processing that does not require inference to propositional processing that does. Another source of the tendency to posit inferences in perception is the resistance to foundationalism of one kind of another. On any plausible conception of a foundation, an inferential belief is not foundational, whereas perceptions and perceptual beliefs may be.

One manifestation of resistance to seeing the import of this moderate foundationalist conception is rejection (e.g. by Dancy) of the view that 'the primary, or basic object of perceptual awareness must be things for the sensing of which no training,

---

[19] This point does not entail that perceptual justification is indefeasible, or even that it cannot be *negatively* dependent, in the way defeasibility implies, on the perceiver's beliefs. This point is explained in Audi (2010), chs. 8–9.

[20] This metaphorical statement does not entail that inference (in the process sense) is propositional and roughly equivalent to 'reasoning': a kind of mental tokening of an argument. A detailed statement of my broadly propositional view of inference is provided in Audi (2006), chs. 5, 7–8. Some philosophers and psychologists use 'inference' more broadly. See e.g. Green (2010), 49: 'The inferences I speak of here will not in general consist of the derivation of one proposition from a set of others. Rather...they will more commonly take the form of a positioning of an object in egocentric space, an attribution of absolute and relative trajectories, and so forth'. On this view, inferences need not be drawn, or figure in consciousness as reasoning does, or be valid or invalid, or voluntary; indeed they need not constitute *doings* at all. I am not arguing that perception cannot involve inference if the term is used in a technical sense with the suggested breadth.

knowledge or experience is necessary'.[21] I agree that at least in that unqualified form this view is a mistake. But I do not hold it, nor need any moderate foundationalist. Moderate foundationalism in the theory of perception implies that in every perception there are some elements basic (so in a sense 'foundational') on the occasion; it does not imply that there are some elements basic in every perception. Moreover, in some perceptions, such as moral ones, the perceptible property—such as wrongness—is simply not accessible except through base elements that are partly constitutive of the property. It is surprising that Dancy says, e.g., that 'one can perceive a resultant property, the dangerousness of the cliff... without perceiving the features that make the cliff dangerous'.[22] Surely one must see the steep slope or smooth, slippery-looking texture to *perceive* the dangerousness. Again, we have *constitutive* base properties. A perception of the dangerousness of a cliff, as opposed to one merely of a dangerous cliff, might be analogous to a moral perception of wrongdoing, as opposed to a perception that is merely of an action that is wrong.

5. Perception and Cognition

That perception is in some way entwined with cognition, at least in normal adults, is rarely questioned. But the intimacy of the relation in some cases, such as seeing that one person wronged another, does not entail that perception is intrinsically cognitive. How, in broad terms, should the relation between perception and cognition be conceived in the moral case?

5.1. Object perception, aesthetic perception, and moral seemings

In exploring the relation between perception and cognition, we might recall the presentationality question. In considering this relation, Cuneo says,

> When I perceive that the cup before me is black, the presentational character is presumably... explained by the cup and its blackness presenting itself to me...there would be a worrisome disanalogy between paradigm cases of perception, on the one hand, and moral perception[23]

The first thing to be said here is that Cuneo's example is misleading: cups are physical objects. Perception of them can be, in my terms, cartographic and even pictorial: from one's percepts (roughly, the internal, sensory elements in perception) one could reproduce their shape, extension, color, and so forth. Perceiving them is like perceiving visible base properties for moral phenomena such as stabbings. The problem is not that the perception is *objectual*, being of a 'thing' rather than a property or proposition; the problem is that the thing is of the wrong kind to sustain the objection.

Second, a better analogy for moral perception is aesthetic perception, such as seeing delicacy in a drawing or gracefulness in a sculpture. Think of the delicacy of a finely inked drawing of a bird on a limb. We see its delicacy in good part by seeing, in a certain way, its lines, design, and coloration. Now think of the violent backstabbing of an old man in a dimly lit parking lot just as he opens his car's door. We see the wrong in good part by seeing the violent stabbing. In the language of presentation, we

---

[21] Dancy (2010), 111.   [22] Dancy (2010), 105.   [23] Cuneo (2014), 4.

might say the wrong presents itself to us, in a certain way, as the violent-stabbing-in-non-threatening-circumstances—a property that partly constitutes the wrong; and the full presentation of that wrong is this percept integrated with our disapprobative shock or distress as reflecting our moral sensibility.

A third point of disanalogy between the case of the coffee cup and that of a basic moral perception turns on the differing forms of the two cases. I have repeatedly stressed that simply perceiving an object does not entail having beliefs about it—as opposed to dispositions to form them. But the coffee cup example ignores this in a way that may obscure the kind of presentation I have sought to capture. I reject Cuneo's unqualified view that 'When I perceive the black coffee cup...I *have the impression* that there is a black coffee cup on my desk.' This view reflects a tendency of many philosophers to *propositionalize* perceptual experience. I would grant here that one has the impression *of* a black coffee cup; but—as where we are intently looking for something else—we may *not* have an accompanying belief *that* there is a cup. Note, moreover, that the propositional impression Cuneo reports is not even appropriate to the case in which (a) I see the cup, (b) it presents itself to me in a normal way, but (c) I *take* it to be a short vase. Yet that is a still clear case of my seeing the cup—even of clearly seeing it. Clarity of our vision of an object does not entail recognition of it.

In the moral case, we could speak of *perceptual moral seemings*, thus using a terminology familiar in epistemological literature. These are usually conceived as *propositional* but still not belief-entailing impressions that something is so, but I have left room for them to be *property impressions*, as with a sense *of* A's wronging B—say, where there is a subtle intimidation. It is quite open to me to say here (what is implicit in *Moral Perception*) that a moral phenomenon can present itself either non-propositionally as a phenomenally definite, normally valenced, seeming *of* wrong-doing or, less basically, as a propositional impression *that* (say) one person is wronging another. Even when such a propositional impression occurs, however, the subject need only be disposed to believe the proposition in question. The impression is conceptual, but not necessarily doxastic.

5.2. 'Cognitive penetration'

Another aspect of the relation between perception and cognition should be considered here:

[C]ognitive penetration...[is] very roughly, the modification of perceptual representational content by states in the subject's cognitive system, where this can include, e.g., beliefs, desires, emotions, and intuitions. Nothing that Audi says in *Moral Perception* rules out this interpretation of the integration that distinguishes moral perception from mere perception of a moral phenomenon.[24]

In considering both ethics and aesthetics, I have presupposed some basic perceptual capacities, and it is true that I leave open the possibility of some kind of cognitive penetration in either moral or aesthetic perception. I see no serious difficulty

---

[24] Cowan (2014), 1170. Here he cites McPherson (2012). Cf. S. Siegel (2010a), e.g. 10.

presented by this openness, provided it is not taken to imply that moral perception *must* be conceptual or must entail some constituent belief. Consider the aesthetic case first.

Suppose that perception is subject to cognitive penetration, which, in aesthetics, has been described as the view that 'cognitive states like beliefs or concepts about art causally influence experiences of art'. The influence is thought to be deep, in the sense that 'what you know or think about art may affect how an artwork perceptually appears to you'[25] and this may be manifested in at least two ways: 'expertise affects the supervenience base [presumably the grounding properties] of aesthetic properties by affecting low-level phenomenal content. Or, if one admits high-level content, expertise causes the perceptual representation of high-level aesthetic properties.'[26] Several questions should be distinguished here if we are to see whether the same kind of cognitive influence undermines my view of moral perception.[27]

First, is 'expertise'—or moral sensitivity, to take the more common counterpart in ethics—exhausted by 'what one knows or thinks about art' (or morality), or does it require familiarity with artworks at the level required for experiencing them in an aesthetically sensitive way? Second, does affecting the base involve changing the consequentiality relation or, instead, changing what base properties for an aesthetic property are perceived? Third, does the main question we must address concern causing or, by contrast, *enabling* the perception of 'high-level aesthetic properties'? These questions should be taken in turn, and what we find will facilitate a further comparison between aesthetic and moral properties.

In both art and ethics, expertise is in part a matter of familiarity with the relevant phenomena and, related to this, of *knowing how*—how to appreciate, view, interpret, evaluate, and the like. Expertise is not purely cognitive. Given this fact, the evidences of expertise affecting experience of art and moral phenomena—even ordinary perceptual experience—are not in themselves evidences of purely cognitive effects. Suppose, however, that cognitive elements (or other intentional elements, including conative ones embodying or entailing desires) affect *what* elements in the scope of one's sensory experience are actually perceived. Perhaps, e.g., I believe that melodic inversion is an element in some of Mozart's piano works. I may then listen for it or simply be more likely to notice and respond to it when I hear these works. This suggests at least two possibilities. One is hearing something without noticing or, more important, responding to it. A second is not hearing something at all. Overcoming the first condition is a kind of perceptual enrichment; overcoming the second might be called perceptual enabling. In relation to either possibility, cognitive and other intentional elements may make one more aesthetically responsive. The parallel point apparently applies in the moral case. There might, to be sure, be a biasing influence of certain beliefs (or other intentional elements), but there need not be.

---

[25] D. Stokes (2014), 27. See also Stokes, Chapter 1 in this volume.

[26] D. Stokes (2014), 29. Supervenience is a weaker relation than grounding (consequentiality) but the term is often used for the latter, as I assume it is here. An explanatory determination relation is likely intended, but is not strictly speaking entailed even by strong supervenience.

[27] In this paragraph and the next few I draw on Audi (2014).

Consider also viewing a painting, where one knows one is viewing an original by Leonardo. This may intensify one's attention to expected features, perhaps with the result of perceptual enrichment, say finer perceptual discrimination in a sense implying actually seeing more. But the aesthetic experience one then has is as such no different from what it would be without the cognitive 'cause'. It might, however, differ—or at least its interpretation by the viewer might differ—in being biased by preoccupation with the thought of the master's technique. The question of bias brings us to the matter of consequentiality of aesthetic (and moral properties) on other kinds of properties. At least in the moral case, these grounding properties are 'natural' properties or at any rate non-moral ones, and they are at a lower level. Now compare the Leonardo case with one in which we observe someone we know is thoroughly immoral interacting with another person. This knowledge will affect our attention and our expectations regarding the person. We may then form beliefs we would not otherwise have formed, but our perception might not be different. Attention, however, is crucial in, for instance, *how much we see*. Thus, one possibility is that our knowledge or a person or thing results in our having more or sharper perceptions than we would otherwise have. This is a contingent matter. It appears, then, that cognitive penetration and similar external influences on perceptual experience may or may not imply that aesthetic or moral perception is *necessarily* biased by certain kinds of beliefs (perhaps not kinds held by everyone) or, as is well known, contingently and, one would hope, remediably biased.

Examples like the kind I have cited show that one's beliefs may, in certain cases, influence what one perceives, whether objects or properties. The examples suggest that, for some aesthetic or moral perceptions, certain experiences or indeed cognitions are needed to have those perceptions at all. But the examples do not show that moral perceptions *must* be influenced by one's beliefs or that moral perceptions are inferential. They also do not show that such perceptions are necessarily biased, in the sense that one would not, for instance, see wrongdoing if one did not *antecedently* believe that the kind of behavior one is viewing is wrong. Even if that should be true for some cases, however, if there can be perception and, through it, perceptual knowledge, of a moral proposition that confirms a general moral belief, the possibility of moral objectivity and of general moral knowledge receives support.

The support that the possibility of moral perception provides for the objectivity of ethics is perhaps clearest when a moral perception is a response to an a priori and, in some sense, basic ground of a moral property, such as a stabbing or a lie or, on the positive side, the bleeding of an injured child which yields a perception of a moral obligation to help. But suppose one perceives a wrong by hearing an insult of a friend. It may be only because one knows the conventions of the culture in which the insult is delivered that one is perceptually sensitive to the insult-property as a kind of injury or degradation and so, by virtue of a reliable connection between the insult-property and harm as a basic ground of prima facie wrongness, one can hear the wrong. Granted, one could in such a case infer that a wrong was done; but given a sensibility informed by relevant knowledge or experience, moral perception is possible and may provide non-inferential moral knowledge of wrongdoing. This seems to me a kind of *cognitive empowerment* affecting moral sensibility rather than a 'cognitive penetration' of perception, but the latter phenomenon has been described with a considerable breadth that may imply its applicability to the former. In any case, perception may yield directly for some observers what is available to others only by inference.

Perception may also be a response to perceptible elements that are themselves manifestations of basic grounds of moral properties, such as injuries, rather than *instances* of basic grounds. Familiarity with conventions is not necessarily required to respond to these manifestations. The higher the level of the perception, the greater the number of layers it may embody, and conventions need not provide the connections that make possible a high-level perception. Seeing a forest fire approaching a child may yield a perception of obligation to rescue; the fire indicates a probability of a kind of suffering—an endangerment—but it is the projected suffering that, as intrinsically *reason-providing*, is a basic (or more basic) ground of the obligation of beneficence. If one saw someone lighting a cigarette near a haystack on which the child was playing, the perception of obligation—for instance, sensing immediately the need to intervene—would likely be still higher level, being one remove further in discerned endangerment of the child than with the threating forest fire; but it could have the same ultimate basis, and one could non-inferentially see that one must help.

6. Moral Perception, Realism, and Rationalism

Given that perception is factive, it would be at best implausible to hold that one can see, for instance, A's wrongdoing toward B, if there is no wrongdoing. To be sure, noncognitivists could argue that the locution 'S sees A's wrongdoing' simply expresses a higher-order moral attitude: a kind of negative attitude toward the behavior one takes S to see, which in turn S would 'describe' by expressing a negative moral attitude through the sentence 'A wronged B'. With enough ingenuity, noncognitivism can be defended for the realm of moral perception as for other domains in which apparent moral facts are expressed. I make no attempt here to refute noncognitivism, but simply seek to provide a more plausible view. Moral realism, then, is presupposed by my theory.

Realism, however, need not be naturalistic, and I do not presuppose naturalism. My view is that moral properties are not natural properties, but if they should be, my overall theory of moral perception is easier, not more difficult, to defend. For if moral properties are natural, I doubt that it need even be argued that they have explanatory power or that moral perception is in part causally constituted. It is difficult to think of any natural properties of spatiotemporal entities, and especially of actions, that even appear to lack causal power. To reiterate part of my view of moral perception, I have argued that the 'process' of morally perceiving something is causal in the way perception must be, but the causal work (insofar as it is done by properties) is apparently done by the properties (possibly tropes) on which moral properties are grounded, not by those properties themselves.

One might object to countenancing even the reality of non-causal properties—or at least non-causal properties that do not characterize abstract entities—on the ground that there are none among natural properties. It may well seem that it is only normative properties, for instance moral, aesthetic, and epistemic properties such as being justified, that are supposed to be real, non-natural, and non-causal. I do not see the objection as decisive even if it is true. But is it true? Consider shape, which is a natural property. A thing has shape not brutely, but on the basis of such causal properties as being spherical, which affects, for instance, its movement tendencies; yet shape itself does not seem causal. If it is, that is on the basis of its grounding properties, but if a property can be causal only on the basis of the causal power of its grounding properties, this would presumably hold for moral properties as well.

The case of shape in relation to particular shapes suggests the question whether we might perhaps say that wrongness, obligatoriness, and other normative properties are determinables. I am not arguing for this, though it is well worth pursuing. There is some analogy (as well as disanalogy) between moral properties and, say, shape and color; but my main point here is that there seem to be real properties even in the natural realm that do not have causal power yet figure in causal relations much as moral properties do. This does not require taking moral properties to have causal power or, if one does attribute it to them, conceiving them as determinables.

It is also true that my overall ethical theory incorporates rationalism, and I have appealed to the a priori and necessary connection between the grounds of moral properties and those properties themselves to explain the reliability of the process connecting, say, wrongdoing with the perception of it. But I would stress here that such a high level of reliability is not required for perception. Similarly, anger does not entail, much less self-evidently entail, the occurrence of the behavioral manifestations by which we know that someone else is angry, but this does not (for non-skeptics) prevent there being a reliable enough connection to make possible perceptual knowledge of anger. I deny, then, 'that the epistemic credentials of moral phenomenal responses [their ability to evidence, e.g., wrongdoing] are derivative of subject's grasping ostensibly synthetic a priori entailments between moral properties and their non-moral grounds'.[28] It is a determination relation that moral perception must appropriately respond to; the modality of the relation is not crucial for the response.

Suppose, for the sake of argument that there is only an empirical and contingent connection between moral grounding properties and the moral properties they ground. Why should this undermine my view that moral perception is non-inferential?[29] I see no good reason to claim that it would. But should we consider knowledge of anger inferential in the kinds of cases I have noted, in which the occasion on which perception occurs makes anger expectable and the person observed blows up with words and gestures appropriate to the occasion, say, a tipsy guest's carelessly breaking a valuable platter? Surely not. Indeed, we recognize platters, vases, and even trees by properties such as color and shape that do not a priori entail their presence. We need not posit inference here, rather than simply grant that some perceptions occur on the basis of others that might be called (relatively) elementary constitutive perceptions.

7. Perception, Conception, and Perceptual Belief

It should be obvious that I do not take perception of objects and events to be intrinsically conceptual. This is not to deny that, for normal adults in many

---

[28] Cowan (2014), 1169. [29] This is suggested by Cowan (2014), 1169.

situations, perception of objects is not in general possible without conceptualizing the objects in question. I myself cannot see a china platter on a dining table in full view at dinner hour without conceiving it in some way that is appropriate to its character as dinnerware. Most of us could not see a man slapping his wife's face upon her smiling at a deft and well-dressed waiter without conceiving of it as wrong. But the commonness of such perceptual patterns does not require concluding that perception can never be non-conceptual. It is indeed at best difficult to explain how conceptualization arises in human life in the first place if perception without it is impossible. Must we, for instance, posit innate concepts of platters, which are as visible to animals and to children just learning a language as they are to adults? And if the couple's 3-year-old child, seeing the incident, bursts into tears and blurts out 'Daddy, don't do that!', must we deny that this could be an indication of the inchoate moral sensibility that presumably lays important groundwork for development of moral concepts?

It is a contingent matter how *conceptually entwined* a person's perceptual experience is. I grant that for some of us moral perception tends to be entwined—or *suffused*, one might say—with moral conceptions: for some of us, human life, or at least human relations, occur as if in a morally constituted framework. This is perhaps not unexpected in those who approach most human relations with standing moral concerns. Is justice being done? Is there an undertone of racism? Is the man condescending to the woman? But perception itself does not have to occur within the constraints created by such questions. There is clear sunlight as well as the colored light that puts us on guard against distortion. Speaking without metaphor, we might say that there are ways of progressively freeing ourselves of the necessity to bring what we see (hear, touch, etc.) under any concepts. Some ways are more successful than others, but the possibility confirms my view that conceptuality should not figure in the analysis of perception, however likely it is for certain persons or certain kinds of occasions of perception.

It is worth reiterating that the non-conceptuality of simple perception does nothing to undermine the view that perceptual belief—at least propositional belief—*is* conceptual. We cannot see (and thereby believe) *that* the platter shattered upon hitting the floor without a concept of a platter and of shattering. This point must be taken in relation to another: much of what we see—and certainly much of what philosophers find worth discussing in the visible domain—is such that we do in fact form perceptual beliefs about it. This helps to explain why philosophers so often, if only implicitly, take perception to be conceptual. Still, although perceptual beliefs are intrinsically conceptual, perception is not.

Let me apply these points to moral perception. It is appropriate that we be interested in and sensitive to moral phenomena in our lives. We should be indignant at the violent husband, pleased on seeing someone resist telling what would be a self-serving lie, and relieved when someone chairing a meeting makes a sincere-sounding apology after overlooking a hand raised to ask a question. These may all be cases of moral perception and so have an appropriate phenomenology, but they are likely to yield some cognition and, accordingly, to embody or, in some intimate way, yield conceptualization. For normal morally constituted adults, it would be rare that the kinds of perceptions just illustrated do not yield conceptualization, but I have given other examples in which the perception precedes conceptualization, as where a kind of activation of our sensibility yields a moral response before the perceiver recognizes what is seen under some moral concept. Another illustration is subtle intimidation, which seems a too frequently encountered case in which the perceptual sense of wrongdoing precedes the judgment that it is occurring. Another kind of case can occur with tiny children. Seeing cruelty by a babysitter may frighten a child and create a sense of something that should not be done. It is at least possible that fear and aversion can develop into a discriminative distress that represents a sense of wrongdoing. The child can be upset by the babysitter's causing a tearful outburst by slapping a sibling, in a way the child is not upset by a qualitatively similar outburst when the toddler is comparably pained and equally distressed by stubbing its toe. It is an empirical question just when and how such moral development occurs, but it is at least possible that a child's moral sensibility develops to some degree before—and paves the way for—acquisition of moral concepts.

8. Conclusion

Moral perception is an element in much human experience. It is possible for any normal person but, like aesthetic experience, occurs less in some people than in others, even when they have highly similar perceptions of morally significant phenomena. It is not inferential, but facilitates inference; it is not doxastic, but creates, in those with sufficient understanding, dispositions to believe moral propositions that it justifies; and it is not necessarily biased by beliefs of perceivers even if it is also not immune to influence by their cognitions and other elements in their psychology. It may or may not yield emotion or be caused by emotion; it may or may not yield intuition or judgment or be caused by them; and it may or may not motivate action or be caused by action. But it often yields moral knowledge and thereby grounds an element of objectivity in ethics. It is not the only route to moral knowledge, but it is a route that different people can traverse in the search for mutual understanding and in the hope of agreement on the moral questions that are central for coexistence.

4

Evaluative Perception as Response-Dependent Representation

Paul Noordhof

In the face of well-known scepticism, some have still intriguingly claimed that we perceive evaluative properties in the world. How can some philosophers be convinced that we perceive the moral properties of a situation, for example, while others are moved to write

> The vice entirely escapes you, as long as you consider the object. You never can find it, till you turn your reflexion into your own breast, and find a sentiment of disapprobation, which arises in you towards this action?[1]

Do they have very different experiences? A natural diagnosis is that they come with different assumptions as to what evaluative perception should be like and/or, relatedly, a different sense of the properties that can be objects of perception. Indeed, there is quite considerable disagreement as to what we can be said to perceive in general.

Recognizing the existence of evaluative perception in a domain—for example, moral, aesthetic, or, more generally, badness for a subject, which we might call *prudential*—is usually to be contrasted with two other positions. The first is Intuitionism. Intuitionists hold that there are non-perceptual cognitive presentations of something as thus and so (for a domain). For example, they might hold that the principle of utility recommends itself to intellectual scrutiny not in terms of any reasons offered for it, nor perceptual experience that it is the case, but simply via an apprehension of its plausibility. The second is Sentimentalism. Sentimentalists take our apprehension of values to be based in feelings and other responses that are not geared to reflect the way the world is, as perception does. The position defended here will take up some of the materials of these other two positions in certain cases but it pays to have them as contrast cases at the outset.

In Section 1, I consider some typical passages in which it is insisted that there is evaluative perception with, often at the same time, the immediate qualification that

---

[1] Hume (1739/1975), bk. 3, s. 1, pp. 468–9.

it is not like perception of other more obviously sensory properties such as colour, shape, and sound. I begin by characterizing some terms of art: phenomenal content, phenomenal properties, manifest objects and properties. I then use these to make more precise the idea of evaluative perception. I identify two types: first, the presentation of evaluative properties as such in experience (Type 1 evaluative perception) and, second, the perception of non-evaluative or evaluation-contributing properties which, it is recognized, are the basis for evaluative classifications (Type 2 evaluative perception). People often turn into Type 2 theorists because of sometimes tacit commitments about what must be involved in Type 1 perception. My aim will be to enlarge the possibilities of Type 1 perception. As should be obvious, the issue upon which I focus concerns the content of putative perceptual states and not whether these states have the characteristic epistemic properties such as being a source of knowledge.

As we shall see from the material of Section 1, one dimension of the controversy about whether there is Type 1 evaluative perception has entirely general roots in the debate about whether perceptual content is to be understood richly/liberally or conservatively/austerely. Those who claim that evaluative properties are perceived, incline towards a rich view of the content of perceptual experience.[2] In Section 2, I draw a distinction between two kinds of manifest content of perceptual experience: sensory and non-sensory manifest content. I then provide two arguments to show that we need to recognize the presence of non-sensory manifest content in perceptual experience and, thus, conclude perceptual content is rich/liberal. Nevertheless, although this clears one substantial obstacle to the recognition of Type 1 evaluative perception in various domains, there are additional factors which might convince somebody to resist extending the richness of content to include various kinds of evaluative properties.

The first is the apparent gap between evaluative properties and the arrangement of non-evaluative properties upon which they supervene. Although we naturally cite non-evaluative properties as the basis for evaluative claims, standardly we don't take evaluative properties just to be complex arrangements of these non-evaluative properties. There seems a simplicity to the evaluative, and unity across different circumstances falling under an evaluative concept, that needs to be explained. The second is a certain lack of phenomenal presence of some candidate cases of evaluative perception, for example, the moral or the aesthetic. In Section 3, I introduce two ideas that promise to assist in the explanation of these features. The first is the idea of intrinsic representational properties, the second is that of response-dependent representation. As an illustration of the issues involved, I touch on the case of expressive perception, a theory of which I have given in previous work.[3]

Section 4, the final section of the paper, applies these ideas to two cases. The first of these, our experience of pain as bad or awful, involves a certain kind of intrinsic response-dependent representation which does not involve loss of phenomenal presence. The second, the case of moral perception, combines both features. Different kinds of response are identified as intrinsically representational for each case. The

---

[2] See e.g. Cowan (2015).   [3] Noordhof (2008).

capacity to accommodate different cases of evaluative perception is a recommendation of the approach recommended here.

1. What Is Involved in Evaluative Perception?

Let the phenomenal content of mental states and events—other people use the term *phenomenal character*—characterize what it is like to have them as part of our mental lives. One important dimension of this phenomenal content will be the objects and properties that these mental states and events concern. For example, if I am perceiving a grey elephant, then a natural characterization of what it is like to have such a state will mention the object elephant—or large object of a certain size and shape (a matter to which we shall return)—and the property of being grey. Call these objects and properties the manifest objects and properties of a mental state or event. Phenomenal properties, on the other hand, let us stipulate to be the properties that determine the phenomenal content of a mental state or event. Amongst other things, they fix what are the manifest objects and properties of the events and states. Different approaches to the nature of phenomenal content will have different views about the phenomenal properties that determine this phenomenal content. Representationalists claim that the phenomenal properties are a kind of representational properties, or supervene upon arrangements of the same, Relationists will say that they are brute relations of awareness. Those who deny that either such approach can suffice for the determination of phenomenal content will want to say that mental events and states possess properties that in some way add to their phenomenal content by neither of these means or, indeed, entirely determine the phenomenal content. These additional property characterizing approaches are sometimes what fans of qualia have in mind. There is much detail that might be added to these preliminary stipulations but it is not needed for the discussion ahead.

With this terminology in place, a natural way of understanding what is involved in evaluative perception is to say that it involves evaluative properties being amongst the manifest properties of experience. Call this *Type 1 Evaluative Perception*. In which case, the issue is just one instance of the general issue about the richness of perceptual experience. The more familiar discussion of this matter—made famous by Susanna Siegel in recent times—concerns the perception of kinds.[4] Interestingly, the relevance of this discussion is illustrated by qualifications and hedges that many of the proponents of evaluative perception seem inclined to make as we shall see shortly.

Although evaluative perception might naturally be thought to involve the straightforward presentation of evaluative properties in perceptual experience, there is another possibility that it seems plausible to characterize as evaluative perception. It is appealing to those who have scruples about how richly the phenomenal content of perceptual experience should be characterized. *Type 2 Evaluative Perception*, as I shall call it, involves phenomenal content that is either appropriately characterized in terms of an arrangement of non-evaluative properties which metaphysically

---

[4] See S. Siegel (2010a).

necessitate that a certain evaluative property is present or an arrangement is experienced as supporting the instantiation of an evaluative property. It is plausible to characterize either as evaluative perception because they provide material that is supportive of the appropriate perceptual recognitional capacities that issue in evaluative judgements about what is perceived.

Once the option of recognizing evaluative perceptions without evaluative properties being part of their phenomenal contents is on the table, it seems that few have firmly committed themselves to the existence of straightforward Type 1 evaluative perception, of which moral perception is the most discussed case. There is, of course, John McDowell who writes:

> The idea of value experience involves taking admiration, say, to represent its object as having a property that (although there in the object) is essentially subjective in much the same way as the property that an object is represented as having by an experience of redness—that is, understood adequately only in terms of the appropriate modification of human (or similar) sensibility. The disanalogy, now, is that a virtue (say) is conceived to be not merely such as to elicit the appropriate attitude' (as colour is merely such as to cause the appropriate experiences), but rather such as to *merit it*.[5]

This seems a commitment to our experience of value being much the same as our experience of colour or sound, in the relevant respects. About as clear a case of Type 1 evaluative perception as it is possible to have. Most are more circumspect. Let me run through a few famous passages. First, of course, there is Gilbert Harman:

> If you round a corner and see a group of young hoodlums pour gasoline on a cat and ignite it, you do not need to *conclude* that what they are doing is wrong; you do not need to figure anything out; you can *see* that it is wrong.[6]

Notice that he does not say that you see the wrongness of the act in perceiving what is going on. All that is denied is that we conclude that it is wrong on the basis, say, of observation of the non-moral features of the circumstances and our understanding of the nature of morality. It is quite compatible with denying this to hold that we are recognizing that something wrong on the basis of our perception of other properties.

Then there is Robert Audi:

> Moral perception is not an exact analogue of physical perception... moral properties are not easily conceived as observable, in what seems the most elementary way: no sensory phenomenal representation is possible for them, as opposed to intellective representations, those these may be integrated with phenomenal elements.... even the perceptible properties on which the possession of moral properties is based may not be strictly speaking observable, at least in this elementary way.[7]

Jonathan Dancy:

> we do perception an injustice... by limiting it to that of which there can be sensory phenomenal representations. No doubt there has to be some sensory activity, some phenomenal

---

[5] McDowell (1985/1998), 143 (all page refs. to 1998).
[6] Harman (1977), 4.   [7] Audi (2010a), 87.

presence or presentation. But it does not follow from this that everything we sense must be phenomenally represented. I can observe that these two books are not the same colour; there is no need to look for a phenomenal representation of the colours as different.[8]

And Sarah McGrath who says, of moral perception, that recognizing it is not to say that moral perception is just like perceiving colours and shapes, or that the blind can't perceive moral facts, or that we can perceive moral facts without a lot of conceptual sophistication. 'We can perceive that other people are in pain, that it's time to water the plants, or that Fred told a joke... [Moral perception] is like that.'[9]

All are keen to deny that evaluative properties show up in experience as other standardly conceived sensory properties show up.

Type II evaluative perception provides one way of understanding the hesitancy expressed in the passages above. It is denied that evaluative properties are sensory manifest properties and, on the assumption that these are all that characterize the phenomenal content of perception, it is denied that evaluative perception can be a case of Type I perception. We just perceive the sensorily manifest base properties of the instantiation of an evaluative property and, on the basis of our perceptual recognition capacities, we judge that an evaluative property is instantiated. In later work, Audi explicitly commits himself to this view.[10] But there is an alternative. The hesitancy of philosophers like Dancy and McGrath stems from an austere picture of the nature of the kind of properties that can be manifest properties of perception. The indefensibility of this austere picture will be the subject matter of Section 2 of this paper.

On the assumption that perception is a source of knowledge, then a proper examination of evaluative perception will also be concerned with whether whatever the account provided gives it the appropriate epistemic credentials. However, it is plausible that a necessary condition for the development of a full account of evaluative perception is an explanation of how evaluative properties may be manifest properties. It is upon this issue that my remarks will focus. Nevertheless, in Section 2, I will identify two features of perception in general—that evaluative perception may share—which provide a basis for the epistemic features those who favour it proclaim for it.

2. Rich versus Austere Accounts of Perceptual Content

The inconclusive character of the debate over the proper characterization of the phenomenal content of perceptual experience seems to be the result of the tension between two plausible lines of argument, the first in favour of rich characterizations, the second in favour of austere characterizations. On the side of richness, there is the familiar argument offered by Susanna Siegel. It rests upon the claim that there is a phenomenal difference between the perceptual experiences of a subject unable to recognize instances of a natural kind from the perceptual experiences of the subject when they are, later, able to recognize the kind in question. The oft discussed example

---

[8] Dancy (2010), 112.   [9] S. McGrath (2004), 220–1.
[10] See e.g. Audi (2013), 40–1, although on pp. 170–1 he is interpretable as a Type 1 theorist appealing to the move I make below.

is of a subject prior to and after they have learnt how to recognize pines. The phenomenal difference, Siegel urges, is a difference in the phenomenal content of perceptual experience and this difference is best characterized in terms of a difference in the natural kind properties that show up in experience.[11]

The success of this argument turns on three issues. The first is whether the phenomenal differences need to be characterized as a difference in the manifest properties the experiences concern. The second is whether the right way to characterize the difference in manifest properties is in term of kind properties rather than some other type. The third is whether the difference in phenomenal content is part of the phenomenal content of perceptual experience rather than, say, a thought or a judgement.

To keep the discussion manageable, I shall take it that it is plausible the phenomenal differences do have to be captured in terms of a difference in manifest properties.[12] The reason why the second and third issues are significant is that there is another line of argument that appears to establish that austerity or conservatism about perceptual phenomenal content must be the case. I think it is best expressed as follows.

(1) It is possible that there are non-K objects that subjects cannot m-distinguish from K-objects without appealing to spatio-temporal position or internal, currently (or even always) m-unavailable, structure.

(2) If subjects cannot m-distinguish non-K objects from K objects except in this way, then K does not characterize the relevant m-experience.

Therefore,

(3) K does not characterize the relevant m-experiences.[13]

Here 'K' stands for objects falling under a certain natural kind. The thought is that there will be non-K objects that prove to be indiscriminable from K objects if just inspected. As a toy example, imagine looking at a real tomato and then later, at the same spot, and unknown to you, looking at a wax tomato looking exactly like it. 'm' is meant to be a placeholder for a certain sensory modality. Thus, it might stand for 'visual', 'auditory', etc.

How should the relevant experiences be characterized then? We might provide a fix on the idea as follows. First, let two objects be sensory duplicates if and only if for any subject with sensory modality M, the subject cannot discriminate between them by that modality without appeal to information about their distinct spatio-temporal location or internal structure. Let sensory properties be those properties that must be shared by sensory duplicates. The austere account of the phenomenal content of perceptual experience says that it can only be specified by sensory properties. Call the content so specified 'sensory manifest content'.[14]

Obviously conservatives are right about sensory manifest content but victory by stipulation satisfies no one. Taking the two arguments together—the argument from phenomenal difference and that from indiscriminability—we don't have to conclude

---

[11] See S. Siegel (2010a), 100–1.   [12] For considerations, see S. Siegel (2010a), 109–10.
[13] Tye (1995), 141.   [14] I have here adapted material in M. G. F. Martin (2010), 198–201.

one or other is correct. Instead, we can argue that they have different notions of the phenomenal content of perceptual experience in mind. Sensory manifest content undoubtedly characterizes something significant although, as we shall shortly see, maybe not quite what was envisaged. Those who argue for the liberal or rich position are just prepared to acknowledge that there is another dimension to the phenomenal content of perceptual experience: non-sensory manifest content. They will say that the austere theorists make the mistake of moving from the claim that subjects cannot perceptually discriminate between K and non-K objects in the circumstances envisaged above, to claiming that what is presented in experience is objects with properties common to the K and non-K objects alone. But this need not be the case. For example, if you have the ability to recognize pines or tomatoes, then, they will argue, your experience presents to you that there is a pine or a tomato before you even if, in fact, it is another tree of the same superficial formation or a wax tomato. Claims about indiscriminability settle the phenomenal differences that need to be recognized but not how these differences should be characterized.

Attribution of non-sensory manifest content goes beyond what subjects can discriminate and, thus, a certain kind of supervenience claim is false for such content. It is not true that if you fix the sensory manifest contents of experiences, then the non-sensory manifest content of experiences is determined. There can be two subjects with the same sensory manifest content but distinct non-sensory manifest contents. Nevertheless, a weaker supervenience claim may still be true. For a subject, if you fix his or her sensory manifest contents, then that subject's non-sensory manifest contents will be fixed. If you have the capacity to recognize tomatoes, then you will see anything, which you experience to have the same sensory manifest properties, as a tomato.

The relative disassociation of non-sensory manifest content from sensory manifest content might encourage some to think of it as a thought or judgement. However, neither model fits the character of our experience of our mental lives. Suppose we have a perceptual experience properly characterized by the term 'pine' and we are told that, in fact, what we are experiencing is a hologram. Our experience still presents it to be the case that a pine is before us even though we no longer judge it.[15] So the rich characterization in terms of pine cannot be the content of a judgement rather than of experience. Note that this is not a simple case where we have conflicting judgements. Our pine experience persists even if we are conscious and have our noses rubbed in the fact that it is not an experience of pines (by other information we receive).

The phenomenal content properly characterized in terms of 'pine' is not easily assimilable to thought either. It does not seem to be something that we simply entertain. Instead, it has the hallmark of making a claim about the way the world is. Equally, it seems to be well integrated with the rest of our experience rather than standing alongside it—as our thoughts are wont to be.[16]

The phenomenal contents characterized using K-concepts, thus, have two distinctive features of perceptual experience which we might call non-neutrality (or making a claim about the world) on the one side but that claim not being a commitment on the

---

[15] S. Siegel (2010a), 104–5. [16] S. Siegel (2010a), 106–8.

part of the subject (as judgement involves) on the other. Might there be some other state that possesses these features?

It is far from clear that intellectual seemings—non-perceptual intuitions that such and such is the case—have the features in question. There will always be a preliminary commitment, by the subject, as a part of the phenomenology, even if the commitment is resisted, which makes it more natural to characterize intellectual seemings as prima facie judgements. Obviously those who take intellectual seemings to be perceptual—or appropriately similar to the perceptual—will resist this second point of difference but, presumably, they will not be in a position to resist the attribution of K-phenomenal contents.[17] In which case, it is a nice question why they should resist the attribution of such contents to perceptual experience of the sensory kind.

A remaining possibility is to claim that *perceptual seemings* are distinct from the content of perceptual experience and, rather than recognize that the latter includes non-sensory manifest content, attribute K-phenomenal contents to the perceptual seemings instead.[18] Perceptual seemings so understood are taken to play a number of different roles. One is that, it is alleged, in contrast to sensory manifest contents common to perception and imagination, they are assertive. They make a claim about the way the world is, thereby, justifying belief.[19] A second is that they capture the epistemically salient aspects of perceptual experience. An experience presenting the three speckles of a hen may justify a belief that the hen has three speckles whereas an experience presenting the forty-eight speckles of a hen does not because, the claim goes, the hen doesn't appear precisely that way to us.[20] These perceptual seemings are taken to be passive, non-neutral but conceptual states.

These grounds for recognizing a distinct state with perceptual seeming content are dubious. Perceptual seemings involve conceptual content that are common to judgement and thought. If there is a solution—for example in terms of the state's mode—to explain when such contents are assertive, then it can apply as easily to differentiate between perception and imagination.[21] Appeal to perceptual seemings relies on rather than supplies this explanation. Equally, perceptual seemings are taken to involve phenomenal rather than epistemic uses of perception verbs.[22] In which case, how do they avoid the problem that the perceptual seemings may have a detail of which the subject is unaware: like it being a seeming of forty-eight speckles. If appeal is made to some further fact like being the focus of attention, then this can figure in the explanation of the epistemically salient aspects of experience in the first place.[23] If it is just claimed that perceptual seeemings are tailor-made to reflect epistemic salience, we could as easily claim the same role for the content of perceptual experience and question whether its content is as richly filled in as assumed, that is, deny that perceptual experience has the content that the hen has forty-eight speckles or reduce such states to perceptual experience plus a further fact such as

---

[17] See e.g. Huemer (2007), 30–1; Chudhoff (2013), 38–9.
[18] Brogaard (2013), 37, and (2014), 284–5; Reiland (2014), 177–87; J. Lyons, Chapter 9 in this volume.
[19] See e.g. T. Tucker (2010), 534–6; Reiland (2014), 180–1.
[20] T. Tucker (2010), 534–6; Brogaard (2013), 37, and (2014), 282–3.
[21] For further discussion, see Noordhof (forthcoming).
[22] Reiland (2014), 180.   [23] Smithies (2011), 264–8.

that mentioned above. Perceptual seemings so understood are also a poor depository for unwelcome K-phenomenal content. As we shall see later, one concern with attributing to perceptual experience rich content is whether such experience is a proper ground for belief. Yet perceptual seemings are introduced here to characterize the epistemically salient features of experience.

A final motivation for taking perceptual seemings to be an independent state depends upon implicit commitment to an anti-representationalist, property-characterizing approach to perceptual experience. The sensory material of a perceptual experience—often dubbed sensations—may, depending upon consequent processing, be taken to have one content or another—this latter being the perceptual seemings.[24] Upon this view, perceptual seemings are causal consequences of perceptual experiences.[25] Part of my response to this is a defence of representationalism, which can't be undertaken here. However, the two arguments below have application to any position that attributes to sensory manifest content a more basic role in the characterization of what is presented in experience.[26] They will likewise throw into question attempts to partition off basic sensory material from the perceptual seemings that putatively characterize how that material is taken.

Recognition of the existence of these two types of perceptual content—sensory and non-sensory manifest content—helps us to make sense of some of the concerns expressed by those who allowed for the existence of evaluative perceptions mentioned in Section 1 while opening up a new possibility to that captured by the notion of Type 2 evaluative perception. We can read them as doubting that evaluative properties could figure as part of the sensory manifest content of a perception. Instead, the thought would run, they exist as part of the non-sensory manifest content of perception.

The two lines of argument in favour of recognizing two kinds of perceptual content are drawn from reflection on the nature of sensory discrimination, perceptual cues and the epistemic role of experience. To introduce the issues, it is helpful to consider the chicken sexers of philosophical lore.

According to the lore, chicken sexers detect the sex of baby chicks on the basis of experience without insight into the visual cues upon which they do it.[27] Some hold that the chicks don't look male or female to the subject. They appear identical and yet chicken sexers judge that the chick is male or female. Lack of insight into the basis for this judgement leads Richard Foley to suppose that they aren't justified in their beliefs even though the beliefs are reliable.[28] Some develop the story in terms of a misidentification of the basis of their judgement. Subjects claim that they are arriving at the judgement by looking at the chicken's genitalia when, in fact, they are doing it by sense of smell. A very natural way, however, to describe the minimal case of what is going on is that visually the chicks look male or female to the chicken sexer. It is just that they cannot identify more basic properties in virtue of which the chicks look that

---

[24] See e.g. Bergmann (2006), 118–32; T. Tucker (2010), 536–7; Bergmann (2013), 158–9.
[25] See also Lyons, Chapter 9 in this volume. [26] See e.g. Chudnoff (2013), 84–98.
[27] See e.g. Gasking (1962), 158–9; Armstrong (1968), 114–15; Aune (1972), 332; Foley (1987), 168–9; Lewis (1996b/1999), 422 (all page refs. to 1999); Zagzebski (1996), 300–1; Sainsbury (1996), 903; Kornblith (1982), 245. Apparently Gasking's paper is the first philosophical reference to the chicken sexer.
[28] See also Lewis (1996b/1999), 422.

way in, at least, some circumstances and may not be conscious of them.[29] To fix ideas, I shall put the first argument—which we may call the argument from unconscious perceptual cues—in terms of this latter way of characterizing the situation and then consider lines of resistance.

The general structure of the argument for different cases (substitutions for K) is roughly as follows.

(1) Two objects may appear to be K and not-K respectively to subjects without those subjects being conscious of any of the perceptual cues to which they are responding in virtue of which one appears K, one not-K.

(2) If subjects are not conscious of any of the perceptual cues to which they are responding, then they are not conscious of the sensory manifest properties of the objects in virtue of which one is K and the other is not-K.

(3) The phenomenal content of the subjects' experiences should not be given just in terms of these sensory manifest properties (if at all).

Therefore,

(4) The phenomenal content of experiences is not just its sensory manifest content.

The leading thought that the argument tries to bring out is that the proper characterization of the phenomenal content of perceptual experience is one thing, the properties of objects which are the basis for a subject being able to discriminate between them (without appeal to spatio-temporal position or internal structure) another. To assume that they amount to one and the same issue is to assume that the basis on which we sensorily discriminate things is somehow open to phenomenal consciousness. It might, just, be plausible to suppose that, if we are relatively reflective about how we discriminate, there will be differences in phenomenal content to correspond to differences of discrimination. It does not follow from that that these phenomenal differences should be characterized in terms of the cues to which we are responding, if unconscious perceptual cues are possible.

The perceptual cues of a scene are those features to which a perceptual system responds in deriving information about it. They will include a subclass of the sensory properties of objects but also relations between properties of distinct objects and so on. Premise (2) just reflects this understanding of perceptual cues so the key premise is the first.

The case of chicken sexing provides one illustration of the phenomena to which premise (1) is pointing. It is not the only one. Consider the case of speech perception. When I hear you talk, I hear what words you are uttering and the meaning they have. I have little insight into the auditory cues on the basis of which I arrive at these conclusions. Recent thinking on the subject notes that the sound waves which constitute speech are relatively continuous. The gaps which occur are poor predictors of the distinctness of words. One hypothesis concerning the basis of our preliminary capacity to segment words, present in infants (experimental work has focused on

---

[29] Armstrong (1968), 115; Masrour (2011), 383.

8-month-old children) and adults faced with a novel language, draws upon the processing of statistical cues such as transitional probabilities.[30] The sound sequences constituting words co-occur more than those sequences which straddle words. The transitional probability of Y/X is given by the formula $P(XY)/P(X)$. It will be high if XY is a sound sequence within a word, low for that between words. For example, the *bay-bi* of baby would have a high transitional probability, whereas *bay-too* would have a low one. Word segmentation is the result of processing these transitional probabilities.

Obviously these transitional probabilities also hold in the absence of meaningful speech or for a language novel to you. So processing these transitional probabilities is not another way of being sensitive to words in a language one understands or meanings. It is dubious, to put it mildly, that transitional probabilities are an appropriate characterization of the phenomenal content of our perception of speech.[31] Indeed, if they were, understanding how we learn a language as an infant might be rather easier than it has proven to be. By the same token, it would be entirely inappropriate to deny that language learning involved processing transitional probabilities on the basis that phenomenal consciousness was not appropriately described in such terms and, as a result, it is inappropriate to take our powers of sensory discrimination to be tracked by such features.[32] Thus, we are not conscious of the basis by which we discriminate sound sequences involving different words.

One objection to this defence of premise (1) is to claim that, for example, appears male/appears female is a sensory manifest property. However, this is a mistake. Whatever perceptual cues subjects use to distinguish between male and female chicks are compatible with the chick failing to fall under the category in question. It may be that there are, in fact, no such cases—hence the highly successful performance of the expert chicken sexers—but since the sex of a chick is a matter, ultimately, of its internal structure, the possibility is open. Chicken sexers have not developed X-ray vision. Apparent maleness and femaleness will not pick out the bundles of sensory properties on the basis of which chicken sexers, in fact, discriminate.

Another objection is that the subjects are conscious *of* the perceptual cues in question but just not aware *that* these perceptual cues are the basis for their discriminations. Experimental research into chicken sexing might be taken to illustrate the point. Irving Biederman and Margaret Shiffrar trained naïve subjects to sex 1-day-old chicks in photographs based upon a simple difference of shape in the genital area—male round ball like watermelon, female more pointed or flat. This enabled the subjects slightly to outperform professional chicken sexers on the photographs (between 72 and 84 per cent accuracy). Real-life chicken sexing is a different story since certain information is lost in photographs.[33] Professional chicken sexers perform, on average, at 99.4 per cent accuracy, rating 960 birds an hour. They are trained on the basis of feedback concerning what they got right/wrong

---

[30] See e.g. Saffran, Aslin, and Newport (1996a) and (1996b).
[31] As is recognized in the literature, e.g. Perruchet and Pacton (2006), 236–7.
[32] I would very much like to thank Riana Belzer for her help in making me more precise in the formulation of this point.
[33] Biederman and Shiffrar (1987), 641–3.

over a three-month period to achieve 95 per cent accuracy and take between one and six years to obtain peak performance. They are not trained by identification of the different shapes the experimenters use and not all have insight that these shape differences are correlated with sex differences. Certainly, as the statistics and the context reveal, these differences are not sufficient to explain the final achieved skilled performance. Nevertheless, it might be urged, while we have not identified the perceptual cues to explain the best successful performance, there is no reason to expect that these do not show up in phenomenal consciousness in much the way the differences identified above show up. What is obscure to subjects are the precise perceptual cues (of which they are aware) which are the basis for their judgements.

To this objection, I make the following responses. First, it should not be assumed that because the elements of a particular perceptual cue—for example, various 3-D shape elements—may appropriately chararacterize the phenomenal content of our experience, the particular arrangement of shape elements that constitute the basis of the difference is also an appropriate characterization. That might be something of which we are unaware. Once the distinction is made between the elements in general and the precise arrangement of elements that might be the basis for a particular discrimination, for example chicken sexing, we can see that our prejudice in favour of sensory properties rests on a confusion. We mistake the fact that we can identify some elements partly in virtue of which a non-sensory manifest property can be realized as a sign that there is some arrangement of sensory properties which it is appropriate to characterize the phenomenal content of experience and on the basis of which we make the relevant discriminations. Thus, we wrongly conclude that appeal to non-sensory properties is unnecessary.

Second, the suggestion that the subject is unaware that his or her judgement is based upon arrangements of sensory properties that are, in fact, phenomenally accessible makes the judgement seem inexplicable to the subject. It also means that the only mental state concerning the sex of the chicken—as far as the chicken sexer is concerned—involves a commitment to the sex of the chicken (a judgement about it) rather than an appearance that the subject may choose to endorse or reject in judgement. But, typically, that's not how chicken sexers would describe their situation. Rather they would, upon inspecting a chick, take the chick to look one sex or another and, on the basis of that, judge the sex accordingly.

Third, the objection seems to rely upon the assumption that phenomenal consciousness is completely filled in. The thought seems to be that if it is proper partly to characterize the phenomenal content of our perceptual experience in terms of sensory manifest properties and, on the basis of experience, we are inclined to judge that a chick is male or female, then arrangements of sensory manifest properties which might be the basis for such judgement are also legitimate to attribute to the phenomenal content of experience. It would not be appropriate to characterize the phenomenal content in terms of some sensory manifest properties, *no* determinate arrangements of such properties which might be the basis for the judgement, but just non-sensory manifest properties. But there is good reason to reject such claims quite generally. For example, we might hold that the proper characterization of our visual experience outside the foveal region is that a certain wallpaper pattern covers a wall— Warhol's Marilyn Monroe for instance—and, yet, it becomes clear that, in fact, the sensory manifest content is much less determinate than that and is, in fact, insensitive to departures from the pattern.[34]

Putting these points together, it seems that there is no reason to conclude that the phenomenal content of a subject's experience should be characterized in terms of determinate arrangements of sensory properties concerning which the subject is unaware that they are the basis for his or her discriminations. This brings us to the third premise. If there is a difference of appearance in two objects—though not, as far as the subject is concerned, in their sensory manifest properties—then we should reflect this in our characterization of the phenomenal content of the subject's experience. It captures the fact that their judgements are done on the basis of their experience. Rejection of this way of describing the situation derives from the unwarranted assumptions described above.

The second argument—from the epistemic role of experience—should undermine further the attraction of stubborn resistance to this last point. Let M be a candidate manifest property of experience, C_M be the perceptual cues on the basis of which a subject discriminates M things from non-M things. As we have seen from the discussion before, M may not be C_M (for example, if M is a kind property) and subjects may not be conscious of C_M. The argument then runs as follows.

(1) M is a candidate manifest property to characterize (partly) the phenomenal content of your perceptual experience, e.g. it visually seems to you as if O has M.

(2) You may be unable to distinguish between an O with a sensory property C_M (the perceptual cues for M of which you are unaware) and M *and* an O with C_M but not M.

(3) If your perceptual experience only has a content involving sensory manifest properties, then you are entitled to judge that O has M on the basis of what you take to be the perceptual phenomenal content that O has M (or of O being M) only if it is not epistemically possible for you that, *although you are having a perceptual phenomenal content*, you are not having a perceptual content that O has M (and hence not epistemically possible for you that M is not a sensory manifest property).

(4) You are entitled to judge that O has M on the basis of what you take to be a perceptual phenomenal content that O has M (or of O being M).

Therefore,

(5) Your perceptual experience has content which does not just involve sensory manifest properties but non-sensory manifest properties too.

In brief, if we did not allow for the existence of nonsensory manifest content, then the perceptual entitlements to judge and believe that we standardly allow would be undermined because it is epistemically possible for most, if not all, properties we take ourselves to habitually experience that they are not sensory manifest properties.

---

[34] Dennett (1991), 354–5.

Many philosophers have emphasized that having a perceptual experience that p makes you entitled, or prima facie justified, to judge or believe that p.[35] The position is often taken to be distinct from the additional claim that you should be aware that you are having a perceptual experience in order to be justified in believing that p on its basis. (3) is not meant to involve this additional claim. Talk of 'what you take to be a perceptual phenomenal content' is not meant to imply an awareness of being in a certain perceptual state. Rather it concerns how you're taking a certain phenomenal content, namely, in an appropriately similar manner to other perceptual phenomenal contents as opposed to other kinds of phenomenal contents.

If I do not know that M is a sensory property, and austere or conservative views about perceptual phenomenal content are correct, then for all I know I am not having a perceptual phenomenal content that O is M (or of O being M). If M is not a sensory property, then there is no such perceptual phenomenal content to be had, although there may be a distinct perceptual phenomenal content related to it. It is plausible that one cannot be entitled, or prima facie justified, to arrive at a belief or judgement that p unless one knows that p is presented in perceptual experience. That does not imply that p is the case but simply that we should know what our experiences purport to be the case in order for them to provide grounds for beliefs or judgements.

Is the last point common ground? Relationists about perception typically say that, while the content of hallucinations may be subjectively indiscriminable from the corresponding experiences, hallucinations lack phenomenal content.[36] They typically adopt the position they do because they want to emphasize the important connection between perceptual experience and knowledge. They can allow that it is epistemically possible for you that you are not in a state with perceptual phenomenal content, when you take yourself so to be, but, in those circumstances, you are not in a state with perceptual phenomenal content at all and so the connection between whatever state you are in and judgement is irrelevant. Nevertheless, when you are in a perceptual phenomenal state, the thought runs, it is not epistemically possible for you to take yourself to be presented with something different from with what you take yourself to be presented. So there is no conflict between an intuitive relationist account of perception and my claim about what we must know about our perceptual phenomenal contents.

The point is not simply that the claim of premise (3) is compatible with extant versions of relationism. Rather the issue concerns the role that perceptual experience plays in the justification of belief. It may, on all sides, be conceded that some conditions on what it is to be justified, warranted, or entitled are inaccessible to a subject as epistemological externalists emphasize. However, if perceptual experience, or for that matter the content of other beliefs, are to play a role in justification, then the link between their contents and the contents for which they provide support should be available to us. In the present context, once the conditions for something to count as a perceptual experience are met, then it shouldn't be the case that its content remains something we do not know.

---

[35] e.g. Alston (2002), 71; Audi (1998), 24-7; BonJour (2003), 74-8; Brewer (1999), 49-51; Chisholm (1989), 64-9; Conee and Feldman (1995), 97-9; Huemer (2001), 98-105; Pollock and Cruz (1999), 201-2; Pryor (2000), 519.

[36] Fish (2009), 81, 94. See remarks naturally interpreted that way in M. G. F. Martin (2006), 389.

The second premise claims that it is epistemically possible that a property M that you take to characterize the phenomenal content of your perceptual experience is, in fact, not a sensory property because two objects may differ in M and yet be indiscriminable by sharing C_M. I take this to be possible for any property which does not reveal its full character in our current experience of it. Properties which require objects to have an internal structure would be a case in point. Even the kind of properties that proponents of the austere or conservative position are prepared to allow characterize experience are, in fact, likely to be ruled out. A classic example would be that of colour. If colour is taken to be an intrinsic property of the surfaces of objects—like a certain surface reflectance profile—then it will be possible for objects to differ in surface reflectance profiles and yet provide the same visual cues for subjects because of the circumstances in which the objects with these profiles are present. Thus Michael Tye's commitment to this account of colour is in tension with his espousal of a conservative or austere theory of manifest content.

Obviously, the point would not apply for any property solely characterized in terms of our responses to the objects which possess it. That might be argued to be the situation with colour and other secondary properties. However, a fair summary of the debate about the various properties we take ourselves to experience is that it is epistemically possible that they should not be characterized solely in terms of our response to them. Our knowledge relating to these properties has not, so far, ruled out response-independent accounts of any of these properties. So any property we take ourselves to experience is one which it is epistemically possible that it does not characterize the content of our experience. It is this which undermines the connection between experience and belief. In summary, any attempt to restrict the properties which characterize our experience to sensory properties, throws into question the epistemic role of experience because it is not obvious that a property satisfies this constraint. This is a matter which is not available to us from within.

One objection to the argument arises from concern that perceptual experience with rich or liberal contents cannot support the corresponding beliefs. Seeing that there is a pine before me, the charge goes, does not entitle me to have the belief that there is a pine before me. In which case, I cannot appeal to the claim that such entitlement would be lost if the austere or conservative approach to content was adopted.[37] The point made just a moment ago, that many properties we intuitively take to satisfy the conservative or austere theorist's strictures in fact fail to do so, merely makes this objection more general.

One response to this objection is to distinguish between two cases. Suppose that S believes that p as a result of which he or she perceives that p—the belief penetrates the perception—when, without the belief, S's perception would have only had a more austere content. In that case, the perception cannot entitle one to have the belief. This is distinct from the following type of case. Suppose that the subject has learnt to recognize objects of kind K on the basis of sensory properties that fall short of K but which, in the circumstances, are only present in Ks. Let this capacity to recognize penetrate the perceptual content so that now the subject perceives things to be Ks.

---

[37] An objection inspired by S. Siegel (2012), 212–15.

Then, if the subject believes that O is a K on the basis of a perceptual experience, the entitlement is still present. The difference is that the subject doesn't have a belief that O is a K until after having the perception. The belief he or she has beforehand, if any, is simply that things with such-and-such sensory properties are Ks. There is no unacceptable circularity of putative entitlement in this case.

A second response to the objection is to note that the argument I have given does not presume that we are entitled to beliefs on the basis of non-sensory manifest contents. Rather the point is that, because it is not accessible from within whether some property counts as a sensory property, the link between sensory manifest contents and the entitlement to have beliefs about such properties is undermined if different epistemic credentials are attributed to sensory and non-sensory manifest contents. Conviction that at least some perceptual experience gives prima facie justification for beliefs is the basis for recognizing that it does in the case of non-sensory manifest contents too. The epistemic flaws of beliefs formed on the basis of such experience arise elsewhere, for example, when they are unreliably formed.

The first argument undermines the claim that sensory properties have most claim to be the appropriate characterization of the phenomenal content of perceptual experience, as it shows up in consciousness, and throws into question the claim that it is possible to separate off such phenomenal content from the perceptual seemings that, it was claimed, are a causal consequence of it. The second argument questions the epistemological motivation for making this differentiation in order to characterize how perceptual experience plays the epistemic role it does.

For some, the recognition of the existence of non-sensory manifest content will be sufficient to establish that there is evaluative perception. They will note the uncertainty about whether there is, for example, moral perception detailed in Section 1. They will argue that the uncertainty stems from attempting to understand evaluative perception as involving evaluative sensory properties. Once we see we don't have to understand evaluative perception in this fashion, there is no further debate. For others, there will still be the question of whether evaluative properties really show up in experience. They will emphasize the hard to resist observation that the question of whether or not we perceive evaluative properties is significantly more contentious than that of whether we see pines or television sets. I suspect that this is because there is a further factor which plays a role in evaluative perception. Arguably, the content of the perception is in some way dependent upon our responses. By being so dependent, at least this aspect of perceptual experience may be plausibly characterized as representational in character whatever one's picture of the perceptual experience of other properties. In Section 3, I will outline two ideas that will assist in developing our understanding of how evaluative perception of such properties may occur given that this is so.

3. Intrinsic Representation of Response-Dependent Properties

The purpose of the present section is to introduce two unorthodox ideas that will assist us in understanding better how evaluative content may be a part of our perceptions. The first concerns the representation of response-dependent properties in general, the second illustrates how different responses may have implications for the nature of the manifest content of perceptions appealing to them.

Response-dependent properties can take a variety of forms. Their distinctive feature is simply that they are properties an object possesses in virtue of the object eliciting, or being co-present with, certain responses in ourselves. A very familiar case is that of those dispositions characterized in terms of eliciting certain kinds of experiences, amongst which some philosophers have been tempted to include colours.[38] I shall use this case to fix ideas. It does not much matter whether we consider the dispositions colours, or apparent/phenomenal colours. The purpose is simply to illustrate the structure of the position.

Representationalists have often felt that they must reject response-dependent accounts of colours because of a concern with circularity.[39] Consider a standard schema for formulating such an approach.

(R)   O is R = O has the disposition to produce M(R) in subjects of type S, in C.

I'll set aside the question of the modality of the claim, or whether it is constitutive and/or a priori. Such issues don't touch on the issue of concern. Suppose R is a response-dependent property, M(R) the mental response in virtue of which it is characterized. If M(R) is equally characterized in terms of R—for instance, it is described as an experience of R or a representation of R—then it relies upon differences of R to distinguish between the different dispositions the schema seeks to characterize, for example, red, blue, and green. It is to address this issue, rather than the interest of response-dependent characterizations in general, that one of R or M(R) requires an independent characterization.[40]

Providing an independent characterization of R is a rejection of a response-dependent account of R. It may be that if O has R it will be disposed to produce M(R) in subjects of type S in C but R itself is no longer a response-dependent property. It may be the basis of the disposition and some philosophers are inclined to identify dispositions with their bases.[41] They would likewise reject the claim that dispositions so understood are response-dependent properties. Tye rightly identifies the resulting view of secondary qualities such as colour as 'perceiver independent'.[42]

The alternative is to provide an independent characterization of M(R). This idea seems a non-starter if M(R) is taken to be a certain kind of experience because, according to representationalism, a necessary condition of this characterization (if not sufficient) will be in terms of what the experience represents. Standard accounts of representation appeal to some kind of complex causal relationship between the item represented in the world and the representation in the head. They are not available if no independent characterization of R is recognized as one of the relata in the complex relationship.[43]

---

[38] See e.g. McGinn (1983), 28–44.   [39] See e.g. Tye (1995), 144–50.
[40] See McGinn (1983), 6–8 for rejection for the general circularity worry.
[41] e.g. Armstrong (1973), 11–16.   [42] Tye (1995), 145.
[43] e.g. Tye's own account, Tye (1995), 101.

The first thought I want to introduce is that M(R) may, instead, be intrinsically representational. There will be a functional story about what makes M(R) a representation, and which intrinsic properties of it have representational significance. Nevertheless, what is represented by M(R) is a matter of the intrinsic properties M(R) has. It is nothing to do with M(R) standing in relation to something independently characterized as R in the world.

A useful example to get the general idea is Goodman's example of tailors' swatches of cloth which represent the colour, weave, texture, and pattern out of which a suit may be made or, to give another example, a colour chart indicating the range of paint colours available.[44] There is a functional story about what makes a particular piece of cloth play the role of a swatch representing the things indicated. Nevertheless, what is represented by the tailor's swatch of cloth is a matter of some of the intrinsic properties of the cloth (and not others, for example size of cloth has nothing to do with size of suit one may have).[45]

The example has features we should not assume are taken across to all cases. In certain respects, the swatch of cloth is taken to stand for clothes of the type of which it is one. Applying the idea to the representation of response-dependent properties such as dispositions, certain intrinsic features of the brain's visual system are taken to index a disposition to give rise to those very features rather than, simply, to stand for the features themselves. This alternative role for the intrinsic features is also likely to be settled by some functional story about how the representations are used, for example, as the basis for certain kinds of sorting behaviour with regard to objects, amongst other things. A related point is that the intrinsic features in question need not even be taken to stand for themselves as the index of the disposition. The functional story which gives certain intrinsic features a representational significance need not give it the representational significance of standing for themselves in the characterization of what is represented.

Thus, the current proposal should be distinguished from two related ones. The first is the idea, put forward by Katalin Balog, and others, that phenomenal concepts involve phenomenal states standing for themselves.[46] Talk of intrinsic representations need not involve taking them to be a concept, or a constituent of a concept. Nor, as I just underlined, need it involve reflexive representation. The second, due to Uriah Kriegel, is simply the thought that the representational properties of our experience represent response-dependent properties, specifically dispositions to produce certain kinds of responses in the visual system.[47] This does not, in itself, involve a commitment to a particular way, an intrinsic way, in which the properties are represented. Indeed, later discussion makes clear that Kriegel still operates with a broadly causal-informational account of representational properties.[48]

Intrinsic representations have a phenomenal consequence with regard to what they represent. The things represented seem, in a certain sense, unstructured. Subjects' experiences take them straight through to what is represented broadly independently of their successful representation of other things. That is so even if

---

[44] Goodman (1976), 53.   [45] For related discussion, see Block (1983), 511–15.
[46] Balog (1999), 525.   [47] Kriegel (2009), 87–93.   [48] Kriegel (2009), 209–32.

the representation in question is a certain internal functional property. It is just that the intrinsic presentation in this case is dependent, while not being apparently dependent, upon its potential to stand in relations to other things.

The second idea, following on from the first, is that the kind of responses which may have representational significance need not be limited to those of the sensory system restrictively understood. An illustration of this point is an account of our perception of expressive properties I have defended elsewhere. There I suggested that the simulation, by the sensuous imagination, of an emotion-guided creative process in response to features of music, paintings, and other things, made these things seem to possess expressive properties. The act of simulation described is, itself, what constitutes the representation of expressive properties.[49] In Section 4, I will consider whether other responses can be identified as the basis of the representation of other evaluative properties.

4. Response-Dependent Representation

The kinds of perception that fall under the general heading of evaluative perception are diverse and there is no reason to expect that they all share the same features. I'm going to focus on two particularly striking and much-discussed cases, although some may contest the description of the first of these as a case of perception. For our purposes, it shares relevant features and serves to dramatize an important issue, that of perceptual presence. When we suffer pain, it is phenomenologically obvious that something bad is going on, in standard cases. By contrast, the moral properties of a situation or action are much less striking in this sense. If I am going to appeal to responses to explain what is represented, how can I capture this difference? As we will see, the crucial work will be done by the characterization of the representational disposition and the conditions C in which the representational dispositions are manifested. My concern is not to defend the existence of evaluative perception in these two cases but rather to illustrate how they might be treated given that you are inclined to accept this characterization of the cases. Successful treatment, though, is an indirect argument for the plausibility of the characterization.

4.1. Pain

According to one line of thought, our experiences of pain represent certain kinds of bodily disturbance/damage. Although I don't endorse this approach—from my perspective, experiences of pain represent the presence of a certain felt property in a certain location—it helps to fix ideas to adopt this framework since it is a familiar one. The question, then, becomes this. In addition to representing certain kinds of bodily damage, pain hurts. It feels awful most of the time. How is this to be characterized? Does it involve a further representation of something else?

---

[49] Noordhof (2008), 343–4.

A recent suggestion is that the representation of pain has an evaluative dimension when it is experienced to be unpleasant. David Bain writes:

A subject has an unpleasant pain iff he or she is undergoing an experience that represents a bodily disturbance of a certain sort and (ii) that same experience additionally represents the disturbance as bad for him or her in the bodily sense.[50]

If such a theory is correct, then pain becomes a form of evaluative perception. Bain goes on to link the representation as bad to motivation. He writes 'Pain is unpleasant and motivating only because it further represents that bodily disturbance as bad for you.'[51] However, he does not expand on the basis of the link.

There are a number of problems with the proposal. Identifying them will enable us to understand more about the nature of the response-dependent representation involved. The first is that a subject's mental state can represent something as bad for him or her in a bodily sense without that state in any way being a negative experience. For example, suppose you see that a meat cleaver strikes your arm, sinks into the flesh, and goes into the bone. Imagine your proponent of moral perception at work here. They will say you don't have to conclude that the disturbance to your body is bad for you. You can just see that it is bad. Nevertheless, for various reasons, you might be shocked or in some strange dispassionate state where you are just an observer and you don't feel, or even respond to, the awfulness of what you have just seen. The second is that the suggested characterization doesn't seem to distinguish pain from nausea. In both, there is a bodily disturbance and the nausea is experienced as bad.[52] Perhaps it will be argued that the feelings of nausea are related to the body in a different way but it is not clear that this is right in every case. It is conceivable that you will feel nausea rooted in a particular injury to the body—imagine the meat cleaver again—so that the nausea is a response, say, to the elements of the damage done (the flesh separated by the blade) and yet it is nausea rather than pain that you feel.

The third is that there are two distinct features of pain which come under the general heading of our negative response to it. The first is the motivational force of pain—for example, to seek to be rid of it—the second is its unpleasantness. As Jennifer Corns points out, although these often go together, they can dissociate cutting the pleasantness/unpleasantness-motivation link to which Bain appeals. One example is the case of addictions. The motivational force can get stronger and yet the experience of the drug as pleasant is weaker. Another is masochism or self-injurious behaviour. Here, although the resulting pain is experienced to be unpleasant, such subjects are motivated to inflict it on themselves further. Corns takes this as evidence that the proper relationship between unpleasantness and motivational force is that the first causes a motivational signal which, in appropriate circumstances, causes motivations.[53] Strength of signal is the motivational force of the feeling of unpleasantness. Her favoured position also captures what she suggests is the natural order of explanation. Namely, that it is *because* pain feels unpleasant that we dislike it (and hence is the object of certain motivational states or dispositions to have motivational

---

[50] Bain (2013), 82.   [51] Bain (2013), 82.
[52] Corns (2014), 253.   [53] Corns (2014), 244–6.

states such as desire). Pain doesn't feel unpleasant because we dislike it.[54] The picture she has in mind is something like this.

    Feeling unpleasant ⟶ Motivational signal ⟶ Motivation

The natural order of explanation is open to question, however. While it might be true that the unpleasant character of pain is something we are not always motivated to be rid of, it is not possible that something can be experienced as unpleasant and be entirely independent of our motivational states, such as desires, regardless of the circumstances. Yet if the connection between the experience of something as unpleasant and the resultant desires is contingent, then it should be possible for the link to be entirely broken. This observation needs to be rephrased if the causal roles of properties are essential properties of their instantiations (as certain power ontologists/dispositional essentialists maintain).[55] Then the point would be that we need an explanation of why, whereas in most cases, we have the illusion of contingency between the instantiation of a property and a typical effect, in these circumstances, we don't.[56] In any event, if there is no contingency, or illusion of contingency, once the circumstances are taken into account, then we need an explanation of the tight connection between something being represented as awful and disliking it (being disposed to have motivational states which make us want to avoid the thing in question).

This suggests that the awfulness of pain is represented by a creature's pain experience involving, as part of its representational properties, the disposition to have a distinctive aversive response: attempting to rid itself of the pain in certain specified ways W in circumstances C, and so on. Call this the pain response. It is a potential for various causal relations that is an intrinsic part of the structure of a subject's brain. When you saw the meat cleaver go into your arm, you did not have the requisite dispositions as part of your visual experience though you might have a Type II evaluative perception of what is happening to your arm as bad. You might also have a distinct kind of Type 1 visual perception. I set this aside. My focus is on the pain experience.

The exact character of the disposition to have a pain response will not be available a priori. For creatures without the mental sophistication to have desires but the appropriate bodily properties, it may be understood in terms of a disposition to quite primitive response behaviours such as writhing, flinching, and attempts to alleviate. For more sophisticated creatures, it will also involve the disposition to have various desires to behave in certain ways. Since motivations are, themselves, dispositional, that will mean that the awfulness of pain is represented by, in part, the disposition to have another disposition. When in circumstances C, the subject will display various kinds of distinctive aversive behaviour. This will include motivations which will be acted upon, given other states. However, without these other states, the motivations will not be operative, and in non-C conditions, the aversive disposition will be present but not manifested. There is no reason to think that this complex aversive

---

[54] Corns (2014), 242.   [55] e.g. Shoemaker (1980) and (1984/2003).
[56] For general discussion of this point see Noordhof (1997).

disposition will fail to differentiate pain from other negative states like nausea even if there are some similarities in manifestation in certain specific cases.

The proposal provides a satisfying treatment of Corns's observations about the causal explanatory order. The metaphysically necessary connection between the negative features of pain and the aversive reaction in certain circumstances is explained by the fact that a state of the body would not be represented as awful unless the subject were disposed to respond in the way indicated. So we have an account of the link. On the other hand, if the disposition plays a representational role, then it will appear that what is represented—the awfulness—is a causal explanation of the resultant response. So we have an account of why the explanatory order seems the way it is.

If circumstances C don't hold, then the pain response will not be triggered or aspects of it truncated. That will be the situation with regard to the masochistic and self-harming. That is one dimension of the dissociation that Corns identifies (awfulness without the motivation). In most circumstances, though, the subject will meet conditions C. In this case, the disposition will be triggered and the subject will go into certain motivational states. Being so disposed, one can reasonably argue, is for there to be a certain motivational signal. The question of whether or not this results in a motivation, and consequent behaviour, will depend upon one's other mental states. Presented awfulness is the result of a representational disposition rather than a representational motivation or response.

Corns suggests that the disposition to make a pain response needs to be cashed out in terms of something else. It is this that she thinks ought to be called the *aversive valence* which, by her lights, plays the role of a motivational signal.[57] If Corns's concern is based upon the thought that there can be nothing it is like to be in the disposition I have mentioned, then I disagree. The phenomenal characterization of aversive valence will appeal to the fact that some state of the body is represented as awful and, in one's current overall mental state (a C state), this inclines one to want to do something about it.

What about the other form of dissociation? The case of the drug addict in which the motivational force to take the drug is strong but this isn't coupled with a representation of the attractiveness of the drug. The pleasure has grown weaker. Indeed, in a moment of self-loathing, the nicotine-addicted smoker finding a cigarette unpleasant may draw deeper. Or the case of a person who is so fearful/anxious about the possibility of a pain that they react strongly but can be brought to the realization that things don't hurt that much.

Focusing on the former, addicts are strongly motivationally disposed to have the drug in the first place. Their mental states are non-C circumstances. Let's call them A (for addict) circumstances. The addict can be in such circumstances without having the disposition to have an attracted response in circumstances C (which would represent the drug as pleasurable). Indeed, the addict may have a disposition to have an aversive response in C thus representing the drug as bad. A-circumstances don't involve a disposition to have an attracted response in C but, instead, simply the

---

[57] Corns (2014), 245.

continuous presence of an attracted response. There is no reason why attracted responses can only result from current dispositions to have attracted responses in C, although it is plausible that these dispositions were present in the past. The addict is stuck with the manifestation without the continuing of the disposition in circumstances C. That does not mean that the addict will be always trying for the drug. It is just that the motivational part of the attracted response—which is, as noted earlier, in itself a disposition—will be continuously present to a lesser or greater strength.

Although the attracted response is always on, as it were, without the presence of the disposition, this does not mean that it is unsupported. The attracted response might be supported by imagining how good a new drug experience will be. These repeated acts of imagination, perhaps relating to a past high, are not reflected in the subject's current experience of the drug which gives little pleasure. We might diagram the situation as follows:

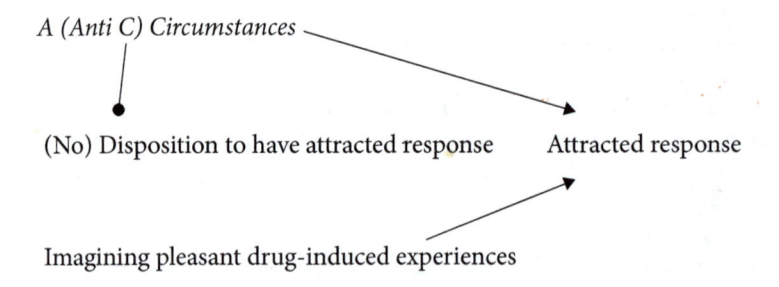

A (Anti C) Circumstances

(No) Disposition to have attracted response   Attracted response

Imagining pleasant drug-induced experiences

In the case of the self-loathing nicotine addict, we have something even more striking. The disposition which, in C circumstances, results in an aversive response causes an attracted response:

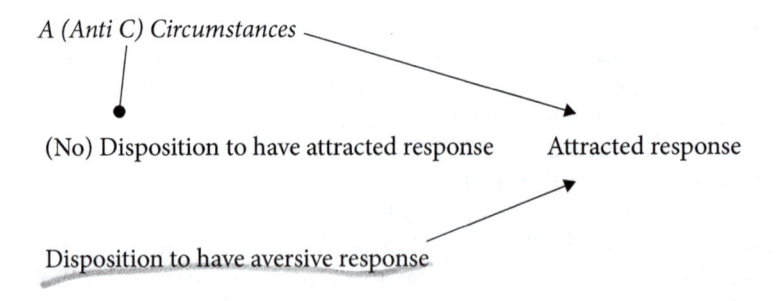

A (Anti C) Circumstances

(No) Disposition to have attracted response   Attracted response

Disposition to have aversive response

There is no reason why a disposition to make an aversive response should not, in particular peculiar psychological circumstances, result in an attracted response since the connection between the disposition and aversive response is only taken to be present in C. Indeed, one might even allow that the awfulness of pain is a more complex disposition which gives rise to this element.

I have discussed the case of addiction in some detail because it was meant to show how the two aspects—representing something as good or bad and the motivational element—can come apart. What we have seen is that representing something as good or bad involves a more sophisticated relationship to motivation but still an essential motivational element. A similar structure can be recognized for pain. Thus, nothing in Corns's interesting reflections on double dissociation undermine the proposal supported here.

Few creatures can avoid being in a state where they have a disposition to make an aversive response in circumstances C. Subjects no more seem to have a control over the instantiation of these dispositions than they have of their experience of other manifest properties. This is a plausible source of the phenomenal presence of the awfulness of pain, to be contrasted with our second case below.

4.2. Moral Properties

Moral belief or judgement has typically been related to motivation. For example, many find compelling the thought that if you believe that you ought to do A and are practically rational, then you are motivated to do A.[58] Therefore, it is plausible that if you perceive various facts which give rise to such judgements, the perceptions themselves will, in some way, be linked to distinctive kinds of motivational states. The link will not be straightforward of course. The link between judging that such and such a thing is morally right or wrong and being motivated to do something about it is based upon evaluative judgements about one's own obligations. You might perceive something in the world which you conclude ought not to occur, feel disapproval towards it, and yet it not be immediately clear that *you* ought to do something about it. Nevertheless, although the link is not straightforward, further information about the state of affairs that you judge ought not to be happening, or is about to happen and which ought not, and your relationship to it, is naturally linked to you being motivated to do something about it. Thus evaluative perception of situations in the world, and how they are developing, typically relate to motivational and other affective responses you are inclined to have. Such perceptions put you in a certain dispositional state.

That suggests that an appeal to affective states is plausible in much the same way as we appealed to dispositions to pain responses in the earlier discussion. The range of responses that seem to pick up the morally relevant properties of a situation is large. Most familiarly linked to motivation is, of course, desire. Allan Gibbard emphasizes the importance of anger and guilt; Jesse Prinz, blame.[59] Other relevant emotions seem to be disgust, sympathy, pity, indignation, and so on. Many of these emotions can rely upon evaluative judgements—for example, I am angry because I judge that somebody has done something wrong—but there are plausible basic cases in which the response has come unmediated by these evaluative reflections upon which further responses may be built.

If dispositions to have these motivational and affective responses are taken to provide the basis for representational properties what do they represent? It might be thought that if we are disposed to feel disgust at something, then we will experience it to be disgusting; if we are disposed to feel anger, then we will experienced it as anger-provoking; and so

[58] See e.g. Korsgaard (1986), 8–9; Smith (1994), 61.
[59] Gibbard (1990), 126; Prinz (2007), 281.

on. The dispositions to these responses would not represent something other than that the thing perceived has the disposition to cause certain responses in us. If that were right, then the chance of these dispositions being the basis of the perception of evaluative properties would be slender. Not only that, but it would encourage the view that such evaluative perception was not really perception but rather an inference from self-observation of our affective responses.

There is an alternative. Instead of representing simple dispositions to motivational and affective responses, these responses might represent their response-worthiness. Thus, if we are disposed to desire that p, then p is presented to us as desire-worthy; if we are disposed to be disgusted by something, it is represented as disgust-worthy; and so on. That does not mean, of course, that the things represented to be R-worthy (where 'R' stands for some type of response) are R-worthy. It is rather that this is how they are presented. Our dispositions to have affective responses provide us with the preliminary representational means for representing certain things as worthy of those responses. If we were not capable of the responses in question, then we would not experience the properties in the world as worthy of certain kinds of response.

One challenge to this proposal is to ask why dispositions to respond in way R represent R-worthiness rather than R-dispositions. However, one should not assume that some representational feature—in this case a disposition to R—should be taken to represent something closest to that feature, say being an R-disposition rather than being R-worthy. As I argued in Section 3, what something represents depends upon the particular functional role that settles which features of the disposition to R are representational, and of what. Different responses give rise to different characteristic patterns of attention to features of the world. The responses, then, may be used to index such characteristic patterns of response as colours in a colour chart may stand for emotions engendered by the colours (say). In which case, what the disposition to R stands for are those features that are typically seen as naturally giving rise to or worthy of the response in question. The C conditions of these dispositions will also bear witness to this representational role. The extent to which these conditions will involve certain constraints on the state of the subject, for example, being reflective, cautious, or other kinds of idealization, again make out the case for R-worthiness rather than, for example, apparent R-worthiness or R-dispositions being represented.

In saying that we perceive these features to be worthy of response, that is not to say that we may not believe these features to be unworthy. For example, in a state of self-loathing, we may perceive some kind of self-abuse or humiliation as worthy of being desired while, at the same time, believing that it is not. The point is rather that our affective responses make us see things in certain ways—because of the representational role that they play—even if we have beliefs which conflict with them. Indeed, even if we reject what strikes us as an illusion stemming from an emotionally disturbed state.

It is the last point that I would emphasize in response to a familiar line of objection to the link between R and the representation of R-worthiness. It is that there are cases in which a subject makes a R response and yet they fail to take the object to which they are making the response as R-worthy. The point is usually made with respect to desire. There is the example of the mother at the end of her tether suddenly wanting to drown the baby she is bathing, pointless desires to engage in little childish rituals, and so on.[60] In each of these cases, the concern is that the subject does not experience the objects as desire-worthy.

My response to this concern is that the representational role that these affective responses play is compatible with the subject resisting what is presented as R-worthy. R-worthiness is meant to capture the fact that, even in these cases, there is something which seems to the subject like a natural calling forth of the response in question. In this respect, my view is very similar to a view put forward by Jennifer Hawkins recently.[61] Where we differ is that she develops her theory within the context of understanding the affective responses as (at most) proto-conceptual capacities presenting the world in various ways as a result of a subject's experience of the responses as fitting the objects.[62] My thought is rather that the affective responses make a fit by changing the representational character of our experience.

It should also be remembered that I am not claiming that a particular response— e.g. desire to drown the baby—represents the drowning as desire-worthy. The claim is that the disposition to have the desire represents this. I noted earlier, with respect to pain, that its awfulness may be represented without a subject being motivated to do anything about it. This suggests, what many point out anyway, that a subject may experience something to be R-worthy without actually having the response in question. Again, the appeal to C conditions in the following general format helps us to capture what we need.

The disposition to have R in conditions C represents O to be R-worthy.

If a subject is *disposed* to be disgusted in conditions C as a result of perceiving O, then they will experience O to be disgust-worthy. If a subject is *disposed* to desire O in conditions C as a result of perceiving O, then they will perceive O to be desire-worthy. The subject does not actually have to desire or be disgusted to see things presented in the way I have indicated. In this case, conditions C are conditions which, when realized, mean that they are engaged rather than distracted, stunned, emotionally withdrawn, or whatever. Also, part of these C-conditions will be facts relating to the relevance of the response, for example, whether there is something the subject can do about the situation, when the response relates to motivation. In the moral case, the C-conditions will include whether or not an agent is practically rational or has suitable moral training. The additional appeal to moral training would give a new kind of representation of desire-worthiness to that which is represented by an untrained but practically rational individual.[63] Note that dispositions with the same response but different manifestation conditions are distinct dispositions with potentially different representational significance.

Notice, too, I am not making the following claim, say,

O is desire-worthy iff O has the disposition to cause in S an experience E (involving the disposition to desire O in circumstances C).

---

[60] Watson (1975); Velleman (1992).   [61] Hawkins (2008), 256–64.
[62] Hawkins (2008), 258–9.
[63] In earlier terminology, those who lack sagacity. See Noordhof (1999), 134–6.

That would be an additional claim. My claim is just that the disposition to desire O in circumstances C represents O (say) to be desire-worthy if caused by O in the right way. Whether a subject's experience of objects as R-worthy corresponds to a genuine property that they have—of R-worthiness—is something else again. If there are things which are morally desire-worthy—that is, if some kind of moral realism is true—then moral training would involve developing our responses to items in the world so our experiences of desire-worthiness picked out a subclass of these properties: the morally desire-worthy properties. If our perceptions of such properties were reliable, they would provide the basis for knowledge. One way of securing their reliability, of course, is to take moral properties to be those which produce the right kind of representations in the appropriate circumstances. In this case, moral training will involve a progressive revisable co-identification of properties perceived to be desire-worthy with the properties which, currently, elicit these experiences until it is judged that the experiences correspond to what it is agreed is desire-worthy. But, as I say, this is an additional claim.

If a subject is disposed to make a certain response then, as I have indicated before, they will be attentive to certain features of the world characteristic of that response. This is part of the explanation of the relationship between the features to which the subject responds to and the response which is worthy of them. However, they may recognize the world to be R-worthy even if they don't have the experience which sets up the disposition in them. Their capacity for sensuous imagination of the reaction will enable them to simulate to what features they would attend. This would be a straightforward case of recognizing something on the basis of perception. This is what I dubbed Type 2 evaluative perception. This kind of activity can also apply to situations in which one has processing problems. They may be complex or uncertain. A particular way of understanding the situation may be unfamiliar to you. You may need to consider the relevant features of the situation, simulate responses you are inclined to make, discuss the matter with others, and, finally, recognize what is the case about that situation. Sceptics about Type 1 evaluative perception may hold that our approach to the perception of moral matters always falls within this category.

The account of the phenomenal content of moral perception defended here can capture the two features distinctive of moral perception mentioned at the beginning. The first was the simplicity and unity of particular cases of moral properties although they are related to complex arrangements of non-evaluative properties. The contrast would be with the way that a macro-property is structured or, for that matter, in the way that functional properties have a structure by being composed from dispositions to have certain consequences. Response-dependent representation enables us to pick out moral properties independent of their relationship to other things. It is for this reason that, although there are features that might be responsible for our responses— recall that I suggested these responses made us focus on certain features of the world rather than others—the property that is picked up by their representation is seen as not simply the arrangement of these features.

The second feature of moral perception was that it seems, to an extent, to lack a certain perceptual presence. This is by contrast with the presentation of other high-level or kind properties and bears comparison with the lack of presence of expressive properties. Both the latter case and the moral case depend upon responses that are, at least, partly under our control as agents, as opposed to the result of extra-agential organization of sensory materials. The result is that our experience of them lacks the commitment to the reality of what is presented.[64] The instantiation of the representational dispositions depends not just on this aspect of their characteristic responses but also has manifestation conditions that are partly characterized by matters under an agent's control, namely their practical rationality and moral training. Where our responses are much less under control—our responses to pain being an example— the corresponding evaluative perceptions are committed to the presence of something bad.

Let me comment on one final feature. Within the domain of the moral, it seems that some candidate moral properties are more obviously part of our experience than others. The kindness of an act strikes us more forcibly than whether it is right or wrong. The reason why we find it harder to see thinner moral properties like rightness and wrongness is because there is no distinctive disposition relating to moral rightness and wrongness. Rather, we recognize that actions are right or wrong in virtue of our perceptions involving dispositions relating to thicker evaluative properties. They are abstractions from our reactions to particular features. Thus the moral rightness and wrongness of an action is a complex function of kindness and other properties which are detected by our immediate reactions.

5. Concluding Remarks

In Section 2, I suggested that perceptual content had two important characteristics that are responsible for its epistemic properties: non-neutrality about the way the world is but absence of a commitment by the subject. Although we have seen, in Section 4, that subjects' responses are partly responsible for what is represented in evaluative perceptions, these responses are not judgements involving a commitment to the presence of the evaluative properties in question. So they do not undermine this feature of perception in general. Nevertheless, one might think, matters are not so clear with regard to non-neutrality. If perception is non-neutral about the world because it is in some sense configured by the world, learning that some of what is represented is due to our dispositions to respond in certain ways might seem to put this characteristic under threat. In particular, this should be so in those cases in which the responses seem more under our control as, I have suggested, the typical dispositions relating to moral perception are. The extent to which these dispositions are reliable habitual responses—partly as a result of training—to features of the world may recover some of the epistemic credentials of such perception. They seem more non-neutral and inescapable. However, it is precisely because there is no easy non-neutrality for these cases—as there is in the case of our perception of many non-evaluative properties and the case of pain—that leads to precisely the lack of presence of evaluative properties and consequent anxiety over whether they are real, with commensurate doubts about the epistemic status of evaluative perception.[65]

---

[64] For further discussion of this point, see Noordhof (forthcoming).
[65] See Noordhof (forthcoming) for related discussion.

Cheekily, then, I suggest that the account recommended above has a further recommendation, namely it implies that the reality or otherwise of the evaluative will be contested and will continue to be contested even if there is evaluative perception.[66]

---

[66] I'd like to thank Anna Bergqvist and Robert Cowan for inviting me to present the work at their Evaluative Perception conference, the participants of that conference for their comments, and, also, the Open University Philosophy Department for their criticism and comments at a research seminar. Special thanks are due to Heather Logue and Ema Sullivan-Bissett who persevered with catching my errors when others had quite reasonably given up.

5
Doubts about Moral Perception

Pekka Väyrynen

1. Introduction

Can moral properties—such as being wrong, or good, or unjust—be *perceived*, in any robust sense? Many philosophers claim so.[1] This paper will press doubts.

It is tempting to count perception as one mode of access to at least some instances of moral right and wrong, goodness and badness, and the like.[2] We often describe our moral experiences—experiences in which things strike us as being a certain way morally—in apparently perceptual terminology. Consider:

Cat: 'If you round a corner and see a group of young hoodlums pour gasoline on a cat and ignite it, you do not need to *conclude* that what they are doing is wrong; you do not need to figure anything out; you can *see* that it is wrong.'[3]

Tiananmen Square: 'Could one not see terrible injustice by viewing soldiers shooting citizens who are peaceably criticizing their government?'[4]

But care is due. Sometimes 'see' designates a kind of intellectual understanding, as when we say things like 'I see that P doesn't entail Q, but surely the truth of P would be an unexplained accident unless Q were true'. And not all experiences that have a phenomenal character which 'see' may be used to designate are clearly perceptual; talk of 'seeing spots' might be an example. Even when 'see' is used in a perceptual context, the mental state to which it is applied may not be a case of perception. We can talk of a scientist 'seeing' a proton by seeing a vapor trail in a cloud chamber, but

---

[1] See Murdoch (1970); McNaughton (1988); DePaul (1993); Blum (1994); Greco (2000), 231–48; Watkins and Jolley (2002); Cuneo (2003); S. McGrath (2004); Wright (2007); T. Chappell (2008); Cullison (2010); Dancy (2010); McBrayer (2010a); Audi (2013); Cowan (2015); Werner (2016).

[2] I'll focus on descriptively 'thin' evaluative properties, such as being good/bad, right/wrong, and just/unjust. Some defenders of moral perception pin their case on 'thick' evaluative properties such as kindness, cruelty, and selfishness. Dancy, for instance, writes: 'I can perceive its being her turn (my favourite example of a thick moral concept), the caring nature of a response, the courtesy or the rudeness of a gesture' (Dancy (2010), 114). This is an appealing move: thick properties are more closely moored to properties that are agreed on all hands to be perceptible. But it is also a risky move: it is controversial whether thick terms and concepts are relevantly evaluative in content, and if they aren't, they won't determine evaluative properties as their referents. Perceiving something to be cruel, or kind, or selfish, wouldn't then be evaluative perception in the relevant sense. See Väyrynen (2013). I also suspect that the doubts I'll raise against the perception of thin evaluative properties can also be run against thick evaluative properties; see n. 35.

[3] Harman (1977), 4.   [4] Audi (2013), 31.

this doesn't mean we can perceive protons. So although examples like *Cat* and *Tiananmen Square* can be felicitously described as cases of 'seeing' something to be wrong, it doesn't follow that these moral experiences involve perceptual representations of moral properties; they may merely be prompted by perceptual input. But as I'll discuss later, developments in the philosophy of perception provide tools for assessing whether moral perception occurs in any robust sense.[5]

The claim that there is moral perception might be found attractive on different grounds. One is epistemological. Assuming we have some moral knowledge, *how* do we have it? Very many people think that if anything gives us knowledge of the external world, perception does. So if moral properties were something things could be perceived to have, this might help with the difficult project of developing a plausible moral epistemology and integrating it with a plausible overall epistemology. The other is phenomenological: certain moral experiences might be best explained as perceptions of moral qualities. The two motivations are logically distinct. Even if some representations of moral properties were best explained as genuinely perceptual, it would be a further question whether this makes an independent contribution to a plausible moral epistemology. (Conversely, the desired epistemological benefits might be secured by some other modes of sensitivity to situations.[6]) But some moral experiences must be perceptual for moral perception to provide epistemological benefits.

This paper aims to undermine the phenomenological motivation for moral perception. I'll argue that cases like *Cat* and *Tiananmen Square* aren't best explained as cases of moral perception even if we assume that the contents of perceptual experience aren't in general restricted to 'lower-level' properties like shape, motion, and color. Positing distinctively perceptual representations of moral properties would add no explanatory power because a simpler and a more unified account treats their representations in the relevant cases as resulting instead from implicit transitions in thought. In closing I'll briefly discuss the negative implications of my argument for the epistemological role of moral perception. (I'll provide no separate argument that moral perception wouldn't be an epistemologically independent source of knowledge or justification.)

2. Moral Perception: Focusing the Issue

My argument will concern the following literal notion of moral perception:

(MP) At least some moral properties can figure in the contents of (veridical) perceptual experience.

---

[5] Other discussions of moral perception that are significantly informed by recent work in the philosophy of perception include Cowan (2015); Werner (2016).

[6] A virtuous person has a better epistemic access to moral facts than someone faced with the same situation who lacks virtue. This sensitivity might be treated as a perceptual capacity: the virtuous person 'sees' things that the non-virtuous doesn't; see e.g. Murdoch (1970); McDowell (1979). Separate discussions of whether it is a robustly perceptual capacity or how exactly a virtuous character interacts with the contents of perceptual experience are beyond this paper's scope; the bearing of the discussion to follow on these issues will remain largely implicit. The same goes for our experiences of certain actions as afforded or even mandated by our environment; for discussion, see S. Siegel (2014).

Perceptual experience has phenomenal character: there is 'something it's like' to have a perceptual experience. As stated, (MP) follows most recent discussions of moral perception in assuming a representational theory of perception: roughly, to have a perceptual experience of an object O as having a property F is to be in a perceptual mental state (a state with phenomenal character) which has the representational content that O is F. For simplicity, I'll assume that the relevant kind of content can be understood as a kind of condition under which the experience which has such a content is accurate.[7]

To focus discussion, I'll also grant two general claims about perceptual experience which have recently attracted considerable attention. The first is that perceptual experience is *cognitively penetrable*. This is to say that what one perceives can be influenced, in a direct and non-trivial way, by the states of the subject's cognitive system, such as moods, beliefs, and desires.[8]

The second claim is that perceptual content can be *rich*. Perception isn't restricted to representing 'low-level' properties, such as spatial properties, color, shape, pitch, odor, motion, and illumination, which are perceived if anything is. Some other properties or relations can also be represented in perceptual experience.[9] This thesis has been defended for natural kind properties (such as being a pine tree), artifactual kind properties (such as being a table), causal relations, semantic properties, and dispositional properties (such as being edible), among others. These are often grouped together as 'high-level' properties. It is unclear whether this is to be understood as a claim about metaphysical hierarchy: odors aren't obviously in a different (and more fundamental) metaphysical boat than natural kinds, and semantic properties and causal relations not obviously in the same. So perhaps a high-level property is supposed to be such that if it is perceived at all, perceptions of it depend on the perception of other (low- or low*er*-level) properties. Moral properties would qualify as high-level properties in this sense. (In fact, they would be high*er*-level relative to some other high-level properties. The non-moral properties on which moral properties depend will often include other high-level properties, only some of which will plausibly be perceptible if any are.)

These two assumptions will be helpful in two respects. First, they help to distinguish doubts about (MP) which are relatively local to the moral case from more general doubts about whether high-level properties can be perceived. My doubts will be of the former type. Second, the two assumptions help to distinguish (MP) from neighboring views which accord perception some weaker role in moral experience than (MP) does.[10] When

---

[7] This is how Siegel describes what she calls the 'Content View' of perceptual experience; see S. Susanna Siegel (2010a), 4, 28–30. Below I'll grant what Siegel calls the 'Rich Content View' (Siegel (2010a), 7, 97).
[8] The cognitive penetrability of perceptual experience is usefully surveyed in D. Stokes (2013). See also S. Siegel (2012); Vance (2014).
[9] The cognitive penetrability of perceptual experience and the richness of perceptual content are distinct issues; see S. Siegel (2010a), 10. Perceptual content could be rich (or even feature moral properties in particular) even if the contents of perceptual experience weren't cognitive-penetrable. And perceptual content might be cognitive-penetrable but not rich if cognitive states only influenced *which* low-level properties figure in perceptual content.
[10] Many discussions of moral perception elide one or another of the distinctions that I draw in what follows, including the works cited in n. 1 by McNaughton, DePaul, Greco, Watkins and Jolley, Cuneo, S. McGrath, Wright, T. Chappell, Dancy, and Cullison.

it comes to experiences like *Cat*, it is one thing to say that an overall mental state that has a perceptual experience as a component can also involve a representation of a moral property as another component, quite another to say that the moral property figures in the content of that perceptual experience. It seems to make sense to speak of 'the overall experience I'm having' when, surrounded by strange noises in a dark forest, I feel frightened, and to say my overall experience would be different if I felt frightened and the forest were silent.[11] The issue is *how* moral properties are represented in certain overall experiences, not *whether* they are.

Those who accept (MP) and those who reject it can agree that we often perceive non-normative and non-evaluative properties on which moral and other normative and evaluative properties depend for their instantiation. (I'll bracket a host of complex issues concerning normative dependence.) The hoodlums can be perceived to ignite the cat, irrespective of whether the wrongness that is grounded in their doing so also figures in the contents of our perceptions. Both sides can also agree that perception can assist us in getting a clearer moral gauge of things. It can, for instance, play a role in developing discriminative abilities that make us see behaviors that in no way alter in a different light—as refreshingly simple rather than unrefined, or spontaneous rather than lacking in dignity.[12]

Both sides can agree that in cases where perception plays some important role in informing us about events or states that bear moral properties, our overall experience can include representation of moral properties. In *Cat*, for instance, seeing the hoodlums ignite the cat and its striking you as wrong can belong to the same overall experience irrespective of whether wrongness figures in the contents of the perceptual experience that is part of the overall experience. Both sides can further agree that the ability to represent moral properties on the basis of perception is an acquired skill whose possession and exercise require training and various sorts of background beliefs and other cognitive states. And both sides can agree that if representing something as being morally a certain way on the basis of perceptual experience were a result of an inference or some other transition in thought, such transitions needn't be conscious, but can be implicit.

Those who accept (MP) and those who reject it can also agree that moral properties can make a phenomenological difference to overall mental states. If what the hoodlums are doing in *Cat* didn't strike me as bad, then (all else equal) my overall experience would feel different to me. I might flinch, but I wouldn't have the kind of emotional or affective responses which psychologically normal moral subjects tend to have in scenarios like *Cat*—responses such as indignation, revulsion, disturbance, a felt disapproval, and affective empathy, as well as other phenomenal responses like a sense of 'unfittingness'.[13] No doubt many of these responses can also co-occur. In this way moral properties can make a difference to the phenomenology of the experience.

---

[11] I hope an example is enough. I don't have an account of experience individuation to deal with such fascinating but complicated phenomena as cross-modal integration and influence.

[12] Compare Murdoch (1970), 16–17.

[13] Audi (2013) mentions all of these states in discussing moral perception. Audi doesn't endorse (MP), however. He only claims that we perceive moral properties by perceiving the non-moral properties that ground their instantiations. For discussion, see Antti Kauppinen's review of Audi, in Kauppinen (2013).

In general, a property F can make a phenomenological difference to an overall mental state S irrespective of whether F figures in the contents of a perceptual experience that S has as a part.

At least in psychologically normal subjects, moral experiences (things striking a subject as being morally a certain way) seem closely bound up with emotional or affective responses. We shouldn't assume that emotions themselves are a kind of perception.[14] But both the proponents and the opponents of (MP) can allow two weaker claims about how emotional and affective responses relate to the overall mental states in question.

The first claim is that the relevant emotional and affective dispositions (for indignation, revulsion, disturbance, felt disapproval, affective empathy, and the like) are normally shaped in part by the same background moral beliefs which presumably also play a role in representations of moral properties. It is in part because I believe that causing seemingly gratuitous suffering to sentient creatures is normally wrong that I'm disposed both to be disturbed and repulsed when I see what the hoodlums are doing and to represent their behavior as wrong. (One simple model would portray the relevant background moral belief as a moral principle which tends to get engaged in cognitive processing when non-moral perceptual input matches the non-moral condition laid down by the principle.[15]) If my background moral views were different, my dispositions to be disturbed and repulsed would also tend to be different, at least in the conditions that trigger them. So even if my having *some or other* relevant emotional dispositions doesn't depend on my particular background moral beliefs, just *which* such dispositions I have depends in part on the influence of those beliefs.[16]

The second claim is that our phenomenological responses tend to be 'phenomenally integrated' with our perceptions of the non-evaluative features of the situation.[17] Once I take in that the hoodlums are igniting a cat, my perception of what they are doing, my repulsion by their act, and its striking me as wrong won't normally seem like distinct co-occurring experiences. (It won't be like seeing Rio de Janeiro and visually imagining myself hang-gliding above it.) The various responses we tend to have in cases like *Cat* normally seem like one fairly seamless overall experience.

The extent of the common ground between those who accept (MP) and those who reject it helps us to identify what is at issue between them. The distinction between overall experiences and the perceptual experiences they may have as parts, for instance, enables each side to allow that 'such ordinary perceptions as seeing a violent seizure of an old man's wallet or hearing an abusive vulgarity screamed at a conference speaker' can have some such moral element as 'a phenomenal sense of

---

[14] For criticisms of the 'perceptual model' of emotional experience, see Brady (2013).

[15] I mention this model just for illustration; options where the background beliefs aren't general principles remain less clear. Note that a background moral principle can play a role in my coming to represent what the hoodlums are doing as wrong even if it isn't exceptionless (contra S. McGrath (2004), 217–20). A moral principle can also influence one's recognitions of moral properties in other ways than by functioning as a premise in inferences from non-moral inputs to moral beliefs; compare Väyrynen (2008b).

[16] Thanks to Preston Werner for comments that helped to make this paragraph more precise.

[17] I borrow the phrase 'phenomenal integration' from Audi (2013), 38–9. It isn't fully clear how Audi understands the phrase. The main text provides the sense in which I'll use it.

wrongdoing integrated with our perceptual representation of the wrong-making facts'.[18] (MP) advances a claim about where the representation of moral properties is properly located in the relevant overall experiences—namely, in the contents of perceptual experiences they have as parts. The version of (MP) on which I'll focus here says that there are some mechanism(s) of cognitive penetration (CP) which enrich the contents of perceptual experience with moral properties. There may be other mechanisms capable of making (MP) true.[19] But this version of (MP) is of double interest: it promises to contribute to a plausible moral epistemology and it provides a test case for how widely the most prominent current argument for high-level perceptual content generalizes.

The foregoing suggests one possible mechanism of the requisite kind. Background moral beliefs might help to enrich perceptual content with moral properties owing to CP facilitated by the emotional and affective dispositions they shape.[20] This would explain not only why certain emotional or affective responses go reliably with certain moral representations, but also why both seem seamlessly integrated with the perceptual inputs that activate them.

The appeal to CP also helps this interpretation of (MP) not to portray moral perception as a function of a special 'faculty' or sensory modality. All sides can agree that if moral properties figured in the contents of perceptual experience, they would have to do so in a different way from colors, shapes, and other low-level properties, information about which is carried by a distinctive sensory modality. Moral perception would be 'amodal' in the same kind of way as perception of many other higher-level properties.[21] In the moral case, then, CP would be better regarded as adding content to a framework provided by non-moral perceptual representations than as altering those representations.[22]

---

[18] Audi (2013), 44–5.

[19] Perhaps moral representations are hard-wired into our perceptual system. Or perhaps (MP) is made true by perceptual learning without a robust CP-type influence of background states with moral content. Neither proposal strikes me as particularly promising.

[20] Both Cowan (2015) and Werner (2016) suggest this kind of possibility. Cowan (2015), 77–9 also describes various possible mechanisms of CP for the moral case. One direct model is that a cognitive state like an emotional experience is triggered directly by perceptual input and then cognitively penetrates perceptual experience, adding moral properties to its content. (I'll bracket the possibility that background moral beliefs themselves somehow directly penetrate perceptual content. It is unclear how this model is supposed to work or to ground the kind of 'phenomenal contrast' argument for (MP) that I'll discuss in Section 3.) One indirect model is that perceptual input first 'matches' memory representations of badness and this matching process leads to the formation of a cognitive state like an emotional experience that cognitively penetrates perceptual experience, adding moral properties to its content. Note that rival views to (MP) can adopt similar models short of adding moral properties into perceptual content. (For instance, a matching process can make a phenomenological difference to one's overall experience either way.)

[21] This kind of parallel between moral properties and some other higher-level properties is drawn in the works cited in n. 1 by DePaul, Greco, Watkins and Jolley, S. McGrath, T. Chappell, Cullison, McBrayer, Cowan, and Werner.

[22] Most proponents of (MP) suppose that perception of moral properties somehow depends on perception of non-moral properties. It is less clear how exactly to cash out this assumption. The constellations of non-moral properties on which moral properties depend are typically very complex and some of the relevant base properties (including various complex social and historical phenomena) plausibly don't themselves figure in the contents of perceptual experience. If we perceive moral properties by perceiving their non-moral grounds but not all parts of such grounds are themselves perceivable, what

This, at any rate, is the kind of account of moral perception against which I'll press doubts in Section 4.[23] I'll argue that certain things which any account of the role of perception in moral cognition should be able to explain don't seem to be best explained by (MP). To make the case concrete, I'll sketch a rival explanation that is at least as powerful as (MP) but simpler and more unified. The view I'll sketch treats the representation of moral properties in the standard examples of moral experience as resulting from transitions in thought whose degree of psychological explicitness or implicitness can vary with how habituated they are and how tightly bound up they are with the relevant phenomenological responses. But we won't have reason to take these transitions to enrich the contents of perceptual experience. Positing distinctively perceptual representations of moral properties would add no explanatory power.[24]

3. The Method of Phenomenal Contrast

How might one try to argue for (MP)? Philosophers who accept (MP) often just defend it against objections instead of giving a positive argument.[25] But we might adapt positive arguments from philosophy of perception to the moral case. Arguments for high-level perceptual content often deploy the *method of phenomenal contrast*.[26] I'm happy to grant the general method.[27] It begins with a description of two overall mental states each of which has a perceptual experience as a part. The description is supposed to elicit the intuition that the overall mental states differ in their phenomenology but not in the lower-level properties represented by the perceptual experiences. The claim that one but not the other of these perceptual experiences involves a particular high-level property (being a pine tree, one event causing another, or whatever) as part of its content will be warranted if it best explains why the mental states differ in their phenomenology. For instance, the claim that we can visually experience the property of being a pine tree might be defended as the best explanation of the kind of phenomenological difference that

---

would this imply regarding (MP)? Worries might arise if, for instance, instantiations of moral properties were perceivable by perceiving their non-moral grounds only if the latter metaphysically necessitated or determined the former. Audi supposes something like this, but he underestimates the complexity of non-moral grounds that will follow; see Audi (2013), 58–60, 108. The non-moral grounds of moral properties might thus be too complex for moral properties to be perceived on the basis of perceiving the perceivable parts of their grounds.

[23] I detect this kind of account, or at least significant strands of it, in Cowan (2015) and Werner (2016). Audi (2013) is a less clear case; his view allows but doesn't require the possibility of rich perceptual contents effected by mechanisms of CP.
[24] More issues arise here than I can address in what follows, many of them concerning perception in general. For instance, perhaps there is no determinate fact as to whether some higher-level property figures in the contents of perceptual experience; compare Logue (2013). The discussion to follow concerns what to say about (MP) presuming the issue isn't indeterminate.
[25] Examples of the defensive strategy include Cullison. (2010); McBrayer (2010a). Werner (2016) offers a positive argument for (MP); see n. 28.
[26] For this strategy, see esp. S. Siegel (2010a), chs. 4–5, and (2006). My presentation of the method of phenomenal contrast has benefited also from Logue (2013).
[27] For various complications that I cannot discuss regarding the relationship between the phenomenal contents of experiences and putative higher-level contents, see Silins (2013).

characterizes your experiences of pine trees before and after you develop a disposition to recognize pine trees.

To assess whether the method of phenomenal contrast can be used to provide a positive argument for (MP), we require a suitable target moral experience and a phenomenologically contrasting experience. A contrast case that involves no moral representation at all would be too dissimilar from the target experience to provide a good test case for (MP). Further, subjects with notably different background moral beliefs will respond differently in many particular cases, but for reasons that are orthogonal to (MP). Recall, however, that both sides can agree that representing something as wrong, or bad, on the basis of non-moral perceptual input tends to be intimately bound up with certain emotional or affective responses at least in psychologically normal subjects. A contrast argument for (MP) might then appeal to phenomenological differences between normal subjects and subjects who share their moral perspective but suffer from affective deficit disorder, such as inability to feel affective empathy for a subject of distress while understanding from behavioral and contextual clues that the subject is in distress.[28]

Thus consider Norma and Alex who both witness a scenario like *Cat*. Their non-moral perceptual inputs (whether low- or high-level) and spatial attention are the same. What the hoodlums are doing strikes Norma as bad and she also has the sorts of phenomenological responses to the scenario which psychologically normal subjects (with a capacity for affective empathy and so on) tend to have. Alex also represents what the hoodlums are doing as bad. For he is capable of recognizing the cat's distress on the basis of behavioral and auditory cues, and he can learn and apply moral norms. But Alex lacks the sort of phenomenological responses (affective empathy, revulsion, and so on) which Norma experiences. Nor is his representation of what the hoodlums are doing as bad psychologically immediate; he needs to 'figure it out'. So Norma's and Alex's overall experiences differ in their phenomenology. (I'll sometimes refer to this contrast as 'Norma/Alex'.) The question for those who advance a phenomenal contrast argument for (MP) is whether this contrast is best explained by the hypothesis that some such property as being (morally) bad figures in the content of Norma's percepetual experience but not Alex's.

(MP) offers a prima facie plausible explanation of the Norma/Alex contrast.

(A) Norma's disposition to have the type of experience she has in response to *Cat* can more or less reliably track badness.[29]

(B) Nor would Norma easily have the phenomenological responses in question if what the hoodlums are doing weren't bad; this counterfactual connection can hold at least locally, across the sorts of circumstances Norma is likely to encounter.

---

[28] After first devising the sort of contrast pair that follows in the text, I discovered that Werner (2016) gives a similar contrast argument for (MP) from phenomenological differences between 'emotionally empathic dysfunctional individuals' and normally functioning human adults. My presentation here adapts some features of Werner's argument. His argument is more subtle than mine—but not, I think, in ways that affect what I want to say. Finally, we both appeal to cases of interpersonal contrast. I agree with Werner that clean intrapersonal cases of phenomenologically differing moral experiences are hard to come by.

[29] I'll pass over the complication that different moral properties can prompt the same response, such as indignation or outrage in the case of both wrongness and injustice.

(C) Norma is also disposed to form moral beliefs (such as that the cat's suffering is bad) based on experiences of this type, and much more spontaneously so than Alex.

States that meet conditions like (A)–(C) seem plausible candidates for states that represent some property F, in this case (moral) badness.[30] Although the phenomenological difference between Norma and Alex is emotional or affective in some sense, it might nonetheless make a difference to the contents of perceptual experience owing to some suitable mechanism of CP.

But is this the best explanation of the phenomenal contrast between Norma and Alex? I want to press doubts by pointing to some respects in which this explanation is problematic or inferior to a rival explanation which I'll sketch.

One immediate worry about the above contrast argument for (MP) is that it threatens to show too much. The distinction between an overall mental state and a perceptual experience that it has as a part implies that Norma's overall mental state can meet conditions like (A)–(C) even if her representation of what the hoodlums are doing as bad doesn't figure in the contents of the perceptual experience that is a part of it. Consider a case from physics that mimics *Cat*:

Proton: When Marie, a trained physicist, sees a trail of vapor bubbles in the cloud chamber, she doesn't need to figure anything out, she can just *see* that a proton is going by.

It strikes Marie that a proton just passed can meet conditions (A)–(C). Her disposition to have this experience can reliably track the presence of protons. It is a disposition she has developed in the course of her training and practice as an experimental physicist. This disposition can have a relevantly associated phenomenology. Marie's overall mental state can include aspects such as a feeling of conviction, and it is psychologically immediate in a way that it wouldn't be if Marie were an untrained physicist who needs to reason her way from a visual experience of a trail of vapor bubbles and the physical theory to the presence of a proton. Owing to how tightly these phenomenological responses can (given suitable scientific training and practice) become bound up with observing vapor trails in a cloud chamber, the responses can also be counterfactually correlated with the presence of protons, at least locally. Marie is also disposed to form beliefs about protons passing based on experiences of this type, and more spontaneously so than if she were untrained.[31]

It doesn't follow from (A)–(C) that the phenomenological difference between the trained and untrained response is better explained by the hypothesis that protons figure in the contents of the trained Marie's visual experiences than by the hypothesis that her response is a kind of trained judgment or transition in thought. The point isn't that you cannot see unobservables. Seeing an F is different from having a visual experience with the content that there is an F. Even so, there had better be some limits on what properties can figure in true instances of 'It visually seems to S that

---

[30] Werner (2016) uses reasoning like this in taking Norma's case to support (MP).
[31] These points chime well with the view of scientific 'intuitions' as a species of trained judgment. Boyd (1998).

there is an F'. Marie's reports aren't a reliable guide to these limits, since what one is trained to say upon having certain experiences ('I see a proton'; 'That's a proton passing') is one thing, the content of those experiences is another. So granting (A)–(C) in *Proton* leaves it open whether Marie *visually* represents a proton passing. It gives no compelling reason to deny that Marie's psychologically immediate proton representation is anything other than trained scientific judgment operating habitually.[32] By parity, then, it remains far from clear that method of phenomenal contrast supports (MP) in cases like Norma/Alex. At the very least, no explanatory schema that we apply to Norma/Alex should straight away imply that we can visually experience protons; that should remain a further issue.

So the question remains: where in the relevant moral experiences is the representation of moral properties best located—the perceptual experiences they have as parts or some other part of the overall mental state? And the question remains: what sorts of considerations would break the issue one way or another?

4. Three Points Against (MP)

I'll now raise three related points against the claim that the phenomenological differences between subjects like Norma and Alex are best explained by (MP). They'll count as points of criticism given the standard theoretical virtues of simplicity, unity, and explanatory power. (One explanation is better than another, all else equal, if it is simpler, and likewise for the other virtues.) The cumulative upshot of these points is that there is a rival model that seems to be able to explain everything that (MP) explains but is simpler and, at least by one relevant measure, more unified.

Comparing rival explanations against multiple criteria can get tricky.[33] In the present context, for instance, positing distinctively perceptual representations of moral properties doesn't automatically make the account less simple. Perhaps each rival must posit some *other* distinctive psychological mechanism. But if a rival explanation can instead appeal to some general mechanism that we need to recognize anyway, independently of the role of perception in moral experience, this is a reason to consider the rival explanation simpler, and possibly more unified. This would make it superior, at least if it also explains at least as much as (MP).

My first critical point builds on points made earlier. When what the hoodlums are doing in *Cat* strikes me as bad, this representation depends somehow on my having certain background cognitive states with moral content. I'm taking (MP) to say that these background states cognitively penetrate the contents of my perceptual experience. But cases like *Proton* suggest an alternative model. The alternative I'll adopt in order to facilitate concrete comparisons is that when Norma sees what the hoodlums are doing in *Cat* and represents it as bad, this representation results from an implicit habitual inference or some other type of transition in thought which can be reliably

---

[32] I confess to not being moved by the tentative defense of 'the possibility of the phenomenal representation of protons in perceptual experience' in Cowan (2015). Delicate issues arise here concerning the relation between perceptual experience and perception.

[33] Thanks to Susanna Siegel for pressing me to clarify my methodological assumptions.

prompted by the non-moral perceptual inputs jointly with the relevant background moral beliefs.[34] (Perhaps the badness of what the hoodlums are doing fits Norma's perceptual evidence and has a high prior probability given her background moral beliefs.) The transition can also be psychologically immediate and bound up with the relevant emotional or affective responses, explaining how things can 'strike' us as being morally a certain way.[35] Sometimes those who defend (MP) tend to contrast it with views that involve a very narrow notion of inference. It is therefore worth noting that we can reasonably speak of inference in a broader sense even when someone doesn't explicitly represent the premises or cannot articulate them.[36] Alternatively the relevant transition might be more like a recognition based on taking in a pattern one isn't able to articulate, where what pattern gets recognized may be influenced by prior training and background cognitive states.[37]

The foregoing is a sketch, but the basic explanatory schema is hopefully clear enough. There are many ways to model the relevant kind of transitions more precisely. One picture is that non-moral perceptual input triggers (directly or indirectly) certain emotional or affective dispositions which have been shaped by background moral beliefs and whose manifestations are intimately causally bound up with representing things as being morally a certain way.[38]

My critical point is twofold. First, there is a principled model for explaining how Norma's representation of what the hoodlums are doing as bad can be phenomenally integrated (owing to related emotional and affective dispositions) with her non-moral perceptions without cognitively penetrating the contents of perceptual experience. Second, the model appeals to no psychological states or mechanisms that we don't need to recognize anyway. My outline only appeals to inferences and other reliable transitions in thought and to emotional and affective dispositions. This explanation of cases like Norma/Alex thus promises to be simpler than (MP).

My second point builds on the first. Cases like *Proton* aren't the only instructive parallel for *Cat*. Representations of some non-moral *evaluative* properties seem to

---

[34] Robert Cowan suggested to me that this account might overgeneralize to exclude many high-level properties whose relation to perceptual content I want to leave open. But whether some higher-level property can be perceived needs to be assessed on a case-by-case basis. The rival explanation that I run for moral properties carries no automatic commitment regarding causal relations, kind properties, or semantic properties. (Apparent differences include the way in which emotional or affective responses are involved.) If a rival explanation along those lines is the best (or not, for that matter) for some other higher-level properties, so be it.

[35] This account of Norma's experience seems structurally parallel to how Marie's experience in *Proton* is bound up with phenomenological responses shaped by her training. Note that a similar account can be run for variants of Norma/Alex where the target property isn't a thin evaluative property such as being bad but a thick property such as being cruel; recall n. 2.

[36] Nicholas Sturgeon offers epistemological motivations for a broad notion of inference which applies to 'cases in which someone is unable to articulate the premises, and also to cases in which someone is unconscious of making an inference and perhaps even of accepting the premises' (Sturgeon (2002), 209). Note that inference so understood remains a process at the personal rather than subpersonal level.

[37] Emotions and affects can work like this. For instance, one might be afraid (or find the used car salesman untrustworthy) without being able to put one's finger on what is wrong. Pattern recognition is discussed in the context of moral perception also by T. Chappell (2008).

[38] Compare the various direct and indirect models of CP described in n. 20.

parallel moral properties but are more plausibly located outside the perceptual components of overall experiences. Consider:

> *Fine Wine:* Greg, an experienced wine maker, reports that when he samples wine he perceives it as having various non-evaluative qualities which form his basis for classifying it as fine or not. Michael, a wine connoisseur, says that he can taste also fineness in wine.[39]

Greg's and Michael's experiences can also differ phenomenologically, such as in the immediacy of their felt satisfaction in tasting a fine wine and its phenomenal integration with the relevant non-evaluative inputs. Given the reported differences, what would warrant attributing the property of being a fine wine to the content of some of Michael's perceptual experiences but not those of Greg's?

Greg and Michael both can recognize fine wine. But I see no good reason to suppose that Michael has some training, background knowledge, or discriminative ability which Greg lacks. According to the rival explanation sketched above, their overall mental states involve the same kinds of prior expectations, beliefs, training, and dispositions to form certain evaluative classifications in response to certain non-evaluative perceptual inputs. A realistic example of this sort will add that sometimes Greg's response is more immediate than his typical response, and Michael's less so. This suggests more forcefully still that their responses differ primarily in degree: in how psychologically immediate their responses tend to be and how integrated the non-evaluative inputs tend to be with the feelings of satisfaction that tasting a fine wine tends to produce.[40] I take this to increase the plausibility of supposing that Greg and Michael share the same discriminative abilities. On this rival account of *Fine Wine*, such representations are even in Michael's case at least as plausibly an upshot of inferences or some other reliable transitions in thought as they are distinctively perceptual. This parallels my suggested account of the Norma/Alex contrast.

My third point is that moral properties can get represented in moral experience on the basis of diverse kinds of input. In vivid moral experiences the inputs often are perceptual. Consider not only *Cat* and *Tiananmen Square* but also seeing a hit-and-run, seeing one person push another off a footbridge, observing a street child living in abject poverty, hearing thuds and cries from a dark alley, or (recall Audi's example) hearing someone scream abuse at a conference speaker.[41] Many of us would represent what we are perceiving in such cases as wrong or bad, and our non-moral perceptual inputs would normally be integrated with certain phenomenological

---

[39] I first used this (real life) example in Väyrynen (2008b), 499.

[40] Two further points. First, as with 'see', so with 'taste': even if Michael doesn't need to stop to figure out that a wine is fine, it doesn't follow that the property of being a fine wine figures in the contents of his perceptual experience. Second, parallel reasoning in the intrapersonal variant of *Fine Wine* suggests that the phenomenological differences between Michael now and in the previous stage of his training aren't explained better as a difference in what properties he perceives than as a difference in the psychological immediacy and phenomenal integration of the same kind of transition in thought.

[41] Note that this model doesn't presuppose that F cannot figure in the contents of one's perceptual experience if one cannot discriminate Fs from not-Fs (e.g. stabbings that are bad from behaviorally identical stabbings that aren't). The relevance of counterfactual conditions to perceptual representation and knowledge is discussed in Cowan (2015), 183–7.

responses. But we seem to exercise the same kind of ability when the street child's circumstances as documented in a photograph strike us as bad and evoke affective empathy. And we seem disposed to respond in the same kind of way also when we imagine rather than perceive the thuds and the cries or the hit-and-run, or come to know about the abusive vulgarity or the footbridge incident by description rather than acquaintance.[42]

These different types of moral experience can of course differ in degree, such as with respect to how reliably they trigger the associated phenomenology and how vivid they are.[43] But they seem all to involve the same *kind* of representational ability. At the very least we have yet to see good reasons to individuate the relevant abilities to represent moral properties so narrowly that we have one ability for 'vivid' perceptual cases like *Cat* and another for others. Explaining these moral experiences seems to require only a general capacity to represent moral properties which is responsive to inputs from perception, imagination, supposition, and belief, and which can be psychologically immediate at least when those inputs are reliably and closely bound up with certain emotional and affective dispositions.[44]

The point isn't just that positing a distinctively perceptual representational ability adds no explanatory power with respect to cases like *Cat* and *Tiananmen Square*. (That was the lesson I took from *Fine Wine*.) It is also that explaining moral experiences that are based on non-perceptual inputs would require positing some distinct representational abilities. The rival to (MP) which I have put on the table explains a wider range of cases by appeal to one general representational mechanism. In this respect it offers a simpler and more unified account of moral experience than alternative packages built around (MP).

This claim is further strengthened when we note that (MP) involves an additional commitment that the parallel claims about many other higher-level properties don't. If we perceive what the hoodlums are doing as wrong in *Cat*, we do so in part by perceiving the cat's distress. If we perceive the shooting of the citizens in *Tiananmen Square* to be unjust, we do so in part by perceiving the citizens as peaceably criticizing their government. These non-moral properties, though low*er*-level relative to moral properties, are still high-level. In typical arguments for high-level content, perceptual content gets cognitively penetrated once over: background cognitive states influence perceptual experience by adding high-level properties to a framework provided by low-level properties. But at least in some cases (MP) would imply that perceptual content is cognitively penetrated twice over: first in the typical way, then by a further addition of moral properties to a framework provided by non-moral high- and

---

[42] Inputs from imagination can be diverse in further ways. They may involve either mental imagery (the kind of quasi-perceptual process we engage in when, for instance, we close our eyes and imagine seeing something 'in the mind's eye') or propositional imagining.

[43] Many philosophers are no doubt desensitized to descriptions of people being pushed off bridges, owing to the ubiquity of such cases in the trolley problem literature.

[44] Robert Cowan suggested to me that this picture implies a disanalogy with aesthetic experience. It isn't clear that we can exercise aesthetic discriminative abilities in response to imagination or testimony in the way we can in response to perception. That may be right, but it remains unclear how this disanalogy would bear on (MP) until its source is clarified.

low-level properties.⁴⁵ The parallel that many discussions of moral perception draw between moral properties and other higher-level properties therefore looks exaggerated.⁴⁶ (MP) requires a more complex picture than such cases of high-level perceptual content as causal relations and kind properties.⁴⁷

In sum: There is a principled model of the role of perception in moral experience on which moral properties don't figure in the contents of perceptual experience. It treats the examples that are meant to make (MP) attractive as special cases of a more general and unified account of moral experience. As a simpler explanation of those cases, the model is preferable to (MP).

5. Two Objections

I'll now consider two objections to my argument against (MP) so far. The first objection is that the rival explanatory schema I have sketched carries some further commitments that make it no more unified or simple than (MP). The second is that some features of moral experience cannot be adequately explained without positing distinctively perceptual representations of moral properties.

One way to press the first objection is to claim that my rival explanation carries a commitment to 'cognitive phenomenology' which (MP) avoids. To acknowledge cognitive phenomenology is to acknowledge that propositional attitudes (such as believing, desiring, and hoping) constitutively involve distinctive phenomenal character or 'what-it-is-likeness'.⁴⁸ But interpreting this worry isn't straightforward. For instance, my account of the phenomenological difference between Norma and Alex in *Cat* requires no particular belief or desire which Norma has but Alex doesn't.

Perhaps the worry is that what it is like for Alex to represent what the hoodlums are doing as bad differs from what that is like for Norma: Alex's experience involves a conscious inference but Norma's doesn't, and this is a difference in cognitive phenomenology. But this worry also fails to bite. On the explanation that I propose, both Norma and Alex come to represent what the hoodlums are doing as bad by an inference or some other kind of transition in thought. In Alex's case the phenomenological

---

⁴⁵ Robert Cowan suggested to me that one might think instead that if one is presented with a non-moral perception of lower-level properties involved in (say) *Tiananmen Square*, CP will involve the activation of a cluster of beliefs and dispositions associated with peaceful criticism, injustice, and so on, which then cognitively penetrate the perceptual experience together, only once over. But I see no principled reason to think this is the only way moral perception could occur if (MP) were true.

⁴⁶ I have in mind the works cited in n. 1 by Greco, Watkins and Jolley, T. Chappell, Cullison, and McBrayer. For a yet further complication, consider that the emotional and affective dispositions manifested in the sorts of overall mental states that generate the phenomenal contrast argument for (MP) are shaped by background moral beliefs. Are these emotional and affective experiences themselves cognitively penetrable? If yes, this may require a yet further layer of CP. The cognitive penetrability of emotional experience is discussed e.g. in Vance (2014).

⁴⁷ This point bears also on the relationship between perceptual experience and perception in the moral case. Even if (MP) were true, the double-layered CP structure might mean that the relevant perceptual experiences fail to be sufficiently directly related to the moral properties that they represent to count as moral *perception*. (Compare the discussion in Cowan (2015), 182–3.)

⁴⁸ See e.g. Horgan and Tienson (2002).

manifestation of the transition is 'figuring things out'.[49] In Norma's case the transition is phenomenologically reflected by certain affective states. In each case the transition needs to be involved in the relevant phenomenology only causally, not constitutively.

The rival explanation to (MP) that I propose for these cases also doesn't require any phenomenology that we don't need to recognize anyway. The phenomenal contrast argument for (MP) outlined in Section 3 is equally committed to whatever phenomenal character is possessed by the emotional and affective states invoked in Norma's case and the experience of 'figuring things out' invoked in Alex's case. The version of (MP) that strikes me as the most promising says that at least in some subjects, perceptual input triggers (directly or indirectly) an emotional or affective response owing to which some relevant moral background beliefs which have shaped those responses cognitively penetrate perceptual experience, adding some moral property to its content. The rival explanation that I propose treats those responses as reflecting an implicit habituated transition in thought from a perceptual input to a moral representation, owing to the way that the relevant emotional and affective dispositions have been shaped by some relevant background moral beliefs which connect non-moral inputs with moral classifications. Each view thus agrees that background moral beliefs can cognitively penetrate some or other aspect of the overall mental state of which a perceptual experience is a part. Each view also treats the capacity to represent moral properties as an acquired capacity that requires suitable training and background moral beliefs. My argument has been that treating this capacity as a perceptual capacity adds no explanatory power.

Characterizations of CP tend to be too weak to discriminate between these rival explanations. To say that a perceptual experience E is cognitively penetrated by a background belief, desire, or other cognitive state C is to say that the phenomenal character of E depends non-trivially on C. The relevant relation of dependence looks to be some suitably internal and mental relation of causal dependence. Now suppose we understand this relation counterfactually: if C didn't occur (antecedent to E), then E wouldn't occur.[50] This characterization is too weak to distinguish, at least in some cases, between the claim that C penetrates the content of the perceptual experience E and the claim that C somehow or other penetrates the overall mental state of which E is a part.[51] On the rival explanatory schema, the relevant background moral beliefs, the emotional and affective dispositions they shape, and non-moral perceptual inputs can stand in suitably internal and mental (indeed, contentual) relations that satisfy the counterfactual. Norma wouldn't have the emotional and affective responses she has to cases like *Cat* if her non-moral perceptual inputs didn't engage her background moral beliefs.[52] The first objection to my argument fails.

---

[49] Nor do I need to suppose that what Alex's experience is like to him is a constitutive feature of making an inference rather than a phenomenal state that may be causally related to making an inference. Here consider e.g. the broad notion of inference in Sturgeon (2002).

[50] See e.g. D. Stokes (2013) whose survey of CP I'm following here.

[51] To my knowledge, this problem hasn't been noted in the literature on CP.

[52] Again one simple model of how perceptual input can 'engage' background moral beliefs in cognitive processing is that it matches the antecedent of a background moral principle.

Figure 5.1

The second objection is that not everything about moral experience that needs explanation can be explained without positing distinctively perceptual representations of moral properties. In particular, one might claim that only (MP) can explain cases where something continues to strike the subject as bad or wrong in spite of stable background beliefs to the effect that it is neither.

One notable feature of perceptual representations is that they are highly insensitive to conflicting background beliefs. For instance, in the Müller-Lyer illusion one line is experienced as being longer than the other. Whatever other adjustments the background knowledge that the lines are really of the same length might effect in my cognitive system, it won't change my perceptual phenomenology. The same is true of certain perceptual illusions, such as the horse illusion (Figure 5.1), where no sense modality carries all of the information that gets represented in the experience.

I cannot help seeing the black box as occluding the midsection of one very long horse, although I firmly believe, on the basis of all the other horse contours, that I should complete the occluded part of the picture with the front half of the horse on the left and the rear half of the horse on the right. We cannot help perceptually completing the occluded parts of objects in the simplest way possible, even if we have some conflicting firm beliefs about how we should complete them.[53] If we completed

---

[53] See Nanay (2010), 243.

this shape by forming a non-perceptual belief that the occluded shape is such-and-such, our completion shouldn't be insensitive to our other beliefs in the way it is.[54]

To defend (MP) on the grounds that moral experiences in the putative cases of moral perception are relevantly analogous to these experiences, it won't suffice to say that the subjects of these moral experiences cannot help having them. For instance, a utilitarian with empirical background beliefs that form a good utilitarian justification for what the hoodlums are doing in *Cat* might well not be able to help responding to it with affective empathy and revulsion or help representing it as wrong.[55] But my rival explanatory schema can explain this much. I can agree that in typical cases the simplest 'moral completion' is the moral representation that we tend to have. In *Cat*, for instance, the likeliest option given the subject's background beliefs and non-moral perceptual evidence is that what the hoodlums are doing is wrong, and this is so irrespective of whether its wrongness is represented perceptually or otherwise. My view is also consistent with the idea that we often cannot help experiencing things the way we do. The kind of transition in thought to which my explanation appeals can occur reliably as a psychologically immediate response to the relevant non-moral inputs, and the representational state it delivers needn't be a full-blown belief. The associated emotional or affective responses that make moral experiences feel so compelling also tend to be at best indirectly sensitive to other beliefs.[56] (Emotional retraining, though not impossible, is often very hard.) So the view that representations of moral properties aren't distinctively perceptual is consistent with the view that moral representations exhibit the kind of insensitivity to the other parts of the subject's cognitive system, such as conflicting background beliefs, which perceptual appearances tend to exhibit.[57]

So what more does this second objection require? Sometimes when we cannot help experiencing an action as bad or wrong, we nonetheless pause to think whether anything supports a morally charitable account of the action. On my account this would be to double-check a psychologically immediate transition in thought. (Compare snap judgments, which get double-checked fairly often even when they are fairly reliable.) According to (MP), by contrast, we would be checking whether a perceptual appearance is illusory (much as one might check the perceptual conditions when doubtful of one's perceptual appearances regarding color, distance, or the like). One might then wonder whether the latter hypothesis is more compelling.

---

[54] Various accounts of such 'amodal perception' are discussed in Nanay (2010). Cowan suggests that the phenomenon can be recruited in support of (MP); see Cowan (2015), 173–5. That would require that the background cognitive states which influence what additional material we represent on top of lower-level perceptual content cognitively penetrate specifically the contents of perceptual experience rather than some other aspect of the overall experience. But that is the issue at stake.

[55] Nor would (or should) she wish to help responding in this way—but that is another story.

[56] Insofar as the proponents of (MP) take affective states to facilitate CP, they incur the same commitments regarding how insensitive those states are to the other parts of the subject's cognitive system, to what extent such insensitivity makes those states irrational, and so on.

[57] I'm not (yet) convinced that the relevant moral experiences really are as insensitive to conflicting background beliefs as perceptual experiences tend to be. This is an empirical issue that I cannot discuss here properly. But there is anecdotal evidence that moral appearances often respond to background beliefs. For instance, many people who used to see eating meat as perfectly permissible but no longer do, come to represent instances of eating meat differently as their beliefs change. Thanks to Jacob Sparks for discussion here.

One might pursue the analogy with perceptual illusions by appealing to examples of people who cannot help experiencing something as bad or wrong in spite of having settled that it isn't bad or wrong and having tried cognitive therapy and emotional retraining. Consider, for instance, a person who continues to be disgusted by homosexual affection long after having settled that there is nothing disgusting or immoral about such behavior.[58] However, it is standard to think that such cases of disgust are irrational insofar as they are recalcitrant, and neither of the competing explanations has grounds for denying this. And since each appeals to emotional and affective dispositions, each is committed to a disconnect between the subjects' background moral beliefs and their moral experiences. (MP) implies that if a property like being immoral figures in the contents of a perceptual experience of homosexual affection, it must have got there in some other way than cognitive penetration by background moral beliefs facilitated by suitable emotional or affective dispositions. And my rival explanatory schema implies that the predominant causal influence on which responses are psychologically immediate and phenomenally integrated with non-moral perceptual input is the recalcitrant disgust rather than the subject's background moral beliefs and the transitions in thought they support. So the example of recalcitrant morally laden disgust by itself privileges neither explanation.

In fact, there may be reason to prefer my hypothesis about what is going on when we 'pause to think'.[59] When we check to see whether a perceptual appearance is illusory, we do so by making other observations, such as looking more closely to see whether what looks like a barn is just a facade or measuring whether the lines really are different lengths. But neither usually does the trick in the moral case. When I cannot help experiencing something as wrong and pause to think about it, I'll usually try to imagine the situation from a different perspective or find (or remind myself of) some other morally relevant feature that I may have overlooked. At least the latter doesn't look normally to happen with perception. But if checking to see whether a moral appearance is illusory were a matter of checking a transition in thought, one would expect it precisely to involve scrutinizing whether the transition holds in view of a fuller range of potentially relevant features grasped from the most apt perspective one can take.

6. Conclusion

I have argued that the phenomenology of the sort of moral experiences we have in response to perceptual input can be well explained without thinking that moral properties figure in the contents of perceptual experience. Treating experiential representations of moral properties as resulting from trained implicit transitions in thought yields a simpler and more unified explanation. But recall that a thesis like (MP) might be motivated not only on phenomenological but also on epistemological

---

[58] Thanks to Preston Werner for suggesting this example to me.
[59] Many thanks to Jacob Sparks for suggesting the line of argument in this paragraph.

DOUBTS ABOUT MORAL PERCEPTION 127

grounds.⁶⁰ If anything gives us knowledge about the external world, perception does. So might the existence of moral perception help us with the difficult project of developing a plausible moral epistemology?

If I'm right that phenomenal contrast arguments that rely on the cognitive penetration of perceptual content by background moral beliefs fail to support (MP), then delivering on the epistemological promises of (MP) requires a different kind of argument for (MP) itself. Such arguments are yet to be developed. But even setting that aside we should be cautious to ascribe (MP) any significant epistemological benefits. Perceptual experiences of some property are in themselves an antidote to skepticism only if they provide an *epistemically independent* source of justification. This is to say, roughly, that perceptually representing O to be F must be able to confer epistemic justification for believing that O is F independently of whether one has (non-perceptual) justification for some belief B that must be justified for the belief that O is F to be justified. For instance, memory will be an epistemically dependent source of justification if it isn't a positive source of epistemic justification in its own right, but can only transmit justification from non-memorial sources of justification.

Insofar as moral perception would involve cognitive penetration of perceptual content by background moral beliefs or emotions, moral perception seems not to provide an epistemically independent source of justification.⁶¹ For it seems that insofar as one's perceptual moral experiences would be sensitive to one's background moral beliefs or emotions, any justification that moral perception could confer on moral beliefs would be mediated by the justification for the relevant background states. And CP seems to abide by the 'garbage in, garbage out' principle: if the penetrating cognitive states are themselves epistemically unjustified, then so would be the beliefs formed on the basis of the perceptual experiences which those cognitive states penetrate. So perceptual moral experience wouldn't confer justification for moral beliefs independently of whether the relevant background states are justified. But this is just to say that perceptual moral experience would be only an epistemically dependent source of justification.⁶² So it seems reasonable to suppose that moral

---

⁶⁰ A third possible type of argument for (MP) is based on the metaphysics of moral properties. T. Chappell (2008) argues that at least some (moral) patterns are properties and at least some (moral) pattern recognition is perception, so there is moral perception. But the contrast he draws between perception and inference ignores various distinctions drawn in the course of my argument. Heather Logue suggests that if instantiations of some aesthetic properties are token-identical with their non-aesthetic base properties and we can visually experience the former, then we can thereby visually experience the latter; see Logue, Chapter 2 in this volume. Whether this generalizes to moral properties depends partly on the issue raised in n. 22: can moral properties be perceived if not all of the typically complex non-moral grounds of their instantiations are perceivable? Otherwise nothing in this paper rules out the possibility of defending (MP) on the basis of some controversial metaphysics of moral properties which requires independent argument.

⁶¹ Here I follow Cowan's argument that (MP) doesn't provide an epistemically independent source of justification; see Cowan (2015), 187–91. After this paper was written, a fuller argument has been developed in Faraci (2015). Note that I'm not supposing that CP *as such* is epistemologically problematic; compare S. Siegel (2010a) and Vance (2014).

⁶² For all I say, moral perception might not be epistemically dependent on versions of (MP) that don't appeal to CP (see n. 35). Versions of (MP) which do appeal to CP require not just that the moral *concepts* one has cognitively penetrate perceptual content, but also that some moral *beliefs* do. Mere conceptual CP

perceptions would all be epistemically dependent. No doubt this claim needs a fuller defense. But if it is right, then moral perception would make no independent contribution to a plausible moral epistemology even if it did occur.

Talk of 'seeing' things to be right or wrong can still come naturally and won't normally mislead. What we have yet to see are good reasons to think that moral perception occurs in the literal sense of (MP). Recent arguments in the philosophy of perception for thinking that various kinds of higher-level properties figure in the contents of perceptual experience aren't plausible when applied to moral properties. Those phenomenological features of moral experience which seem to provide the most promising kind of phenomenal contrast argument for (MP) can be adequately explained without appeal to (MP). Nor would (MP) seem to help us with the project of developing a plausible moral epistemology. Moral experience is a complex and rich phenomenon with various features that I haven't considered here. So I cannot rule out the possibility that other arguments for (MP) might fare better. But on the present showing doubts about the existence of moral perception look robust.[63]

isn't enough to explain why different things tend to strike people as wrong as background moral beliefs vary, at least in subjects whose emotional and affective dispositions aren't significantly out of line with their background moral beliefs. This strengthens the case that moral perception won't be epistemically independent insofar as (MP) appeals to CP.

[63] Thanks to audiences at University of Leeds, the Evaluative Perception conference at the University of Glasgow, and the Evaluative Perception workshop at Cardiff University for helpful discussions of this paper. Many thanks also to Anna Bergqvist, Robert Cowan, David Faraci, David Killoren, Heather Logue, Jacob Sparks, Preston Werner, and an anonymous referee for valuable written comments.

6

Seeing Depicted Space (Or Not)

Mikael Pettersson

1. Introduction

What is it to see something in a picture? How is it that we, say, see a boy in Rembrandt's *Titus at His Desk*? We do not strictly speaking see him; the boy is not really there, so we cannot really, actually, see him. But we 'see' him 'in the picture'. The question as to how we 'see things in' pictures has dominated much philosophical theorizing about pictures in the last couple of decades.[1] The question of how we see things that are *not* in the picture has received less attention—perhaps unsurprisingly, as it is simply unclear that we could ever see something in a picture which is not there. But our inability to see things in pictures is often one reason why we *value* looking at pictures in the first place. I am not thinking of our inability to see particular things in pictures—in some cases we do marvel at how a particular object is absent in a picture, as when we see (if we do) the absence of the Twin Towers in post-9/11 photographs of Manhattan's skyline. Instead, what I intend is how we are seeing the absence of visible objects in general in pictures, and related to this, how our experience is apparently of seeing *empty space* in pictures. Seeing empty space has aesthetic significance: photographers talk of the importance of having enough 'negative space' in a picture (and what they mean is space uninhabited by material objects), and, to take an example from painting, much of the aesthetic pleasure we may get from looking at Raphael's *Expulsion of Heliodorus* is to see the empty space surrounded by the depicted vault; to stare into the void, if you like. But how do we see empty space in pictures, if we do? It does not seem to display any 'look', at least not in the way material objects do. The boy in Rembrandt's painting has a look; the space surrounding him in the picture does not seem to have one, and that is why we can *see through* that space to the boy. But if we can see *through* it, can we see *it*? In this chapter I will discuss what it could mean to say that we see empty space in pictures, and, if we do, why it has aesthetic significance. Section 2 introduces the idea of 'seeing things in pictures' and explores the abilities of various theories' of seeing-in to account for 'seen-in' empty space. Section 3 offers a sketch of a 'top-down' theory of pictorial perception of empty space; as I shall argue, seeing empty space in pictures is to a large extent something 'coming out of the head', as it were, or requires 'looking

---

[1] See e.g. Wollheim (1980a); Hopkins (1998); Peacocke (1987); Budd (1992).

for things' in the first place (rather than being the 'result' of 'mere seeing'). More precisely, what I shall argue is that our apprehension of empty space in pictures is a matter of imagining it in a way that 'colours' or 'permeates' the perception of the picture. Section 4 offers a few clarifications and also addresses the aesthetics of seeing empty space in pictures (or not).

2. Seeing-In

When you look at Rembrandt's painting you have a visual experience (as) of a boy. This experience is to some extent similar, and to some extent dissimilar, to seeing him 'in the flesh', or face-to-face. It is visual in the sense that it more resembles actually seeing a boy than it does merely *thinking of* (without visualizing) a boy, for instance. Both seeing a boy in the flesh and seeing him in a picture comes with phenomenal character, as it is usually called; merely *thinking* of a boy may present him with no such character. Whatever the similarities with respect to phenomenology may be, it is clear that one does not really, strictly speaking, *see* the boy when looking at the picture. After all, there is not anyone *in* the picture to be seen.[2] And yet, we *seem* to 'see' him 'in' the picture. What is seeing-in?

According to Richard Wollheim, to whom the term 'seeing-in' is due, it is a 'perceptual capacity',[3] a 'species of seeing',[4] which 'is triggered off by the presence within the field of vision of a differentiated surface'.[5] These descriptions, unfortunately (and notoriously),[6] do not tell us very much about what seeing-in really is: again, the experience is 'triggered off' by certain surfaces, but (the last quote continues) Wollheim 'doubt[s] that anything significant can be said about exactly what a surface must be like'[7] in order to yield the experience. Indeed, many recent theories of depiction, or of pictorial experience, can be seen as attempts to say more about what seeing-in is, but before coming back to that issue, let me stress one aspect of Wollheim's theory that most theorists agree on, namely his characterization of its *phenomenology*.

According to Wollheim, it is a defining characteristic of pictorial experience (seeing-in) that it comes with what he calls a *twofold* structure. Wollheim describes twofoldness differently in different contexts. Sometimes it is said to be a medium/content amalgam; as he puts it in the piece where he originally introduced the idea, '[s]eeing-in permits an unlimited simultaneous attention to what is seen and to features of the medium'.[8] At other times, however, twofoldness seems to be not so much a medium/content distinction, but instead implies a spatial awareness of a 3-D 'picture world' in a 2-D surface. Here is how he describes it in one context: 'I discern something standing out in front of, or (in certain cases) receding behind something else.'[9] (I will come back to this spatial understanding of twofoldness later.)

---

[2] Some may beg to disagree: Kendall Walton thinks that when we look at photographic pictures, we are, literally (although only indirectly), seeing the depicted item. See Walton (1984). Dominic Lopes thinks that this 'transparency thesis' pertains also to many 'handmade' images. See Lopes (1996), 182–7.
[3] Wollheim (1980b), 217. [4] Wollheim (1980b), 205. [5] Wollheim (1987), 46.
[6] See below for criticisms. [7] Wollheim (1987), 46. [8] Wollheim (1980b), 212.
[9] Wollheim (1987), 48.

If most theorists agree with Wollheim that pictorial experience is twofold,[10] fewer have been happy with Wollheim's account or *explanation* of seeing-in. Kendall Walton, for instance, claims that Wollheim leaves the notion of seeing-in 'seriously underexplained',[11] and Dominic Lopes thinks that '[a]n analysis of depiction in terms of seeing-in may well be true, but at the very least it stands incomplete'.[12] Wollheim seems to think of seeing-in as sui generis, not explicable in terms of anything else. Indeed, he thinks that seeing-in 'is such an everyday experience that it would only be necessary for me to gesture towards it for a reader to understand what I had in mind'.[13] But, again, as an *account* (or theory) of pictorial experience, a mere gesture has been seen as insufficient, and most recent theories of depiction have been attempts to elaborate on that 'gesture'. Three theories stand out: the experienced resemblance theory, the recognition theory, and the imagination theory. However, neither of the first two theories would to have enough resources to say anything about how we see empty space in pictures; the third only with significant supplementation, which I will come back to presently.

2.1. Seeing-in as experienced resemblance

It is part and parcel of how we pre-theoretically think about pictures that what a picture is of is a matter of what it *looks* like, or *resembles*. Resemblances come cheap though—and how a thing looks (in a picture or face-to-face) might vary depending on what we focus on. The experienced resemblance theory picks out one kind of resemblance, the experience of which is said to account for depiction and pictorial experience, namely (in various versions) 'outline shape'.[14] While 'actual shape' is a matter of relations between different parts of an object, outline shape, by contrast, concerns different *directions* between different parts of an object and another point in space, say the location of one's eye. So, for example, while a coin is seen as having a constant circular 'actual shape' regardless of the viewpoint from which it is seen, its outline shape will vary as the directions between its parts and the eye change. On the experienced resemblance view, depiction works by displaying the outline shapes of things. And, more importantly in the present context, seeing-in, or pictorial experience, according to this view, is a matter of experiencing a resemblance between the outline shapes of objects and (parts of) pictures. As Robert Hopkins, who defends this view, puts it: 'Seeing-in is experienced resemblance in outline shape'.[15]

The main aim of the experienced resemblance theory is to account for the seeing-in of (material) objects, and as such it may or may not be successful.[16] But how about

---

[10] Not everyone agrees that twofoldness is a necessary feature of seeing-in, as Wollheim contends. Trompe l'œil pictures would seem to be a counterexample. According to Dominic Lopes, twofoldness is a matter of degree, where some pictures clearly occasion a twofold experience, where some do not. See Lopes (1996), 50–1.
[11] Walton (2008), 134.
[12] Lopes (1996), 44. For similar criticism, see Budd (1992); Hyman (2006), ch. 7.
[13] Wollheim (1991), 404.
[14] The notion of outline shape is due to Rob Hopkins. See Hopkins (1998), ch. 3.
[15] Hopkins (2003), 153.
[16] For criticisms as to whether the theory is an adequate one with respect to object-seeing-in, see Lopes (2005), 44–5.

its potential for explaining the seeing-in of empty space? Empty space, typically, does not seem to display any outline shape. True, *sometimes* it would seem to make sense to talk of empty space as having an outline shape. Consider Michael Heizer's sculpture *North, East, South, West*, a sculpture made of four holes of different shapes. As we look at the holes from different vantage points, the empty space 'filling' the holes could be said to display varying outline shapes. And when we look at the photographs of it on Dia Art Beacon's website, *perhaps* we see the empty space in the holes due its displaying outline shape. But at other times it sounds strange to say that empty space displays outline shape. I point my camera to the sky, and a picture of a uniformly blue sky is formed. In it we seem to see empty space, but not because the space displays any outline shape. It would be to strain the notion of outline shape quite a bit to say that the portion of empty space—now 'displaying' a rectangular shape in the photograph— would have any visible shape prior to my taking the picture, thereby delineating it and 'separating it' from the surrounding space. At any rate, it did in not any sense stand out as a 'portion of space' before I took the image. And if this is so, it seems implausible to say that we see it in the photograph as a *result* of experiencing a resemblance in outline shape between the image and that portion of space.

2.2. Seeing-in as recognition

A different kind of approach to accounting for seeing-in is the recognition theory, as defended (e.g.) by Gregory Currie and Dominic Lopes.[17] When you see, say, a horse face-to-face, part of what you do is that you recognize it as a horse, at least if you possess the concept of a horse. Seeing in general (and indeed also other sensory modalities) triggers our recognitional capacities for things. On the recognition theory, depiction exploits these recognitional capacities: a picture of a horse is precisely that, because it triggers our recognitional capacity for horses. True, you do not actually, literally, recognize a horse when looking at the picture, because you are not really seeing a horse. But your recognitional capacity does not discriminate between looking at a real horse and a depicted one. More importantly, according to the recognition theory, seeing-in consists precisely in having one's capacity to recognize a certain kind of object triggered by a picture. As Currie puts it: 'To see a horse in the picture is to have your horse-recognition capacity triggered by the picture.'[18]

Again, I will not try to evaluate the recognition theory as an account of our seeing-in of material objects like horses. But it seems plain that it does not seem to fare much better than the experienced resemblance theory with respect to our seeing-in of empty space.[19] Again, the photograph of the uniformly coloured sky mentioned in

---

[17] The issue of how triggering recognitional capacities is thought to account for seeing-in is a bit unclear. Both Flint Schier, who first formulated the theory, and Dominic Lopes, in his (1996), seem to think that the two notions are independent. See Schier (1986), ch. 10; Lopes (1996), ch. 9. In *Sight and Sensibility*, however, it sounds like Lopes does think that the recognition theory does account for seeing-in. See Lopes (2005), ch. 1. In Currie's case it seems clear that he thinks of the recognition theory as a theory of seeing-in (see the quote at the end of this paragraph).

[18] Currie (1995), 90.

[19] Maybe a little better: A possible way to account for our seeing-in of empty space is to say that we see the state of affairs of its being empty (see below). And it may be true that we have recognitional capacities for states of affairs (cf. Le Poidevin 2007). However, as I will argue, such an attempt to reduce seeing empty

Section 2.1 is full of empty space, and in some sense of the phrase, we see it in the image. But our undergoing the experience does not seem to depend on any recognitional capacity being triggered, as empty space does not seem to possess any 'look' (in a way that horses do) which can do the triggering.

Neither theory, then, seems to have the resources for accounting for how one may see empty space in pictures—and this should not be surprising, since the main objective in both theories is to explain how we see material objects in images. Seeing-in, on both accounts, is taken to be the result of pictures' displaying the 'looks' of things—be it their outline shape, or some other visual appearance that triggers recognition—but empty space does not display looks of this kind. As indicated in Section 1, the empty space is the 'thing' you *see through* before your gaze 'lands' on an object, and it does not in any way obstruct the view. So do we really *see* it *in* pictures? Section 3 explores two different ways to account for a visual apprehension of empty space in pictures.

3. Seeing Empty Space In Pictures

One of the few who has said anything about the possibility of seeing empty space in pictures is Richard Wollheim. And he takes a sceptical stance. In a discussion of an image, similar to the imagined photograph discussed in Section 2.1, he writes 'we could not produce a sheet of blank paper and say that it was a representation of Empty Space. Though, of course, what we could do is to produce such a sheet and entitle it "Empty Space", and there could be a point to this title'.[20] Moreover, although he does not say as much, given Wollheim's main idea that pictorial representation is a matter of what can rightly be seen in a picture, I take it that Wollheim thinks we cannot (rightly) see empty space in such a sheet.[21] This pessimism on Wollheim's part is, I think, overly pessimistic, as I think his own view of seeing-in suggests two different ways to understand how we see empty space in pictures (one more plausible than the other, as I will explain). One route goes via what Wollheim says about the possible contents of seeing-in; the other via what he says about how seeing-in comes about in the first place, and in particular his claim that seeing-in is 'permeable to thought'.[22]

3.1. *The glimmering of facts*

Most theories of seeing-in, or pictorial perception, like the ones considered earlier, focus on what it is to see material objects in pictures: a boy, horses, and so on. Wollheim, however, when introducing the notion of seeing-in, stresses the fact that the possible contents of seeing-in are not restricted to (material) objects; it can also

---

space to seeing-*that* space is empty is not very plausible, at least not as a general account of seeing empty space in pictures.

[20] Wollheim (1980a), 14.
[21] The exegetical matters here are somewhat difficult, as at the time of this quote, Wollheim had not yet made his claim that pictorial representation should be analysed in terms of seeing-in; instead he thought it was a matter of *seeing-as*. This, however, matters little for what follows, I think.
[22] Wollheim (1998), 224.

have states of affairs, or facts, as its content: 'Seeing-in', says Wollheim, 'can be, as experiences in general can be, of either of two kinds: it can be an experience of a particular [a material object or an event], or it can be of a state of affairs.'[23] So, for instance, in looking at Rembrandt's *Titus*, not only are we seeing the boy, but we are also seeing the states of affairs, or ('pictorially alleged') facts, *that* he is wearing a hat, *that* he is reading, *that* he has fairly long hair, and so on. So, seeing-in, on Wollheim's view, not only pertains to objects—it is not restricted to what is sometimes called 'object seeing'; it can also be a matter of 'fact perception'. This would seem to open up a possible route to understanding the pictorial experience of empty space: for, why not just simply say that seeing empty space in pictures is a matter of *seeing that* space is empty?

A possible problem with this suggestion, however, is that it does not make the seeing-in of empty space sufficiently perceptual. Our problem is to say how we *see* empty space, and saying that it is a matter of somehow apprehending states of affairs, or (putative) *facts*, might be to appeal to 'things' which are not really visible, and if so, we have not given a perceptual account of the seeing-in of empty space. For do we really *see* facts (or states of affairs)? A memorable passage from Thoreau's *Walden* effectively brings out how 'seeing facts' straddles the border of visibility: 'If you stand right fronting and face-to-face with a fact, you will see the sun glimmer on both sides of its surfaces, as if it were a cimeter, and feel its sweet edge dividing you through the heart and marrow.'[24] Now, whatever the mode of our perceptual access to facts, we do not see the sun glimmer on their surfaces—as on the surface of an object—and this, of course, is what makes the poetry work. Or as Fred Dretske more prosaically puts the apparent problem of perceiving facts: 'Facts don't reflect (or emit) light, objects do [...] In a sense, facts aren't visible.'[25] But if facts are not visible, and if (pictorial) empty space perception is to be accounted for in terms of 'fact perception', we do not seem to have made much progress, if the task is to say how we *see* empty space in pictures. The problem is that fact perception (and if it is a species of it, then, by extension, also empty space perception) seems to be, in Dretske's idiom, an 'internal affair', rather than a perceptual affair; it involves a *conclusion* or *judgment* that something or other is the case, and this, as Dretske puts it, with a reference to William James, 'comes out of the head' (or perhaps better, mind) rather than happening in the eyes. However, at least on Dretske's account, even if fact perception is something that partly happens in the head/mind, this does not preclude it from being fully perceptual:

Although fact perception is [in involving a conclusion we reach] an internal affair, this does not mean it is not essentially visual. It does not mean that seeing facts [...] isn't really perception at all. Fact perception is a *coming to know by the use of the senses*[,] a process that ends in the head (with a perceptual judgment) but begins with the perception of those objects and properties that 'reveal' this fact. Seeing that a ball is red is coming to know it is red by using your eyes, by (typically) seeing the ball (object perception) and its color (property perception) and, on this basis, making the requisite judgment: the ball is red.[26]

---

[23] Wollheim (1980b), 223.   [24] Thoreau (1897), 1: 154–5.   [25] Dretske (2004), 12.
[26] Dretske (2004), 13. See also Dretske (1969), ch. 2; (1993).

And if Dretske is right in this, the objection that fact perception/perception-of-empty-space as a species of seeing-that is not sufficiently visual is not too worrisome. A more problematic objection to this suggestion, I think, comes from the other frontier: i.e. that on such an account, the mind does *not* play a sufficiently significant role in the seeing-in of empty space. For some perception of empty space in pictures seems to depend in crucial respects on our minds. Let me explain.

On Dretske's view, fact perception is the *result* of object perception and property perception; it is a coming to know some state of affairs or other by looking. But seeing empty space does not (or at least does not always) seem to be a result of the seeing-in of objects and properties. This can perhaps most easily be demonstrated by again considering the photograph of a uniformly coloured sky mentioned in Section 2.1. In the picture, we see empty space. But this does not seem to be the result of any object- and property-seeing-in.[27] There are simply no (material) objects that we see in the picture. We are, instead, simply looking into (depicted) empty space. True, there is a sense in which we can see *that* the space is empty in the picture, due to our not being able to see any objects there. But this requires that we *already 'look for' things in that space*, which suggests that the very apprehension of the space somehow precedes or conditions the seeing-in of it, rather than being a result of seeing-in ('it comes out of the head/mind', as Dretske/James would have it). Section 3.2 sketches such a 'top-down' account of pictorial perception of empty space.

3.2. Permeated pictorial perception

According to Wollheim, one of the most salient phenomenological features of seeing-in is, as he put it, its being 'permeable to thought'.[28] He illustrates the phenomenon by means of a scenario where a viewer of a landscape painting of ruins is prompted, by means of questions, to allegedly alter the content of her seeing-in. Upon being asked, the viewer can see not only columns in the picture, but also 'the columns as coming from a temple', and even '[the columns] as having been thrown down some hundred years ago by barbarians'.[29] In this way, says Wollheim, 'we can recruit a thought to our perception so that what we see in the picture changes', and this thought can either be 'directly caused by the surface or [as in the described scenario] prompted by another'.[30] Now, we do not have to agree with Wollheim that seeing-in may have such 'rich' content as he claims it has—after all, the property of having been thrown down by barbarians does not even seem to be a *visible* property[31]—to grant the general point that seeing-in is permeable to thought. Indeed, the third theory of seeing-in, Kendall Walton's imagination theory of seeing-in, makes its permeability to thought a central aspect of the theory. Or, rather, what he argues is

---

[27] There is an additional problem here of accounting for seeing-in in terms of fact perception, namely that we do not, strictly speaking, see that space is empty in pictures, for there is no such space, much as we are not really seeing that unicorns are white when we see them in pictures, for we do not even believe that there are any unicorns; so we do not come to know about the colours of unicorns when we see them in pictures. This problem, however, is not insurmountable, I think, as we could say that the 'conclusion' in Dretske's account, in the pictorial case, instead of being a belief is an imagined proposition. I will have more to say about the role of imagination in pictorial perception below.
[28] Wollheim (1998), 224.   [29] Wollheim (1998), 224.   [30] Wollheim (1998), 224.
[31] Thanks to Max Deutsch for making me realize that I should stress this point.

that seeing-in is the result of our experience of the picture being permeable to imagination. With substantial supplementation, Walton's account is a plausible way to think about our seeing-in of empty space (if not necessarily our seeing-in of objects).[32]

According to Walton, pictures are 'props in games of make-believe', they occasion 'imagined seeing', rather than actual seeing, of what they depict.[33] So, when one looks at Rembrandt's painting, one is not actually seeing a boy, but one is imagining seeing him. Now, this imagining seeing is not visualizing seeing a boy, or some other free-floating experience happening solely 'in the head/mind', but is grounded in actually seeing the picture. More precisely, 'seeing' something 'in' a picture, on Walton's view, is to imagine *of* one's perception of the picture *that* it is a perception of whatever the picture depicts. And, said imaginings 'permeate[s]' or 'colour[s]' the experience so as to transform the perception of the picture into an experience as of a boy. In short, seeing-in, for Walton, is an experience that is both perceptual and imaginative. Here is how he describes how imagination interacts with perception in pictorial experience:

> The experience of recognizing an (actual) tree as a tree is not a combination of a pure perception and a judgment that what one perceives is a tree. It is rather a perceptual experience that is also a cognitive one, one colored by the belief that what one is experiencing is a tree. Likewise, to see a horse in a design is to have a perceptual experience colored by imagining one's perception to be of a horse, a perceptual experience that is also an imaginative one.[34]

Should we say that seeing empty space in pictures is simply an experience (of the picture) which is thusly 'coloured' by imagining seeing it face-to-face? If so, what distinguishes seeing our uniformly blue photograph as just a blue flat surface from seeing empty space in it, on this 'Waltonian' account,[35] is that in the latter case, but not the former, one imagines seeing space in it—or better, that one imagines of one's seeing the image that it is seeing of empty space. This, I believe, is correct as far as it goes, but more can be said about what it means to say that one imagines seeing empty space, by saying more about how we see it 'in the flesh'. One plausible way to do so is to adopt, and adapt, an account of what it is to see empty space 'face-to-face' that Louise Richardson gives in a recent paper.[36]

Richardson argues that our apprehension of empty space is, what she calls, a 'structural' feature of perception, meaning, roughly, that it is less a result of perceiving things than a condition for it. In particular, she rejects a 'cognitive' account of seeing empty space—that it is merely seeing *that* space is empty—and instead views it

---

[32] One objection against Walton's view is that it puts too much stress on the viewer's mind, that it is too much a top-down account. But be that as it may, in the case of our seeing empty space in pictures, being a top-down account is, I think, rather a virtue. See Schier (1986), 23 for the objection; Walton (1990), 303, for a reply.

[33] This pertains to 'handmade' images, such as paintings and drawings. Photographs, by contrast, do, according to Walton, occasion actual seeing; photographs are transparent. See again Walton (1984). For Walton's most elaborate views on depiction in terms of imagination and 'fictional seeing', see his (1990), ch. 8.

[34] Walton (2008), 138.

[35] As far as I know, Walton has not discussed what it means to say that one sees empty space in pictures—hence the scare quotes.

[36] Richardson (2009).

as an 'awareness' of it as 'a potential location for visible objects'.[37] That is, seeing empty space, on this view, involves, as one might put it, a counterfactual-coloured awareness of visible objects;[38] or, in Richardson's idiom, a 'seeming to one' that the space before one's eyes is 'a place in which if a visible object were there, I would see it'.[39] So when we look into empty space (face-to-face), although we do not see anything there, we are *visually aware* of it as a space where visible objects could be.[40] A few comments on this account are in order, and some tweaking is needed, in order for it to work as a theory of the perception of *pictorial* space.

It might (again) be objected that this view does not make the apprehension of empty space sufficiently visual: does an awareness of a *counterfactual* seeing of visible objects—an awareness that *had* visible objects been there, one would see it—count as *seeing* anything? This kind of objection, however, puts too high a threshold on what counts as visible. True, there is a sense in which empty space is not visible: it does not reflect or absorb or emit light, like objects do (and these, arguably, are the basic ways in which things are seen). There is also, however, a sense in which it is visible— despite there being nothing to see in it. This sense in which empty space is visible can be effectively brought out by an example that Roy Sorensen uses in a different context.[41] Look into empty space—a uniformly coloured sky, for instance. Now compare the awareness you have of the space before your eyes, and the awareness you have of the space behind your head. You do not see any material objects either before your eyes or behind your head. Still, you are visually aware of the space before your eyes, in a sense that you are not thusly aware of the space behind your head. And this awareness, I submit, is precisely the one Richardson describes: you are aware of it as a potential place for visible objects, or as a place where had something been there, you would have seen it.

As indicated earlier, if this account is to work as an account the pictorial perception of empty space, it needs some modification. For, when we look at a picture of empty space, we are not strictly speaking aware of any space 'in the picture'. The picture is a flat surface, and, literally speaking, there is no 3-D space to be seen in it, and no space in which we would (literally) see anything, had it been there. But, in line with Walton's claim above—that picture perception is both a perceptual and an imaginative one— we do, I suggest, experience an *imagined awareness* of empty space as a potential place for visible objects; we are imaginatively aware that, had things been in the pictorial space, we would see them. Moreover, still in line with Walton's account, this imagined awareness is not simply an 'add-on' to what we perceive. Instead, it 'permeates' or

---

[37] Richardson (2009), 239.
[38] I do not know whether Richardson would be happy with this way of putting it, as she does not cash out this 'awareness' in terms of cognitive penetration.
[39] Richardson (2009), 237.
[40] This 'counterfactual' account of Richardson might call J. J. Gibson's account of perception in terms of 'affordances' to mind. But Richardson's account is more based on Michael Martin's notion of a 'visual field'—a cone-shaped area of space protruding from our eyes—which determines or is a limit for what we are visually aware of. See Richardson (2009), sect. 4. In looking at some *pictures* there might be (an imagined) counterpart to such a visual field, but the experience that other pictures occasion is more 'unsaturated' than our face-to-face visual field (more on this below).
[41] Sorensen (2008), 245–6.

'colours' the experience, so that what can be seen as a flat blue piece of photographic paper can also yield the impression of seeing empty space in it.

4. Seeing Depicted Space (Or Not): Three Clarifications and Four Examples

I should provide a few clarifications and will also offer some applications, or cases that the account illuminates.

4.1. Three clarifications

Let me begin by summing up the account just given. There is a sense in which seeing empty space in pictures can be viewed as an instance of seeing-that in pictures: we come to imagine that space is empty as a result of what we do and do not see in the 'picture world'. However, as our perception of the uniformly coloured photograph shows, there is also a sense in which we can see empty space independently of any seeing-in of material objects and their properties. Instead such seeing-in, as Wollheim describes the permeability of seeing-in, 'recruit[s] a thought to [the] perception so that what we see in the picture changes'. More precisely, seeing empty space in pictures, I have suggested, involves imagining space as, in Richardson's idiom, 'a place in which if a visible object were there, I would see it'. This imagining is not something that merely accompanies the experience of the picture. Instead, it permeates it or colours it; it is, as Walton puts it, 'a perceptual experience that is also an imaginative one'.

The account, then, makes imagination an integral part of seeing-in. With that said, it is neutral with respect to the question of how we see (material) *objects* (and their properties) in pictures, which, again, have been the central topic in theories of pictorial perception. For all I have said, as theories of object-seeing-in, the experienced resemblance theory and the recognition theory are as good contenders as the imagination theory and I will remain neutral regarding this matter here.

Another issue regards twofoldness. Twofoldness, as Wollheim first formulated it, again, is a matter of 'a simultaneous attention to what is seen and to features of the medium', and in this sense, our seeing empty space in a photograph of a blue sky is unproblematically to undergo a twofold experience: we are seeing the flat surface, and at the same time we are aware of space in it. Wollheim's alternative characterization of twofoldness, i.e., one's 'discern[ing] something standing out in front of, or (in certain cases) receding behind something else', might seem to sit less well with the idea that we can see purely empty space in a picture, and yet undergo a twofold experience. However, the account is still true to the spirit of Wollheim's thesis. To be sure, in the case of pictures of completely empty space, there are no 'things' that we discern at all (so nothing standing out or receding), but, still, we are aware, on the one hand, of the picture's flat surface, and, on the other, of potential places for visible objects that are located at different points 'in the picture world'. And this, I suggest, is enough for a twofold experience of the relevant kind.

Wollheim, then, says that seeing-in is permeable to thought, and Walton holds that seeing-in is a result of our perception of the picture being coloured and permeated by imagination, and I have helped myself to these metaphors in describing how imagination plays a role in the pictorial apprehension of empty space. How should one unpack these metaphors?

Unfortunately (and I suspect disappointingly), I will not be able to say much about this here. The question as to how, or whether, cognitive states have effects on perceptual states is currently a much-discussed (and highly controversial) topic. And in the vicinity of this debate is the as-controversial related topic of the admissible contents of perception. *Perhaps* the imagination has effects on our perception so that the very perceptual content is affected; that is, that the perception of the picture (non-veridically) represents spaces as potential locations for visible objects (non-veridical as behind the picture's surface we would not see anything if it were there).[42] Or, *perhaps* the transformation in phenomenal character one experiences when one goes from seeing a flat surface as flat, to seeing empty space in it, is instead due to a cognitive phenomenology associated with the imagined awareness of places as potential locations for visible objects (rather than stemming from imagination altering the content of the perception itself). But if this latter suggestion is the right way to think about the phenomenal transformation, it should be stressed that it is arguably not due to something only 'coming out of our heads'; for it would be closely linked to our *looking* at pictures at least in this sense: when you look at one part of the blue photograph, you imagine one place, and when you look at another part of the image, you imagine a distinct location. So it is not completely free-floating, nor a mere 'add-on' to the perceptual experience, totally unrelated to it. (Contrast this to visualizing empty space with your eyes closed: *this* time the imagined location for potentially visible objects is indeed completely unrelated to any perception, as you do not see anything.)

4.2. Four examples

I said in Section 1 that one reason why we value looking at pictures is how they treat space. Also, picture-makers have been highly occupied with different ways to render space in pictorial form; indeed, the art historian (and art psychologist) Ernst Gombrich talks of art history's 'obsession with space'.[43] Let me use a few examples to illustrate how the account sketched in Section 4.1 can illuminate different ways to depict space, and the aesthetic effects of our perception of it.

One pivotal event in the history of painting is often said to be the invention of linear perspective, precisely because it provided a new means to depict space (even empty space).[44] Leon Battista Alberti's advice to painters to think of a picture as a 'window' through which we can observe the depicted world 'opened up' the worlds of pictures to a, by and large, Euclidean space behind that 'window'. One striking example of this method of rendering space—empty space—in pictorial form is the already-mentioned *Expulsion of Heliodorus* by Raphael. The artistic and aesthetic

---

[42] For a recent discussion of how Walton's account in terms of cognitive penetration, see Chasid (2016). The literature on cognitive penetration is extensive. For a good recent survey, see Stokes (2013). On the admissible contents of perception, see e.g. Hawley and Macpherson (2011).

[43] Gombrich (2002), 279.

[44] Whether or not this is a means to depict space as we actually perceive it is another issue. Eric Schwitzgebel has interesting things to say about this in his (2006).

success of this picture is due to many feats, one striking example being Raphael's treatment of light and shadow on the walls of the temple. But what really stands out in this image is the void that structures our experience of it, and which gives the image unity and balance. Now, note that this unity and balance is not merely due to relations between design properties of the image—expanse of colour and the like *on the surface*—but rather due to our *seeing* the empty space *in the picture*. The aesthetic effect of Raphael's painting is not so much due to what he chose to put in the picture, as to what he chose not to put in it; or, in other words, how he chose to render empty space visible. Or, what is the same, if the present account is correct, how he makes us imaginatively aware of potential places for visible objects.

Other styles of depiction treat space in a very different manner. In these images, space does not fill the whole picture. Instead, some parts of the image seem 'mute' with respect to pictorial content; they are 'unsaturated' in a similar way as mental images are sometimes said to be.[45] Some Chinese landscape paintings have this effect, as do indeed also stick figures and (figurative) tattoos. As an illustration, consider a simple stick figure: some black ink lines on a white sheet of paper depicting a man. In such an image, we do see empty space. But how much? We seem to see it in the parts surrounding the man, but do we see it all the way to the edges of the paper? That seems wrong. Somewhere on the way from the ink lines to the edges of the paper, we stop seeing space. The picture's surface, in one sense, 'looks' the same (white) but at some point it does no longer sustain the experience of seeing space in it (so in another sense does not 'look' the same); it becomes 'mute'. Similarly for a tattoo on one's skin; at some point, the features of one's skin no longer depict the space we saw around whatever is depicted. The shift in the experience is rather similar to a shift between not seeing anything before one's eyes and not seeing anything behind one's head, to use Sorensen's analogy. And this shift, I suggest, is ultimately explained by how our seeing some parts of the paper/skin, but not other parts, is permeated by an imagined awareness of places where things could 'show up'.

A particularly intriguing example of how empty space is made visible by pictures, is provided by pictures where parts of the pictorial content seem to protrude into the space in which the picture is seen. Mostly, when we see empty space in pictures, that depicted space is (or, better, is imagined to be) *behind* the surface of the picture.[46] But some pictures disrupt this view of depicted space, one striking example being Caravaggio's 1601 *Supper at Emmaus*, where the arm of one of the disciples seems to be stretching out into the space in front of the painting, and the chair on which another disciple sits seems to be 'moved out' into the space in which the picture is seen (actually seen).[47] Our apprehension of the space surrounding the arm and the chair in Caravaggio's painting is rather perplexing. The space seems to belong not only to the 'picture world' which is separated from the space in which we see the picture, but also to the latter. The present account illuminates the somewhat paradoxical nature of this experience: on the one hand, as far as we take the space to be part of the 'picture world' we are merely *imaginatively* aware of it as a space for

---

[45] Cf. McGinn (2004), 25–6.   [46] Cf. Kulvicki (2009), 390–2.

[47] I borrow this example from Michael Newall who discusses the phenomenon in a different context. See Newall (2015), 134; see also 150–1 for another example.

potentially visible objects, but, on the other, as we are at the same time seeing the surface, and its location in relation to us, we are also *genuinely* seeing the empty space in front of it; we are genuinely aware of it as a place where had visible objects been there, we would have seen them.

One final example. In addition to the Albertian 'opening up' of pictorial space, another stance towards pictorial space stands out in the history of picture-making and the perception of pictures, namely the 'closure' of the space of pictures, which is connected to the 'purification' of the medium that happened in the early 1900s. If what is unique to painting is its 2-D medium, in contrast to the 3-D medium of sculpture and theatre, then what painting should aim for, painters and theorists argued, is flatness;[48] a lot of the abstract art of modernism aims at such flatness, and Yves Klein's monochromes might perhaps succeed completely at exemplifying such flatness. Their aesthetic virtues are obviously very different from, for instance, Raphael's painting, being more 'conceptual' than perceptual, making a point about pictures' relation to space; part of the aesthetic or artistic success of these images is arguably how they cleverly refuse to depict (3-D) space at all.[49] But their aesthetic significance is not solely conceptually grasped, but also perceptually so: their 'flatness' is, after all, something that we *see*. Part of how we do so is simply due to Dretskean fact perception: we see *that* they are flat. But the *salience* of the flatness is also related to our capacity to see space in other more conventional pictures: they 'look' flat in contrast to other, more conventional paintings. As a comparison, consider how Warhol's film *Empire*—almost eight hours of footage of an unmoving Empire State Building—looks still in a way that a photograph of the building does not. And it does so because the medium of film is sensitive to movement in a way that (still) photography is not.[50] Although (almost) nothing happens in the film, we know it could have, and this knowledge is responsible for our experience of stillness. Similarly, I suggest, the reason why Klein's paintings look so flat is because we categorize them as paintings (although not figurative ones), and this category typically includes the possibility of seeing space—even empty space—in them.[51] Much as the stillness of Warhol's film is due to our knowledge of the medium's capacity to depict movement, the flatness of Klein's images is due to our knowledge of paintings' (and pictures' more generally) capacity to depict—and let us see—space in them, and which he refuses to engage. More precisely, and if what I have argued in this chapter is correct, what he refuses to engage is our ability to recruit a thought—an imagined awareness of places as potential locations for visible objects—that could transform our experience of the picture.

---

[48] The most influential theorist of flatness is Clement Greenberg. For a nice discussion of his position, from a philosophical perspective, see Newall (2011), 174–6.

[49] Note that I am not claiming that these pictures *could* not be seen as pictures of (empty) space; after all, in a sense, they (at least the blue ones) 'look' very much like the photograph of an empty blue sky mentioned in Section 2.1; but if we conceive of them (as we reasonably should) as a kind of 'comment' on medium-specific feature of painting (i.e. 'flatness' and colour) we will not try, and will have more difficulties, to see space in them.

[50] Cf. Arthur Danto's discussion of a similar Warhol-inspired example in Danto (1979), 8.

[51] The locus classicus of this kind of category-dependent aesthetic perception is Walton (1970). For a recent elaboration of Walton's account in terms of cognitive penetration, see Stokes (2014).

5. Conclusion

Pictures let us undergo experiences of things which are not really there. When we look at Rembrandt's *Titus*, we have an experience (as) of a boy who is not really in front of us, but only 'in the picture'. But pictures have a richer content than merely things; they also let us see the empty space surrounding those things, although there is (in one sense) nothing—no *things*—to see there. Such seeing-in differs from the seeing-in of objects, as it does not depend on pictures' displaying the 'looks' of anything, as empty space does not have any 'look'. Instead, as I have argued, our apprehension of it 'comes out of our heads'—or, more precisely, depends on our imagination which can 'colour' or 'penetrate' the experience. In some pictures, as in a photograph of a blue sky, empty space is all there is to see. Some pictures are even more parsimonious with respect to pictorial content. Klein's blue monochromes, in one sense, 'look' very similar to such a photograph, but at the same time appear 'flat' in a way the photograph does not—so in another sense 'look' different. In Klein's paintings there is, as the saying goes, 'nothing to see here'—not even empty space.[52]

---

[52] I am very grateful to the editors of this volume for their patience and for their very helpful advice. An ancestor of this chapter was presented at the University of Hong Kong in spring 2015, and I thank the audience for many valuable comments, especially Max Deutsch and Dan Marshall. Special thanks to Jonas Åkerman. Part of the research leading up to this chapter was funded by Vetenskapsrådet [grant number 350-2012-6582].

7

Perception of Absence as Value-Driven Perception

Anya Farennikova

1. Introduction

You are at a bar, and you spot an attractive person across the room. You sneak a glance at his hand. No ring. Encouraged, you begin a conversation.

You feel encouraged because you perceive the absence of a ring. But that's not the whole story. You feel encouraged because you interpret the absence in a certain way: as a sign that the person is available. Noticing the absence of a ring depends on knowledge of social conventions: married people are expected to wear wedding bands. It is also culturally conditioned: checking for the ring on the wrong hand might generate an unreliable result.

Experiences of absence are often laden with values. They embody cultural knowledge and expectations, and therefore seem like good candidates for being a form of evaluative perception. In this paper, I'll argue that experiences of absence are evaluative apart from the cultural or social values they take on. They don't need to be framed by moral, political, or aesthetic reactions in order to express an evaluation. They are evaluative in their core, solely by virtue of being experiences of absence.

One consequence of this argument is that it demonstrates that there is a form of *sensory* perception that is *intrinsically* evaluative. Values are at the heart of perception of absence, because they are the reason we experience absences.

Moreover, the argument illuminates a role of value that is unique to this form of perception. Evaluative character of experiences of absence isn't replicated in other forms of evaluative perception. There are several ways in which values might interact with perception. One paradigmatic case is moral perception, which argues that evaluative properties can serve as objects of perception.[1] Evaluative perception also includes cases of 'biased' perception: perceptual experiences whose character has been altered by one's values or preferences.[2] Finally, Gibson's theory of affordances[3] argues that the direct objects of perception are pragmatic aspects of the world: opportunities for action. The examination of value in experiences of absence will show that it has a unique role in experiences of absence. Perception of absence is fundamentally value-driven, and it constitutes a new form of evaluative perception.

---

[1] McNaughton (1988).   [2] Payne (2001).   [3] J. J. Gibson (1966).

An argument for evaluative nature of experiences of absence carries a broader lesson for the thesis of evaluative perception. It demonstrates how not to trivialize the notion of evaluative perception. It seems natural to think of experiences of absence as states that are driven by expectations. One experiences an absence when the world does not conform to an expectation about how the world ought to look. Recent research, however, demonstrates systematic dependence of most of perceptual processing on expectations. If expectations express norms, and if they underwrite most of perceptual processing, then all perception becomes evaluative. But the sense of value that's operative here is too thin. In my argument, I will isolate the notion of value that leads to this consequence, and explain how the thesis of evaluative perception can be made substantive even for the accounts that assume systematic reliance of perception on expectations.

I will proceed as follows. In Section 2, I characterize experiences of absence and delimit a class of states called 'perceptual experiences of absence'. In Section 3, I present an argument that perception of absence is a form of evaluative perception. I clarify the sense in which perception of absence depends on evaluative states and draw some preliminary conclusions. In Section 4, I respond to the problem of trivial value. I highlight two factors that can lead to the trivialization of the thesis of evaluative perception, and offer a way to thicken value for perception. In Section 5, I show that experiences of absence constitute a new form of evaluative perception. When perceiving an absence, one experiences a feature of the world that is not fully objective, but nor is it a subjective projection of the mind.

2. Values and Absences

Consider the following three cases:

(1) Top Doctors
You are on a plane, and there's a long flight ahead of you. You flip through an airline magazine, and come across an advertisement of doctors. The ad spans several pages, and you are suddenly struck by the absence of women in the ad. All pictures are of male doctors. You wonder if the ad is sexist, and check the lists of doctors on each page. Out of twenty-seven names, only one is female.[4]

(2) Neglectful Parents
You are driving along a street, and see a child sitting dangerously close to the road. You look around to see if his parents are close by, but no one is there. You feel outrage about the fact that the parents are not there.

(3) Headless Monarch
While doing research on portraits, you stumble upon a modified version of Van Meytens's painting of Marie Antoinette in which the eponymous monarch is headless. The portrait now looks gory, and the missing head is an obvious political pun. You think that the work is clever and succeeds as an art piece.

---

[4] This description is of Delta's February 2013 issue of *Sky Magazine*. In 2012–14, these ads were frequently featured in various airline magazines in the United States.

In these examples, absences are experienced in a morally, politically, and aesthetically valenced way. Seeing the absence of women in a magazine advertisement is politically charged; seeing a child abandoned by parents expresses moral outrage, and headless Marie Antoinette elicits aesthetic appreciation. Many experiences of absence are evaluatively charged in this way. They depend on social (moral, aesthetic, political) values or expectations, and thus possess a strong evaluative dimension.

In Section 3, I'll show that experiences of absence are evaluative even when stripped of their political, moral, or aesthetic garb. They are value-laden in their core. Before I introduce the argument, it's worth spending some time clarifying what I mean by 'experiences of absence'. I will begin with an example, and then clarify the kinds of cases my argument will focus on.

Imagine that it's Friday night, and you decide to go see a movie. You park your car and head to the movie theatre. A few hours later, you get out to the parking lot and walk toward the spot where you had parked your car. The spot is empty. Your car is no longer there.

This experience involves an *immediate* recognition. You perceive the absence effortlessly, without inference: it's visible as soon as your eyes fall on an empty spot. Moreover, this experience involves a certain kind of a *representation*. Because the car is not there, the content of your experience lacks a representation of a car being there. But your experience also records something positive about the world: it represents an absence.

Generalizing, experiences of absence involve immediate recognitions that something is missing. When one experiences an absence, one notices that something in the world is lacking or incomplete. These experiences can take many forms. They can be emotional (missing a person), cognitive ('there's no solution to this problem!'), or perceptual ('seeing the absence of a car'). In this paper, I will be focusing on *perceptual* experiences of absence. The ambition of the project is to show that there is a form of perception, called 'perception of absence', that is evaluative in its core.

The argument therefore requires a clarification, and a defence, of this phenomenon. So, what are *perceptual* experiences of absence, and how do they differ from other kinds of experiential states? Moreover, why think that these experiences exist? Is it really possible to *see* absences? Beginning with the first set of questions, let's return to the stolen car example to set up the some distinctions.

You are at the parking lot, staring at the empty spot. The missing car is flashing before your eyes, and you feel shock that it's gone. This event triggers a complex experience, which involves several kinds of mental states. One obvious component of this experience is emotion. You feel surprise at the sight of the missing car. The event elicits shock and even terror: you had various valuable possessions inside the car. Visual imagery is another prominent contributor to this experience. The car is flashing before your eyes, as you stare at the empty spot in disbelief. But there is another, more fundamental component to your experience, which grounds all these states. The component is *detection* of an absence. Detection of an absence is a sensory act that frames other mental states in this complex experience. The car is not there, and you register its absence with your senses.

We may now define perceptual experiences of absence. Perceptual experiences of absence are *sensory* recognitions that something is missing from a location or a scene.

As is evident from the example above, these experiences can be integrated into more complex imagery- and emotion-laden states. However, they can occur independently of such states, and be (almost) purely perceptual. To illustrate, suppose that you are shown pictures of car spaces as a part of an experiment, and your job is to press a button if there is no car in the display. Presumably, absence detection in this task won't engage emotion or the imagination in the way that the stolen car example does. There'll be no need for strong feelings: detected absences will correspond to affectively neutral states. There will also be no time or need for vivid imagery. Time constraints and the lack of affect will obviate the need for this effect.

Let us now return to the headless empress and analyse the example in light of these points. As in the stolen car case, this experience will prompt a complex psychological state. One of its components will be aesthetic evaluation: an aesthetic reaction to qualities of an artwork. Another component might be emotion: for example, a feeling of disgust at the sight of missing head. The picture might even trigger a moral reaction: one might consider the joke to be in bad taste. All these aspects, however, will be grounded in a more basic perceptual state: detection of an absence. The empress is missing a head, and its absence will be represented as a core part of one's experience.

I now turn to the second question that needs to be addressed. Are there perceptual experiences of absence? So far, I've been assuming that they exist, but what positive reason do we have for treating certain experiences of absence as perceptual states? The account I favour appeals to mechanisms. According to this account, perception of absence relies on a certain process that's pervasive in ordinary perception: perceptual template-matching. I'll unpack it briefly.

Imagine that you are about to head out of the door, and you start looking for your house keys. You check the kitchen counter where you remember leaving them, but they aren't there. How do you perceive their absence? You begin by forming a mental image of the keys. Next, you try to think of where they're likely to be found, such as the place you had seen them last. You then project their image (or rather, a perceptual template) onto the likely locations. Since the keys are not there, projection results in a mismatch, and you perceive an absence.

The same mechanism can be applied to the earlier examples, such as seeing the absence of a ring on a stranger's hand in a bar. You form an image of a ring, project it onto the person's hand, and perceive an absence by registering a mismatch.

Here, then, is the model:

The Mismatch Model Perceptual experience of O's absence consists in an object-level mismatch between perceptual template of O generated by working memory and a percept of the observed stimulus.

Why is the mechanism cited in the Mismatch Model perceptual? I present a longer answer to this question elsewhere,[5] but here is the gist of the response. Mismatches are outputs of a matching operation: a process that's routinely used in perceptual recognition of positive objects and scenes.[6] It is therefore sensible to think of this operation as perceptual. Consider also the mismatch structure itself. The two elements related

[5] Farennikova (2013).   [6] Bubic et al. (2009).

via a mismatch structure are a visual representation of the missing object and positive representation of the world. Given that both representations are perceptual in format, and the comparing process occurs in perception, it seems plausible to regard the entire mechanism as perceptual.

Let me summarize. I have introduced experiences of absence and delimited a class of experiences called 'perceptual experiences of absence'. I then explain why we should think of them as perceptual states. In the rest of the paper, I will be focusing on the more 'pure' cases of perception of absence: experiences that lack prominent affective, moral, or cultural components. The main claim that I'll be defending is that perception of absence embodies an evaluation independently of its moral or aesthetic colouring. Even the most routine cases of perceiving an absence betray one's values.

3. From Values to Absences: An Argument from Salience

3.1. The argument

I now turn to the main argument I will be defending: the claim that perception of absence is inherently evaluative. Core motivation for this claim comes from considering the nature of dependence of experiences of absence on certain evaluative states: desires and expectations. In this section, I will unpack the relevant form of dependence that supports the argument, and then consider an alternative approach to identifying the evaluative dimension in experiences of absence.

A natural way to introduce the argument is by considering experiences of absences in situations in which these experiences frequently occur: searches.[7] Searches pervade our daily life. Recall this morning and think about the things you had to find before heading out of the house: your phone, a laptop charger, and your house keys. If you were lucky, you succeeded in finding these objects.

But searches often fail. Phone is missing, the charger is probably lost, and a frantic search for house keys produces no result.

Let's focus on the latter case: the missing keys. What caused you to experience their absence? Various cognitive states played a role. Desires matter: you really need your house keys, and this motivates you to look for them. Beliefs also matter: you are confident that you left your keys in the kitchen, and this is the place you check first. Beliefs and desires engage expectations: you expect your keys to be on the counter, which prompts you to look for them there.

Beliefs, desires, and expectations determine the nature of your search. They determine where you look, how long you look, and when you stop looking. Importantly, they determine that you look at all. It is because you desire to find your keys that you look for them and experience their absence. If you weren't invested in looking for your keys, if the keys did not matter to you at all, you would have not experienced their absence.

---

[7] While my focus hereafter will be on visual searches and on visual experiences of absence, the evaluative analysis of experiences of absence that I will be defending can be extended to experiences of absence in other sensory modalities, involving tactile or auditory absences.

In sum, searches for objects are controlled by various cognitive states: desires, beliefs, and expectations. These states trigger and shape the resultant experiences of absence. The reason this point helps the argument is due to their role as evaluative states. In context of a search, desires to find the object express *significance* of the object to the viewer. The reason one looks for an object is because that object has *value* for the agent. Cognitive states operative in searches are therefore evaluative: they embody one's values by representing those objects that matter to the agent.[8]

This gives us the ingredients for the first sketch of the argument. It should now seem straightforward. If desires and expectations encapsulate agent's values, and if desires and expectations drive experiences of absence, then evaluative states are integral to experiences of absence. Conclusion: perception of absence is value-laden.

The argument is on the right track, but contains an obvious gap. The claim that experiences of absence routinely *causally* rely on evaluative states, such as desires and expectations, does not imply that perception of absence *itself* is value-laden. Thus, it seems plausible to accept the idea that experiences of absence are systematically triggered by the evaluative states, but this feature by itself cannot ground the claim that perception of absence is *inherently* evaluative. There is a gap in reasoning. To close the gap, I will show that experiences of absence exhibit special dependence on the evaluative states, and contrast it with how other perceptual experiences rely on the evaluative states. To simplify the argument, I'll focus on desires as the relevant evaluative states.

Desires routinely influence what we see. For instance, you may form a desire for a cold beverage, walk to the fridge, and find the beverage there. It seems wrong to say that seeing the beverage is a case of evaluative perception: the experience is *caused* by an evaluative state, but isn't *itself* evaluative. One might be tempted to view experiences of absence through the same lens. Experiences of absence are triggered by evaluative states: states that represent what matters to the agent. For example, one forms a desire to check one's phone for messages, and see its absence in the place where one had left it. It seems like a bad inference to say that this causal relation to a desire makes the experience of absence of a phone evaluative.

I would now like to show that there is an important difference in the patterns of causal dependence of positive perceptual states on evaluative states and those of experiences of absences. The difference has to do content-specificity of the causal relation.

The term 'content-specificity'[9] comes from the modularity debate, and refers to computational, or semantically relevant, influence from extra-modular processes on

---

[8] Here, I am categorizing desires as evaluative states; thus desiring implies valuing. Michael Smith's (1988) analysis takes the opposite direction: to value is to desire (this is an obvious oversimplification; his analysis goes through a couple of intermediary steps that appeal to reason and dispositional states). I won't be arguing for a specific direction of the analysis. What matters here is that there is a tight connection between desiring and valuing in context of a search.

[9] Fodor (1983). Fodor defines informationally encapsulated systems as systems whose main processes consult a database proprietory to that system in the course of computation. Unencapsulated processes and systems recruit extra-modular information when running a computation. A breakdown of encapsulation for visual perception occurs when cognition exerts computational influence of the operations of vision: when what we believe or desire influences what we see.

computations within a given module. Content-specificity was initially introduced to explain why certain trivial influences from cognitive states on perception shouldn't be understood as showing a violation of informational encapsulation. Content-specificity can also help with the present argument, by showing how the nature of dependence of experiences of absence on desires and other evaluative states contrasts with that of positive perceptual states.

Perception of absence depends on the evaluative states computationally: desires and expectations influence experiences of absence in a content-specific way.[10] Thus, the content of desires and expectations determines the sorts of absences we see: it is because you desire to find your phone that you perceive its absence, and not the absence of other objects missing from the locations you had searched. Moreover, presence of desires and expectations makes it the case that we experience an absence at all. If you hadn't had desires or expectations about the phone, you would not have perceived its absence. This contrasts with the causal dependence of the sort we've seen in the fridge case. While seeing the beverage in the fridge is preceded by forming a desire for the beverage, the perceptual experience is ultimately caused by a change in sensory input: looking inside the fridge. There is no substantive *computational* connection between desiring the beverage and seeing one. Once you open the fridge in search of a beverage, there is enough information there for the perceptual system to register its presence.

Due to content-specificity, the dependence of experiences of absence on the evaluative states is more intimate than the dependence exhibited in positive perceptual experiences. This observation allows us to sharpen the argument for value-ladenness of perception of absence. The first premise remains the same. Desires and expectations have an evaluative role for experiences of absence, by encoding significance of the object we are looking for. The second premise can now express the point about dependence more specifically. Absences in the world are *made visible* by means of evaluative states. Desires and expectations computationally enable us to experience absences.

This effect from the evaluative states can be put in terms of salience. We experience absences when they are singled out as *salient* objects. And they become salient when presences of those objects *matter* to us. Salience, or significance of an object, is precisely what desires and expectations represent, and it is in this sense that perception of absence is inherently evaluative.

There is an alternative approach to identifying the evaluative dimension in experiences of absence. Considering this approach will help clarify the present argument, and will also allow us to diagnose a weak point in the argument that needs to be addressed.

---

[10] I elaborate on content-specificity and experiences of absences in Farennikova (2014). The point about content-specificity is relevant for the topic of top-down effects on perception. In Farennikova (2014), I argue that computational influences of expectations on perception of absence might be initially taken to suggest that perception is cognitively penetrated, but then show that there is a need for a more nuanced account, given that the influence from expectations on experiences of absence is indirect and is mediated by visual imagery. My conclusion in Farennikova (2014) therefore departs from the view that cognitively sourced imagery does demonstrate cognitive penetration. For a defence of the latter view, see Macpherson (2012).

3.2. The affect-based approach

The argument I've defended says that antecedent evaluative states—desires and expectations—inject experiences of absence with value. By depending on the evaluative states, experiences of absence express which objects *matter* for the viewer.

Call the analysis that locates value in the antecedent states 'evaluative seeing' or 'ES'. Perhaps there is a more straightforward way to locate value in experiences of absence. My argument has focused on psychological states that *precede* experiences of absence, to demonstrate their evaluative nature. But the same conclusion can be reached in a simpler way, if we consider what happens *after* one experiences an absence.

Experiences of absence tend to be associated with a violation of expectation. We experience an absence when reality does not match an expectation. There is discrepancy between what we expect the world to be like, and what it is actually like. Crucially, violation of an expectation triggers the feeling of surprise: a kind of *affective evaluation*, signalling that something unexpected has happened. Then, the argument goes, if the feeling of surprise always accompanies experiences of absence, this shows that perception of an absence always involves an evaluation.

Call this affect-based analysis 'affective seeing', or 'AS'. The selling points of AS are that it seems to deliver a simpler and more unified account in comparison to ES. While ES appeals to a variety of psychological states—desires, expectations, beliefs, which indicate values reflected in the experiences of absence, AS appeals to a single type of evaluation: surprise.

I think, however, that the unity and simplicity are merely apparent. AS does not succeed as a general model of absence perception, since the latter doesn't always involve surprise. So, it does not win in unity. Another worry is that AS doesn't provide a compelling defence of the cases where surprise *is* involved. So, it does not win in simplicity either. Let me go over these points.

The first problem is that AS lacks proper explanatory scope. It appeals to a violation of expectation to make perception of absence evaluative, but there are no good reasons to think that violation of expectation is an intrinsic feature of experiences of absence.[11] Let's consider a couple of cases to illustrate this point. (1) You walk along a street on Monday morning and you peek inside bars and clubs. You expect to see no people inside at this hour, and you are right. The bars are all empty. (2) You want to check if there is a pencil inside a drawer. You aren't sure if it's there, and you won't be too upset if it isn't. You open the drawer and confirm its absence. There are no reasons to posit surprises in (1) and (2). In (1), you know what to expect. In (2), you are ignorant about what to expect. Cases like these therefore lack a kind of violation of expectation that AS requires.

I now move to the second problem with AS: its failure to handle experiences of absence where surprise is involved. Why doesn't AS provide an effective model for these cases as instances of evaluative perception? The reason is that it does not provide a model for these cases as instances of *perception* of absence. To see why, let's see how AS might unpack experiences of absence in searches. We may capture its analysis as a three-stage process. The first stage is cognitive: one forms expectations

[11] Farennikova (2013).

about what the world is going to be like. The second stage is experiential: one registers an absence in the world. The final stage is evaluative: one's cognitive system appraises the experience, manifest in the feeling of *surprise* about the absence.

This three-stage model is a coherent story, but this isn't the most natural way to read AS. Instead of attributing surprise to perception of absence, it can be attributed to an unexpected *presence*. One isn't surprised about an unexpected absence of a car, one is surprised to see the object that's in place of a car. If AS is implicitly committed to this story, then we lose perception of absence. Experiences of absence are constituted by affective reactions (plus cognitive judgements) to what's perceptibly present. AS therefore fails as a defence of the evaluative status of *perception* of absence.

In sum, the flaws of AS are twofold. AS excludes from the explanation a large set of cases that lack surprise, and it does not validate the experiences of absence it does include, by failing to explain why they are perception. On AS, perception of absence does not exist.[12] It does, however, exist on the ES account. If the Mismatch Model is correct, then experiences of absences are not affective reactions to perception. They are perceptual states underwritten by object-level mismatches. AS therefore needs to be supplemented with a positive story about why experiences of absence are perception.[13] In the absence of this account, AS is neither more unified, nor simpler than ES is.

Let's summarize. My argument has been that experiences of absence are driven by evaluative states: desires and expectations, expressive of what matters to the agent. These values are then reflected in consequent experiences of absence. If this approach is correct, then experiences of absence are best explained in terms of what's *salient* to the viewer, instead of what the viewer predicts as *most likely*. But, even if prediction can't explain *all* cases of perception of absence, this does not mean that predictions can't have a certain powerful role in a certain class of experiences of absence. And it is this set of cases that can potentially undermine the argument that I've been making.

4. The Problem of Trivial Value

To introduce the problem, consider the following examples:

(a) You run into a colleague after summer break and after a few minutes of a conversation, notice that his front tooth is missing.

(b) After a long day at work, you finally get home. You turn on the light inside the house and freeze. The house is completely empty. All your things are gone.

A characteristic feature of experiences of absence in searches is that they are set by cognitive states. But the examples above operate differently. Their main determinant is the world. They are triggered automatically by the character of the stimuli: by what

---

[12] Similar tension exists between sentimentalist versions of Projectivism and the thesis of moral perception. On moral Projectivism, moral values are constituted by responses elicited by certain events. But Projectivism is often just a form of sentimentalism. So, if one's moral response is constituted by emotions, that response cannot be perceptual, at least on standard approaches to perception.

[13] It is unlikely that AS will be supplemented with such a story, since a big motivation for treating surprise as a core component of experiences of absence is to show that experiences of absence are not perceptual. An account along these lines is defended in J. R. Martin and Dokic (2013).

the world appears to be like. Here is why these cases (a) and (b) pose a problem for the main argument I had offered.

(a) and (b) demonstrate that experiences of absence can be independent of higher cognitive states. While experiences of absence are frequently triggered by desires to look for objects, they do not have to be: they can be elicited automatically, by patterns in the world. Given that such automatic cases are pervasive, it is not clear why we should treat perception of absence as *inherently* evaluative. Instead, it seems that the evaluative thesis I've been advocating should be construed more narrowly, as true of only a subset of experiences of absence—those that are driven by higher cognitive states and that happen during searches.

In this section, I will outline an argument for why even stimulus-driven cases like (a) and (b) are value-laden. Besides vindicating the evaluative character of perception of absence, this argument will carry important lessons for ordinary perception. Prediction-driven cases of positive perception have the potential of trivializing the notion of value, so that all perception, not just perception of absence, becomes evaluative. In my response to the objection from stimulus-driven experiences of absence, I will highlight the factors that lead to the trivialization worry, and explain how the thesis of evaluative perception can be made substantive for even the automatic cases of experiencing an absence that do not require higher level cognitive states.

Let us return to (a) and (b). We observed that these cases differ from search-based experiences in being independent from cognitive states. In searches, you wouldn't have perceived an absence of an object had you not been looking for it. In (a) and (b), you would have perceived an object's absence even if you hadn't been looking for it. We need to be careful in how we interpret this difference. The counterfactual does not imply that (a) and (b) are fully bottom-up driven. What it shows is that (a) and (b) do not rely on a specific type of cognitive state: conscious desires and expectations. This does not mean that they do not require other kinds of cognitive states. While (a) and (b) may not recruit desires, they do recruit implicit expectations. In (a), expectations are set by observing a pattern in a sequence. In (b), expectations are set by previous encounters with the item. The registration of an absence even in the more low-level cases is thus not fully stimulus-driven. It is driven by predictions and depends on implicit expectations.

Can the appeal to implicit predictive states secure the evaluative status of automatic experiences of absence? Can prediction give us evaluation? One might submit that it can. There is an intuitive link between prediction and value. Predictions are psychological states that represent what's likely in the environment. When one makes a prediction, one estimates the likely character of the future. One might interpret this as indicating that predictions embody an evaluation. They involve appraisal of chances: of probabilities of events occurring in the future. Such appraisals might be implicit: one may be completely unaware of making any kind of a prediction in cases like (a) and (b). Nonetheless, these predictions are still actively used as evaluations of what's coming next and ground one's experience of absence.

If this argument is correct, then we have a reason for treating stimulus-driven, automatic experiences of absence as evaluative. Desires aren't the only source of value in perception of absence. Implicit predictions also contain an implicit evaluation, which affects experiences of absence.

The main problem with this analysis is that it cheapens the notion of value. Automatic experiences of absence become evaluative by relying on prediction, but in a trivial way. While whether something is trivial is a subjective matter, there is a real concern in our case, due to how this argument bears on ordinary perception. We commonly think of experiences of absence as relying on expectations. But predictions aren't exclusive to seeing absence. They are also involved in positive perception (Bar,[14] Summerfield[15]). In fact, if certain prediction-based approaches to cognition are correct (Clark,[16] Friston and Kiebel,[17] Hohwy,[18] Huang and Rao,[19] Seth et al.[20]), then predictions are essential to virtually all forms of perceptual processing. We can now formulate the problematic implication. If predictive processing is pervasive in most operations of perception, and if prediction implies an evaluation, then most perception is value-laden.

Just how problematic is this consequence? The proponents of predictive coding might embrace this result. The opponents will dismiss it, because of the assumptions it makes: the role of prediction in the human cognition is massively overestimated. I'd like to highlight, however, that there is a reason for *both* parties to be worried. One does not need to embrace predictive coding or the Bayesian brain hypothesis to conclude that ordinary perception is inherently evaluative. The claim easily follows from a more established approach to perception: constructivism.

Constructivists, such as Richard Gregory[21] and Irwin Rock,[22] conceive of perception as a process that's mediated by unconscious inferences. The inferences in question recruit background knowledge with the goal of producing the best guess about the nature of the sensory input. Making this guess may require making a choice between alternative hypotheses on the basis of evidence; alternatively, perception might put forward a single guess for confirmation. What's key is that both processes imply evaluation: assessment of the quality of evidence or of alternative options. The result is that perception becomes evaluative solely by virtue of involving an interpretation.

Let me summarize. I've just considered two senses of evaluation: (i) appraisal of probabilities in prediction, and (ii) appraisal of confirmation strength in constructive inference. Both, in my opinion, trivialize the idea of evaluative perception. It is certainly non-trivial whether perception systematically relies on prediction. It matters whether our experiences acquire the character they do *if* the brain is predominantly forward-looking. It is also a substantive matter whether perception involves reasoning-like procedures when constructing a percept. But calling these aspects of perception 'evaluative' reveals nothing interesting about perception. Value is just a label. It is a generalization over independently rich research programmes.

The lesson is this. It is important to keep track of the different notions of value. Given orthodox conceptions of value, certain forms of perception become substantively evaluative. In those cases, values function either as objects of observation (as in moral perception), or as subjective states that influence observation (certain cases of

---

[14] Bar (2009).   [15] Summerfield and Egner (2009).   [16] Clark (2015).
[17] Friston and Kiebel (2009).   [18] Hohwy (2013).   [19] Huang and Rao (2011).
[20] Seth, Suzuki, and Critchley (2011).   [21] R. L. Gregory (1970).   [22] Rock (1983).

cognitively penetrated perception). But there is another sense of evaluation that also applies to perception. In this sense, evaluation means judgement or appraisal: of chances when making a prediction, or the strength of evidence when drawing a perceptual inference. Given this sense of evaluation, broadly constructivist approaches would be sufficient to secure the thesis of evaluative perception for all perception. Mere presence of judgement or an interpretation would be enough to confer value.

Let's recap. All this discussion arose as a reaction to the problem of scope. Search-based experiences of absence acquire their evaluative character by relying on desires and conscious expectations. Automatic experiences of absence, in contrast, rely on implicit predictions, and thus seem to lose the evaluative dimension. So, the question is whether the appeal to implicit prediction can help bring in value. Technically, it can, but this would trivialize the thesis of evaluative perception. Experiences of absence in searches are a clear case of value-driven perception. But when we move from the mundane to the automatic, the notion of value becomes too minimal. The evaluative thesis loses its bite.

Is it possible to link prediction to value in a more substantive way? The option I will defend is tentative, and I hope to defend it at greater length in the future. As a result, this won't be a complete account, but I hope that it can indicate a strategy for locating a more substantive notion of value in automatic, prediction-driven states.

To sketch the answer, let's return to (a) and (b), and look at the mechanism underlying automatic experiences of absence. We observed that these cases rely on implicit expectations. Let's now consider how these expectations are set. The argument might come from research on natural statistics. When we view the world, we automatically extract certain patterns in what we observe. We do this by assessing similarity in perceived objects or events. The extracted patterns then serve as the grounds for making a prediction about the likely character of future observations. For instance, observing a sequence of similar objects will generate a prediction to perceive similar objects in further displays.

This prediction about the future possesses one important feature. It isn't just a description of facts, likely to occur in the future. Implicit in the description is a recognition that this is how the future *ought* to unfold given what has already been observed. It embodies a kind of normative commitment, which can be understood as preference, about what the world should be like.

My proposal, therefore, is to treat implicit expectations driving experiences of absence as containing latent norms. In experiences of absence, presence of this norm is manifest through a specific sensory reaction. When an absence is perceived, the visual system undergoes surprise. The perceptual system was making an accurate assessment of the future given the statistic of the scene, and that assessment was proven wrong through an observation of an absence. In experiences of absence, surprise communicates a sense that something has gone wrong in prediction. It involves disruption in processing that indicates perception's awareness of its own error.

Surprise isn't involved in all cases of perceiving an absence[23] and therefore cannot secure value for all perception of absence. But surprise can be expressive of value for

---

[23] The claim that experiences of absence do not require surprise might perceived as being in tension with my earlier account of experiences of absences, where I appeal to mismatches. In Farennikova (2013),

the cases where it is involved, when it indexes a violation in a norm: of how things ought to look.

This invites us to rethink the probabilistic character of cases like (a) and (b). Initially, it seemed that they undermined the evaluative account of absence perception. Such cases depend on how the world does look (the stimulus), and not on how we prefer the world to look (value). The analysis I've offered shows that bottom-up cases depend on how we think the world ought to look. By getting to preferences expressed in norms, we get to value.

The benefit of this proposal is that it delivers a notion of value that's thicker than the one captured by appraisal or interpretation. But arguably, it also isn't as rich as the one at work in the top-down cases. So, does this notion of value possess enough richness to remove triviality concerns? It seems so. If predictions are essential to perception, then predictive coding still has the potential of making all perception evaluative. But that depends on certain commitments: that the relevant predictive states are representational (and not just bodily reflexes), and that these representations embody expectations about how things ought to look. The reason this is non-trivial is because not all predictions work in this way. In (a) and (b), expectations to see certain objects are generated by observing a sequence and are justified by that observation. They aren't random. But it is possible to imagine cases where predictions aren't similarly justified: they are not rooted in observation in the same way. Furthermore, this analysis of value does not easily transfer to constructivism. Perceptual inference may run free of expectations of how things ought to look. This, too, adds cost to the claim.

This completes my defence of the claim that perception of absence is inherently evaluative. It's worth noting that the argument I had offered does not imply that experiences of absence depend on value *in exactly the same way*. One source of value is drawn from conscious desires and expectations which guide searches. Another source of value stems from implicit preferences and commitment about how the world ought to look, embodied in predictive states. Understood from the evaluative perspective, perception of absence thus comes to look like a multifaceted phenomenon. In the remaining space, I will clarify why it is still useful to think about perception of absence in evaluative terms despite its diverse character, and state some important implications for other forms of evaluative perception.

This presents us with a picture of perception of absence as emerging from interactions between experience and value. One may wonder, however, if value is really fundamental here. The phenomenon looks quite heterogeneous. While search-based absences are enabled by top-down cognitive states, more bottom-up cases are driven by probabilities. So, what is the significance in thinking about perception of absence in evaluative terms?

The implication can be understood contrastively. Certain common ways of thinking about perception of absence are wrong. Experiences of absence are not primarily

---

I argue that mismatches do not essentially express error and can be recruited in experiences of absences that do not involve violation of expectation.

expectation-driven. They are sensitive to values and interests more than to probabilities. It requires a mix of knowing and wanting. It is not enough to assign a high chance to seeing an object. It is not enough to be equipped with advance knowledge about how objects look and where they are in order to perceive an absence. Predictive assessments by themselves are inert. An object's presence (or absence) must matter to the observer and draw upon values in addition to (and often contrary to) drawing on chances.

5. A Third Kind of Value

You are at a bar, and you want to know if an attractive person across the room is single. You quickly look at his hand and notice no ring. According to the account I've defended, this experience of absence is value-laden independently of its social meaning. It is evaluative because of its reliance on certain kinds of psychological states: desires and expectations that embody one's interest in a certain object. I've also argued that the evaluative analysis extends to the more stimulus-driven cases of perceiving an absence that do not engage conscious desires. These experiences are evaluative because they depend on states that express norms or preferences about how the world is expected to look.

One consequence of this argument is that it allows us to achieve greater clarity on the evaluative role of expectations. Expectations express predictions, but predictive content is not sufficient to communicate value. Predictions must reflect interests or norms in order to confer value on observation. In the absence of norms or interests, influence from predictions is evaluative only in the trivial sense.

Another consequence concerns a taxonomy of the forms of evaluative perception. Given the nature of its interaction with value, perception of absence constitutes a new form of evaluative perception.

As mentioned earlier, evaluative perception encompasses diverse phenomena, which we may sort roughly into two large classes. The first class includes perceptual paradigms in which value functions as an object of perception. In moral perception and aesthetic experiences, properties like beauty or justice serve as objects of our experience. Second, we have cases in which value functions as a modulator of perception; for instance, in the phenomenon called 'wishful seeing', one's desires and preferences about the world change how one perceives the world.

Let's call the first form of evaluative perception 'value perception' and the second form 'value-modulated perception'. Where does perception of absence fall? Seeing absence is neither like seeing justice nor like wishful seeing. It constitutes a new form of evaluative perception. Take value perception first. In moral perception, observers directly perceive evaluative properties like wrongness or justice. This doesn't reflect what's going on in experiences of absence. Absences are not evaluative properties. The argument that we perceive absences with the help of values doesn't imply that absences are values. Absences do not express oughts, and do not have hold on us as reasons. Value perception therefore isn't the right model of perception of absence.

The second option holds more promise. There are obvious structural parallels between perception of absence and the cases of value-modulated perception. In both forms of perception, antecedent psychological states shape how one experiences the world. Biases and desires produce 'wishful seeing' for positive perceptual experiences, and they also engender experiences of absence. Due to this similarity, it is tempting to treat perception of absence as a special case of value-modulated perception.

I think, however, that doing so would actually misconstrue the phenomenon in question. Experiences of absence aren't really value-modulated. They are value-enabled. Consider again wishful seeing. In this form of perception, certain subjective states alter how physical objects look. For instance, objects may appear closer or look larger due to emotion or bias. This influence is contingent: physical objects can be seen in the absence of evaluative states. This isn't the case with absences. Absences require values to be seen.

I have just shown that this way of interacting with value is unique to perception of absence. It also presents the fact–value dichotomy in a new light. When perceiving an absence, one is seeing a feature of the world that is not objective, but neither is it a response-dependent property. I'll conclude by unpacking this claim.

The analysis of perception of absence I had offered implies that absences require values to be seen. Note, however, that their reliance on value does not introduce distortion into one's experience. In perception of absence, subjective values help us pick up what is already true about the world: an absence. This point may be brought into sharper relief by comparing the evaluative relation in absence perception to two dominant accounts of moral evaluation: Projectivism[24,25] and Objectivism.[26,27]

Suppose you see an adult screaming and hitting a child. This may immediately strike you as morally wrong. For a projectivist, wrongfulness isn't a property that inheres in the event independently of one's observation. Rather, wrongfulness is constituted by a psychological (for a sentimentalist, affective) response to events in the world. This naturally affords analysis in terms of response-dependence. Just as colours require certain psychological responses in order to be perceived, moral values, similarly, require certain responses to be perceived.

Compare absence perception. We just noted that absences require subjective values to be perceived. The necessity of this relation may prompt one to treat evaluative states as constituents of experiences of absence. Projectivist ontology would follow: absences are projections we impose on the world by applying subjective values to the world. But there is a big disanalogy with Projectivism and response-dependence. In Projectivism, moral facts are constituted by perceiver's affective states and cannot exist independently of perceivers. Facts about absences can exist without the perceivers. When we perceive absences, we register objective properties of the world. Noticing an absence is enabled by value; whether something is absent is independent of noticing or value.

The form of valuing in perception of absence therefore is not projectivist. But neither is it fully Objectivist. Experiences of absence are not response-dependent, because absence facts exist independently of perceivers. Absences are not made up, they are picked up; however, they do require *prior cognitive states* to be picked up. This differs from objectivist approaches to moral evaluation. Objective values do not

---

[24] Blackburn (2013), 263.　　[25] Prinz (2008).
[26] Shafer-Landau (2003).　　[27] Boyd (1988).

rely on prior cognitive states to be experienced. Their pickup is more immediate: it is driven by character of the world.

6. Conclusion

When considering the question whether perception of absence is evaluative, two strategies seem especially appealing. First, one can focus on cultural or moral experiences of absence. Because these experiences will be expressive of one's moral or social judgements, we may attribute to them a strong evaluative dimension. Alternatively, one can appeal to the emotionality of experiences of absence, and argue that perception of absence acquires value through feelings of surprise.

In this paper, I used a third strategy to show that even very mundane experiences of absence, like seeing the absence of a pencil in a drawer, involve values. Absence perception presents a novel interaction between value and perception, which, in an important and interesting sense, is objective. This form of valuing presents the fact–value dichotomy in a new light. It has been argued that we need value in order to create moral facts about the world (subjectivism). It has also been argued that we need to detect facts about the world in order to create value (response-dependent accounts). Experiences of absence show that we need value in order to perceive facts about the world.

This conclusion bears on the evaluative status of ordinary object perception. Consider searches for objects that do succeed in the end. Prior to completion, these searches involve experiences of absence. Since experiences of absence are essentially evaluative, positive experiences of objects will have a value-laden history. Such aetiology, however, doesn't thwart the epistemic standing of positive experiences. Perception of absence, after all, is objective. It does not use value to obscure what's true of our world.

PART II

The Epistemology of Evaluative Perception

8
Moral Perception and Its Rivals

Sarah McGrath

1. Introduction

Consider an example that seems like as good a candidate as any for being a full-fledged case of moral perception. While walking through a grocery store parking lot, you witness a frustrated adult lash out and strike a child across the face, causing the child to draw back in pain and surprise. In response, you take up the belief that what the adult did was *wrong*. Let's set moral skepticism of various kinds to the side for the time being, and allow both that the adult's action really was wrong, and moreover, that this is something that you know after taking in the scene. We can then ask: how do you know that the adult acted wrongly?

The answer that I favor is that your knowledge that the adult acted wrongly is *perceptual* knowledge. More specifically, you know the relevant proposition by way of visual and auditory perception, in the same way that your knowledge that there are other people in the parking lot is a matter of visual and auditory perception. Given the assumption that you know that the action was wrong, the claim that you know this by perception is a hypothesis about how you know, one that competes with various rival hypotheses about how you know. Because of this, the credibility of the hypothesis that your knowledge is perceptual knowledge is in large part a comparative matter: it depends in large part on the plausibility of rival, non-perceptual accounts of how you know.

In recent years, the once unfashionable view that some of our moral knowledge is perceptual knowledge has found an increasing number of able proponents.[1] The greater part of this literature consists of attempts to defuse longstanding objections to the very possibility of moral perception—for example, that moral perception cannot be reconciled with the fact that perception is a causal process, or with the fact that we do not seem to have perceptual experiences that represent moral properties. I believe that these recent defenses have generated significant insights. Indeed, the modest version of moral perception that I endorse here incorporates an insight on which a number of contributors to this literature have recently converged. In large part,

---

[1] See e.g. Audi (2013); T. Chappell (2008); Cullison (2010); Dancy (2010); McBrayer (2010a); Watkins and Jolley (2002). The current paper is an attempt to improve on my own earlier defense of moral perception (S. McGrath 2004), a paper that I now believe significantly underestimates the resources available to those who favor rival views.

however, the current paper is an attempt to illuminate the terrain by approaching it from a different direction. Discussions of whether moral perception is possible often seem to proceed against a background assumption that there is some attractive alternative account of how we arrive at moral knowledge in cases of the relevant kind, cases in which (e.g.) you come to know that the adult acted wrongly more or less immediately upon witnessing the relevant scene. Here I want to raise some doubts about whether that is really so. Toward this end, Sections 2–4 are devoted to scrutinizing some alternative accounts of how we arrive at knowledge in the relevant class of cases. Special attention is paid to Kieran Setiya's 'Reductive Epistemology' defended in *Knowing Right From Wrong*,[2] an account that, for reasons that I explore, might seem particularly attractive to those seeking a thoroughly non-perceptual moral epistemology. It is my conviction that the more one scrutinizes alternative accounts, the more implausible they seem as accounts of how we actually manage to arrive at knowledge in cases of the relevant kind. In Section 5, I sketch a modest version of moral perception, one that, I suggest, does not suffer from any similarly implausible commitments. I conclude in Section 6 with some reflections on why it matters whether some of our moral knowledge is perceptual.

2. Perception versus Inference

How then do you know that the adult's action was wrong? I take it that the obvious alternative to a perceptual account is that you arrive at this knowledge on the basis of inference. For example, in a discussion of cases like the one at issue here, Nicholas Sturgeon writes that

[apparent] moral observation, even when it doesn't require stopping to 'figure anything out', always does involve inference, automatic and unconscious, and...among the premises are moral views one already has.[3]

Let's call the view that inference is always involved in cases of the relevant kind the *inferentialist* view. It is fair to say, I think, that proponents of the inferentialist view seldom provide much in the way of detail when it comes to characterizing the inference which allegedly underwrites the acquisition of knowledge.[4] For this reason, I want to canvass some of the more natural possibilities.

Here is one natural way of spelling out the inferentialist view. You arrive at the knowledge that the adult acted wrongly by bringing together two prior pieces of knowledge, one of which is perceptual but not moral, the other of which is moral but not perceptual. What you literally observe is that the situation had certain non-moral features—for example, that the adult acted in such-and-such a way, where the description of the behavior is given in completely non-moral terms. You then put this piece of observationally delivered non-moral knowledge together with some background belief (or beliefs) about the connections between the relevant kind of behavior and wrongness. Perhaps the most straightforward picture is that this

---

[2] Setiya (2012).   [3] Sturgeon (2002), 205.
[4] To be clear, I don't offer this as a criticism of Sturgeon, whose primary concern in (2002) is with a thesis other than the one at issue here.

background belief is belief in a conditional, a conditional to the effect that *if someone acts in such-and-such a way, then he or she acts wrongly.* Assuming that you know this background moral belief, you're in a position to know that the adult acted wrongly on this occasion.

On the suggested picture then, the hypothesized reasoning looks something like the following:

(1) The adult acted in such-and-such a way. (Piece of non-moral, observational knowledge)

(2) If someone acts in such-and-such a way, then he or she acts wrongly. (Piece of background moral knowledge)

(3) The adult acted wrongly. (Inferential moral knowledge, from (1) and (2))

On this reconstruction of the inference, the propositions from which the conclusion is inferred *entail* that conclusion. For this reason, I will refer to this reconstruction as the Deductive Model. While I do not believe that the Deductive Model is the best version of the inferentialist view, I do think that it is a very natural picture, and one that is relatively clear and straightforward. For these reasons, consideration of the Deductive Model provides a useful context for introducing a series of objections. As will become clear, versions of these objections will arise for *any* proposed reconstruction of the inference; they thus constitute challenges that any inferentialist view must meet, in order to be viable.

First, and perhaps most obviously: the Deductive Model, like any inferentialist view, seems at first blush at least somewhat psychologically unrealistic. When you come to believe that the adult acted wrongly as a result of witnessing the scene, it certainly doesn't seem as though your belief is the upshot of reasoning or inference from a belief that has as its content a non-moral description of the adult's behavior and another belief that has as its content that anyone who acts in that way acts wrongly. Rather, it seems as though you arrive at the judgment that the act was wrong *immediately* or *non-inferentially* upon witnessing the scene.[5] In this respect, the moral perception account seems to better fit the phenomenology.

Although I do not believe that this fact is completely worthless as evidence, I also do not believe that we should put much weight on it. As noted above, Sturgeon emphasizes the automaticity and unconscious character of the inference, and we can expect any inferentialist to follow suit. Particularly where what is at issue is whether we've engaged in any *implicit* reasoning or inference, the phenomenology, or what introspection seems to suggest, would not seem to be a reliable guide about whether any inference or reasoning has actually taken place.[6]

A more formidable objection is epistemological. After all, it is not simply that you end up with the belief that the action was wrong; rather, you *know* that the action was wrong. If you end up knowing that the action was wrong, and this belief was inferred

---

[5] Cf. Harman (1977), 4.

[6] For further discussion, see Vayrynen (2008). Sturgeon (2002) concedes that the phenomenology seems to favor the perceptual account over the inferentialist account but argues that we have good reason to suppose that inference is involved nonetheless.

from other beliefs, then it seems as though you must have had prior knowledge of the beliefs from which it is inferred. We can thus ask: is this assumption epistemologically realistic?

Consider premise (2) in the reconstruction offered above. Crucially, the antecedent of the conditional will contain no moral vocabulary, since according to the account under consideration, this is the condition that you directly observe to obtain, and the content of your purely perceptual knowledge contains nothing moral. In effect, what you are required to know is a sufficient condition for acting wrongly, specified in entirely non-moral terms, and one that is instantiated by the adult on this particular occasion. How likely is it that some such sufficient condition is grasped by *everyone* who is in a position to know that the adult acted wrongly, upon witnessing the scene? For reasons that I explore below, I believe that this is quite unlikely.

Before turning to those considerations, however, it is worth pausing to note a further burden that arises for any inferentialist view, and not simply the Deductive Model. As we have noted, given that a proponent of the inferentialist view will agree that the conclusion of the inference is known, she will presumably hold that whatever premises are employed in the inference are also known. But even if it can be made plausible, for some reconstruction of the inference, that the premises are known, there is also the question of *how well* those premises are known. After all, it is plausible that, in suitable circumstances, you can know that the adult acted wrongly with a relatively high degree of certainty. If you know this on the basis of implicit reasoning from premises $p1 \ldots pn$, then it seems as though you must know each of these premises with at least as high a degree of certainty, because whatever uncertainty collectively attaches to the premises will be inherited by the conclusion. For example, in terms of the Deductive Model, you would have to know the conditional premise (2) with a level of certainty that equals or exceeds the certainty with which you know that the adult acted wrongly.

In fact, there are reasons to think that a claim like (2) will be relatively difficult to know (let alone know with a high degree of certainty) even for philosophically sophisticated individuals. One initial ground for suspecting that this is the case is that the antecedent of (2) is likely to be quite complicated: it would be at least somewhat surprising if there turned out to be a relatively simple and straightforward sufficient condition for wrongness, given the constraint that the sufficient condition has to be put in *morally neutral terms*. Now, one might think that I'm overestimating the difficulty here. For example, let's suppose that the following is a sufficient condition for acting wrongly: *intentionally causing another person pain for the sake of one's own satisfaction*. So the corresponding conditional would run as follows: If one intentionally causes another person pain for the sake of one's own satisfaction, one acts wrongly. Perhaps it is not far-fetched to think that this conditional, or some similar conditional, is within the cognitive grasp of anyone who has the ability to recognize that the adult treated the child wrongly.

But here is the worry. Recall that there is another constraint on the relevant conditional: it is not simply that the antecedent of the conditional must contain only morally neutral terms; in addition, if the hypothesized inference is to deliver knowledge, then the antecedent of the conditional must be something that *you know on the basis of perception*. Thus, if the antecedent of the conditional is: 'a person intentionally causes pain to another for the sake of his or her own satisfaction', then you must be able to directly observe that the adult intentionally caused the child pain for the sake of his own satisfaction. Notice, however, that although this observational content is morally neutral, it is nonetheless extremely *rich*, because it includes things like the fact that the observed event was a source of pain, that it was done intentionally, and indeed, that it was done for a particular motive.

Consider next the kind of philosopher who is likely to be drawn to the inferentialist picture in the first place: a philosopher who, although not skeptical about morality or our ability to achieve moral knowledge, holds a relatively *thin* or *austere* view of what can be known on the basis of perception (in particular, one's knowledge of the moral facts is never a matter of perception). The question for such a philosopher is this: once we accept a view on which the possible content of our perceptual knowledge is rich enough to include things like the fact that someone is in pain, that that pain was *intentionally caused* by someone else, and even the motive behind the relevant action—what principled reason is there to exclude the possibility that some perceptual knowledge could have moral content? That is, once one is sufficiently liberal about the possible contents of perceptual knowledge, to the point that we can literally have perceptual knowledge that someone is acting with a certain intention (and so on), it is hard to insist, in a principle, not ad hoc way, that moral facts must always remain on the outside looking in.

Suppose instead that the proponent of the inferentialist picture holds a generally austere view about the kinds of contents that are possible objects of perceptual judgment, and about which we can have perceptual knowledge—so that it is not only moral facts, but also facts about the intentions of other people (etc.) that are never known on the basis of perception. For example, the inferentialist might adopt a view according to which the propositions that we know on the basis of perception only make reference to color properties, shape properties, and other properties of a comparably rudimentary sort. In that case, the exclusion of moral facts from the domain of the observable will not seem ad hoc or unprincipled. But then the worry arises: given that the relevant condition is one that you know on the basis of perception, it seems as though carrying through the relevant inference requires you to know a sufficient condition for acting wrongly that is stated in an extremely sparse vocabulary. And it is natural to think that the project of trying to provide a sufficient condition for acting wrongly in terms of shape properties, color properties, and so on, is simply hopeless. Moreover, even in the unlikely event there is some sufficient condition for acting wrongly that can at least in principle be given in terms of the sparse vocabulary, it seems vanishingly improbable that it is grasped by everyone who is capable of knowing that the adult acted wrongly upon witnessing the scene.

The inferentialist thus faces a dilemma. The more liberal the inferentialist is about what can be known on the basis of perception, the more it becomes at least somewhat plausible that you have background knowledge of some conditional that specifies an observable sufficient condition (one that is satisfied by the adult in our example) for acting wrongly in non-moral terms. However, the more liberal the inferentialist gets on this front, the more dialectical pressure there is to allow for the possibility that we sometimes have perceptual knowledge with moral content. (Again, it is crucial to bear in mind that the relevant theorist is not someone who is skeptical about morality itself. So the reason why moral facts cannot be observed, while causal facts and intentional facts can be observed, cannot simply be that there are no moral facts around.) On the other hand, if the inferentialist does embrace a sparse account of the possible contents of perceptual knowledge, then (i) the more implausible it is that there actually is a way of specifying an observable sufficient condition for wrongness, and (ii) the more implausible it is that the sufficient condition is known by anyone who is in a position to know that the adult acted wrongly upon witnessing the scene.

Thus, any version of the inferentialist view will face both a psychological challenge—is it psychologically realistic to suppose that the hypothesized inference is something that you actually engage in in coming to know that the adult acted wrongly?—as well as an epistemological challenge—is it realistic to think that your epistemic relationship to the premises of the hypothesized inference is such as to underwrite your knowledge? With respect to the Deductive Model, I believe that while the psychological challenge is not telling, the epistemological challenge provides a good reason for rejecting the account: it is not plausible to suppose that anyone who is capable of knowing that the adult acted wrongly upon witnessing the scene knows the premises of the hypothesized inference with the required level of certainty, given the constraints on the contents of those premises.

In addition, it is worth noting that any inferentialist account will also face a kind of hybrid challenge, which combines both psychological and epistemological considerations. As a first step towards appreciating this challenge, consider the familiar distinction between *propositional* and *doxastic* justification. Even if one is propositionally justified in believing some claim (say, in virtue of having good evidence that it is true), and one believes that proposition, one's belief might nevertheless fail to be doxastically justified. This would be true, for example, in a case in which one's good evidence for the belief plays no psychological role in one's holding it: one holds the belief for some bad reason, or for no reason at all.

Now, in the usual case, when you form the belief that the adult acted wrongly in response to witnessing the scene, your belief is both propositionally and doxastically justified: you have good reason for holding the belief, and you hold the belief for that reason. (It is not as though you have good reasons for holding the belief, but hold it in on some bad basis, e.g., out of a conviction that people who belong to an ethnic group to which the adult belongs are disposed to act wrongly.) Indeed, it is widely assumed that *knowing that p* entails that one's belief is doxastically as well as propositionally justified: when one believes for bad reasons, one's belief does not amount to knowledge, regardless of the strength of the reasons or evidence that might have been offered in favor of the belief. Given that assumption, it follows from the fact that you know that the adult acted wrongly that your belief is doxastically, and not merely propositionally, justified.

The worry behind the epistemological objection raised above concerns whether it is realistic to think that the epistemic standing of the two premises in the hypothesized inference is strong enough to put you in a position to know that the adult acted wrongly with the level of certainty that your belief seems to enjoy. However, even if a theorist does tell some story on which you are in a position to know both premises with a high degree of certainty, that is not enough; given the assumption that you are not only propositionally but also doxastically justified in believing that the adult acted wrongly, it must also be plausible that your justification for believing the premises plays the right *psychological role* in your coming to believe that the adult acted wrongly.

For example, on some views of concept possession, anyone who grasps a concept is in a position to work out (in principle) the necessary and sufficient conditions for its application, at least if she were to engage in a process of ideal reflection. One might hold then that the sense in which you are in a position to know the relevant conditional (2) is simply this: because you are a competent user of the concept *wrong*, you could at least in principle work out the relevant sufficient condition that is satisfied by the adult. In this sense then, you are in a position to know the problematic premise of the hypothesized inference. However, even if such a story is granted, it does not do justice to the idea that your belief is doxastically (and not merely propositionally) justified, given that the former requires knowledge of the relevant premise to be psychologically efficacious in bringing about your belief. Thus, the mere fact that you could (in principle) work out the relevant sufficient condition in virtue of your grasp of the concept *wrong* is neither here nor there, when it comes to accounting for how you know that the adult acted wrongly.

3. Beyond the Deductive Model

A natural response on the part of the inferentialist to the kinds of considerations offered here against the Deductive Model is to insist that that model misrepresents the reasoning by which you come to know that the adult acted wrongly. On the Deductive Model, you observe certain non-moral features F1...Fn of the situation, features that together guarantee that the witnessed event is a morally wrong action. In reconstructing your reasoning, the Deductive Model thus credits you with the grasp of a conditional whose antecedent states a sufficient condition for acting wrongly, or (more or less equivalently) a universal generalization to the effect that anyone who acts in such-and-such a manner acts wrongly.

But why should the inferentialist endorse that model? Perhaps the relevant inference is non-deductive. For example, perhaps what you observe is that the action has certain non-moral features F1...Fm, conditions that do not amount to a sufficient condition for moral wrongness; thus, even in the best case, what you actually observe is perfectly consistent with the action's not being wrong. Nevertheless, you know that *most* actions with those features are wrong, so what you observe inductively supports (and in a favorable case, puts you in a position to know) that *this* action is wrong. For example, perhaps the best reconstruction of the hypothesized inference looks something like this:

(1*) The adult intentionally struck the child [or:... intentionally struck the child in such-and-such a way]. (Piece of non-moral, observational knowledge)

(2*) Most cases in which an adult intentionally strikes a child [or: intentionally strikes a child in such-and-such a way] are cases in which the adult acts wrongly. (Background knowledge)

(3*) Therefore, (probably) the adult acted wrongly. (Inferential moral knowledge, from (1*) and (2*)).

Again, on this view, the content of your perceptual knowledge leaves open the possibility that the adult's action was not actually wrong. Indeed, it is consistent with what you observe that the adult's action was one of *benevolence*. (Perhaps the adult violently lashed out in order to kill a poisonous mosquito that had just descended on the child's cheek.) Nevertheless, if cases of wrongful action sufficiently outnumber cases of non-wrongful action within the relevant reference class, then your observation puts you in a position to know that *this* act is wrong, given that it is.

What should we say about this proposal? Again, there is a concern about how well motivated the proposal is, given the dialectical context. Once a philosopher grants that you can observe that the adult struck the child intentionally, it is not obvious what reason remains to deny that it is possible for you to observe that the adult treated the child wrongly. But let us waive the concern about motivation. An apparent advantage of reconstructing the reasoning as non-deductive is that so interpreted the reasoning requires less in the way of background knowledge. Gone is the need to grasp anything like a sufficient condition for acting wrongly; rather, what you grasp and deploy in your reasoning is in effect a statistical generalization that non-moral behavior relevantly similar to the adult's is strongly correlated with wrongful action.

Notice, however, that on this view the relevant piece of background knowledge is clearly a piece of empirical knowledge. In contrast, on the Deductive Model, in which one grasps a sufficient condition for acting wrongly, it is tempting to think of this piece of background knowledge as available from the armchair: indeed, as noted above, on some views it is something that you are in a position to know simply in virtue of having the concept *wrong*. On the current proposal, however, it is quite clear that the corresponding premise (e.g., 'most cases in which a child is struck are cases of wrongful action') is *not* a potential piece of a priori knowledge: given that at least some strikings of children are not cases of wrongful action, it is an empirical question whether most are. A claim such as 'Most strikings of children are cases of wrongful action' is a statistical generalization, and it is known, if it is known at all, in the way that statistical generalizations are.

Now, I do not think that it is implausible that some such generalization is known by anyone who is in a position to know that the adult acted wrongly upon witnessing the relevant scene.[7] What I do think is implausible is the idea that an empirical generalization like 'Most intentional strikings of children are wrong' would be generally known *if it were in principle impossible for anyone to ever observe, of a particular action, that it is wrong*. If 'Most actions with such-and-such features are wrong' is an empirical generalization, then it is presumably known (if it is known at all) because certain past token actions with such-and-such features were *independently recognized*[8] as cases of wrongful action. But it is far from obvious what account the inferentialist

---

[7] Of course, the viability of the current inferentialist proposal does not require that there is some generalization that is known to everyone who would be in a position to know that the adult acted wrongly upon witnessing the scene—different individuals might know, and deploy in their reasoning, at least somewhat different generalizations. For ease of exposition, I will sometimes write as though there is some one generalization that is at issue, but nothing in my argument trades on this.

[8] That is, recognized as instances of wrongful action in a way that did not make use of the generalization that 'Most actions with such-and-such features are wrong'.

can offer of how such knowledge is gained, once we have ruled out as impossible anyone's ever having observed that any token action is wrong.

Notice, for example, that the most straightforward route to establishing an empirical generalization of the relevant kind—generalizing from an *observed correlation* between the relevant properties—will be a complete non-starter in the eyes of the inferentialist. Often, we can establish an empirical generalization to the effect that events of type F are usually events of type G by observing, of a sufficient number and variety of F-events, that they are also G-events. Applied to the current case, this procedure would involve our knowing that (e.g.) 'Most intentional strikings of children are wrong' by its having been observed, of a sufficient number of intentional strikings of children, that they were cases of wrongful action. But obviously, the inferentialist will be the first to deny that *that* is a viable picture.

Of course, not all non-deductive reasoning is a matter of projecting past correlations of observable properties onto the future. On the orthodox view of the matter, no one has ever observed a proton; nevertheless, the scientist can arrive at knowledge that a proton has just passed by by reasoning non-deductively from what she observes in the laboratory, together with background assumptions. Could the inferentialist claim that you know that the adult acted wrongly on the basis of an *inference to the best explanation*?[9] On the face of it, that suggestion also seems wrong. *That the adult acted wrongly* does not causally explain his intentionally striking the child, in the way that the proton's passing by causally explains the observed effects in the cloud chamber. Rather, the adult's striking of the child is that in which the adult's acting wrongly *consists*. Thus, an inferentialist who eschews the Deductive Model should hold out for a more sophisticated picture of the relevant reasoning than either simple enumerative induction or inference to the best causal explanation.

4. Setiya's Reductive Epistemology

Where then should the inferentialist turn? An intriguing option is to adopt the 'Reductive Epistemology' recently proposed by Kieran Setiya, in an unusually sophisticated and insightful discussion of these issues.[10] In discussing cases of the kind at issue here, Setiya embraces a view on which our knowledge of the moral worth of an action typically rests on non-moral evidence, while clearly rejecting as unpromising or unworkable both the Deductive Model[11] and the idea that such knowledge is the result of either ordinary induction or inference to the best explanation.[12] Moreover, Setiya's discussion is unusually sensitive to the general kinds of concerns about psychological and epistemological plausibility raised earlier. Because I regard Setiya's general epistemological framework as the most promising option for the inferentialist that has yet been offered, I want to consider it in some detail.[13]

---

[9] Cf. Harman (1977), ch. 1.   [10] Setiya (2012).   [11] Setiya (2012), 44–6.
[12] Setiya (2012), 48–9.

[13] To be clear: although there are aspects of Setiya's Reductive Epistemology that make it particularly congenial to the inferentialist, his account does not actually *entail* inferentialism. According to Setiya, our knowledge of the moral worth of an action typically *rests on* non-moral evidence. Arguably, it does not follow from this that our knowledge of the moral worth of an action is typically the result of an *inference*

At the heart of Setiya's view is an account of what our evidence for moral claims is, and the conditions under which we have such evidence. Like most, Setiya accepts the supervenience of the moral on the non-moral: when an action falls under some moral concept, E, it does so in virtue of falling under non-moral concepts N1...Nn, such that, necessarily, whatever falls under N1...Nn falls under E.[14] Thus, whenever an action has some moral property, it instantiates some (often quite complicated) supervenience claim, a supervenience claim which captures the way in which the action's being the relevant moral type is guaranteed by its having certain non-moral features. If Setiya required that a believer know this supervenience claim, together with the fact that an observed action falls under the relevant non-moral concepts N1...Nn, then he would accept a version of the Deductive Model, and his account would immediately be vulnerable to the charge that it is not an epistemologically realistic account of much ordinary moral knowledge.

However, Setiya explicitly denies that the relevant supervenience claim must be known, or even believed, by a person who knows the moral truth in question.[15] Rather, when you know that an action is E (where E is some moral property or concept), you know this on the basis of evidence, but your evidence is *non-moral evidence for the claim that the action has the non-moral features N1...Nn, which feature in the true supervenience claim*. That is, on Setiya's view, evidence that an action has non-moral features N1...Nn is itself evidence for the moral claim that the action is E, when it is true that an action would be E in virtue of being N1...Nn. As he puts it:

What is the evidence by which I am justified in believing that an act is right or wrong, an agent generous or unjust? It is evidence that the act or agent falls under non-ethical concepts, N, where necessarily, what falls under N is right or wrong, generous or unjust. Call this Reductive Epistemology, since it reduces evidence in ethics to evidence elsewhere.[16]

When compared with the other accounts that we have considered, the novelty, indeed radicalism, of Setiya's proposal consists in this: on his proposal, you need not employ premises that have any moral content in arriving at a moral conclusion on the basis of evidence.[17] Whenever an action has a certain moral property, there is some true supervenience claim which captures the way in which its having that moral property depends on its having a certain non-moral property; by requiring only that

---

from non-moral evidence. On the usual view, inference is a transition among *beliefs*. Thus, whether your knowledge of the moral worth of an action is inferential knowledge might depend on whether the non-moral evidence on which it rests is the content of a belief. On some views, appearances can give rise to perceptual beliefs directly, where this is not a matter of inference. (The transition from something's looking red to the belief that it is red may not involve *the belief that it looks red*. In that case, the transition from something's looking red to the belief that is red will not count as an inference, given the assumption that inference is a transition among beliefs.) Similarly in the moral case: one might allow that non-moral evidence plays a role in the epistemology of moral belief that is similarly direct and unmediated by *beliefs* about the non-moral evidence, and so not a matter of inference. (For clarification on this point, I am indebted to correspondence with Setiya.)

[14] Setiya (2012), 49. [15] Setiya (2012), 50. [16] Setiya (2012), 49.
[17] Thus, Setiya would deny the claim by Sturgeon noted in Section 2, that 'among the premises [of the inference] are moral views that one already has'.

the supervenience claim be *true* (as opposed to known or believed by the person who has the evidence), Setiya seems to avoid the worry that the model is either epistemologically or psychologically unrealistic.[18] Thus, in order to have compelling evidence that the adult acted wrongly, you need not know or even believe some (possibly quite complicated) supervenience claim. Rather, you have such evidence simply in virtue of having evidence that the action had certain non-moral features, features in virtue of which the action counts (from the god's-eye point of view, as it were) as wrong.

An immediate worry about Setiya's picture is the following: in general, even if some higher-level fact supervenes on certain lower-level facts, merely having evidence that those lower-level facts obtain does not put you in a position to know the higher-level fact, so long as you are ignorant of the way in which the higher-level fact supervenes on the lower-level facts. Indeed, even *knowing* that the lower-level facts obtain (as opposed to merely having evidence that they do) does not generally put you in a position to know the higher-level fact, so long as you are ignorant of the way in which the higher-level fact supervenes on the lower-level facts. Compare the case of aesthetics. Just as it is plausible to think that the moral supervenes on the non-moral, so too it is plausible to think that the aesthetic supervenes on the non-aesthetic. Perhaps the aesthetic properties of a painting—say, the fact that it is beautiful—supervene on facts about the way in which the molecules of the paint are distributed on the canvas. Still, even if I have perfect knowledge of the way in which the paint molecules are distributed—perhaps the information has been provided by the testimony of an all-knowing oracle—this does not put me in a position to conclude that the painting is beautiful. (Of course, if I learn about the distribution of the paint on the canvas by *looking* at the painting, then I *will* typically be in a position to know that the painting is beautiful. But here, the obvious thought is that this is not a matter of potential inference from lower-level facts, but simply because I can now *see* that the painting is beautiful.) The analogue to Setiya's 'Reductive Epistemology' in aesthetics would be this: because the fact that the painting is beautiful supervenes on facts about the distribution of paint molecules, you have strong evidence that the painting is beautiful when you know how the paint molecules are distributed.[19]

In general, it seems implausible to credit a believer with having evidence for some class of F-facts simply in virtue of having evidence for some class of G-facts on which the F-facts supervene, so long as she remains ignorant of how the F-facts supervene on the G-facts. (Indeed, to strengthen the point, we might consider a case in which the individual not only has no idea of how the F-facts supervene on the G-facts, but

---

[18] Indeed, Setiya indicates that the believer need not even grasp the non-moral concepts that figure in the supervenience claim (see Setiya (2012), 50).

[19] Indeed, in at least one way, this example understates the potential gap between the content of our evidence for moral claims and the content of those claims on Setiya's picture. For Setiya often writes as though our evidence for some true moral claim consists, not in the non-moral truth on which that moral truth supervenes, but rather on *evidence for the non-moral truths on which the moral truth supervenes*. (See e.g. the statements to this effect in Setiya (2012), 49, 54, 56.) The analogue to this view in the aesthetic case would be the following: simply in virtue of having evidence about the distribution of the paint molecules on the canvas, I have evidence that the painting is beautiful.

(in which she is also completely ignorant of the fact *that* the F-facts supervene on the G-facts at all.)

But let us return to the moral case. In giving examples of the kinds of non-moral facts on which the moral facts supervene, we naturally cite facts that are themselves relatively 'high-level facts': for example, facts about the intentions of an agent, or about whether a given action will cause pain to sentient beings. Setiya himself provides the following example: perhaps the fact *my action was wrong* supervenes on the fact *I hurt you for fun*.[20] Of course, *I hurt you for fun* is presumably not a good candidate for a metaphysically fundamental fact, either: it too supervenes on lower-level facts, which in turn supervene on still lower-level facts, down to (at least) the microphysical level. Given the transitivity of the supervenience relation, it follows that the moral facts will supervene on the microphysical facts as well: any world exactly like ours with respect to the microphysical facts would not differ from ours with respect to the moral facts. Would Setiya go so far as to say that having evidence of how things are at the microphysical level amounts to having evidence for moral facts, given that the moral facts supervene on how things are at the microphysical level? While he nowhere commits himself to that view, notice that evidence of how things are at the microphysical level stands in exactly the same relation to the moral facts as the kind of evidence that Setiya treats as paradigmatic evidence for moral claims: both are evidence for a set of facts on which the moral facts supervene. Just as there is some (possibly quite complex) truth that captures the way in which a given moral fact supervenes on relatively high level, non-moral facts about the intentions of agents (etc.), so too there is some vastly more complex truth that captures the way that same moral fact supervenes on the microphysical facts. Of course, because of its complexity, there is no possibility that an actual human being could grasp a truth of the latter kind. But as we have noted, for Setiya, it is not necessary that the believer grasp the way in which a moral fact supervenes on a set of non-moral facts in order for evidence for the non-moral facts to count as evidence for the moral fact.

The worry, then, is this. Setiya's account of the conditions under which we have evidence for a moral claim seems overly liberal, crediting us with strong evidence in circumstances in which (intuitively) we have little or none. Intuitively, when one has sufficiently conclusive evidence in favor of some true claim, one is in a position to know that claim, provided that one attends to that evidence in a context in which the claim is salient. On Setiya's picture, however, one might have, at least in principle, *conclusive* evidence that some moral claim is true, while not being in a position to recognize the moral claim as true, no matter how carefully one attends to one's evidence while thinking about the claim. This will be the case, for example, when one has conclusive evidence for some set of non-moral truths on which the relevant moral fact supervenes (one's evidence thus *guarantees* that the moral fact obtains) while being ignorant of how the moral fact supervenes on the non-moral facts for which one has conclusive evidence.

Setiya has, I believe, a formidable response to the kind of concern raised here. The response exploits the distinction, which he emphasizes throughout his discussion,

---

[20] Setiya (2012), 49–50.

between propositional and doxastic justification, or between what is involved in having evidence that some moral claim is true and what is involved in knowing or justifiably believing the moral claim on the basis of that evidence. As he puts it:

> there is no suggestion that having evidence that an act falls under [the non-moral concept] N... is sufficient by itself to justify one's belief. In general, there is a gap between having evidence for a proposition and believing it with justification. In order to be justified, one's belief must relate to that evidence in the right way.[21]

Consider how this applies to the aesthetic example discussed above, in which the oracle has provided you with strong evidence for facts about how the paint molecules are distributed on the canvas (facts on which the beauty of the painting supervenes) but you have had no opportunity to actually look at the painting and see whether it is beautiful. Even if a proponent of Reductive Epistemology about aesthetics is committed to saying that you thus have strong evidence in favor of the claim that the painting is beautiful, there is no danger that the account will entail the unpalatable conclusion that a belief that the painting is beautiful would be known or doxastically justified in your circumstances. For in order for you to know or justifiably believe a claim, you have to be able to respond to that evidence in the right way, and this is exactly what you lack the wherewithal to do in the case as it has been described.

Similarly, a proponent of Reductive Epistemology in ethics, like Setiya, can say the following: the apparent proliferation of evidence for moral claims that the view seems to countenance is benign, for the distinction between propositional and doxastic justification (and the fact that the latter is necessary for knowledge) ensures that we will not be credited with moral knowledge or justified belief in cases where we have none.

Given that on Setiya's view, we often *do* know moral claims on the basis of evidence for non-moral facts on which their truth supervenes, what must be added to that evidence in order for us to know? Again, a natural and traditional thought is that, in those cases in which we arrive at moral knowledge on the basis of non-moral evidence, this transition is facilitated by our grasping some proposition that encodes how the moral supervenes on the non-moral in the case at hand, a proposition that we deploy as an (implicit) premise in drawing the moral conclusion. But as we have seen, Setiya eschews anything like this picture. As he himself notes, this eschewal leaves the psychology of doxastic justification, and how we arrive at moral knowledge, at least somewhat obscure.[22] On the alternative picture that he endorses, what bridges the gap between our non-moral evidence and the moral conclusion is not a *belief* that connects the moral and the non-moral, but rather an *epistemically reliable disposition*:

> A natural thought is that, when S forms an evidentially justified belief, she manifests an epistemically reliable disposition: a disposition to form beliefs on the basis of evidence by which they are propositionally justified... In relation to ethical knowledge, we can work with a simple formula: if you know that X is E [where E is some explicitly ethical predicate], your knowledge manifests a reliable disposition, a disposition to believe the truth on adequate grounds.[23]

---

[21] Setiya (2012), 50–1.   [22] Setiya (2012), 63.   [23] Setiya (2012), 64.

According to Setiya, these epistemically reliable dispositions are dispositions to form moral beliefs on the basis of non-moral evidence in a way that tracks, at least roughly, the way in which the moral supervenes on the non-moral in a given case.[24]

Although I will ultimately suggest that something much like Setiya's notion of an epistemically reliable disposition might be useful for understanding the true epistemology of the relevant class of cases, I do not believe that the account is ultimately satisfactory. As argued here, the Reductive Epistemologist credits us with having evidence for moral claims in circumstances in which it is natural to think that we do not have such evidence. Although the apparatus of epistemically reliable dispositions allows the account to avoid some of the concerns that arise from this, it does not help with others.

Notice that there are two distinct ways in which the relative liberality with which Setiya's account credits us with having evidence for moral claims threatens to lead to counterintuitive consequences about what we are justified in believing.

First, there is the worry on which we have focused thus far. In a case in which you have compelling evidence for the non-moral facts on which some moral truth supervenes, the account credits you with having compelling evidence for the relevant moral truth. Nevertheless, in a case in which you have absolutely no idea how the non-moral facts determine the moral truth, you are not in a position to know the relevant moral claim; if you believed it anyway, your belief would not amount to knowledge.

But why are you not in a position to know, according to the Reductive Epistemologist? That is, given that, according to the Reductive Epistemologist, you have compelling evidence for believing the moral claim that you believe, what exactly are you missing, that prevents you from knowing? (Again, the answer cannot be: what you are missing is knowledge of how the moral supervenes on the non-moral facts, for Setiya holds that you often can know, even in the absence of such knowledge.) Here, the machinery of epistemically reliable dispositions *does* provide a satisfying answer. The reason why you are not in a position to know the moral claim (despite having good evidence for it) is that you lack an epistemically reliable disposition to respond to that evidence in the right way.

A second case is more troublesome. In general, one way of being irrational is this: you have strong evidence for a given claim, and you attend to that evidence, but you nevertheless fail to believe the claim that the evidence supports. Again, according to Reductive Epistemology, when you have strong evidence for the non-moral facts on which some moral truth supervenes, you ipso facto have strong evidence for the relevant moral truth. However, surely you are not being irrational in failing to believe some moral claim simply in virtue of having strong evidence for lower-level claims on which its truth supervenes, provided that you are ignorant of the connection, and your ignorance of the connection is not itself a failure of rationality.

But what account can the Reductive Epistemologist offer of why you are not irrational when you fail to take up the relevant moral belief, given that he will credit you with having strong evidence for the claim? Notice that here, the machinery of

---

[24] Setiya (2012), 65.

MORAL PERCEPTION AND ITS RIVALS 175

epistemically reliable dispositions is *not* helpful to the Reductive Epistemologist. The fact that you are not irrational for failing to take up a moral belief for which you have (according to the account) compelling evidence cannot be explained by your *lacking* a disposition to respond to that evidence correctly; for in the usual case, failing to believe a claim for which one has compelling evidence simply because one lacks a disposition to respond to that evidence in the appropriate way hardly gets one off the hook with respect to the charge of irrationality. (Compare: if the Holocaust denier refuses to believe that the Holocaust occurred even after being presented with compelling evidence that it did, we do not judge that his failure to believe the proposition is rational, so long as he lacks an epistemically reliable disposition to respond to that evidence in the right way.)

Again, the basic point is perhaps best grasped when we consider the same issue as it arises in the aesthetic domain. Consider again the case in which the oracle has provided you with compelling evidence about the way in which the paint molecules have been distributed on the canvass, but where you have not yet had an opportunity to view the painting. A proponent of Reductive Epistemology in aesthetics will say: given that you have compelling evidence for the facts on which the truth that *the painting is beautiful* supervenes, you ipso facto have compelling evidence for the claim that the painting is beautiful. Nevertheless, given your utter ignorance as to how the facts about the distribution of the paint molecules determine whether the painting is beautiful, you are obviously in no position to know or justifiably believe that the painting is beautiful; if you nevertheless went ahead and believed that the painting is beautiful anyway, this belief would not be justified or amount to knowledge.

What account can the Reductive Epistemologist give of your inability to know in the circumstances, given that he attributes to you compelling evidence for the truth that you believe? Here the Reductive Epistemologist has a satisfying answer to offer us: your inability to know, despite your compelling evidence, is due to your lack of an epistemically reliable disposition to respond to your evidence in the right way. So far, so good. But we should also ask a follow-up question of the Reductive Epistemologist. Given that you have never seen the painting, it is not simply that you are not in a position to know that it is beautiful; it is also the case that if you suspend judgment as to its beauty, you are not irrational in doing so. (Indeed, suspending judgment as to its beauty seems like the *uniquely* reasonable stance for you to take, given your circumstances.) But what account can the Reductive Epistemologist offer of why it is rational for you to suspend judgment as to its beauty, given that on his account, you have compelling evidence for believing that it is beautiful? Notice that here the answer: 'The reason that it is rational for you to suspend judgment as to whether the painting is beautiful, despite having compelling evidence that it is beautiful, is that you lack a disposition to respond to your evidence correctly' falls flat. For lacking a disposition to respond to one's evidence correctly is no defense of one's rationality, when one takes up some stance other than the one supported by one's evidence.

The objection to Reductive Epistemology in ethics that I have developed in this section can be summarized as follows. In general, even if some higher-level fact supervenes on a set of lower-level facts, having compelling evidence for those

176   SARAH MCGRATH

lower-level facts does not necessarily amount to having compelling evidence for the higher-level fact. In the absence of some special reason to think that things are otherwise in the moral domain, we should similarly assume (contrary to the account) that having compelling evidence for the non-moral facts on which a moral fact supervenes does not necessarily amount to having compelling evidence for the moral fact. The apparatus of epistemically reliable dispositions blocks only some, but not all, of the counterintuitive consequences that result from the fact that the account is overly liberal in crediting us with evidence for moral claims.

5. Moral Knowledge by Perception: A Relaxed View

Thus far I've examined a number of different ways of developing the inferentialist picture and noted some of the challenges that arise for those accounts. I don't pretend to have made a conclusive case against the accounts that I've considered. Moreover, even if the considerations that I've rehearsed are persuasive, there are presumably any number of other ways in which the inferentialist picture might be developed, ways that would need to be considered in any complete treatment of the topic.

But suppose that it turns out that objections broadly similar to the ones I've canvassed here will arise for any inferentialist account. Since all of these objections concern the nature of the hypothesized inference, none of them arises for a rival hypothesis about how you know that the adult acted wrongly: namely, that you *saw* that he acted wrongly. That is, perhaps your knowledge that the adult acted wrongly is a piece of non-inferential, perceptual knowledge. Again, the hypothesis that your knowledge is perceptual seems to fit the phenomenology (the felt immediacy of the judgment, and so on) better than the hypothesis that your knowledge is a matter of inference. Given this, and given the challenges facing inferentialist accounts, why not simply take the appearances at face value and adopt the perceptual account?

Consider then the following argument that there is at least some moral knowledge that is perceptual. In the case described in Section 1:

(1)   You know that the adult acted wrongly.

(2)   If you know that the adult acted wrongly, then you know this either on the basis of perception or on the basis of inference.

(3)   You do not know that the adult acted wrongly on the basis of inference.

(4)   Therefore, you know that the adult acted wrongly on the basis of perception.

I think that this is a good argument.[25] In fact, the reason why I believe that we sometimes have moral knowledge by perception is because I think that there are

---

[25] Of course, because the argument concerns a hypothetical example, the most that it can really establish is that you know that the adult acted wrongly on the basis of perception *in the fiction*. But given that the fiction includes no unrealistic assumptions, I take it that it would be enough to show that moral knowledge by perception is *possible*. Moreover, given the similarity of the example to countless actual cases, I assume that no one who agrees that you have perceptual moral knowledge in the fiction would deny that we have perceptual moral knowledge as things actually stand.

some arguments of this general type that are compelling. Of course, I haven't offered anything like a full defense of the argument, so my endorsement of it is more of an exercise in laying my cards on the table than anything else. Among other things, I have not said anything at all in defense of premise (1). Thus, a moral skeptic might agree that the inference view seems unpromising, while denying that this gives us reason to believe that we sometimes acquire moral knowledge by perception. Moreover, as I have admitted, I don't think that any of the kinds of considerations that I've offered in favor of premise (3) is decisive. Even if the inferentialist view has some implausible commitments, perhaps the moral perception view turns out to be even worse. No doubt, one of the motivations that leads many people to learn to live with some of the counterintuitive aspects of the inferentialist view is their commitment to the idea that one really can know that the adult acted wrongly, and that, however exactly one manages to attain that knowledge, it certainly isn't something that one just *sees*.

However, I believe that the commitments incurred by the friend of moral perception are often overestimated. For example, here is one reason for rejecting the perceptual account that might be offered. A theorist might hold that you could have perceptual knowledge that the adult acted wrongly only if you had a visual experience that represented the property of wrongness (in the way that your visual experience might have as part of its content a certain shade of red), but that no visual experience ever represents an action as wrong. And one might think that visual experiences do not represent actions as wrong for any of the reasons that drive many philosophers of perception to accept relatively austere accounts of the admissible contents of perceptual experience.[26] Thus, one might argue as follows:

(1) You can observe that an action is wrong only if you have a visual experience that represents the property of wrongness.

(2) Visual experiences do not represent moral properties like wrongness.

(3) Therefore, you did not have a visual experience that represents the property of wrongness (from (2)).

(4) Therefore, you did not observe that the adult acted wrongly (from (1) and (3)).[27]

However, this argument is not compelling, for we lack good reasons to believe premise (1). In general, it is not true that you can have perceptual knowledge that *x is F* only if you have a perceptual experience that has as part of its content that *x is F*. This is a point on which a number of philosophers of perception have

---

[26] For example, it is sometimes argued that the only experiential representations are those that are produced in a lawlike way from the stimulation of our retinas, but that we have empirical evidence that the process by which retinal stimulation gives rise to experience is insulated from any information that is processed cognitively. For a case along these lines, see O'Shaughnessy (2000). Other philosophers who hold that we only ever represent lower-order properties include Byrne (2009), Clark (2000), Dretske (1995), and Tye (1995).

[27] Compare McBrayer's (2010a) presentation of the 'Representation Objection to Moral Perception', which he proceeds to criticize at length.

recently converged.[28] Applied to the moral case, the point suggests a need to distinguish sharply between the following two questions:

(1) Are moral properties ever represented in perceptual experience?
(2) Do we ever acquire moral knowledge *via* perception?

An affirmative answer to either of these questions does not entail an affirmative answer to the other. First, an affirmative answer to question (1) does not entail an affirmative answer to question (2). For example, a theorist might coherently hold that although our visual experiences sometimes represent token actions as wrong (and so the answer to question (1) is 'yes'), we are never in a position to have perceptual knowledge that an action is wrong. One straightforward way in which this combination could be realized is if no actions really are wrong (despite the fact that some of them are visually represented as such). If that were the case, then we would not have any knowledge (and a fortiori, no perceptual knowledge) to the effect that a given action is wrong. The truth about wrongness would be parallel to a kind of error theory about color, according to which our visual experiences systematically mislead us about what the world is like.

More relevantly for our purposes, we should also deny the validity of the inference from 'S has perceptual knowledge that x is F' to 'S has had a perceptual experience with the content that X is F'.[29] A quick way of appreciating this point is the following. Suppose that some very *thin* view about the admissible contents of experience turns out to be correct, so that the content of visual experience is exhausted by things like shape properties and color properties. Thus, contrary to what Siegel (2006) and others have argued, *kind* properties are never represented in visual experience—for example, no visual experience ever literally represents something as *a lemon*, although a visual experience might represent something that is in fact a lemon as having a certain shape and being a certain color. Should we conclude from this that no one ever *sees* that there is a lemon on the table? No, we shouldn't. For it might be like this: the features of the scene that you do take in in your visual experience *trigger* or *prompt* you to take up the immediate, non-inferential belief that there is a lemon on the table. The features of the scene that you are responding to in taking up the immediate, non-inferential belief that there is a lemon present need not (and typically will not) amount to anything like a sufficient condition for the presence of a lemon. (Perhaps all of the same features would also be present if the object that you are looking at were actually a fake lemon.) But if circumstances are favorable

---

[28] See esp. Audi (2013), Dancy (2010), Johnston (2011), McBrayer (2010a), McDowell (2009), A. Millar (2000), and Silins (2013). Audi, Dancy, and McBrayer make the point in the context of discussions of moral perception. Of the authors listed in this footnote, Johnston's rejection of the orthodox view that perceptual knowledge that X is F entails having a perceptual experience that represents X as F is the most radical. While the others retain the familiar picture on which any instance of perceptual knowledge is underwritten by a perceptual experience with representational content (but hold that the content of the perceptual knowledge can outrun the content of the experience), Johnston rejects this picture altogether, on the grounds that we do not actually have perceptual experiences of the relevant kind. While I have considerable sympathy for Johnston's more radical critique, the view that I endorse here is compatible with both it and the less radical alternative.

[29] Again, I want to emphasize that here I'm following a number of others; cf. n. 28.

(it really is a lemon on the table, there are no fake lemons in the vicinity, and so on), then your belief that there is a lemon on the table might be safe enough[30] to qualify as knowledge.

Moreover, the knowledge in question is perceptual knowledge. It is not as though you infer the belief that there is a lemon on the table from a more basic belief that there is an object of such-and-such a shape with such-and-such a color. Indeed, you might not have any belief about the features whose presences triggers your immediate belief, and which are actually represented in the perceptual experience. On this point, consider also Audi's (2013) example of facial recognition. Entering my department lounge, I might know that Sarah-Jane is there by perception: I see her and recognize her face. (It is not as though I infer that she is there, by reasoning from beliefs of the form: 'This person's face has such-and-such features, and Sarah-Jane's face has such-and-such features'). But equally, it is not as though there is some property of *being Sarah-Jane* that is literally represented in some visual experience that I have.

Similarly, it is not a necessary condition of your knowing via perception that the adult acted wrongly that you have a perceptual experience that includes the property of wrongness. Indeed, once we take up a suitably liberal view about the connections between (i) what we can know on the basis of visual perception, and (ii) the admissible contents of visual experience, we should not put up much resistance to a literal interpretation of perfectly ordinary claims such as 'I saw him treat her wrongly when we were at the restaurant'. That is, once we don't see such talk as committing us to highly contentious claims about the nature of visual experience, we should be willing to take such talk at face value—at least, if we are not outright moral skeptics.

In fact, once we adopt a suitably relaxed view of what moral perception would involve, I think that the most pressing challenge to the friend of moral perception is not the traditional worry that it is utterly fanciful to suppose that anything like it ever occurs. Rather, the question is why it *matters* (either theoretically or practically) whether any of our moral knowledge is perceptual in the relevant sense. After all, if both the inferentialist and the proponent of the perceptual account think that you know that the adult acted wrongly more or less immediately upon witnessing the scene, how much difference does it make exactly how you arrive at this knowledge?

This question seems particularly pressing if the inferentalist emphasizes (as she surely will) that the hypothesized inference is both automatic and unconscious, and if the proponent of the perceptual account emphasizes (as I think she should) that she is not committed to the claim that we have visual experiences that represent moral

---

[30] Here I put the point in terms of a general 'safety theoretic' account of knowledge to which I am sympathetic, according to which (roughly) you know that p just in case your belief that p is safe, i.e., you could not easily have been wrong in a sufficiently similar case. (For defenses of safety-theoretic approaches to knowledge see esp. Williamson (2000) and Sosa (1999).) I want to emphasize, however, that any number of other accounts of knowledge will similarly return the verdict that your immediately formed belief that *there is a lemon on the table* counts as knowledge in favorable circumstances, even in the absence of a visual experience that represents the kind property *lemon*. Among other possibilities, notice that one might adopt a theory that incorporates something very much like Setiya's notion of an *epistemically reliable disposition*: perhaps an essential part of the story as to why your immediately formed belief counts as knowledge is that you have an epistemically reliable disposition to form that belief in response to the scene with which you are visually presented.

properties. A common prototype of inferential reasoning consists of the deliberate and self-conscious drawing of a conclusion from explicitly represented premises (despite the fact that much of our actual inferential reasoning does not correspond to that prototype). Similarly, for many philosophers, the prototype of coming to know that x is F via perception involves representing that feature in a perceptual experience. Once the inferentialist makes clear that her preferred reconstruction of your knowledge that the adult acted wrongly is very different from the common prototype of inferential reasoning, and the moral perception theorist makes clear that her reconstruction of your knowledge is very different from the common philosopher's prototype of what is involved in the acquisition of perceptual knowledge, why should we think the residual dispute is still of interest and importance?[31]

While I feel the force of this challenge, I believe that it is mistaken. In Section 6, I want to offer one reason why it matters whether some of our moral knowledge is perceptual, in the sense endorsed here.

6. Moral Knowledge by Perception and Theorizing in Normative Ethics

Here is one way in which taking moral perception seriously can make a difference to theorizing in ethics. If we have moral knowledge by perception, then it follows not only that some of our moral knowledge is immediate and non-inferential, but also that some of this immediate, non-inferential moral knowledge consists of *singular moral judgments*: paradigmatically, judgments to the effect that a token event has a certain moral property. (Indeed, perhaps when you witness the scene in the parking lot, the immediate judgment that you form is the demonstrative judgment *that's wrong*, where the demonstrative picks out a certain token event.) My own view is that a significant part of our most fundamental evidence for ethical theorizing consists in singular moral judgments that we know to be true. But I also think that there is a fairly widespread tendency to neglect this fact, and to think that our evidence, or what we ultimately have to go on in our ethical theorizing, consists exclusively of judgments with more general content. In fact, I think that this neglect is in practice characteristic even of approaches to ethical theorizing that on their face would seem to be immune to the charge.

As an example of one such view, consider *the method of reflective equilibrium*, as it is standardly explicated. Proponents of the method of reflective equilibrium emphasize—correctly, I believe—that in moral theorizing we are never in the position of 'starting from scratch'. Rather, we begin our theorizing from certain considered judgments about morality. These considered judgments are of different levels

---

[31] Proponents of the inferentialist picture sometimes stress that in order for their view to be viable, we have to work with what they call a 'broad' notion of inference (Sturgeon 2002; Väyrynen 2008). I have urged that the best version of the moral perception involves a similarly 'broad' notion of perception or observation, on which we can have perceptual knowledge that x is F in the absence of a perceptual experience that represents X as being F. The present objection is, in effect, that the interest and importance of the issue that seems to divide the two camps lapses, once sufficiently broad notions of both inference and perception are employed by the disputing parties.

of generality: some concern very abstract general principles about morality, while other considered judgments concern particular cases. A second major theme of proponents of reflective equilibrium (which I also take to be correct) is that no judgment is privileged over any other simply in virtue of its level of generality. So, for example, against a certain kind of revisionary consequentialist, who will advise us to abandon any number of extremely intuitive, common-sense judgments about cases because those judgments conflict with the very general principle of maximizing expected utility, the reflective equilibrium theorist will defend the propriety of giving significant weight to some of our judgments about cases, sometimes to the point of treating them as straightforward counterexamples to otherwise plausible general principles.

Against this familiar backdrop, it is natural to think that, even if the revisionary consequentialist is potentially vulnerable to the charge of unduly privileging the abstract and general over the concrete and particular, at least the reflective equilibrium theorist is in the clear with respect to the same charge. However, I think that this natural thought is incorrect. For as Shelly Kagan[32] has argued, what philosophers often call 'judgments about cases' (as opposed to 'judgments about general principles') are actually judgments about *types* of cases, as opposed to token cases. Typically, what we are offered is an abstract description of an event type. (For example: 'Suppose that one could save the lives of five people dying from organ failure, by overpowering some unwilling bystander and harvesting his or her organs.') We then arrive at a moral judgment about what it would be permissible or impermissible to do in the circumstances. Thus, even what are called judgments about particular cases are often judgments about the truth of general principles (e.g., 'It would be morally wrong to sacrifice the innocent bystander in such circumstances') as opposed to genuine singular moral judgments. The difference is simply that these general principles are much less sweeping in their scope and application than very sweeping, overarching general principles such as the principle of utility.

Thus, a methodological view according to which the correct starting point for moral theorizing consists of both our considered judgments about general principles and our considered judgments about particular cases is still at risk of neglecting the particular, so long as 'considered judgments about particular cases' is understood (as in practice it often is) as referring to judgments about case types, as opposed to singular moral judgments.[33] Moreover, notice how this picture—that the least abstract items of moral evidence that we have to go on are judgments about case types—fits very naturally certain inferentialist pictures of how you know that the parent acted wrongly in the parking lot. For example, on the Deductive Model, as opposed to the moral perception picture, that the parent acted wrongly is a derivative

---

[32] Kagan (2001), 61–2.
[33] To be clear, I don't regard myself as raising a significant worry about the method of reflective equilibrium here. For it is easy enough, I take it, for a proponent of the method to allow that the considered judgments that on her view constitute the proper starting point for moral inquiry to include, not only judgments about principles and judgments about "particular cases", but also singular moral judgments. In terms of the method of reflective equilibrium then, the upshot of these remarks concerns the most defensible version of the method if in fact some of our moral knowledge is perceptual. For some more substantive reservations about the method of reflective equilibrium, see T. Kelly and S. McGrath (2010); S. McGrath (unpublished).

piece of moral knowledge, one that rests on a more fundamental piece of moral knowledge: namely, a conditional to the effect that *if someone acts in such-and-such a way, then he or she acts wrongly*. And of course, that conditional is not a singular moral judgment. Rather, it is a putative general moral principle, equivalent to the claim that 'Anyone who acts in such-and-such a way is guilty of acting wrongly'.

On the other hand, if we take moral perception seriously, we will naturally think that some of our fundamental, non-derivative moral knowledge consists in singular moral judgments. For this reason, friends of moral perception should hold that singular moral judgments are an important part of what we have to go in ethical theorizing. Similarly, if in fact some of our moral knowledge is perceptual knowledge, then a theorist who fails to take moral perception seriously is more likely to end up with an overly narrow view of what we have to go on in ethics, one that neglects an entire class of judgments as potential evidence.[34]

---

[34] Earlier versions of this paper were presented at the University of Glasgow, at a meeting of the Central States Ethics Reading Group, and as a keynote address at the 2014 Rutgers–Princeton graduate conference. I am grateful to the audiences present on those occasions for their feedback. Special thanks to Robert Cowan, Elizabeth Harman, Mark Johnston, Thomas Kelly, Pekka Väyrynen, and an anonymous referee for written comments.

9
Perception and Intuition of Evaluative Properties

Jack C. Lyons

Is it possible for us to perceive evaluative properties, such as the moral rightness of some act or the aesthetic beauty of a piece of art? I won't try to answer this question definitively, in part because I think the answer depends on the answers to a number of empirical questions. However, I want to lay out some reasons to be optimistic about an affirmative answer, and even more optimistic about an affirmative answer to a nearby question. I want to distinguish what we can perceive from what we can have perceptual experience of, and I want to distinguish perception from a more general category, that I will call intuition (using 'intuition' in a broader sense than is common in philosophy). I think it is unlikely that we have perceptual *experience* of evaluative properties or their instances as such. It is more likely that we perceive these properties, however, and even more likely that we have perception-like, empirical intuitions of them. The resulting epistemological status of evaluative property attributions is very much like it would be if we actually perceived such properties. Thus, the proponent of the claim that evaluative properties are perceivable is taking on an excessive and unnecessary burden, especially if a perceivable property is taken to be one that is the object of a perceptual experience.

In Section 1, I make some preliminary, clarificatory remarks. Section 2 is concerned with the distinction between perception and perceptual experience, Section 3 with the distinction between perception and intuition in the current sense. In Section 4, I discuss the epistemology of intuitive judgments. In Section 5 I turn to the question of whether we intuit evaluative property instances and argue that, though we would need empirical data for a firm conclusion, it seems likely that we do. In Section 6, I note some important ways in which perception and (other types of) intuition differ both psychologically and epistemologically. In Section 7, I return to the epistemology of intuition and sketch some of the implications of the earlier sections.

1. Three Questions

Let me start by clarifying the nature of the question about whether we can perceive evaluative properties.[1] There are at least three different versions of the question, only two of which figure into the present concerns.

---

[1] Throughout, 'perception of property *P*' should be understood as shorthand for 'perception as of something's being an instance of *P*'.

The *metaphysician's question* is whether evaluative properties are 'out there' in the way that uncontroversially perceptible properties are and causally efficacious in a way that allows us to be appropriately related to them. The *cognitive scientist's question* is whether the psychological or neural or computational systems or processes or capacities by which we come to form some judgments about evaluative properties are the same as or similar to those involved in perception. The *epistemologist's question* is whether some beliefs about evaluative properties have the same or similar status as perceptual beliefs and for the same or similar reasons.

My concern here will be with the second and third questions. I'll formulate them in such a way that they are neutral with respect to the metaphysical question. This means, among other things, that psychological processes and capacities have to be individuated more or less internalistically, at least in the sense that we could determine that an agent is employing a particular capacity without first knowing what kind of environment the agent is in and whether the capacity is getting at the truth or not.[2] It also means that the epistemic status of interest will be justification, rather than knowledge.

This amounts to making substantive assumptions at the outset, e.g., that some kind of nondisjunctivist psychology and epistemology are correct. I won't try to defend these nondisjunctivisms, but I don't mind taking them as a starting point. It seems to me that the psychology and epistemology of, say, color vision might possibly be relevant to theories about the ontological status of color, but the links are complex and controversial enough that we can pursue the former while setting aside the latter. Similarly regarding the psychology and epistemology of causal judgment or other minds. We ought to be able to figure out how we do and should come to beliefs about causation, for example, without having to first figure out what causation is. The flipside to this autonomy for our epistemology and psychology, however, is that we're not going to get a cheap argument for metaphysical realism from them. So even if some kind of direct realist epistemology of moral properties is true, it won't imply realism about moral properties.

Although I think that the metaphysical question is largely separable from the other two, I think that the cognitive scientific question and the epistemological question are closely linked.[3] In particular, I hold (as will become clearer later) that the epistemic status of a belief is partly determined by the nature of the process or capacity by which that belief arises. In the present case, there is reason to suspect that some evaluative judgments result from 'intuitive' systems/processes/capacities and that these judgments therefore have an epistemic status similar to that of perceptual judgments.

Intuition—in the broad and inclusive sense common everywhere, I think, outside of philosophy—is sometimes described as 'knowing without knowing how you know'. This is a handy characterization of the phenomenon that I am interested in, although since I'm avoiding the metaphysical questions, we will need to remove the factivity. And to answer the psychological questions, we will need to remove the normativity.

---

[2] For a very different use of 'capacity', see Millar (2011); Schellenberg (2013).
[3] Even if an externalist epistemology is true, the metaphysical question is largely separable, or can be, depending on the theory. This will become clear as I develop the externalist epistemology that I favor, in Sections 4–7.

A more accurate slogan, then, would be 'cognizing without cognizing how you cognize', but of course, this is too ugly and awkward to actually use. I'll stick with the easier phrase, but please keep in mind, I'm using 'knowledge' the way psychologists frequently do, in a way that implies neither justification, truth, nor belief. Intuition thus understood is a capacity that delivers judgments in a way that is automatic and, more importantly, doesn't involve an introspectible train of reasoning.[4] Intuition will include perceptual capacities as well as so-called 'System 1' capacities.

2. Perception versus Perceptual Experience

I will suppose that all introspectible states have a phenomenology, at least in the minimal sense that there's something it's like to be in them.[5] There's something that it's like to (consciously) believe that p, and that's different from what it's like to believe that $\sim p$. But there isn't *much* that it's like. Beliefs and the like don't have a rich phenomenology, and they don't have a sensory phenomenology, but if phenomenology is understood merely in terms of what-it's-like-ness and not in terms of rich qualitative character, then it seems quite plausible to me—insofar as I understand the phrase 'what it's like'—that purely cognitive conscious states have an associated phenomenology. I'll call this a 'bland' phenomenology to distinguish it from the rich phenomenology of sensory experience.

If this is right, if perceptual judgments have even a bland phenomenology, then perceptual judgment affects experience. But we may well not want to count that as affecting *perceptual experience* in any interesting sense.

Suppose, for example, that color inversion without doxastic error is possible:[6] you and I have the opposite color sensations, but we both form in response to these sensations the correct belief that the surface in front of us is red. Presumably, what it's like for me to form the perceptual belief that the surface is red is the same as what it's like for you. You and I have the same bland phenomenology but different rich phenomenology. However, if we found just the right pair of stimuli (getting the exact right shades of red and green, for example), we would have the same rich phenomenology but different bland phenomenology.

Consider another example, although it is less obviously perceptual: you and I can both visually distinguish mice from shrews when they're right next to each other. Yet the things you judge to be mice I judge to be shrews, and vice versa. Thus we can have the same rich phenomenology and different bland phenomenology (when we're both

---

[4] I take 'judgment' and 'belief' to be pretty much equivalent, though the former term seems to me to better connote occurrent tokening, while the latter term is often used to describe dispositional or standing states of the cognizer.

[5] This, of course, is controversial. See Bayne and Montague (2011a) for an overview.

[6] Some theorists who endorse externalist accounts of phenomenal character (Dretske 1995; Hill 2009; Tye 2000) will claim that *systematic* inversion without error is possible, on the grounds that the sensations are individuated by their contents, which are determined by the features of external objects. Thus the same thing couldn't *always* look, say, red to me and green to you. Any externalist theory worth taking seriously, however, must allow for the possibility of misrepresentation and thus must allow for the possibility of one-off inversion without error, which is all the current discussion requires. In any case, I invoke inversion here simply to illustrate the difference between rich and bland phenomenology; it doesn't even have to be possible to serve that purpose.

looking at a mouse) or the same bland phenomenology and different rich phenomenology (when I'm looking at a shrew and you're looking at a mouse).

It is not only perceptual *beliefs* that have bland phenomenology. Even if I am so diffident about my color perception abilities or my mouse-detecting abilities that I'm withholding belief, perception will make it *seem* (i.e., *look*, i.e., *appear*) to me as if there's a mouse or a green patch present. If you and I are highly skeptical but are looking at green and red patches respectively, we will again have the same rich phenomenology but different bland phenomenology; even though we are both withholding belief, my patch looks green to me and yours looks red to you, and that makes for a bland phenomenological difference, in contrast with our rich phenomenology, which is the same. The same is true in the case where we are both looking at a mouse, which looks to one of us like a mouse and to the other like a shrew, even though we are both withholding belief.

'Seem' and 'appear', as well as the modality-specific verbs, like 'look' and 'sound', are famously polysemous; the terms all have (among others) a phenomenal sense (according to which, to say that x looks F is to describe the character of one's x-experience), a comparative sense (where x looks F just in case x looks the way F things normally or characteristically look), an epistemic sense (there's reason to believe that x is F), and a hedging use (I'm not completely sure that x is F). Importantly for the present discussion, they also function to attribute certain mental states. They do so ambiguously, however, for they can either refer to the states with bland phenomenology or the states with rich phenomenology. In the color inversion case, for example, things look in one sense the same to us, but they look in another sense different.[7] In what follows, I'll use 'looks', 'appears', 'seems', and the rest (normally the latter) only to pick out the states with bland phenomenology.

The states here with the rich phenomenology are clearly and intrinsically perceptual: they have a spatiotemporal character and are highly modality-specific. Visual experiences, for example, have a distinctive phenomenology that is strikingly different from that of tactile experiences, even when they're experiences of the same property (e.g., *squareness*). There is no serious doubt that these states count as perceptual experiences. The states with the bland phenomenology, on the other hand, have neither spatiotemporal character nor modality-specificity. I will claim that some states with bland phenomenology should count as genuinely perceptual as well, though this clearly cannot be in virtue of their intrinsic character, since the intrinsic character doesn't have any distinguishing marks that set a state off as, e.g., visual, rather than auditory, or even inferential. The visual belief that p is not intrinsically or phenomenally different from the auditory belief that p. The same thing strikes me as true regarding the bland seeming states just described: there is nothing *phenomenally* visual about the state you and I share when the single patch looks red to us both.

This is not to deny that perceptual seemings or judgments might have a kind of phenomenology that distinguishes them from some other mental states; they might have a feel of 'forcefulness' that some beliefs—e.g., voluntary beliefs, if there are

[7] Lyons (2005a).

such things—lack. To the extent that this forcefulness provides perceptual states with anything approaching rich phenomenology, however, it is quite unlike the rich phenomenology just discussed, for it is unconnected to the contents of those judgments or seemings. Whatever presentational or assertoric feel or forcefulness these perceptual states have, it is common to them all (even if varying in intensity), irrespective of content or sense modality, and it's shared by nonperceptual seemings and judgments as well. The rich phenomenology of visual states, however, is very different.

So then, what does make a state with bland phenomenology a perceptual state? A plausible answer is that what is distinctively perceptual here is the nature of the process(es) by which that state comes about.[8] A belief or seeming is a perceptual belief or seeming just in case it results directly from a perceptual process, or perceptual capacity, or perceptual module.[9] The processes that produce perceptual judgments are fast, effortless, automatic processes whose operations are triggered by the activity of sense transducers. They are more or less 'modular', in Fodor's sense;[10] most importantly, they are relatively resistant to the influence of the beliefs and goals of the larger organism, and they operate in a way that, though involving a great deal of subpersonal inference, hides this fact from introspection: their outputs are not the result of an introspectible train of reasoning.

There is therefore an important asymmetry between the rich states and the bland states. What makes a rich state a perceptual state is presumably its intrinsic character; what makes a bland state a perceptual state, however, is its causal history. Another important difference is closely related: the states with rich phenomenology are essentially phenomenological, while the states with bland phenomenology are only contingently so. Two zombies, for example, could not undergo the color inversion described above. Perceptual beliefs, on the other hand, could clearly be unconscious, and the same, I think, is true of seemings, even though these standard terms tend to suggest otherwise. I could be unconsciously perceiving the Müller-Lyer lines; if my visual system works normally even in these conditions, the one line would still look longer than the other, whether or not I (unconsciously) believed so. (This will become more plausible in Section 3, when I elaborate on the nature of these seemings.)

Thus I'll use the term 'perceptual experience' in a narrow way, to include the states with rich phenomenology but not the states with bland phenomenology. Perceptual beliefs and seemings are perceptual states in that they have a perceptual etiology; they're just not perceptual experiences in any robust sense of 'experience'. But mustn't perceptual seemings be experiences if they're conscious states that aren't beliefs? I'm inclined to answer yes, these bland states are experiences—at least in the sense that they have some, albeit bland, phenomenology—and yes, they're perceptual, but to simultaneously insist that they're not really *perceptual experiences* in any ordinary or reasonably interesting sense of the term, largely because—unlike

---

[8] Lyons (2005a) and (2009).

[9] I am not assuming that these are equivalent; however, they turn out to be roughly coextensive (close enough, at least, for present purposes): a belief that comes out of a perceptual module is one that results from a perceptual capacity, and is one that results from a perceptual process.

[10] Fodor (1983).

perceptual experiences proper—what makes them experiences (they're conscious but not beliefs) has nothing to do with what makes them perceptual (their causal history). So they're perceptual, and they're experiences, but they aren't perceptual experiences. Now in part this is a terminological stipulation, but it is also a substantive position: there's an important difference between those states that count as perceptual in virtue of their experiential aspects and those that count as experiential in virtue of their etiology. Despite superficial appearances, however, it is not an incoherent position.

The high-level content view of perception holds that perception doesn't only represent low-level properties like shape, color, surface orientation, and the like, but also high-level properties, which could include kind properties, historical properties, semantic properties, and perhaps others.[11] High-levelists sometimes say that high-level properties are represented in perceptual *experience*. If this is simply the view that high-level properties are represented by conscious perceptual *states*, including perceptual beliefs and seemings, then I concur (some reasons for this will be given below). However, if it's the view that high-level properties are represented by perceptual experiences in the current sense of states with rich phenomenological character, then I object. Sometimes differences in perceptual judgment, e.g., between experts and novices, are accompanied by differences in rich phenomenology, but the most obvious cases of this are cases where the rich experiential difference is only causally linked to the high-level (i.e., seeming or judgment) difference, rather than constitutive of it. Expert ornithologists and anthropologists and the like probably attend to different features of distal stimuli, which might produce a difference in rich phenomenology. Yet even if I were to accidentally attend in just this way, and thus have the same rich phenomenology as an expert, I would still have no clue that the thing I was looking at was, say, part of a femur of *P. boisei*, or a 1-year-old female pileated woodpecker. Thus, I would neither perceptually judge nor would it perceptually seem to me that there's a *P. boisei* femur, or a pileated woodpecker, in front of me.

So is the view I'm articulating a high-level view or not? It is a high-level view about the contents of perception, but not a high-level view about the contents of perceptual *experience*, understood the way I'm understanding 'perceptual experience' here. I'm not sure how high-levelists typically understand the term, and maybe this is roughly what they've had in mind all along.[12] One important difference between my view and standard versions of high-levelism[13] is that mine is not, and couldn't very well be, defended on phenomenological grounds. There's nothing distinctively perceptual about the (bland) phenomenology of high-level perceptual states. There is an argument

---

[11] Bayne (2009); S. Siegel (2006) and (2010).

[12] In the past (Lyons 2005b), I have taken the current view to conflict at least with Siegel's version of the high-level view, in part because her argument for high-levelism crucially involves denying that the overall phenomenological difference between the expert and the novice is due to a difference in cognitive phenomenology, where she assumes that the only states with the relevant phenomenology would have to be beliefs (for all intents and purposes) or mere entertaining of propositions. Seemings, as here described, do not seem to be on her radar. Indrek Reiland presses this objection to her in greater detail in his (2014). It is possible, however, that she means for seemings to be counted as experiential, despite their having only a bland phenomenology. If so, then her neglect of seemings is benign, and our views are compatible.

[13] e.g. S. Siegel (2010).

for thinking these states are perceptual, but it can only be an empirical argument concerning the cognitive mechanisms involved in the production of these states.

3. Perception and Intuition

I've insisted that what makes a certain judgment a perceptual judgment is the nature of the process that gives rise to it, not its phenomenology. The processes that give rise to perception are fast, effortless, automatic, more or less modular processes, triggered by sense transducers. They are highly encapsulated and inferentially opaque. The 'more or less' and 'highly' hedges are quite deliberate here. If in order to count as modular, a process needs to satisfy all of Fodor's nine diagnostic features of modules (speed, shallowness, innateness, domain specificity, mandatory operation, encapsulation, characteristic breakdown, fixed neural architecture, introspective opacity), or if these nine are interpreted in a very strict way, then I don't want to claim that perceptual processes/systems are modular.[14] I especially don't want to make any claims about innateness, or (as this would beg soon-to-be-central questions) shallowness.

Being inferentially opaque and being highly encapsulated are essential to my view; they require elaboration and qualification. To say that a system is informationally encapsulated (aka 'cognitively impenetrable') is to say that it does not take the beliefs, desires, expectations, or other 'cognitive' states of the larger organism as inputs. When I say that perceptual systems are 'highly' encapsulated, I mean that perception is largely, even if not strictly, cognitively impenetrable. The empirical and theoretical debate about informational encapsulation and cognitive penetration centers on the question of whether an extremely rigid version of the encapsulation hypothesis is true.[15] Whatever the outcome of this debate, we can't lose sight of the striking fact that perception is *highly* encapsulated. It is uncontroversial that we can't just see whatever we want, that imagination has little if any effect on perceptual experience, that perception quite frequently violates our antecedent expectations, etc. This explains the persistence of known illusion: I know the stick in the water is straight, but it continues to look bent; I am firmly convinced that the lines of the Müller-Lyer illusion are the same length, but one of them looks longer. For very good reasons, there are heated debates in philosophy and the cognitive sciences about whether perception is ever penetrated by cognition. But the mere fact that this is a live debate is a testament to how generally resistant (even if not impervious) to penetration

---

[14] Fodor (1983). The term 'module' has a complicated history in philosophy and in cognitive science. In some circles, it is only used to pick out systems that satisfy these nine constraints, all read quite restrictively. In other circles (e.g. Carruthers 2006; Lyons 2015b), it is used quite broadly to apply to any functionally independent cognitive system or subsystem. In this latter sense, it is an open question whether a particular module is 'modular', where this latter term could be used in the restrictive sense of satisfying all those nine criteria or in the somewhat relaxed sense I am employing here in the text. Fodor's early work on the subject allowed that these features could come in degrees, but as he defended his view (Fodor 1988 and 2000), the criteria became stricter and more rigid, resulting in a less plausible theory about the mind. The more demanding criteria for modularity are likely never satisfied, but this should not obscure the genuine insight of Fodor's original view, which goes beyond mere functional independence and claims that most of the nine features are manifested to an interesting extent in a number of cognitive systems. I discuss this further in Lyons (2015b).

[15] Lyons (2015b); Macpherson (2012); Pylyshyn (2003); Athanassios (2009); Stokes (2014).

perception is. We can't simply see whatever we want or fear or expect, and this is a central and foundational fact about perception. This is what is meant by claiming that the processes are highly encapsulated.

When I say that they are inferentially opaque, I mean that the outputs of the perceptual systems are, as BonJour calls them, 'cognitively spontaneous': not the result of an introspectible train of reasoning.[16] Although perception is certainly a kind of Helmholtzian inference, it doesn't introspectively seem to be. We are often unaware of either the cues we are relying on or the processing that transforms these cues into higher-level information. Some cues, as in auditory localization, are simply unconscious. Other cues, as in visual perception of depth or 3-D shape, are conscious, but their significance for perceptual processing tends to be unknown except by artists and perceptual psychologists. Most untutored adults (and certainly children) do not know what aerial perspective is, for example, or how it serves as a cue to distance; things just look far away, and they're not sure why.

The end result of perception being modularized in this way is that we perceivers find ourselves with specialized subpersonal mechanisms that perform tasks for us that we are usually not capable of performing for ourselves. Even if we had at our disposal and were capable of taking in all the information that serves as input to our perceptual modules, we would not be able to infer from all this what kind of distal layout was being presented to us. We would certainly not be able to do it in real time, but probably not ever, since we don't generally appreciate the significance of the various cues.[17]

In other work I used the term 'identifications' to refer to the high-level, conceptual content, outputs of modular perceptual processes.[18] They have bland phenomenology when conscious, the rich phenomenology being attached to the lower level states. These outputs represent objects as standing in various relations to each other, having certain properties, and belonging to certain categories. Exactly which relations, properties, and categories is a difficult empirical question. These high-level outputs are typically beliefs. Sometimes, however, as when we believe appearances are illusory, we don't form judgments, but things continue to look, or seem, or appear a way that corresponds to the judgment we would have unreflectively made. These identifications are mere appearances/seemings/looks.[19]

Perceptual identifications are a species of a more inclusive genus. Intuition, again, is a capacity to 'know without knowing how you know'. This capacity (or, more

---

[16] BonJour (1978).

[17] The kinds of inferences embodied by such modular processes are of a sort that would not normally confer justification if consciously undertaken at the person level. See Fodor (1983); Lyons (2009) and (2016).

[18] Lyons (2005) and (2009).

[19] I am trying to remain neutral here on the relation between perceptual judgments and perceptual seemings. Though judgment and seeming are clearly distinct types, nothing I have claimed here is incompatible with their being token identical. In fact, I have argued elsewhere (Lyons 2009) that in the normal case, where I accept seemings at face value, the seeming *is* the belief: the perceptual system delivers a representation that *p*, and this representation takes on a functional role appropriate to belief: it is allowed as a premise in theoretical and practical deliberation etc. In other cases, however, that very same representation might take on a more restrained functional role, making it a mere seeming. Nothing in this paper will hinge on this perhaps idiosyncratic view.

likely, cluster of capacities) is subserved by so-called 'System 1' processes: they are fast, automatic, effortless, and more or less modular.[20] They needn't be triggered by the operation of sense transducers and are often more sensitive to the agent's occurrent beliefs than perceptual systems are, but otherwise are quite similar to perception. There is reason to think that we have intuitive processes for making probability estimates, predicting stock performance, evaluating the validity of an argument, assessing the desirability of various bets, and so on.[21]

Some of these processes take beliefs as inputs; some don't. Because I am interested in perception and perception-like capacities, I will focus on the latter. It is frequently difficult to tell, however, whether or not a given process is taking beliefs as inputs, in part because it is difficult to precisely specify the content of the output. A given process, for instance, might be delivering 'x is a qualified candidate' on the basis of beliefs about x's work experience, or it might be delivering 'a candidate with x's work experience is qualified' without taking any beliefs as input.

I will use the term 'intuition' broadly to include any of these fast, automatic, modular processes, when they're not taking beliefs as inputs. So it includes perception, but also a priori intuition, as well as capacities for the non-inferential formation of empirical judgments, provided that all of these result (as seems plausible) from the kinds of cognitive systems described above. 'Intuitions' will refer to the high-level, conceptual content outputs of these systems. Some but not all of these will be beliefs; one can have the intuition that p without believing that p. Thus, there are intuitive seemings as well as intuitive judgments, although I doubt that there is anything in intuition that corresponds to perceptual *experience* in the narrow way I'm understanding it here. The persistence of cognitive illusions is similar to, though sometimes less robust than, the persistence of perceptual illusions. Even though I understand framing effects, there is still a part of me that would rather suffer a disease with a 90-percent survival rate than one with a 10-percent mortality rate; even though I know about the conjunction rule for probabilities, I'm still somewhat tempted to think that Linda is more likely to be a feminist bank teller than simply a bank teller.

In subsuming perception under intuition, I am claiming that perception involves a kind of knowing without knowing how you know. But is this right? The perceptual experience, after all, seems to provide evidence in support of the perceptual judgment. I'm inclined to think of this as an 'illusion of evidence', and like other illusions, I am subject to it myself, even though theoretical considerations convince me to the contrary. Experiences *appear* to provide evidence for perceptual judgments, but this appearance is probably the result of something like the hindsight bias in social psychology: once you know what the outcome was, that outcome seems to be predictable from the prior data, even if it wasn't at all predictable at the time.[22] In the perceptual case, we 'know the outcome' by knowing which perceptual identification matches up with the experience, and so the content of the identification seems to be easily derived from the perceptual experience. But this is only because we are so good at moving from the experience to the identification, and we are only good at it

---

[20] Evans (2003); Stanovich and West (2000).
[21] See Kahneman (2011) for a broad overview. [22] Fischhoff (1975).

because we have special machinery for doing so. As discussed above, if the novice were to have the expert's visual experience of a pileated woodpecker, she would have no idea what kind of bird she was seeing. Thus, there may well be less evidence available for perceptual judgment than it initially would seem.[23]

4. Two Epistemologies of Intuitive Judgment

The epistemologist's question from Section 1 was whether some beliefs about evaluative properties have an epistemic status similar to that of perception. This is only an interesting question on the assumption of an epistemology that grants some kind of special, or at least interesting, status to perception. (On coherentism, for example, all beliefs have the same—inferential—status, so the answer to the epistemologist's question is trivial.)

It is illustrative to compare a standard internalist version of modest foundationalism with the externalist version I prefer. I won't try here to argue for or against either view. Both are modest foundationalist views in that they hold that beliefs about the external world can be epistemologically basic—i.e., can be (prima facie) justified even in the absence of evidential support from other beliefs.

On the externalist view, the outputs of the more or less modular systems described above—when those modules are not taking beliefs as inputs—are basic and therefore immediately justified, without needing support from other beliefs. I want to insist on a reliabilist component as well, so that the intuitive processes yield justification only if reliable. Contrast this with an internalist view that holds that its seeming to S as if p is sufficient to give S prima facie justification to believe that p.[24]

Both views have minimal cognitive and metacognitive requirements for justification. So, unlike coherentist and classical foundationalist theories, these don't require the agent to distinguish her beliefs from the reality they purport to describe or to have justified metabeliefs about the reliability of her perceptual processes. Both thereby allow animals and small children to have justified beliefs.

The externalist view, however, is more demanding than the internalist view in several respects. First, there are fewer intuitions in the present sense than there are seemings as the internalist theory views them.[25] All (conscious) intuitions are

---

[23] Some epistemologists reserve an evidential role for perceptual seemings but deny an evidential role for perceptual experiences (Tucker 2010; Brogaard 2014; Conee 2013). I argue against the first conjunct in Lyons (2009) but I won't object to it for the present purposes, since this would still put perceptual belief on the same evidential footing as apriori intuition, which is generally thought to involve intuitive seemings that are closely analogous to perceptual seemings.

[24] See Lyons (2009) for the externalist view. See Chudnoff (2013); Huemer (2001) and (2007); Pollock (1986); Pryor (2000); and Tucker (2010) for defenses of the internalist view.

[25] I will use 'seeming' here the way this internalist view uses it, for a conscious mental state that has conceptual and propositional content and has assertoric force but that is nondoxastic. As such, it is intensionally and extensionally distinct from 'intuition', as I've been using it. In addition to the differences already mentioned, I would want to allow for the possibility of unconscious intuitions, while I doubt the internalist would think unconscious seemings were intelligible. I am sometimes (e.g. Lyons 2015a) inclined to think that externalists should instead co-opt the term 'seeming' for our own purposes, treating it as equivalent to 'intuition' and claiming that the internalists are simply wrong about the individuation criteria, but I won't press that here.

seemings, though not all seemings are intuitions; intuitions need to have the right causal history, while seemings don't. Further, not all intuitive beliefs are going to be the result of a reliable process, so they won't all be prima facie justified. Those who are impressed by the claims of epistemic irrationality coming out of the heuristics and biases tradition in social psychology[26] may welcome this reliabilist requirement. What's wrong with these ill-formed judgments we naturally and intuitively make is not that they are formed in the absence of the relevant metabeliefs (i.e., that they were nonbasic and in need of further inferential support, which they then failed to receive), but that they result from unreliable heuristics. They might have been justified even without these higher order beliefs, if only they'd been the result of a better (i.e., more reliable) heuristic.

Higher order introspective knowledge about the nature of our intuitions is harder to come by on the externalist view than on the internalist view. Reliability, of course, is not something one can determine by introspection. But neither is whether a given spontaneous judgment is strictly speaking intuitive, as this is a matter of causal history. The point concerns not just beliefs or seemings that have popped into one's head from nowhere (though the internalist and externalist views will classify these differently), but it is also difficult to determine introspectively whether a given judgment/seeming is perceptual/intuitive or post-perceptual/intuitive. When I hear the rain hitting my roof, I immediately form the belief that the seats in my jeep are getting wet, without consciously forming the beliefs that the top is down, or that it's raining, or that if the top is down and it's raining then the seats are getting wet. The belief that the seats are getting wet is neither perceptual nor basic. It is psychologically immediate, but it is clear that it depends causally and epistemically on these other beliefs.[27] Psychological immediacy doesn't indicate intuitive status.

This bad news about higher order knowledge on the externalist view is balanced by good news: although we can't rely very heavily on introspection to reveal the epistemic status of a given belief, introspection is no longer our only tool for doing so. We can, on the externalist view, bring the full power of empirical cognitive science to bear on these questions. Introspection is notoriously unreliable and notoriously subjective, and if you and I have a different introspective sense of the contents of our seeming states, we're pretty much at an impasse, for it's not at all clear how to adjudicate such a disagreement. But there is a feasible (even if far from trivial) empirical route to settling corresponding questions and disagreements about the contents of intuitions.

5. Do We Form Intuitive, Perception-Like Judgments about Evaluative Properties?

Do we perceive evaluative properties? This remains a difficult question to answer, for reasons considered above. First, it is at least three different questions: the metaphysician's, the cognitive scientist's, and the epistemologist's question. Second, even if we

---

[26] e.g., Gilovich, Griffin, and Kahneman (2002); Tversky and Kahneman (1974).
[27] Lyons (2014).

focus on, say, the cognitive scientist's question, what we are left with might be the question whether we have perceptual *states* that represent evaluative properties, or it might be the question whether we have perceptual *experiences* of evaluative properties. Although I'm not sure how to go about answering this last question, I have suggested that the answer to this second-to-last question is an empirical question, since it depends on facts about the etiologies of the states in question. Because it's empirical, I can't give it a definitive answer here. But there are general reasons to be optimistic about a positive answer to it, and thus reasons to be optimistic about the outlook for evaluative perception (i.e., for the perception of evaluative properties).

The distinction between perception and perceptual experience is good news for evaluative perception, because such properties don't seem, pretheoretically, to be objects of perceptual experience. But this is no obstacle to them being objects of perception, if perception includes more than perceptual experience. In general, anything that is good news for a high-level view about the contents of perception is good news for evaluative perception, and the distinction between perception and perceptual experience, as drawn above, is good news for high-levelism. Similarly, if intuition is a more inclusive category than perception, but one that has an importantly similar psychological status and carries the same epistemic benefits, then some evaluative judgments are that much more likely to enjoy the special epistemic status of perception.

It is no surprise, for instance, that Hume's views about the perception of causation and about the perception of virtue and vice were similarly restrictive:

When we look about us towards external objects, and consider the operation of causes, we are never able, in a single instance, to discover any power or necessary connexion; any quality, which binds the effect to the cause, and renders the one an infallible consequence of the other. We only find, that the one does actually, in fact, follow the other. The impulse of one billiard ball is attended with motion in the second. This is the whole that appears to the outward senses.[28]

Take any action allow'd to be vicious: Wilful murder, for instance. Examine it in all lights, and see if you can find that matter of fact, or real existence, which you call vice. In which-ever way you take it, you find only certain passions, motives, volitions and thoughts. There is no other matter of fact in the case. The vice entirely escapes you, as long as you consider the object. You never can find it, till you turn your reflexion into your own breast.[29]

Hume's reasoning here is tempting, but it will be thought question-begging by anyone who holds that we perceive causal relations or moral properties, for one could simply insist that yes, we do perceive cause, and so the conjunction of the motions of the two balls is simply not 'the whole that appears to the outward senses'. Similarly for 'matters of fact' regarding vice.[30]

Two different factors contribute to the initial plausibility here. One is that Hume seems to assume that the alternative view would have to be committed to the perception of highly superordinate/determinate, rather than subordinate/determinable

---

[28] Hume (1748/1975), 63.   [29] Hume (1739/1975), 468–9.
[30] Hume's second quote here obviously isn't concerned with *perception* of moral properties, but if it's true that the only matter of fact related to vice that we can find *even in conception* is our own emotional reaction, then this is even more obviously true regarding perception.

properties, e.g., that it would be perception of *vice*, rather than *selfishness*; *power*, rather than *kicking*. Second, Hume seems to equate perception with perceptual experience, so that its contents would have to be limited to spatiotemporal properties that have distinctive, modality-specific phenomenology.

Even if Hume is right that we don't perceive or intuit superordinate properties, we might still perceive or intuit subordinate properties. Thus, while it seems right that we don't perceive causes as such, it also seems that we do perceive certain determinate types of cause as such. For example, I can see that x is kicking y, or I can feel that z is burning me. Similarly, even if it's implausible that we perceive the wrongness of burning the cat, we might instead perceive the sadism, from which we could infer wrongness. It is often the case that we perceive relatively subordinate categories without perceiving the superordinate ones. Thus, the object looks like a chair to me, not like furniture; the surface doesn't look colored, but rather looks red; this looks like an insect without looking like an animal; and so on. The superordinate property is easily and quickly inferred from the subordinate one, but that's now inference and not perception or intuition. These claims are all the more plausible in the context of the view that what an intuition is, is an output of a modular process. There's no reason to think that perceptual modules couldn't be aimed at a fairly high level of specificity, representing their objects at relatively subordinate levels, without also or instead representing them at superordinate levels.

In any case, there are no a priori constraints concerning at what level of generality the modules would have to couch their outputs; this increases the number of ways in which intuition might represent evaluative properties.

We have already seen how Hume's equating perception with perceptual experience puts evaluative perception at an unfair disadvantage. Perception is more inclusive than perceptual experience, and intuition is more inclusive than perception. So even if evaluative or other high-level properties are not plausibly represented in perceptual experience, it is more plausible that they are represented in perception, and even more plausible that they are represented in intuition.

Insofar as our concerns are epistemological, we get as much out of the claim that a certain property is intuitable as we would out of the claim that it is perceptible; and by focusing on intuition rather than perception, we further divest ourselves of a significant but unnecessary argumentative burden. There are a number of processes whose status as perceptual is controversial, but whose status as intuitive is unproblematic. Fodor famously classified language comprehension as a perceptual capacity.[31] Now, speech perception (forming judgments of the form 'S said "it's raining"') is obviously perceptual, but Fodor meant judgments of the form 'S said *that* it's raining'. It's not clear what Fodor means by calling these latter judgments perceptual, but there's no question that they're intuitive. Similarly, chess experts are sometimes said to 'see' that the opponent has certain weaknesses, etc.[32] We can be fairly sure that these judgments are intuitive, whether they are perceptual or not. Turning to the evaluative domains, mind reading—third-person mental state attribution—may or may not be perceptual, but again, the judgments are uncontroversially intuitive. This last case is

---

[31] Fodor (1983). [32] e.g., Chase and Simon (1973).

especially important for the present purposes, for it is plausible that the mindreading systems deliver intuitions involving *cruelty*, *sadism*, *generosity*, *bravery*, *cowardice*, *wisdom*, *knowledge*, and other 'thick' evaluative concepts.[33]

Then there are intuitive processes that no one would think are perceptual but which seem to yield evaluative judgments. There is evidence that we have intuitions about how valuable this stock is, how qualified this current or potential employee is, whether a particular argument is cogent, which of two bets is better, among others.[34] If we care for epistemological reasons about the perception of evaluative properties, and if the epistemology of intuition mirrors that of perception, the fan of evaluative perception is well advised to broaden the view to include intuition as well.

6. Beliefs and Basing

The special epistemic status of intuitive judgments is a matter of these judgments being epistemologically basic, but this is only true in cases where the relevant systems are not taking beliefs as inputs. Nonperceptual intuition, however, is far more sensitive to background beliefs than perception. This poses two related threats to the current project. First, if the influence of beliefs is rampant, then the processes in question cease to be significantly modular, and their outputs cease to count as intuitions. Second, if these processes are taking beliefs as inputs, then their outputs aren't epistemologically basic.

Even if nonperceptual intuition is more cognitively penetrable than perception, cognitive illusions tend to persist in much the same way that perceptual illusions do, and this shows that the relevant processes have limited access to the cognitive states of the larger organism. This is enough for the level of modularity I require. The second challenge requires a lengthier and more complicated response. In particular, it requires clarification of what's meant by claiming that a system is taking beliefs as inputs. I will claim that the kind of taking-as-inputs involved in cognitive penetration is different from the kind of taking-as-inputs involved in inference.

There are independent reasons for thinking that the cognitive penetration of perception does not thereby render perception epistemically inferential. Suppose I'm hiking in the woods and believe for terrible reasons (or none at all) that there are a lot of snakes nearby.[35] (Fill in the psychological details in whatever way is needed to ensure that it's a genuine case of cognitive penetration.) Suppose further that this unjustified belief penetrates perception in one of two ways. It might

(a) cause me to generate a lot of false positives, mistaking sticks and roots for snakes,

or it might

---

[33] Although there has been a fair amount of recent discussion about the modularity of our mind reading capacities (e.g., Carruthers 2006; Leslie 2005; Prinz 2006), there has been, to my knowledge, little discussion analogous to the high-levelism debate regarding the contents of perception. My claim about *cruelty* and the like expresses my hunch that high-levelism about mind reading may well turn out to be correct.

[34] Shefrin (2007); Reb et al. (2013); De Neys (2012); Turnbull et al. (2005) respectively.

[35] Lyons (2011).

(b) make me better at spotting the snakes that are actually in my environment, without the false positives.

The contrast is important, because while case (a) is one where cognitive penetration reduces perceptual justification, case (b) is not; my resulting perceptual beliefs are justified, *even though the penetrating belief was completely unjustified*. This latter feature, however, is a mark of nonevidential influence of belief. Nothing that is unjustified can confer evidence. But here, in case (b), there are beliefs that I wouldn't have had, had I not believed that the woods around me were full of snakes. So my perceptual beliefs causally depend on this unjustified belief, but since they're justified anyway, they must not depend *evidentially* on that belief.

But how do we make sense of this? Here's a proposal: in these sorts of nonevidential cases, the belief is affecting processing but is not doing so *qua* belief. The belief that p is not being used by the receiving system as a premise; the fear that p or a vivid conception that p would have the same or similar result. That is, the propositional attitude of believing that p influences processing within the system, but it does so in virtue of the *content* of that attitude and not in virtue of the attitude *type* (e.g., belief, desire, fear). There are various mechanisms by which this might happen: perhaps specific high-level object templates (e.g., snake templates) are activated in advance of sensory activity. Those who prefer a Bayesian framework could view this sort of cognitive penetration as working by modifying priors (e.g., increasing the prior for the hypothesis that the current object is a snake). The latter sounds somehow more evidence-involving, but there's actually no conflict between these two proposals; the template account is one possible implementation of the prior raising account. Priors can get raised for all kinds of reasons, evidence being just one of them, with fear, interest, and idle curiosity being others. We will of course eventually want to know the mechanism by which real cases of cognitive penetration occur, but this won't help us much in settling the current worries. Whether a system is using a belief qua belief is not determined by the mechanism, but by counterfactuals about what effects might have been had by other propositional attitudes with the same content.

In any case, and independent of my current proposal to reconcile basic beliefs with cognitive penetration, we will all need some way to understand taking beliefs as inputs while not taking them *qua beliefs* as inputs. My first-order belief that p is an input to the introspective process whereby I come to believe that I believe that p, but this higher order belief does not depend for its justification on the first order belief's being justified. Anyone who wants to hold that introspective beliefs are epistemologically basic will need some solution to this problem. If it's better than the one I've just sketched, I would be happy to try to co-opt that solution instead of the one I've just offered, to explain how cognitively penetrated beliefs might remain basic.

Some of the more common doxastic influences on intuition seem to leave the intuitions basic, on the view just sketched. When evaluating the quality of a college professor, your intuition is affected by your beliefs about the instructor's gender.[36] In the moral realm, your judgments are influenced by (your knowledge that there are)

---

[36] MacNell, Driscoll, and Hunt (2015).

dirty pizza boxes nearby.[37] In these cases, it is plausible that these beliefs are having their effects without functioning as beliefs, in which case, they don't threaten the intuitive status of these judgments, and the penetrating beliefs' justificatory status doesn't affect the justificatory status of the intuitions. In the latter case, especially, it is likely that verbally convincing the subject that there are dirty pizza boxes nearby would have much less of an effect on her moral judgments than would presenting her with what she knew to be holographic images of dirty pizza boxes (in fact, the literature generally takes the effect to be one of the *emotion* of disgust on moral judgment). If so, then it is a particular vivid representation of dirty pizza boxes that is doing the work, not a belief per se.

Nonperceptual intuition is more sensitive to the agent's other beliefs than perception is. Some of this is because these intuitive processes are central, rather than peripheral, stimulus-driven processes. These processes may therefore be designed to take beliefs qua beliefs as inputs. Some of this sensitivity, however, is likely the result of beliefs influencing processing in a way that is independent of attitude type. That is, nonperceptual intuitive processes may simply be more cognitively penetrable than perceptual ones.

Obviously I have made a number of empirical assumptions here, in particular about what counterfactuals are true in cases of cognitive penetration of intuition. These assumptions might turn out not to be true. As with any empirically vulnerable work in philosophy, were these assumptions to prove false, I would have the options of (i) biting the bullet and taking it as a discovery—in this case, claiming that the beliefs in question aren't epistemologically basic after all, (ii) tweaking or abandoning my theory, or (iii) trying to find a way to argue that my theory is actually compatible with the empirical finding after all, despite initial appearances to the contrary. Clearly, choosing among these is impossible in the absence of a specific problematic empirical finding.

7. Epistemology, Again

At the very beginning of this paper, I set aside the metaphysician's question to address the cognitive scientist's and the epistemologist's questions, which I claimed were closely related to each other but relatively independent of the first. But then in Section 4, I introduced a reliabilist epistemology. It was one of two options on the table, but it was the more demanding option, so it would be especially nice if the reliabilist epistemology can make room for evaluative perception. But how can the metaphysics not matter in the context of reliabilism? If there aren't any evaluative properties, then judgments attributing them won't be true, and they won't be reliably formed.

This may pose a problem for indicator reliabilism, but according to *process reliabilism* (the kind of reliabilism I had in mind above), it's the reliability of the process that determines justification. The more nonevaluative judgments a given process is responsible for, the less it matters for the reliability of that process whether

[37] Schnall et al. (2008).

realism about the relevant evaluative property is true. For example, I suggested above that moral epistemology might get a foothold from thick ethical judgments that are basically justified in virtue of resulting from a modular mind-reading capacity. If so, then the processes responsible for our intuitions about lewdness, rudeness, and the like are the same processes responsible for our intuitions about sadness, shyness, and the like, and there is little reason why these processes couldn't feasibly be reliable, even if there aren't really any evaluative properties. Even if this means that there's no such thing as rudeness, and even if this means that judgments attributing rudeness are therefore false, the mind-reading processes might be responsible for enough other, true beliefs, that they are still reliable and still confer justification. We would need to know more about the kinds of processes involved in other sorts of evaluative intuitions to know whether the same might apply to them, but it is a promising possibility. Again, the intention here was not to argue for anything decisive regarding evaluative judgments but only to show that (and how) there might be some grounds for optimism.

In all, I take the case for evaluative perception (or intuition, at least) to be a rather hopeful one. There is already good empirical reason to think we have intuitions about several evaluative properties (e.g., argument cogency, strength of candidates, values of bets), and I predict that empirical data will significantly expand this list by revealing that we have intuitive mind-reading capacities that deliver judgments about thick ethical properties. Although it may be unlikely that any of these properties are represented in perceptual *experience*, I have argued that they are more likely to be represented in perceptual seemings and judgments, and more likely still to be represented in intuition. This has much the same epistemological significance as the claim that we can perceive evaluative properties, since, on the most plausible views that accord perception a distinctive epistemic status, intuition, as understood here, shares it.[38]

---

[38] Earlier versions of this paper were presented at the Evaluative Perception: Aesthetic, Ethical, and Normative conference in Glasgow and at the Southeastern Epistemology conference in Athens, GA. Thanks to those audiences for helpful comments, especially Jon Altschul, Anna Bergqvist, Michael Bishop, Robert Cowan, Dominic Lopes, Fiona Macpherson, Kevin McCain, Dustin Stokes, and Sarah Wright.

10
On the Epistemological Significance of Value Perception

Michael Milona

0. Introduction

A recent flurry of articles and books defend the possibility of *value perception*, with a guiding thought being that the question of whether there is value perception is of significant import to *value epistemology*.[1] I examine this thought. Most of the paper focuses on what I call the *high-level theory of value perception*, an increasingly popular theory (or, rather, family of theories). At a first pass, a high-level theory says that at least some *ordinary* perceptual experiences–whereby 'ordinary' denotes the traditional five senses—can in certain instances have veridical evaluative content.[2] (We'll see below why this is called 'high-level'.) My central claim is that value epistemologists needn't take sides in difficult debates about high-level value perception; it just isn't an important epistemological question.[3] But I close the paper by noting that it may matter a great deal whether a certain other picture of value perception is true.[4] This alternative picture has it that desiderative and/or emotional experiences often involve perceptual experiences of value.[5]

---

[1] For a sampling, see Greco (2000); Johnston (2001); Oddie (2005); Döring (2007); Tenenbaum (2007); Chappell (2008); Audi (2010) and (2013); Cullison (2010); McBrayer (2010a) and (2010b); Church (2010) and (2013); Roberts (2013); Werner (2016).

[2] The reader will notice that I regularly shift between 'perception' and 'perceptual experience'. The former, of course, is factive; I can only perceive that p if it really is the case that p. There can thus only be value perception if there are values. In this paper, I simply assume there are. More specifically, I assume that if there are value-perceptual experiences, then there are value perceptions. One who disagrees can substitute 'perceptual experience' for any instance of 'perception'.

[3] Numerous philosophers hold that high-level value perception is possible. My dispute is *not* with the view itself but, rather, with its *significance* for value epistemology. (For a different way of attacking the import of high-level value perception, see Cowan 2015.) For a sampling of works that not only defend high-level value perception but also assume that the debate about high-level value perception matters for value epistemology, see Greco (2000); Audi (2010) and (2013); Cullison (2010); McBrayer (2010a); McBrayer (2010b). Matters are a bit complicated when it comes to Cullison, however (see Section 4).

[4] As far as I am concerned, a given theory counts as a theory of value perception if it posits either (i) *literal* value perceptions or (ii) value experiences that share with ordinary perceptual experiences the features that make ordinary perception such a good way to acquire knowledge. Defenders of the high-level view defend the existence of literal value perceptions.

[5] Defenses of this view include Stampe (1987); R. C. Roberts (2013); Oddie (2005); Döring (2007).

The paper begins by describing the notion of an *ambitious theory of value perception*, which plays an important dialectical role in my central argument. An ambitious theory says (roughly) that any justified belief about whether something is valuable (e.g., good, bad, right, wrong) epistemically depends on value-perceptual experiences, whatever exactly those experiences are supposed to be. In Sections 2-3, I describe the high-level theory in more detail and then explain why it is not a plausible basis for an ambitious theory. But as I go on to note, it still appears to matter quite a bit for value epistemology whether there is such a thing as high-level value perception. Appearances, however, are misleading. Reflection on how one of the alternative ways of justifying evaluative beliefs—a way that the defender of high-level value perception in particular needs to allow—relates to high-level value perception leads to the conclusion that the question of whether there is any high-level value perception is not so significant, after all.

1. Ambitious Theories

This section sketches the outlines of what I call an *ambitious theory of value perception*. The crucial point that I want to make is that even an ambitious theory should allow for some evaluative knowledge not grounded in value perception, namely what I call below *non-substantive evaluative knowledge*. Placing such a limitation not only helps to avoid certain objections, but is also natural for the theory. Let me explain.

Some philosophers have argued that theories of value perception cannot explain the full range of evaluative knowledge.[6] Consider the following remark from Simon Blackburn:[7]

Literal talk of perception runs into many problems. One is that the ethical very commonly, and given its function in guiding choice, even typically, concerns imagined or described situations, not perceived ones. We reach ethical verdicts about the behavior of described agents or actions in the light of general standards. And it is stretching things to see these general standards as perceptually formed or maintained. Do I see that ingratitude is base only on occasions when I see an example of ingratitude? How can I be sure of the generalization to examples that I did not see (I could not do that for color, for instance. Absent pillar-boxes may be a different color from present ones; only an inductive step allows us to guess at whether they are). Or, do I see the timeless connection—but how? Do I have an antenna for detecting timeless property-to-value connections?[8]

---

[6] Pekka Väyrynen suggests that defenders of perceptual views often seem to commit themselves to the bold claim that all of our evaluative knowledge is grounded in value perception, or at least the claim that no ethical knowledge is a priori. See Väyrynen (2008). Many of the 'Cornell Realists', for instance, seem to suggest that all of our evaluative knowledge is acquired by *observation*, in a way analogous to how we acquire knowledge in science. See esp. Boyd (1988). I won't engage in the lengthy exegetical task to try to pin the bold view on these thinkers, however.

[7] For a similar sentiment (although about a different theory of value perception not of immediate concern here), see Smith (1994), 22.

[8] Blackburn (1988). After listing these questions which he takes to indicate problems for the target theories, Blackburn says, 'Perhaps these questions can be brushed aside' (1988, 365). I'll point out in a moment that they clearly can be. That said, my best guess is that Blackburn is led to pose these 'challenging' questions because defenders of value perception often seem to be defending the view that *all* of our evaluative knowledge can be grounded in value perceptions.

There is a lot going on in this quote, but I simply want to highlight the thought that a perceptual view can't be squared with our knowledge of supervenience.[9] Blackburn is baffled by how we could ever (literally) perceive a supervenience relation. Do we generalize from cases, or do we (as Blackburn mockingly suggests) have an antenna for detecting eternal property-to-value connections?

The response should just be that perception is not the basis for our knowledge of the supervenience of evaluative properties on non-evaluative properties, which seems to be a non-substantive, or conceptual, evaluative truth.[10] Another candidate example of a non-substantive true is the transitivity of value: if x is better than y, and y is better than z, then x is better than z. It is presumably acceptable to have different standards for answering different kinds of questions. Blackburn himself makes this point. For Blackburn, a truth is conceptual just in case 'we cannot imagine it otherwise; we could make nothing of a way of thought which denied it'.[11] But in both ethical and non-ethical domains, it may turn out that some truths aren't conceptual, and so must be discovered by other means. Blackburn tells us:

In particular in the moral case it seems conceptually or logically necessary that if two things share a total basis of natural properties, then they have the same moral qualities. But it does not seem a matter of conceptual or logical necessity that any given total natural state of a thing gives it some particular moral quality. For to tell which moral quality results from a given natural state means using standards whose correctness cannot be shown by conceptual means alone. It means moralizing[12]

So some ethical questions can be settled by conceptual standards alone, while others need to be settled by other standards. Blackburn places an *unreasonable* constraint on the ethicist who has value perception playing a central role in value epistemology; we would never place an analogous constraint on paradigmatic forms of perception, as if visual perception couldn't play a central role in acquiring empirical knowledge unless it informed us of certain conceptual truths.[13]

I propose, then, that we can usefully define an *ambitious theory of value perception* as a theory that accepts the following: for any value property, V, perceptions of value are epistemically indispensable for knowing that something (an object, way

---

[9] I believe that Blackburn is referring to a supervenience relation when he talks about 'timeless connections', but if he really means to refer just to a temporal relation then my point in this section could be reframed accordingly.

[10] Some philosophers argue that conceptual truths can be substantive. See Cuneo and Shafer-Landau (2014). Although I think it is a mistake to allow for non-substantive conceptual truths, nothing important turns on this disagreement here. However, allowing substantive conceptual truths leaves less room for value perception to play an important role, unless we allow that value perception helps us to learn conceptual truths.

[11] Blackburn (1984), 217. Alternative ways of characterizing conceptual knowledge are available, and I won't try to adjudicate between them here. See e.g. Boghossian (1996).

[12] Blackburn (1984), 184.

[13] That said, as I mention in n. 8, Blackburn remarks at the end of his list of challenging questions that the defender of value perception may be able to set the questions aside. Blackburn may think his questions are only a problem if his targets accept a very bold thesis about the extent of our evaluative knowledge that value perception can explain. The text is unclear on this point.

of acting, particular action, etc.) is V, assuming the something in question is not V by definition.[14,15] A natural thought for a defender of this ambitious view to have is that without value perceptions, we wouldn't have any input to begin to form justified (substantive) ethical beliefs, for even if there were valuable things, nothing would *seem* good or bad, right or wrong. For such an ambitious theorist, even the question of whether an agent's perceptual faculties are working well is probably going to be a question for value perception, unless one believes such a question can be answered conceptually.[16]

2. High-Level Value Perception

An ambitious theory of value perception would be of great interest, since it would provide an answer to the question of how we know substantive truths about value; a question with relevance to not only the epistemology of value but also the metaphysics of value. After all, if we can find no plausible account for how we know about value properties, this is a step toward calling into question whether there really are any. An unambitious theory may still be interesting, of course; but even if an unambitious theory were defensible, we would still be left with the task of defending some other account (or accounts) of what grounds the other substantive evaluative knowledge that we have. And, furthermore, there may also be a desire for a unified theory of what grounds such knowledge, in which case an ambitious theory would be a *desideratum* (though perhaps one we could eventually be talked out of). Before we can consider whether any theory of value perception can be ambitious, however, we need to know more about the theories on offer. For this paper, I focus on high-level value perception, which in recent years has been growing in popularity. This section explains what a high-level theory of value perception is. The ensuing sections explain why such theories not only fail to be ambitious but fail to be interesting at all.

It's uncontroversial that familiar types of perceptual experience can have *low-level content*. I take the *content* of any perceptual experience to be the accuracy conditions of an experience that are conveyed (or presented) to the subject.[17] For example, a visual experience as of a red sailboat in the distance is accurate just in case there is a

---

[14] I do not require that the perceptual experiences be of an object's being V. An ambitious theorist can allow that we need value experiences to know about the presence of *any* value (goodness, badness, rightness, etc.), even though we only have perceptual experiences of *certain* values. Suppose, for instance, that we can perceive goodness but not rightness. If the concept of rightness is analyzed in terms of that of goodness, then value perceptions may still be essential for knowing what is right, even though we never perceptually experience anything as being right. See Milona (2016).

[15] Testimony, for instance, is plausibly a way of justifying evaluative beliefs, too, but testimony is not plausibly an epistemically independent route. Robert Cowan offers a helpful definition of epistemic dependence: 'a state, d, epistemically depends on another state, e, with respect to content c iff e must be justified or justification conferring in order for d to be justified or justification-conferring with respect to content c' (Cowan (2015), 2).

[16] But this is not a bad result, for matters are much the same with ordinary perception. We can only learn when our perceptual faculties are functioning well by relying on perception. For more on this, see Milona (2016).

[17] On this way of thinking about content, see S. Siegel (2010), 28.

red sailboat in the distance; and the phenomenal character of the visual experience consists (at least partly) in those accuracy conditions appearing to the observer to be the case (i.e., being conveyed to her). *Low-level* visual content includes (inter alia) color and shape. (Or, in the case of audition, low-level content includes pitch and tone. But to keep things simple, I'll stick with vision.)

While some theorists contend we can only perceive such low-level content, others are drawn to more liberal views.[18] At the least, we often *talk* as if we can perceive other things. For example, we often speak of seeing that there is an apple, that one event caused another, etc. Following Nicholas Silins, I define high-level (visual) perception as perception with content other than shape, color, and location (low-level content).[19] The defender of high-level perception claims that some ordinary perceptual experiences can have high-level content. The defender of high-level *value* perception defends this claim for values, in particular. Finally, I use the words 'ordinary' and 'familiar' to denote the traditional five senses, i.e., vision, audition, gustation, tactility, and olfaction. The high-level view, as I discuss it, is a view about (at least some of) those familiar sense modalities.[20] If we drop 'ordinary' from the definition of high-level value perception, then in our discussion of theories of value perception, we risk collapsing the distinction between importantly different kinds of views.[21]

The plan for getting a better handle on what high-level theories of value perception essentially are is by way of considering an exemplar of such a view. Robert Audi (in his recent *Moral Perception* (2013), as I interpret him, develops the most detailed account of high-level value perception of which I'm aware, and so the aim is to take advantage of his extensive treatment of the topic to help in getting a handle on the target view.[22] The criticisms I develop in the ensuing sections turn not on any idiosyncrasies of Audi's position but, instead, only on the features that make his view, or any view, a high-level theory of value perception.

---

[18] Those who reject the possibility of any high-level perception include Dretske (1995); Clarke (2000).
[19] See N. Silins (2013). One might worry about such a definition by list. The reason for defining low-level content in this way is, at least in part, to denote the problem-space in a theory-neutral way. More illuminating definitions often arise after further theorizing. See e.g. Noë (2009); Cowan (2015).
[20] If we allow for such high-level perceptual content, then there will plausibly be cases in which our experiences in one sense modality affect our experiences in another modality. My auditory experiences may affect what I see, e.g., I see that a person as saying such-and-such, and that experience is intimately related somehow to my auditory experience of the sounds of the speech. In any case, for this paper, I do not try to answer whether or not such experiences are irreducibly intermodal. Nothing important for my arguments turns on the possibility of intermodal experiences. For more discussion on these issues, see S. Siegel (2010), 24–6.
[21] If we define the high-level theory of value perception as the theory that we can have perceptual experiences with evaluative content, then we risk counting the theory that emotions have evaluative content as a theory of high-level value perception. But the view that emotions are perceptual experiences that can have evaluative content is prima facie very different from the view that some visual experiences can have evaluative content.
[22] Some read Audi as defending a view of value perception which is subtly different from the high-level view. See Pekka Väyrynen, Chapter 5 in this volume. For reasons which will become clear below, however, I resist this reading (see esp. n. 31). But in any case, we should not get bogged down by interpretative questions, for the view that I interpret Audi as defending is held by numerous philosophers, including, among others, McBrayer (2010a); Cullison (2010); Werner (2016).

To begin, Audi points out that a thought inimical to the possibility of value perception is the thought that all visual perception has to be *cartographic*. Cartographic perception involves a 'mapping' from phenomenal properties (low-level properties like shape and color) to properties perceived.[23] Audi's example of cartographic perception involves going from the impression of four squares to the property of being divided into four squares. It isn't plausible that value perception can work on a cartographic model, since there is no mapping of phenomenal properties to evaluative properties. But Audi at least, believes that this mapmaking idea of perception is undermotivated and does not square well with the phenomenology of actual perception.[24] We *seem* to have non-doxastic visual experiences of properties that we cannot easily have arrived at in a way consistent with the cartographic model.[25] For example, when a trained botanist and a layperson walk through a forest together, it is natural to expect that the surroundings will *look* different to the botanist, for her expertise would seem to help her to *see* the different kinds of foliage.[26]

If there is such a thing as visual value perception, then there must be 'phenomenal sensings' of wrongdoing/badness/goodness/etc., since for anything we see (e.g., a lemon) there is *something it is like* to see it.[27] To get a grip on what it might be like to see value, consider an example. A patron in a bar is casually watching a married couple.[28] The husband is quite intoxicated, yet he nonetheless requests another whiskey. His wife kindly asks him to stop drinking, and he responds by slapping her across the face. The observer can see the wrong act, but can he see its wrongness? Well, Audi finds that the observer's perception of the wrong-making features may be coupled with a distinctive kind of phenomenology, which we would naturally describe as a recognition (not necessarily involving any belief) of wrongdoing; this phenomena is plausibly a phenomenal sensing of wrongdoing, exactly what we're after.[29] This is a kind of 'felt connection' between the base (wrong-making) properties and the property of being wrong. Audi's claim is that the relationship ('felt connection') between the ordinary perception (of the wrong-making features) and the phenomenal sensing

---

[23] Audi (2013), 37-8.   [24] See Audi (2013), 38-9.
[25] I find much of what Audi says about the cartographic model to be underdeveloped. It perhaps would have been useful for him to appeal to Susanna Siegel's much discussed "phenomenal contrast" argument for why we should believe visual experiences with high-level contents are possible. Siegel uses the argument specifically to argue we can perceive natural kinds, but a parallel argument could be developed, I think, for values. (It has recently come to my attention that Werner, (2016), tries to do just this.) Siegel's argument, like Audi's, appeals to phenomenology, but it is a far more robust abductive argument that attempts to head off alternative explanations of the phenomenological data. See S. Siegel (2010).
[26] An opponent of high-level perception will want to try to explain the different way in which the botanist and layperson experience their surroundings without appealing to differences in how things look. S. Siegel (2010) argues in much more detail than Audi against many of these alternative explanations (although Siegel does not consider value perception, in particular), but for our purposes, we need not go into so much detail.
[27] Sometimes philosophers say, which comes to the same thing, that all perception is *experiential*.
[28] This example is from Audi (2013), 61-2.
[29] It is helpful to notice that high-level value perception is probably going to be one of the most controversial forms of high-level perception. This is because it depends on our ability to have high-level perceptual experiences of the properties (e.g., persons, mental states, causes) that (metaphysically) ground the values.

of an evaluative property is such that it is correct to speak of value perception. Speaking of a sensing of injustice, in particular, Audi says:

> The sense of injustice, then, a kind of impression of it, one might say, *as* based on, and as phenomenally integrated with, a suitable ordinary perception of the properties on which injustice is consequential—*grounded*, to use another term for the same relation—might serve as the experiential element in moral perception.
>
> An important constituent in this phenomenal integration is the perceiver's felt sense of connection between, on the one hand, the impression of, say, injustice or (on the positive side) beneficence and, on the other hand, the properties that ground the moral phenomena.[30]

As I interpret Audi, it's best to separate his view into two key commitments: (i) there are a variety of different kinds of phenomenal sensings of evaluative properties, which can apparently occur independently of value perception (see Section 5), and (ii) the content of these phenomenal sensings is often integrated into the content (i.e., the accuracy conditions conveyed to the subject in her experience) of familiar perceptual experiences so as to generate a value perception.[31]

It is a delicate task to characterize in greater detail how Audi understands 'what it is like' to experience an evaluative property. If I understand the view correctly, phenomenal sensings of evaluative properties are manifold; in fact, phenomenal sensings of the *same* evaluative properties can vary. Audi tells us that felt sense of connection may be partly constituted by an emotion, though it need not be.[32] (So we should not take the word 'feel' to necessarily indicate an emotional experience.) It may also be partly constituted by an intuition.[33] Audi tries to capture the rich variety of phenomenal sensings by engaging in phenomenological inquiry, drawing distinctions on the basis of an examination of different cases.[34] For instance, in one case, we may 'feel' disapproval when a man deliberately spills hot liquid on his friend's hand. Or there may be a 'felt *unfittingness* between the deed and the context, as where we see a male and female treated unequally in a distribution of bonuses for

---

[30] Audi (2013), 38–9.

[31] Audi isn't explicit that by 'integration' he means *integration into the content*. But I think this is what he intends, and it is, in any case, hard to see how he can avoid it. Consider that Audi thinks that we can literally see wrongness. But if he doesn't think the phenomenal representation of wrongness is part of the content of the visual experience, then it seems he'd have to think a visual experience as of something's being wrong could be correct (assuming a visual experience is correct just in case its content is true) even if there's no wrongness, because the wrongness isn't part of the *content*. But then it's hard to see how talk of seeing wrongness could be anything other than metaphorical, contrary to what Audi says. Furthermore, if by 'integration' Audi doesn't mean integration into the content, then his view may actually be interpretable as a counter-hypothesis to the common way of formulating the thesis that there is high-level value perception. On this last point, see Cowan (2014).

[32] See Audi (2013), 39.

[33] See Audi (2013), 134–6. For Audi, intuitions can come in a variety of forms. We can have an intuition *that p*, which is a kind of belief. We can also have *objectual* intuitions, which are direct apprehensions of concepts, properties, or relations (see Audi (2013), 85–8). Both kinds of intuitions can presumably constitute phenomenal sensings of an evaluative perception. Though, as far as I can tell, Audi only mentions the possibility that an intuition that p can be part of an evaluative perception.

[34] After identifying the different ways we can have a phenomenal sensing of an evaluative property, he goes on to sketch theoretical accounts of each of those ways. It would be tangential to my purposes to spell all this out in detail.

the same work'.³⁵ But experiences of unfittingness can happen in different ways; it can be conceptual, as it often is with an adult who sees *that* an act is unjust, or can be non-conceptual, as it may be with a young child who is uncomfortable at seeing peers treated unequally.³⁶ More could be said about how Audi analyzes various different types of phenomenal sensings, but this basic characterization of Audi's high-level theory of value perception is sufficient for my purposes.

Generally speaking, I understand any high-level view to be committed to both a *phenomenological* thesis and an *integration* thesis.³⁷ The first step is to identify certain evaluative experiences (I'll often follow Audi in speaking of *sensing* value properties) and the second is to argue that the content of the experiences can be integrated into the content of familiar kinds of perceptual experiences to produce a value perception. (Integration secures the possibility of *literal* visual, auditory, etc. experiences of evaluative properties; the high-level view isn't the far more familiar and less controversial view that we can have evaluative responses to visual, auditory, etc. experiences but that are external to the visual, auditory, etc. experience's content.)

3. The Need for an Alternative Way

Defenders of high-level value perception claim that the perception of values is tied to one or more of the ordinary five senses.³⁸ (Audi discusses visual, tactile, and auditory value perception.) In the case of vision, we see high-level properties by seeing other, low-level properties. This means that in *imagining* a scenario, an agent will never literally see any values, for she is not having a visual experience.³⁹ The following thesis seems rather obviously true:

Limits: In imagining something, we do not perceive it with any of our five senses.

Of course, it's almost surely true that our ability to reflect, whether imaginatively or not, causally depends on our having certain experiences. (Even mathematical reflection likely depends on having some experiences.) But the point is that the ordinary senses aren't part of what constitutes such reflection.⁴⁰

There are manifold ways in which we engage the imagination in evaluative reflection. The paradigm is when we *sensorily* imagine various sights, sounds, smells, etc. For example, in reflecting on the moral status of torture, we may conjure up images of

---

[35] Audi (2013), 39–40.   [36] See Audi (2013), 45–9.

[37] Cowan (2015) mentions (but then sets aside) the possibility of a view on which humans are 'hardwired' for visual value perception, a view which would apparently not require the integration thesis. I consider this importantly different (though rarely defended) kind of view in Milona (2017).

[38] I assume defenders of the high-level view don't believe that there is any other kind of value perception. But they actually could; the view that desires and/or emotions often involve perceptions of values is compatible with the high-level view. At certain points, Audi seems to suggest that emotions can be a kind of value experience (perhaps similar in some ways to perceptual experience) contained within a visual experience, making that visual experience evaluative.

[39] As Audi points out, visual imagination is 'possible even given blindness'. And so 'It is not perceptual' (Audi (2013), 9).

[40] For helpful discussion on the relationship of experience to ethical and mathematical reasoning, see S. McGrath (2011).

the sights and sounds of a suffering prisoner.[41] In other cases, we imagine in a way that does not seem to be straightforwardly sensory, if even sensory at all.[42] Most obvious here are the cases when we imagine content that is not perceivable, e.g., that Athens wins the Peloponnesian War or that McCain wins the 2008 US election.[43]

The crucial point for us is that the imagination, whether sensory or not, can sometimes be a route to evaluative knowledge, and this is a problem for any high-levelist who advocates what I have labeled an *ambitious theory of value perception* (at least insofar as she thinks high-level value perception is the only kind of value perception that there is). Much of ethical inquiry is deliberation about what to do in the future; and when we engage in such reflection, there is nothing yet to perceive, at least in so far as our five senses are concerned.[44] Although one *could* hold that substantive evaluative knowledge or justification for beliefs about what is valuable can only be acquired through high-level value perception, and not by, say, imaginatively simulating how events would unfold if we performed a given action, such a view seems difficult to motivate on theory-independent grounds.[45]

One intuitive way to push this thought is to notice an apparently important *asymmetry* between evaluative and empirical inquiry. While with the latter we rely on *actual* experiments, evaluative inquiry only seems to require *thought* experiments.[46] It is one thing to deny that any of our evaluative beliefs count as knowledge, or (less plausibly) that they are ever justified; it is another thing altogether to deny the following premise: if ordinary deliberators can gain evaluative knowledge through high-level value perception (e.g., that her helping the man across the street is good), then in most cases, they could have gained similar evaluative knowledge through imagining (e.g., that her helping the man across the street would be good). A theory which denies the possibility of evaluative knowledge by mere reflection is going to be highly revisionary; and many would rightly count such a commitment as a serious strike against the theory.

We can push the point a bit more with an example. Consider a toddler who has never had any high-level perceptual experiences of wrongness. To be sure, this toddler has perceptually experienced things which are wrong (e.g., lying), but she has never perceptually experienced anything *as* wrong. Now imagine our toddler cackling to herself as she remembers, say, pushing another toddler into the mud. But

---

[41] There is a great deal of complexity that I am glossing over here. For example, in visually imagining a suffering prisoner, we might imagine having a visual experience of the suffering or simply imagine it from some viewpoint. On this distinction, see e.g. Wollheim (1987); Gregory (2010).

[42] I think it is a mistake to suppose that the imagination is essentially sensory. But if one thinks it is, then I am happy to call the phenomena I am about to describe 'reflection'. Nothing turns on the disagreement.

[43] See Yablo (1993); Fiocco (2007).

[44] Dancy makes this point, but he seems to have in mind value perception *as such*. See Dancy (2010). In my view, his claim is correct if we're considering a high-level view of value perception, but it may be overstated if we are talking about desiderative or emotional evaluative perception (see Section 6).

[45] Richard Swinburne articulates the core idea as follows: 'When examples of particular situations (e.g., the trolley problem) are adduced in order to persuade us that some general moral principle is or is not true, it is quite irrelevant whether the examples are examples of an actual event or of an imagined event. What matters is what it would be right to conclude about which actions in that situation would be good or bad; whether or not the situation actually occurred is irrelevant.' See Swinburne (2015), 620.

[46] S. McGrath (2011) makes this point.

after a moment or two of imagining the scenario, as her attention is drawn in a special way to her peer's pain and embarrassment, she suddenly experiences her act as wrong. It seems to me that the high-levelist should allow that this is perfectly possible, and that this experience is a source of justification similar to as if she had actually visually experienced the wrongness. The high-levelist should allow that we can acquire justification for an evaluative belief through imagining some possibility; and that justification will in many cases be independent from any evaluative perceptions.

The following thesis is difficult to deny:

> *Liberality*: Justification for evaluative beliefs can be gained, independently of high-level value-perceptual experiences, by imaginatively reflecting (whether sensorily or non-sensorily) on cases.[47]

Liberality is silent about the exact way in which we acquire evaluative justification through the imagination, and, more specifically, what high-levelists should say about this. But if what I have argued in this section is correct, we can at least say that high-level value perception is not an attractive basis for an ambitious theory of value perception. (And it will become even clearer in Section 4 why that is.) Section 4 defends a much stronger claim: building off Limits and Liberality, I claim that so long as we accept a few more attractive theses, whether there is high-level value perception is simply not an important issue *at all* for value epistemologists.

4. High-Level Value Perception and Imagination

4.1. Isn't it obvious?

The argument in Section 3 hardly shows that the question of whether there is high-level value perception is not important for value epistemology. A natural thought is that if we discover that there are such perceptions, we will have discovered a unique and distinctive way in which we can acquire evaluative knowledge. Consider why we might care about *any* brand of high-level perception, whether evaluative or otherwise.[48] Many philosophers are inclined to believe that our perceptions can give us *immediate* (basic or non-inferential) justification for relevant beliefs. Such philosophers have tended to focus on the perception of low-level properties like color and shape, assuming that other things, e.g., kinds, causation, emotion, are outside the reach of perception. To account for our knowledge of such phenomena, one has to explain how we can rationally transition from our immediately justified perceptual beliefs to our

---

[47] For the central argument of this paper, it is only important that we can gain evaluative justification independently of high-level value perception by way of either the sensory imagination or non-sensory imagination. It is not required that we be able to acquire evaluative justification in both ways. But because our ability to acquire knowledge in both ways becomes relevant when we consider a revised version of the high-level view (Section 5), I simply work with the strong principle for the sake of simplicity.

[48] My discussion in this paragraph of why we might care about high-level value perception is inspired by Nicholas Silins's recent (2013) discussion of the potential significance of high-level perception more generally. I say 'inspired' because his discussion is far more detailed and subtle than I can reproduce here. (Silins ultimately has his own reasons for wanting to temper excitement about high-level perception in general.)

beliefs about kinds, causation, emotions, etc. However, if we can literally perceive such things, then perhaps one can argue with some plausibility that the range of immediately justified beliefs is much greater than initially realized. This observation might lead us to think that whether there is high-level value perception is of deep importance to value epistemology. But that would be a mistake. My claim is that the defender of high-level value perception should adopt three theses that jointly (along with Limits and Liberality) mute the epistemological significance of whether there is high-level value perception.

4.2. Normative similarity

I noted in Section 3 that a defender of high-level value perception should allow that, in addition to acquiring (substantive) evaluative justification through perception, we can also acquire it through imaginative reflection (Liberality). I suggest that the defender of high-level value perception should probably accept a further *normative* similarity between imagination and value perception:

> *Normative Similarity*: Imaginative reflection can in principle (though perhaps with one exception to be explained below) supply just as good evidential support for a normative belief that something would be good/bad/wrong/etc. as any value perception of the relevant evaluative property can supply for the belief that the relevant thing is good/bad/wrong/etc.

Just as the patron in the bar can literally see that the husband behaves badly when he slaps his wife, he could also see 'in the mind's eye' that such behavior would be bad. And, of course, seeing 'in the mind's eye' is not *literally* seeing; it doesn't actually engage the visual faculties and so isn't a high-level perception. But the rational support for the belief would apparently be the same. When we engage in imaginative reflection, we do not ordinarily think that we need to actually observe the case to be sure that the verdict about the imaginary case is correct. We don't think we need to use perception as a 'check' on our value judgments about hypothetical cases.[49]

In the statement of Normative Similarity, I noted that we may want to complicate the principle by allowing for an exception. Here's the candidate exception:

> *Normative Similarity-Exception*: the 'vividness' of a value-perceptual experience is often revelatory of something's evaluative significance in a way that cannot be replicated imaginatively, at least not by ordinary human agents.

Consider a person, Cindy, who imagines killing her rival, Lenny. When she *imagines* what it would be like, killing him appears very good, especially given all the awful things Lenny has done. Now suppose she carries out the act by driving a knife through Lenny's heart. After carving into Lenny's chest, well past the point of no return, the killing starts to appear differently. The apparent disvalue of her act intensifies as she sees Lenny wriggling on the floor, gasping for his last few breaths. Because the action is now presented to her in a more 'vivid' way, she is able to *see* the badness of her act. Perhaps the vividness of this experience could never (for a human

---

[49] Dancy (2010) makes an observation along these lines.

being, at least) be fully replicated imaginatively. The term 'vividness' may be interpreted in different ways. It might have to do, for instance, with our inability to accurately imagine in full detail what it would be like to actually experience something. Or, it might have to do with the greater reliability (at least sometimes) of our evaluative responses to actually perceived scenarios. So maybe value perception is in many cases better for revealing *degrees* of value (due to the 'vividness' of perception). For my purposes, I'll assume that value perception is, at least in some cases, superior to imagination for revealing degrees of value. (However, merely imagining a possibility, as opposed to actually experiencing it, occasionally provides us with the 'reflective distance' needed to make a soberer and more accurate evaluative judgment. This will especially be the case when we do not enjoy doing what is best or right.) But as I will endeavor to show, we should doubt that there is any plausible way of filling in what 'vividness' means that salvages the epistemological significance of high-level value perception.

As we'll see over the next two subsections (4.3–4.4), granting a certain descriptive similarity between imagination and high-level value perception means that Normative Similarity-Exception can't salvage the significance of the question of whether there's high-level value perception. This descriptive similarity helps to drive home the epistemological inconsequence of high-level value perception.[50]

4.3. Descriptive similarity

Audi emphasizes the parallels between value perception and moral imagination.[51] He says:

[T]he exercise of moral imagination can, through vivid imaging of morally significant events, and through envisaging diverse possibilities, produce an experience significantly like a moral perception.[52]

This claim isn't surprising. Our imaginations allow us 'replay' and 'preplay' perceptual experiences; the different components of the perceptual experience will have analogues that are 'in the mind's eye'.[53] In some cases, those 'analogues' turn out to be the *very same kinds of phenomena* involved in actual experiences. Intuitions (of whatever kind, if one believes, like Audi, that there are many kinds) had in response to actual cases are plausibly the same kind of thing as intuitions had in response to imaginary ones. Likewise for the emotions. Recall now the notion of *sensing* (or experiencing) an evaluative property, which is necessary for the possibility of high-level value perception. (High-level value perception involves the *integration* of one of these sensings with a suitable ordinary perceptual experience.) For any sensing of an evaluative property involved in value perception, there will be an analogue of that sensing that could have occurred had the agent imagined the same scenario. But should we go further, claiming that the sensings had in response to imaginative cases are the very same kinds of phenomena? To make the question vivid, return to the case of the husband who wrongly slaps his wife when she asks him not to have

---

[50] One can also read Section 5 as providing further support for Normative Similarity.
[51] Ethical imagination is not a special type of imagination; it's just imagining about ethical matters.
[52] Audi (2013), 160.   [53] See Audi (2013), 47.

another whiskey. As we saw, the observer's perception of wrongness (assuming he does see the wrongness) is partly constituted by a *sensing* of wrongdoing. But had the observer imagined the case, rather than perceived it, could he have had the same kind of experience (sensing) of wrongdoing?[54] I claim the following:

Descriptive Similarity: For any sensing of an evaluative property suitably integrated with an ordinary perception to create a value perception, the same kind of sensing of an evaluative property could occur through imagining such a case.

If Descriptive Similarity is true, then it can help us see why Normative Similarity seems correct. This is because in both perceptual and imaginary cases, it's plausibly the sensings that are doing the important justificatory work (see also Section 4.4). But why think Descriptive Similarity is true?

As I have already suggested, there are phenomenological grounds for believing this thesis. To begin, consider emotions and intuitions. Just as we can experience an emotion, say, revulsion, at some *actual* event, we can experience revulsion when reading fiction or the newspaper, imagining possibilities, etc. Furthermore, the same kind of intuitive response might be had to a given scenario, whether actual or possible. Part of the reason such claims about emotions and intuitions go mostly unquestioned in the literature is, I believe, because denying them would fly in the face of actual experience.[55] My view is that matters are much the same with sensings of evaluative properties. Audi assumes without much ado that the myriad of ways we can sense an evaluative property have analogues in imagination; I am going one step beyond: the reason this seems obvious is that the very same kinds of experiences can occur when we consider imaginary cases.[56] Although I'm open to counterexamples, I can't conceive any way of sensing of an evaluative property that cannot be reproduced in imagination.[57] And if I've got the phenomenology correct, that's outstanding evidence for Descriptive Similarity, since after all, sensings of evaluative properties *just are* certain kinds of experiences.

In sum, from a phenomenological angle, it seems Audi should allow that what's distinctive about value perception is never the sensing of the evaluative property, as

---

[54] Of course, we should be careful about generalizing from one case, but I think matters will be much the same for other examples.

[55] Some philosophers do claim that emotions had in response to fictions and some imaginings are different in type. See Walton (1978); Doggett and Egan (2012). But the reasons why they believe this do not provide an attractive model for resisting Descriptive Similarity (see n. 57).

[56] But notice that the analogue claim may be enough for the main point. Suppose the experiences are different, e.g., in virtue of different functional roles. Well, even if that's defensible, it may still be that what is epistemically significant about the sensings remains constant in responses to imagined cases and actual ones. In that case, I would simply have to rephrase Descriptive Similarity to be about that feature rather than the sensings.

[57] There is a complication worth flagging. As I mentioned in n. 55, some philosophers (e.g. Walton 1978; Doggett and Egan 2012) believe that emotions in response to (some) imaginings and fictions really are different in type. But the best case for this counterintuitive view appeals to the apparently different functional and motivational profiles of our offline responses. This doesn't provide a model for resisting Descriptive Similarity, at least not in a way that matters. For one, it is not clear that we should be typing phenomenal sensings by their motivational profiles. And, furthermore, even if we do, an 'online' sensing and its 'offline' analogue will still be the same in that they present the same evaluative properties or relations; and it is that psychological constant which matters.

such, which could occur in merely imagining the same case. What's special about high-level value perception is the sensing's *integration* with the ordinary perceptual experience (see Section 2), which secures the possibility of seeing, hearing, etc. values.

4.4. Immediacy

Descriptive Similarity and Liberality (the claim that imagination is a source of justification for evaluative beliefs) make it highly attractive to adopt one last thesis:

> *Immediacy*: the various sensings of evaluative properties are sources of *immediate* justification for relevant evaluative beliefs, whether in response to real or imagined cases.

To deny this claim, while accepting each of Descriptive Similarity and Liberality would generate a peculiar asymmetry in the way our evaluative beliefs are justified.[58] It isn't clear what could warrant positing the asymmetry, and I suspect positing such an asymmetry would seem unattractive to a defender of high-level value perception.

To get a grip on Immediacy, a bit more needs to be said about what sorts of evaluative beliefs are justified by our responses to imaginings. Consider a concrete case. Sandra and Ronaldo are enjoying themselves at a party, until Ronaldo suddenly, and unexpectedly, finds himself embroiled in an uncomfortable conversation about his political beliefs. Sandra, who isn't directly involved in the conversation, is looking for a way to diffuse the situation. Sandra quickly imagines several possible courses of action: (i) stepping in to defend Ronaldo's views, (ii) telling Ronaldo's questioner to pipe down, since Ronaldo is uncomfortable, or (iii) subtly trying to change the subject by bringing up an interesting but apolitical news story. She imagines events unfolding in different ways, depending on the course of action she has in mind. Her evaluative responses to the different imaginings give her some *immediate* justification for an evaluative belief about the possibility as she imagines it.[59] As it turns out, when Sandra imagines subtly changing the subject (and the subsequent unfolding of events), she experiences that choice and subsequent unfolding of events (however she imagines those things as unfolding) as especially good. She has *non-immediate* justification for believing that right now it would be good to attempt to subtly change the conversation insofar as she is justified in believing that her situation is similar (in non-normative respects), and would unfold in similar ways, to the situation she just imagined. There is much more that would need to be said to give a complete account of how we get justification for evaluative beliefs through imaginative reflection, but these brief remarks should suffice to illustrate the only point needed for

---

[58] As far as I'm aware, those who argue that high-level value perceptions are important in moral epistemology hold that value perceptions are in standard cases sources of *immediate justification* for relevant evaluative beliefs.

[59] Our evaluative responses to imaginings that are vague and undetailed will presumably not be a particularly good source of justification for evaluative beliefs, although the high-levelist should allow that even in those cases, we get *some* justification. Similarly, we may have high-level value-perceptual experiences on the basis of very limited information. Imagine a high-level visual experience as of S's taking money out of the wallet's being wrong. Well, if for all the agent knows the wallet is S's, then this experience won't be a great source of justification for believing S acts wrongly, even though it presumably provides *some* evidence (which is sure to be defeated).

my purposes: the high-levelist should allow that evaluative experiences had in response to imagined scenarios supply us with immediate justification for relevant evaluative beliefs.

4.5. Summing things up

We're now in a position to recognize why accepting the three theses I've put forward makes the question of whether there is high-level value perception unimportant for value epistemology. If the defender of high-level value perception accepts each thesis, then she's committed to the following: *whether or not sensings of value are ever suitably integrated* with ordinary perception to generate a high-level value perception, *those sensings (or experiences) of value are already a source of immediate justification that is just as good*. And, furthermore, although Normative Significance-Exception seemed to leave open the possibility that value perception is a crucially important way of gaining insight about something's degree of value, this isn't so. The myriad of ways in which we might sense value are already equipped to supply the same insights, whether or not they are *integrated* with an ordinary perception. To illustrate, return to Cindy's murder of Lenny. Consider Cindy imagining murdering Lenny. As her imagination of the deed becomes more vivid, she is poised to gain more insight into the degrees of the act's disvalue. But actually carrying out the act, and so seeing, hearing, and feeling it, supplies her with *maximal* vividness, which for ordinary humans is only going to be achievable by observing the actual deed. The actual experience may make possible greater insight, but the possibility of the greater insight is not dependent on the phenomenon of high-level value perception; it's made possible by the degree of vividness with which the *bad-making* properties are presented (in imagination or perception).

Defenders of the high-level view are forced to defend difficult, controversial theses in the philosophy of perception. It's very important, for example, that all visual perception isn't 'cartographic', it's very important that it be possible for sensings of values to be suitably integrated with ordinary perceptions, and so on. High-level value perception, moreover, is plausibly going to be one of the most controversial kinds of high-level perception, since it typically depends on our ability to perceive the properties that ground the value properties. For instance, value properties are in some cases partly grounded in natural kind properties, but even the latest arguments for natural kind perception have been called into doubt.[60] However important this debate about high-level value perception might be for understanding perception, it isn't important for value epistemology. Whether or not the sensings of values are ever 'suitably integrated' with ordinary perceptions, the high-level theorist should already think such experiences are a source of justification that needn't itself be justified.[61]

---

[60] See Brogaard (2013).

[61] One might try to salvage the epistemological significance of high-level value perception as follows. It's a common thought that in order to imagine, say, colors, shapes, flavors, sounds, we must first actually perceive those colors, shapes, flavors, sounds. So one might argue that in order to be able to imaginatively experience value properties, we first have to perceptually experience those properties. In that way, the ability to perceptually acquire substantive evaluative knowledge is fundamental. (Audi may be making this claim about the fundamentality of value perception. See Audi (2013), 173. But if this is what the high-levelist needs to argue to salvage the significance of her view, then she has a serious argumentative burden,

Four points of clarification. First, I concede that value perception may be a common way in which we come to have evaluative knowledge. What I have claimed is that the defender of high-level value perception should accept certain theses that ensure *any* knowledge or justification we get by value perception is in an important sense also had on non-perceptual grounds (since *integration* is not doing epistemological work). And this mutes the epistemological significance of whether there is value perception. Second, there are questions closely related to the question of whether there is high-level value perception that *are* clearly important for value epistemology, but we should distinguish the significance of such questions from the question of high-level value perception. For example, some philosophers may want to claim that evaluative perception isn't possible unless value properties are causally networked, or are reducible to properties that are. And the question of causation is hugely important in value epistemology (and metaethics as a whole).[62] But it's causation that's important, strictly speaking, not perception.[63]

Third, I am not arguing that the question of whether there *perceptual knowledge* of value is insignificant, at least given a liberal understanding of what can count as perceptual knowledge. To illustrate, Andrew Cullison argues for high-level value perception as a way of securing perceptual evaluative knowledge.[64] But when considering a certain objection to high-level value perception, he argues we may be able to get perceptual knowledge of value *without* high-level evaluative perception. His thought is that by perceiving things regularly correlated with some value property, V, perhaps we can know on that basis that V is instantiated. I suspect he would also say we need to have some epistemically significant evaluative response, or intuition, to what we perceive.[65] But even if many philosophers would balk at calling knowledge acquired by such means perceptual, I suspect they would find the description of the view, at least in the very abstract way Cullison describes it, a familiar and not terribly implausible picture of how we acquire evaluative knowledge.

The fourth and final point of clarification is that, strictly speaking, the theses I offer are not *necessary* to generate the result that the question of high-level value perception doesn't matter for value epistemology. We get the desired (or undesired, depending on your perspective) result so long as one accepts that it does not matter whether the content of phenomenal sensings of value is ever integrated into the content of ordinary perceptual experiences. What the theses do is draw attention to

---

for the empirical claim about what is required for us to be able to imaginatively experience values needs defence. For example, we need to know why the case of values is like color rather than like, say, mathematics. While humans might need perceptual experiences of some kind to be able to engage in mathematical thinking, there's no need to invoke mathematical perceptual knowledge or experiences to explain how we're able to justify mathematical beliefs (see McGrath 2011)). Furthermore, we need to know why the phenomenal sensing of value's being integrated into the content of a familiar kind of perceptual experience is at all important.

[62] See Oddie (2005); Enoch (2011).

[63] Most defenders of value perception claim that the question of value perception doesn't turn on whether values are causally networked. See Audi (2013); McBrayer (2010b).

[64] Cullison speaks of 'moral perception' rather than 'value perception', but I take the difference to be merely terminological.

[65] Cullison (2010), 17–19.

our ability to acquire evaluative knowledge through the imagination, independently of familiar perceptual experiences (see Limits and Liberality), and then to draw our attention to the descriptive and epistemological similarities between the knowledge we get by imagining cases and the knowledge we get by perceiving actual cases (see Normative Similarity, Descriptive Similarity, and Immediacy). The theses help us to see *why* the integration thesis—a central component of high-level value perception— simply doesn't matter for value epistemology. But even if it turns out, say, that Descriptive Similarity is false, because value experiences integrated with ordinary perceptions somehow have a different nature from those not so integrated, the high-levelist who maintains the import of her view still has a serious challenge: explain the epistemological import of integration.

5. A Revised High-Level View

As we know, an essential component of the high-level view is a claim about *integration*: evaluative content can literally be part of the content of visual, auditory, and tactile experiences. I have been trying to argue that whether the content of value experiences is so integrated just isn't an epistemologically significant question. I have pushed this thought by appealing to our ability to acquire evaluative justification through the *imagination*. Suppose now that a high-levelist contends that when we imagine scenarios, we often (passively) imagine seeing, hearing, and feeling evaluative properties. So, for example, when I imagine Wesley copying answers off Jackie's test, I also (let's suppose) passively imagine seeing Wesley's action as wrong.[66] The revised high-level view says this: high-level perceptual experiences of value occur when we have visual and other familiar perceptual experiences of value properties, or when we passively imagine having such experiences.[67] Although when we imagine having such experiences, we are not having *genuine* perceptual experiences, the defender of the revised high-level view claims that they're on a par with literal high-level value experiences.

This revised high-level view doesn't secure the view's epistemological importance. The first point to notice is that if there are value experiences, or sensings, of the sort the high-levelist imagines, it is unlikely they are tied essentially to actual or imagined visual, auditory, and tactile modes. For example, suppose we read a newspaper story about a complicated but sketchy Wall Street business deal. It seems we can reflect on the various propositions comprising the story without conjuring any sensory-like images of the events taking place. Nevertheless, when engaging in such reflection, we might have a phenomenal experience as of the deal's being bad. Take another case. Suppose we imagine that John McCain defeats Obama in the 2008 US presidential election. Even if we conjure some images into our head when we imagine such a

---

[66] It is important that the imagining be passive, or involuntary. If someone actively decides to imagine that they see some action as wrong, then it is hard to see how that experience could supply them with evidence of anything.

[67] Janet Levin pointed out to me the possibility of revising the high-level view in this way.

scenario, it is not clear that those sensory images are *of* the imagined event, since it does not seem as if someone's winning an election is the kind of thing that can be perceived.[68] Nevertheless, it seems that when we imagine McCain defeating Obama in 2008, we may well have a passive experience as of its being bad.

There is another kind of case worth mentioning. Even when we imaginatively visualize something, we may not (and I suspect we normally do not) imagine having a visual experience of it. Dominic Gregory has a helpful analogy for illustrating the point:

> We naturally interpret photographs as showing how things looked. We usually treat them as merely displaying the layout of a past scene, as showing how things once looked from a viewpoint within a previous situation... But we can also treat the same photos as showing how things looked in the course of past visual sensations, that is, in the course of visual sensations which occurred at viewpoints in past scenes. (Photos are sometimes used in that way in recounting first-personal narratives in comics, for example.)[69]

Gregory's view is that the same goes for visual images. A given visualization may be an imagining of how things looked from some viewpoint, or it may be an imagining of a visual sensation from that viewpoint. But when we visualize something in the former way and have an evaluative experience in response to the imagining, the response will not be imagined as integrated with any imagined visual experience, since ex hypothesi there is not any imagined visual experience. So, it seems to me a stretch to maintain that evaluative experiences are in some way bound to ordinary perceptual experiences or imaginings of ordinary perceptual experiences. The high-levelist should allow that while experiences of goodness, badness, rightness, wrongness, etc. can often be integrated into sensory experiences, or imagined sensory experiences, they could also occur independently.

Now we can see that the revised high-level theory does not salvage the view's import. When we have evaluative experiences detached from ordinary perceptual experiences (real or imagined), as the high-levelist should allow is possible, it would be dogmatic to insist that in such cases, the experiences are not a source of immediate justification for evaluative beliefs. There does not seem to be anything special about real or imagined evaluative experiences that occur in visual, tactile, or auditory modes. (As another example, suppose that we sensorily imagine something but then as it fades, we are suddenly struck by the badness of what we just imagined. We do not imagine seeing/hearing/touching badness, but it is hard to see how a high-levelist can avoid allowing that the experience is a source of justification just the same.) But then this suggests that if we come to find out that the high-levelist is wrong, and value experiences (along with their evaluative content) are never *integrated* into sensory experience or imagined sensory experience, but can at best be *responses to* sensory experience or imagined sensory experience, then it hard to see how that finding could be of much epistemological import.

---

[68] See Yablo (1993); Fiocco (2007). [69] Gregory (2010), 744.

6. Conclusion: A More Epistemologically Exciting Model of Value Perception?

The high-level theory of value perception isn't the only kind of value-perceptual theory on offer. An alternative theory says that desires and/or emotions involve perceptual (or perceptual-like) experiences of value. Although I haven't the space to discuss any such view in detail (and there are a variety), it's worth noticing that, in contrast with high-level value perception, I suspect it is a very interesting question for value epistemology whether desires and/or emotions are perceptual experiences of value. As noted above, we have desiderative and emotional responses not only to actual cases but also imaginative and fictional ones. For instance, when we imagine a complicated business deal, or the possibility that McCain won the 2008 election, we may well have desiderative and emotional responses. Furthermore, as ethicists and psychologists alike have noticed, desires and emotions are *ubiquitously* present in human evaluative thought.[70] A theory according to which emotions and desires are perceptual experiences of value can arguably explain why; it is because affective experiences are *the way*, or *mode*, by which we come to recognize evaluative properties, analogous to how visual experiences are the way we come to recognize colors.[71,72]

---

[70] For a sampling of the relevant psychological literature, see Nichols (2004).

[71] For contemporary defence of this kind of view, see Oddie (2005). Jessica Moss attributes such a view to Aristotle in her (2012).

[72] I would like to thank Greg Ackerman, Robert Cowan, Stephen Finlay, Janet Levin, Mark Schroeder, Ralph Wedgwood, and Preston Werner for incredibly helpful feedback on earlier drafts of this paper. Thanks also to audiences at the University of Glasgow and the University of Southern California. Finally, I benefited significantly from conversations with Anna Bergqvist, Michael Lacewing, Fiona Macpherson, Indrek Reiland, Susanna Siegel, and Pekka Väyrynen.

11

Epistemic Sentimentalism and Epistemic Reason-Responsiveness

Robert Cowan

Assume that ordinary agents have some epistemically justified substantive evaluative beliefs,[1] e.g., Katherine justifiably believes that *Trump's comments about immigration were wrong*, Umut justifiably believes that *the pianist's performance was admirable*. Given this assumption, we face a further question: how can ordinary agents come to possess justified substantive evaluative beliefs?

Recently there has been interest in the following answer:[2]

> Epistemic Sentimentalism: emotions are a source of immediate prima facie propositional justification for evaluative beliefs; emotions sometimes constitute the justificatory basis for undefeated doxastically justified evaluative beliefs.[3]

According to Epistemic Sentimentalism (hereafter 'Sentimentalism'), an emotion like guilt, for instance, can provide prima facie propositional justification, sufficient in the absence of defeaters to make it epistemically permissible to believe that, e.g., *my having lied to my partner was wrong*, independently of having justification for believing other supporting propositions, e.g., that *lying is pro tanto wrong*. Further, guilt (for example) may sometimes constitute the justificatory basis of evaluative beliefs. Finally, Sentimentalism claims that emotions are *a* source of immediate justification. That doesn't entail, but nor does it preclude, the stronger view that emotions are *the* source of immediate justification for evaluative beliefs.

Sentimentalism is motivated by the following considerations. First, for there to be justified substantive evaluative beliefs, this plausibly requires something akin to experiential 'evaluative data', in a similar way to that allegedly provided by sensory

---

[1] I'm understanding 'epistemically justified' in the following way: S possessing an epistemically justified belief that p can be understood either as (i) S believing p and there being the absence of a non-moral or non-prudential obligation on S not to believe that p, or (ii) S believing p on the basis of something that makes probable the belief that p. By 'substantive' I mean something like 'non-formal'. See Cowan (2017) for a fuller discussion of substantivity. Finally, I'm understanding 'evaluative' very broadly so as to encompass beliefs about deontic and value properties.

[2] See e.g. Döring (2003); Pelser (2014). Note that in Cowan (2016) I label this view 'Epistemic Perceptualism'. I've come to think that 'Epistemic Sentimentalism' is a more informative and specific label, and thus preferable.

[3] Moral sense theorists like Frances Hutcheson can be interpreted as endorsing Epistemic Sentimentalism.

experience vis-à-vis empirical beliefs. Second, Sentimentalism is motivated by a commitment to Perceptualism about the emotions. On this view, conscious and occurrent emotions are, or are best understood by analogy with, perceptual experiences, e.g., like perceptual experiences they are intentional, non-doxastic, and possess phenomenal character.[4] Endorsing Perceptualism provides some reason for exploring Sentimentalism's prospects, i.e., if emotions are perceptual perhaps they have a perceptual epistemology (there is, however, no entailment). Finally, the idea that emotion can be revelatory of evaluative features—which Sentimentalism precisifies—has support in everyday thinking (and coheres with the alleged intentionality of emotion). For example, it is plausible that remorse can sometimes be the way in which we realize the moral import of our actions, while indignation at the judge's ruling might reveal to its subject how unjust it is. If that's right, then perhaps subjects gain justified evaluative beliefs via their emotions.

Sentimentalism is attractive. Firstly, it promises a way of halting the epistemic regress for evaluative beliefs, i.e., it identifies a source of evaluative justification that is not itself in need of justification. This will, of course, only be of interest to those who think epistemic justification is linear. The second attraction is broader in scope: if one thinks that we need something akin to experiential evaluative data to get justified substantive evaluative beliefs, then Sentimentalism potentially provides a naturalist-friendly account that doesn't require an extravagant philosophy of mind, e.g., it doesn't require positing a faculty of rational intuition.[5]

Sentimentalism is, however, apparently vulnerable to serious objections. Perhaps emotions are too unreliable for it to be true.[6] Or maybe *Epistemic* Sentimentalism clashes with an attractive analysis in the metaphysics of value: Neo-Sentimentalism.[7] In this paper I'm setting these (and other objections[8]) aside and instead focus on a family of objections that all take as a premise the claim that emotions possess a normative property that is apparently antithetical to Sentimentalism: *epistemic reason-responsiveness*.[9] Epistemic reason-responsiveness (hereafter 'reason-responsiveness') can be thought of as encompassing two interconnected claims: firstly, emotions can be held or undergone for epistemic reasons, e.g., my guilt might

---

[4] There are various reasons for adopting Perceptualism which I don't have space to go into. Note that Döring (2003 and 2007) partially identifies Perceptualism with Sentimentalism, i.e., emotions are analogous to perceptual experiences in virtue of their normative properties. This complication shouldn't make a difference to my discussion—but the reader should note that, as I'm characterizing it, the views are distinct.

[5] Oddie (2005) argues that *desires* play a similar epistemic role vis-à-vis judgements about *goodness* to that afforded to emotions by Sentimentalism. The reader is invited to consider how my arguments impact on Oddie's view.

[6] But see Pelser (2014) for a response.

[7] See e.g. Brady (2013). But see Cowan (2016) for a reply.

[8] See e.g. the objection from Brady (2013) that proponents of Sentimentalism misidentify the primary goal of evaluative thinking as epistemic justification or knowledge, when it is actually evaluative *understanding*.

[9] See e.g. Brady (2013); Deonna and Teroni (2012); Salmela (2011); Vance (2014). Both Brady, and Deonna and Teroni, discuss explicitly the Neo-Sentimentalist claim that evaluative properties can be analysed in terms of *appropriate* or *fitting* emotional responses. In my view this neither entails nor is entailed by the claim that emotions are epistemically reason-responsive. However, I suspect that, e.g., Brady thinks that emotions are *also* epistemically reason-responsive.

be based upon a belief that *I have lied to my partner*, where this constitutes an *evidential* base for my guilt. If an emotion is based upon defective evidence, e.g., my belief that *I have lied to my partner* is unjustified, then the emotion is itself in some way epistemically defective, e.g., perhaps my guilt is also unjustified. Second, emotions are mental items for which epistemic justifications can be given/demanded, e.g., if I'm feeling guilty, it's perfectly legitimate for someone to ask me to provide a *reason* for my guilt—e.g., '*why* are you feeling that way?'[10]—where this is an appeal for epistemic reasons or evidence.

Given reason-responsiveness, it is apparently possible to develop powerful objections against Sentimentalism. First, the reason-responsiveness of emotions may appear to entail the falsity of Perceptualism, since perceptual experiences aren't reason-responsive: it apparently makes little sense to pose justificatory why-questions about perceptual experiences, e.g., 'why are you having that experience?', and experiences don't seem to be held or undergone for epistemic reasons. Experiences stand beyond epistemic justification.[11,12] Given the seemingly reasonable assumption that Sentimentalism depends on Perceptualism then Sentimentalism is false. Call this the 'Experiences Aren't Reason-Responsive' Objection.

Second, if emotions have evidential bases, e.g., a belief that *I have lied to you*, then emotions are *epistemically dependent*, i.e., they justify evaluative beliefs only if (and partly because) their bases are justified or justification-conferring. Given this, it is difficult to see how emotions could play an immediate justifying role, i.e., epistemic dependence and epistemic immediacy seem incompatible. Call this the 'Epistemic Dependence' Objection.

Finally, it is implausible that a mental item could be a source of immediate justification—i.e., it can generate justification for reason-responsive states such as beliefs—while being itself reason-responsive. This is because this combination— being generative of justification and reason-responsive—would seem to entail that such a mental item could justify *itself*, which is highly dubious. Call this the 'Self-Justification' Objection.

It might seem that the natural way to respond to these objections is to argue against emotional reason-responsiveness, e.g., perhaps *why-questions* are merely causal or clarificatory questions. I here adopt a different approach. I respond to these objections whilst *granting* that emotions are reason-responsive.[13] This is not only dialectically significant vis-à-vis the prospects for Sentimentalism, but also supports a broader claim about the compatibility of a mental item's being reason-responsive and its being

---

[10] Deonna and Teroni (2012), 69.
[11] Thanks to David Chalmers for highlighting this line of objection to me.
[12] Sceptics might pose why-questions which are aimed at undermining the trust that we put in perceptual experience, e.g., 'why do you think that the world is the way your experience presents it?' But that is a different matter from the one under consideration, i.e., whether one can ask for a justification for *an experience*.
[13] My strategy vis-à-vis Sentimentalism is similar to the approach adopted by Perceptualists to show that the seeming *irrationality* of recalcitrant emotions (e.g., fear in the face of knowledge that there is no danger) is compatible with their being experiences. See e.g. Brady (2009); Tappolet (2012). For an attempt to explain away the claim that recalcitrant emotions are irrational, see Döring (2015). I regard the issue of emotional recalcitrance as distinct from—though related to—epistemic reason-responsiveness.

a *generative*[14] source of epistemic justification. In Section 1 I clarify Perceptualism and Sentimentalism. In Sections 2–5 I respond to the reason-responsiveness objections. In Section 6 I conclude.

1. Perceptualism and Epistemic Sentimentalism

There's a reasonable degree of consensus among contemporary philosophers of emotion that paradigm cases of emotions, e.g., guilt in response to infidelity, implicate the following elements: (i) a representation of some target object or event, e.g., a belief that *I have lied to my partner*; (ii) an evaluation of that target object or event, e.g., that my lying was *wrong*; (iii) a motivation to act which is intelligible in light of the representation and evaluation, e.g., to apologize or make reparations to my partner; (iv) affective phenomenology, e.g., an unpleasant 'yucky' feeling; and (v) bodily changes (and perhaps an awareness thereof), e.g., a lump in one's throat, a dry mouth.[15]

Disagreement emerges when we theorize about which of these elements are constitutive of emotions, which are mere eliciting causes and effects, and what the nature is of the component parts and their relations.

Perceptualists think that conscious and occurrent emotions are, or are best understood by analogy with, perceptual experiences. More specifically, Perceptualism can be understood as providing an account of the evaluative element in emotion (component (ii)): it's a perceptual experience, or is in some respects like a perceptual experience, with evaluative content. For example, a proponent might claim that fear is, or involves, a perceptual experience of *dangerousness*, guilt an experience of *wrongness*, and so on.

There are various ways in which Perceptualism could be developed, e.g., whether the affective component constitutes the evaluative component,[16] or whether we include component (i) the 'cognitive base'[17] as part of the emotion. I'm agnostic about which version of Perceptualism is most plausible (note that this includes my being open to the possibility that different versions are plausible for different types of emotions). However, depending on which version we adopt, this will make Sentimentalism more or less vulnerable to objections, including reason-responsiveness objections. As it happens, I think that versions of Perceptualism which claim that component (i) is *not* part of the emotion and that component (ii) is a sort of affective seeming state with *conceptual* content (which is part of the emotion but distinct from other components) will be the most vulnerable to reason-responsiveness objections.[18,19] I'll tentatively assume this in what follows.

---

[14] The reader can assume that *generative* and *immediate* justification are equivalent. I will, however, argue that these come apart.

[15] This is indebted to remarks made in Brady (2013); Deonna and Teroni (2012).

[16] See e.g. Doring (2003); Goldie (2000).   [17] Deonna and Teroni (2012).

[18] Indeed, without the assumption of conceptual content, one might wonder whether it is plausible to claim that they are reason-responsive in the first place—but see Corns (forthcoming) for the view that hedonics can be reason-responsive.

[19] For a version of Perceptualism along these lines, see R. C. Roberts (2003).

Sentimentalists claim that emotions are a source of immediate justification for evaluative beliefs and sometimes constitute the immediate justificatory basis of evaluative beliefs.[20] Sentimentalism can take two general forms: Reliabilism and Phenomenalism.

Reliabilists think that a subject, S, has immediate prima facie propositional (perceptual) justification for believing that p iff S has (i) an experience with an appropriate content, e.g., p, and (ii) the experience is produced by a reliable process.[21] On this view, an emotion can constitute the evidential ground or basis for an evaluative belief, but does so in virtue of a non-evidential property of emotions: their being produced by a reliable process, i.e., one which issues in a favourable ratio of veridical to non-veridical states.

Phenomenalists think that a subject, S, has immediate prima facie propositional (perceptual) justification for believing that p iff S has an experience with presentational phenomenal character with respect to p. On this view, emotions constitute the evidential base for evaluative beliefs in virtue of their presentational phenomenology. 'Presentational' character with respect to p apparently differs significantly from representational content found in a belief or judgement that p, e.g., compare visually perceiving the red postbox at the end of the road with judging that *the postbox at the end of the road is red*. Although there are competing accounts of presentational phenomenology with respect to p,[22] it can be roughly understood as it seeming that p, where this involves the feeling that one is being *told* that something is true, as opposed to asserting that it is true. It is also typically associated with passivity and (importantly) a lack of reason-responsiveness.

I'm ecumenical about these epistemological views, but I suggest that the reader assume the version of Sentimentalism that they take to be most vulnerable to the various reason-responsiveness objections. I now proceed to those objections and my responses.

2. Experiences Aren't Reason-Responsive

The Experiences Aren't Reason-Responsive Objection goes as follows:

P1: Emotions are epistemically reason-responsive.
P2: No perceptual experiences are epistemically reason-responsive.
C1: Emotions are not perceptual experiences.
P3: Epistemic Sentimentalism is true only if emotions are perceptual experiences.
C2: Epistemic Sentimentalism is false.

P1 encompasses the claim, already explained in the introduction, that emotions can be held for epistemic reasons and that justifications can be demanded or given for emotions.

---

[20] Some proponents, e.g., Döring (2003), talk of *non-inferential* justification. Others, e.g., Pelser (2014), refer to *basic* justification. I assume that these are equivalent to immediate justification. See e.g. Pryor (2005).

[21] Brady (2013) assumes Reliabilism. [22] See Chudnoff (2013) and Reiland (2015) for examples.

P2 expresses a standard view about the nature of perceptual experience. On this view, perceptual experiences—and this is usually thought to include seeming states[23]—just aren't the sort of things which can be epistemically based upon other mental items such as beliefs,[24] or for which justificatory why-questions can be sensibly asked. It arguably doesn't make sense to think that a subject could be experiencing the redness of an object on the basis of further evidence that they have about the object. Similarly, asking someone for a justification for having the experience of redness would strike us as odd. Indeed, we might think that possession of these features (or perhaps it is the *lack* of features) is partly constitutive of being a perceptual experience.

P3 hinges on the claim that it is only perceptual experiences that possess/lack features which enable them to confer immediate justification for beliefs. Importantly for our purposes this allegedly includes their lacking the feature of epistemic reason-responsiveness. Here is Sosa expressing a similar thought:

> Experiences are able to provide justification that is foundational because they lie beyond justification and unjustification. Since they are passively received, they cannot manifest obedience to anything, including rational norms, whether epistemic or otherwise. Since unmotivated by reasons, they can serve as *foundational* sources, as regress-stoppers.[25]

If that's right, then emotions will be capable of conferring immediate or generative justification only if they are perceptual experiences. Hence, Sentimentalism hinges on the truth of Perceptualism. Given the intermediate conclusion that Perceptualism is false (from P1 and P2), Sentimentalism is also false.

Since I am granting P1 (reason-responsiveness), in order to defend Sentimentalism I must deny either P2 or P3. I'll first briefly explain how P2 is controversial and can plausibly be resisted. I'll then outline how P3 can be denied. However, as will become clear, a plausible denial of P3 requires dealing with further reason-responsiveness objections.

One option open to Sentimentalists is to deny P2 by identifying cases of non-emotional perceptual experiences which seem to be reason-responsive. The most plausible candidates of this are, I think, *cognitively penetrated* perceptual experiences. Roughly, cognitive penetration of (sensory) perceptual experience is possible if and only if it's possible for two subjects to have experiences which differ in content and/or phenomenal character, where this difference is the result of a causal process that traces more or less directly to states in the subjects' cognitive system, and where we hold fixed the perceptual stimuli, the condition of the subjects' sensory organs, the environmental conditions, and the attentional focus of the subjects.[26] Putative cases of cognitive penetration include: beliefs about the typical colour of bananas can allegedly make subjects experience them as being more *yellow* than they are; possessing a stock of beliefs about pine trees may enable perceivers to have visual experiences which represent the property of *being a pine tree* in a way that novices do not.

---

[23] Although note that those who countenance the existence of seemings think that they are distinct from sensations. See papers in Tucker (2013) for discussion.

[24] See e.g. Lyons (2011).   [25] Sosa (2007), 46.   [26] See Vance (2014).

Why would anyone think that cognitively penetrated experiences are epistemically reason-responsive? Although this matter is highly contentious, some philosophers[27] think that attributing something like the property of reason-responsiveness to at least some cognitively penetrated experiences can best explain our intuitions about the epistemological features of beliefs based upon such experiences. To get a sense of what is meant by this, consider the following case:

> Wishful Willy: Willy is a gold prospector but hasn't yet become an expert at identifying gold nuggets, e.g., he isn't yet able to distinguish them from yellowish pebbles. Nevertheless, Willy also has a very strong wish to find gold. Indeed, his wish is so powerful that when he observes a yellowish pebble (and has a seeming that there is a yellowish pebble) his desire cognitively penetrates his seeming such that it comes to seem to him to be a gold nugget.[28]

About this case, consider the following question: would Willy's belief that *there is a gold nugget* be epistemically justified? The intuitive verdict, I think, is 'No'. Yet, Willy had an experience with this content, and there aren't any obvious defeaters for his belief. At this point, the appeal to reason-responsiveness comes in. For example, Matthew McGrath[29] suggests that in order to explain the verdict about Wishful Willy, we ought to say that Willy's seeming that there is a gold nugget is a special kind of seeming (he calls it a 'non-receptive' seeming, in contrast to more basic 'receptive' seemings). Thanks to his strong desire for gold, Willy *quasi-infers* the seeming that there is a gold nugget on the basis of his receptive seeming that there is a yellowish pebble. About quasi-inference, McGrath says the following:

> Let us say that a transition from a seeming that P to a seeming that Q is 'quasi-inferential' just in case the transition that would results from replacing these seemings with corresponding beliefs that P and Q would count as genuine inference by the person.[30]

Applied to the Wishful Willy case, the thought is that the relation between the non-receptive seeming of a gold nugget and the receptive seeming of a yellowish pebble is similar to the relation between two beliefs, where one is inferred from the other. As McGrath characterizes this, quasi-inferred seemings

> function epistemically in the way inference by the person does: they can at best *transmit* the relevant epistemic property of the inputs to the outputs; they cannot *generate* this property for the outputs when it isn't possessed by the inputs.[31]

A quasi-inferred seeming can fail to confer epistemic justification in two ways: (1) if the quasi-inference isn't a good one for the subject, i.e., if the content of the input seeming doesn't sufficiently support the content of the output for the subject, and, (2) if the input seeming isn't justification-conferring. Finally, note that McGrath also allows that there can be seemings that are based upon beliefs.

Back in the Wishful Willy case, McGrath would say that the seeming with gold content is quasi-inferred from the seeming of a yellowish pebble. Although the

---

[27] See e.g. Siegel (2012); M. McGrath (2013).　[28] This is adapted from a case in Markie (2006).
[29] M. McGrath (2013).　[30] M. McGrath (2013), 237.　[31] M. McGrath (2013), 237.

seeming of a yellowish pebble is justification-conferring (let's assume), the seeming with gold content fails to justify because the quasi-inference isn't a good one for Willy: it simply involved wishful thinking, not the deployment of some recognitional capacity (compare with an analogous case of standard inference due to wishful thinking).

If that's right, then we would have a nice explanation of our intuitive verdict about the Wishful Willy case: the gold seeming fails to justify because it is produced by a bad quasi-inference from a more basic seeming.

This proposal could make sense of our verdict about another case (although note that this is a cognitive and not a sensory seeming):

> Sloppy Sherlock: Sherlock has the epistemically unjustified belief that Melanie's story about where she was at the time of the murder is a ruse (let's suppose he makes an inexplicable inferential error while listening to her testimony). Given his background beliefs about the other suspects and his general expertise in crime solving, it seems to him that Melanie is guilty. He forms a belief on the basis of this seeming.

In this case, I hope the reader will agree that Sherlock's belief isn't justified. Relatedly, it seems that we should also agree that the seeming that Melanie is guilty cannot confer justification for believing that content. This is well explained by the view that the seeming about Melanie's guilt is quasi-inferred from Sherlock's belief about Melanie's alibi.

Are quasi-inferred seemings susceptible to justificatory *why-questions*? Although I doubt that this will convince proponents of P2, I don't think that it would be odd for someone to ask Willy 'why does the pebble seem like a piece of gold?' Neither would it be strange for someone to challenge Sherlock by asking 'why does Melanie seem guilty to you?' Furthermore, in response, Willy and Sherlock may appeal to the contents of their more basic seemings or other beliefs that they hold.

Although much more would need to be said,[32] I think that the possibility of putative cases of quasi-inferred seemings provides us with some reason to think that a lack of epistemic reason-responsiveness is not a constitutive part of being a perceptual experience. Hence P2 doesn't appear unassailable.

But maybe the reader rejects this: perhaps there are no non-emotional quasi-inferred seemings or perceptual experiences. If so then Sentimentalists might deny P2 by identifying emotions themselves as counterexamples. On this view, emotions would be unique kinds of perceptual experience that are epistemically reason-responsive.

Nevertheless, some may be wedded to the standard view of perceptual experience and will thus be unimpressed by these attempts to push back against P2. In light of this, I think that the Sentimentalist might be best advised to make the following three

---

[32] Even if non-receptive seemings are in some important sense *passive*, this is still compatible with their being epistemically dependent. Many beliefs are—in some sense—passively formed yet are epistemically dependent. A similar point could be made if it was thought that non-receptive seemings are in some sense outside subjects' control. Again, it seems possible for subjects to possess beliefs that they can't get rid of—synchronically or diachronically—yet are held for epistemic reasons.

claims which together would enable them to deny P3: (1) Emotions are *not* genuine perceptual experiences. They are simply best understood by analogy with perceptual experience; (2) One way in which they differ from genuine perceptual experiences is that they are epistemically reason-responsive; and (3) One way in which they are like perceptual experiences is that they can play an epistemically generative role.

Indeed, (1) may be the best way to understand the Perceptualist proposal.[33] Emotions possess important features in common with perceptual experience: e.g., they are intentional, non-doxastic, they possess a phenomenal character, they can conflict with evaluative judgements without contradiction. However, they also possess features that make it difficult to classify them as genuine perceptual experiences (given the standard view), e.g., they are dependent upon our cares and concerns, they are (allegedly) motivational. As (2) claims, one further disanalogy on this list may be that emotions, unlike bona fide perceptual experiences, are reason-responsive (and recall, I am granting this).[34]

Now, in order for this to constitute a rejection of P3, it needs to be the case that, despite the fact that emotions aren't perceptual experiences, and despite one of the disanalogies being that emotions are reason-responsive, one *similarity* between perceptual experience and emotions—understood as sui generis intentional phenomena—is that emotions are capable of playing an epistemically generative role with respect to evaluative beliefs (claim (3)). But given the assumption that emotions are epistemically reason-responsive it might be hard to see how that could be true. Making good on this response to P3 thus requires responding to further reason-responsiveness objections, to which I now turn.

3. Epistemic Dependence

The Epistemic Dependence Objection goes as follows:

P1: Emotions are based upon epistemic reasons.

P2: If emotions are based upon epistemic reasons then they are epistemically dependent sources of epistemic justification.

P3: If emotions are epistemically dependent sources of epistemic justification then emotions do not confer immediate justification.

C: Emotions do not confer immediate justification, i.e., Epistemic Sentimentalism is false.

As before, I'm taking P1 for granted. On the version of Perceptualism that I'm assuming, guilt, for instance, could be mediated by a belief that *I lied to you*, or fear might be mediated by a perceptual experience of a *snake*. So, emotions are *causally* dependent upon cognitive bases. It's plausible that the cognitive bases of emotions are also *evidential* bases because emotions are apparently susceptible to

---

[33] See e.g. Doring and Lutz (2015). On p. 260 they say that 'in its strong version at least, perceptualism in emotion theory has lost lots of its original attraction'.

[34] Doring and Lutz (2015), 265 agree.

justificatory why-questions, and, answers to these questions tend to identify features (re)presented in the cognitive base of the emotion. Consider the following case:

> Guilty Party: During a conversation with some colleagues at a work Christmas party James reveals some intimate details about his partner to them. James knows that his partner would be horrified to learn that strangers knew about such private details. After the conversation ends, James is overcome with guilt.

Were someone to ask James why (in the justificatory sense, let's assume) he was feeling guilty, it wouldn't be unusual for him to reply 'I broke my partner's trust.' This, we might think, is good reason to think that James's emotion is evidentially based upon a (re)presentation of this fact, e.g., a belief. However, even if a subject's attempts at demonstrating that they're justified are not necessarily a good guide to what actually justifies a particular mental item (more later), proponents of P1 may think that it's independently plausible that Alex's belief that *he has broken his partner's trust* is the evidential basis for his guilt.

P2 says that if emotions have evidential bases then they are epistemically dependent. Minimally, this is the claim that if emotions are based upon a *bad* evidential base, e.g., an unjustified belief, they will fail to confer justification for evaluative beliefs. More strongly, it says that emotions can *themselves* be epistemically (un)justified depending on the justified status of their cognitive bases.[35]

P3 makes the further—seemingly plausible—claim that epistemic dependence entails that a particular source of justification is only a source of *mediate* justification, which is antithetical to immediate justification.

Given the acceptance of P1, Sentimentalists must deny P2 or P3.

Although P3 is questionable (since epistemic dependence and epistemic mediacy may come apart, cf. memory justification) Sentimentalists may attempt to deny P2 in the following way. It might be thought that P2 is vulnerable to the fact that states other than beliefs can be cognitive bases of emotions. For example, my perceptual experience of a snake could be the cognitive base of fear. Or an imaginative episode wherein I consider pushing someone off a bridge to save five people might be the cognitive base of a sort of moral revulsion. This is significant because, unlike beliefs, it's standardly thought that perceptual experiences and imaginative episodes can't be (un)justified, e.g., it apparently doesn't make sense to say that my experience of the snake is *justified*. Perhaps emotions which take perceptual experiences or imaginative episodes as evidential bases aren't epistemically dependent because they're based on states or processes that are *beyond* justification (although see Section 2).

In response it might be argued that, if the evidential base of one's emotion is, e.g., an experience of a snake, the experience must be *justification-conferring* in order for the emotion to confer justification. This is true, even though perceptual experiences can't themselves be justified. If that's right, then emotions based on perceptual

---

[35] There may be additional normative constraints on the cognitive bases of emotions, e.g., perhaps the content of cognitive bases must be such that *were they true/veridical* then the emotional response would be a *fitting* or *appropriate response* to the object or event.

experience would be epistemically dependent. Perhaps similar points could be made about imaginative episodes.[36]

I leave it others to pursue this line of attack on P2. Instead, I propose to grant the *soundness* of the Epistemic Dependency Objection, but deny that this is fatal for Sentimentalism. Let me explain.

Suppose that emotions are epistemically dependent sources of justification. That would seem to require that Sentimentalists jettison their view. However, even if emotions are epistemically dependent upon their cognitive bases this is compatible with their functioning as 'evaluative data' and serving as *fundamental* or *generative* sources of justification for evaluative beliefs.[37]

According to this proposal, an emotion, e.g., guilt, would fail to justify an evaluative belief, e.g., *my having lied to you was wrong*, if the cognitive base for this emotion, e.g., a belief that *I have lied to you*, was itself unjustified. This is the sense in which it's epistemically dependent—it requires that the subject have justification for believing non-evaluative propositions. However, when the cognitive base of an emotion *is* justified then emotions can justify beliefs with *evaluative* content, *independently of having further justification for believing supporting evaluative propositions*. This is the sense in which emotions are epistemically fundamental or generative. If that's right, then emotions being epistemically dependent upon their cognitive bases is compatible with their playing the epistemic role that Sentimentalists require of them: they sometimes generate evaluative justification.

On this proposal there is a sense in which emotions are epistemically *independent* with respect to their evaluative content, since emotions don't require further justification for supporting evaluative propositions in order to justify evaluative beliefs. However, if the content of emotions links evaluative and non-evaluative contents—e.g., my having lied to you was wrong—then emotions are clearly epistemically dependent upon their cognitive bases, i.e., they can't justify evaluative beliefs unless their cognitive bases are justified or justification-conferring. Even if emotions have 'thinner' non-evaluative content—e.g., what I did was wrong—then emotions may still be epistemically dependent upon their bases (yet also generative of justification).

It may help to compare this proposal with Michael Huemer's account of *inferential appearances/seemings*.[38] These are non-doxastic, perceptual-like, propositional states which allegedly play a key role in inferential (or 'mediate') justification. They are distinguished from other seeming states, e.g., sensory perceptual seemings, because they (or at least some of them) involve or require the exercise of reason or understanding. They are thus labelled 'intellectual' seemings. They are also distinct from other intellectual seemings: intuitions. Unlike intuitions, which simply represent the

---

[36] Emotions also have *motivational* bases, e.g., moods and character traits (see Deonna and Teroni 2012). I don't take these to be good candidates for evidential bases. Moods seem to be best thought of as potential defeaters for emotional justification, e.g., if my anger is a product of my bad mood, then this might serve to undermine the justification I'd otherwise get from the emotion. Note, however, that moods might sometimes be epistemically beneficial, e.g., perhaps my being in a bad mood makes me more sensitive to the presence of (genuine) offences. Character traits—construed as (partly) emotional dispositions, thus standing in a partially constitutive relation to emotional episodes—might impact on the reliability of emotions, but don't seem to be best thought of as evidential bases.

[37] Pelser's (2014) discussion is suggestive of this point.   [38] Huemer (2013) and (2016).

truth of some proposition, inferential appearances involve some proposition seeming true to a subject *in light of the* presumed truth of some other proposition. Specifically, inferential appearances 'occur during inference and represent that a conclusion must be true or is likely to be true *in light of* something else that one believes'.[39] To illustrate consider the following case. I get home from work and see Jen's shoes. I immediately infer that Jen is probably home. On Huemer's view what may be going on is that I have a belief that Jen's shoes are in the hall and then undergo an inferential appearance that in light of Jen's shoes being in the hall, Jen is probably home. On this basis I form the belief that Jen is probably home.

Suppose that there are inferential appearances. There are two similarities between these and what I have just said may be true about emotions (remember that I am thinking of the perceptual component of emotions as involving an evaluative conceptual seeming state). Firstly, Huemer suggests that inferential appearances, e.g., it seems that p, given q, lead to doxastically justified beliefs *only if* the subject has justification for believing the premise(s), e.g., q. This epistemic dependence is similar to the relation between the cognitive bases and evaluative judgements on the current proposal about emotions. Second, emotional experiences might be thought to be experiences *in light of* their cognitive bases, e.g., in guilt my actions (represented in the cognitive base) appear *wrong*. Are emotions thereby a kind of inferential appearance? No. There is a crucial point of disanalogy: inferential appearances are apparently *not based* upon the premises which they are formed in the light of. Instead, an inferential appearance 'plays an essential role in the process of basing a belief on another belief, because it is what constitutes one's *seeing* the premise *as* an adequate ground for the conclusion'.[40] Inferential appearances are not themselves epistemically dependent. This contrasts with emotions which, on the current proposal, *are* epistemically dependent (but also epistemically fundamental).

Instead, on one version of the proposal I'm offering, emotions are (or involve) evaluative seemings that are *themselves* the result of something like a quasi-inference from their cognitive base. This quasi-inference may be made against the subject's background beliefs, commitments (some of which may have evaluative content), and character traits. Is this compatible with emotions being fundamental sources of justification for evaluative propositions? It could be so long as the subject didn't require justification for believing supporting evaluative propositions in order for the quasi-inference to be a good one (and thus for the emotion to be justification-conferring). And I suggest that it's not implausible that this is indeed the case. To illustrate: in Guilt Party, James might have the following kinds of commitments in light of which he experiences guilt: my partner is deeply important to me, my partner doesn't want strangers to know about aspects of her private life, trust is important in a relationship, etc. None of these directly support the proposition that *my having revealed to strangers private details about my partner was morally wrong*. Yet James's guilt could plausibly be justification-conferring with respect to this proposition, in light of the cognitive base of the emotion, and given his background commitments. Hence, guilt could be epistemically fundamental with respect to this evaluative proposition.

[39] Huemer (2013), 338.   [40] Huemer (2013), 338.

Finally, note that the combination of dependence and fundamentality being posited here is not without precedent: it is similar to the ontological relation that apparently holds between *emergent properties* and their base properties, e.g., between mental states and physical states of the brain. On this view, mental phenomena are ontologically dependent on physical states, but are nonetheless ontologically fundamental.[41] Hence, one way of understanding the current proposal about emotional justification is that emotions constitute *emergent* sources of epistemic justification for evaluative propositions.

How could emotions be epistemically emergent with respect to evaluative propositions? This will be because emotions possess epistemically important properties with respect to evaluative propositions: either being the outputs of a conditionally reliable process which generates veridical experiential outputs given true/veridical non-evaluative evidential bases, or possessing something akin to presentational phenomenal character with respect to evaluative propositions. Regarding the latter, Phenomenalist option, it might be thought that, if emotions really are reason-responsive (as I'm granting), this precludes them from having presentational character of the same kind as that allegedly found in sensory experience (since one of the features of presentationality, noted earlier, may be a lack of reason-responsiveness). Although a lot more would need to be said, note two thing in defence: (i) presentationality is a condition on immediate justification, but emotions are not here being claimed to provide immediate justification, and (ii) emotions lacking the presentationality of sensory experience is compatible with their possessing something similar, e.g., to the subject of an emotion it may feel like they are being told that some evaluative proposition is true. Of course, if one has serious doubts about the Phenomenalist option, Sentimentalists may instead wish to adopt a Reliabilist account. In order to do that, proponents will, however, need to address the issue of whether emotions are indeed reliable. But demonstrating how and explaining why, e.g., emotions could be reliable, is beyond the scope of this paper.[42]

Despite these limitations, I take myself to have said enough to show that Sentimentalists could accept the soundness of the Epistemic Dependence Objection whilst maintaining the spirit (though not the letter) of their view. On this proposal, emotions are not sources of immediate justification. They don't halt the epistemic regress tout court. However, this is compatible with emotions functioning as generative sources of justification for evaluative propositions and being an empiricist-friendly source of value input. That's all Sentimentalists need to secure the aforementioned attractions of the view.[43]

---

[41] See e.g. Barnes (2012).

[42] One might wonder whether there is anything epistemically special about emotions on this proposal, i.e., it seems that an evaluative *judgement* could be just as easily emergent from a cognitive base and one's background commitments. Unless one adopts a Phenomenalist view of emotional justification, this may turn out to be correct. However, even if true, it may be the case that emotions play a motivational role that renders them important for evaluative justification.

[43] In Cowan (2016), I discuss another version of this sort of objection which claims that emotions are always *based* upon mental items with *evaluative* content. I don't have space to discuss this here, except to note that this seems to be question-begging against Sentimentalism (since it can be understood as the claim that emotions are sometimes the way in which we non-derivatively recognize evaluative features).

4. Why-Questions

Consider now Why-Question Objections to Sentimentalism[44] which concern the claims that (1) when challenged with *why-questions* for evaluative judgements subjects don't (and shouldn't) cite emotions, and, (2) emotions are themselves susceptible to *why-questions*. Note that (1) doesn't take emotional reason-responsiveness as a premise. I discuss it because my response to it connects with my response to the Epistemic Dependence Objection and leads on nicely to (2), which does assume epistemic reason-responsiveness.

Sentimentalists claim that emotions can (and sometimes do) constitute the epistemic *base* of justified evaluative beliefs. Emotions allegedly function in an epistemically analogous way to perceptual experience vis-à-vis empirical beliefs. An alleged sign that perceptual experience is the basis for perceptual beliefs is that in response to why-questions regarding these beliefs, subjects typically appeal to their experience, e.g., in response to 'why do you think that the ball is green?' a natural answer is 'I can see it'. However, the emotional case is apparently different: we *don't* typically respond to why-questions for evaluative beliefs, e.g., *the dog is dangerous,* by appealing to emotions. It would be unusual to respond to the question 'why do you think that the dog is dangerous?' by saying 'because I am afraid'. Not only are these responses atypical, they seem like the incorrect thing to say. Instead, when faced with why-questions regarding evaluative beliefs, we tend to (and should) identify features, objects, or events that are represented in the cognitive base, e.g., 'because the dog is rabid'.

This allegedly provides reason for thinking that emotions aren't the justificatory basis for evaluative judgements. If they were then we would identify emotions when challenged with why-questions. But we don't. Further, the fact that an appeal to one's emotion would seem illegitimate suggests that emotions are insufficient to justify evaluative judgements.

I present two responses. Firstly, the above data about why-questions is what we should expect if emotions are epistemically dependent sources of justification. If challenged on one's evaluative judgement, of which the justificatory basis is an emotion, then it's unsurprising that subjects appeal to the cognitive basis of their emotion rather than the emotion. For if they were to only appeal to the emotion they would still face justificatory questions regarding the emotion. Further, Sentimentalists should admit that emotions are not, by themselves, sufficient to justify evaluative beliefs: they are, after all, epistemically dependent. However, as I have argued, this is compatible with their being generative sources of evaluative justification. Sentimentalists should also claim that it's compatible with emotions being the justificatory *base* for evaluative beliefs (or at least the partial base): in at least some cases, without an emotional response, subjects wouldn't have (and may not have formed) a justified evaluative belief, since it's the emotion which generates evaluative justification.

An alternative response is that, when subjects respond to justificatory *why-questions* about their evaluative beliefs, perhaps they are covertly appealing to their emotions rather than simply to cognitive bases, i.e., if a subject responds to the question 'why do you think what you did was wrong?' by claiming 'I lied to my

---

[44] See Deonna and Teroni (2012); Pelser (2014).

partner', this is elliptical for 'I lied to my partner, and my having lied to my partner was wrong'. Sentimentalists could then claim that, in at least some instances, subjects are thereby partially appealing to the *content of their emotion*, e.g., my having lied to my partner was wrong. It's only a partial appeal, because they're also appealing to what justifies the emotion, e.g., the belief that *they lied to their partner*. Far from eschewing emotions when attempting to show that evaluative beliefs are justified, subjects sometimes implicitly appeal to them.

If we implicitly appeal to emotions, one might wonder why it seems illegitimate to defend an evaluative judgement, e.g., *I did something wrong*, with an *explicit* appeal to emotion, e.g., 'I feel guilty'. Sentimentalists should again highlight the epistemic dependence of emotions: appealing to emotion will be insufficient to justify the evaluative belief. An alternative explanation is that evaluative discourse is subject to additional norms not operative in non-evaluative discourse. For example, perhaps in order to be entitled to evaluative beliefs one requires evaluative *understanding*.[45] When engaged in evaluative discourse perhaps subjects ought to offer justifications for beliefs that demonstrate their understanding (at least when they are in a position to do so). Appealing explicitly to emotions fails to do this.

Even if these responses are accepted, it's possible to develop a second Why-Question Objection. Suppose that I'm being challenged with a justificatory why-question about my emotion: 'why are you feeling guilty?' As suggested, a natural response would identify features represented in the cognitive base, e.g., *I lied to my partner*. However, if this is elliptical for the content that *my having lied to my partner was wrong* (as was suggested previously) and if that involves a covert appeal to emotion, then the justification being offered for the emotion is circular.

Moreover, even if identifying the cognitive base of an emotion doesn't involve a covert appeal to the emotion, an interlocutor might challenge the attempt to justify the emotion: 'why does your having lied to your partner justify your guilt?' If one responded by claiming 'because lying to my partner was wrong' it would seem that Sentimentalists are committed to claiming that the subject would (at least sometimes) be thereby appealing to their *emotion* (according to Sentimentalists emotions are sometimes the way we register evaluative properties). But that is to engage in illegitimate circular justification.

In attempting to respond to why-questions regarding emotions, subjects may end up engaging in illegitimate circular justification. Is that a problem for Sentimentalism? No. Let me explain.

Firstly, we should distinguish between *demonstrative* and *agential* justification, i.e., between a subject *showing* that they're justified and a subject *being* justified with respect to a mental item/proposition.[46] The fact that some mental item, e, is justified by another item, d (agential justification), doesn't entail that subjects will appeal to d when challenged about e (demonstrative justification), e.g., subjects might be inarticulate. Conversely, the fact that a subject appeals to some mental item f, in

---

[45] See Brady (2013) for something like this suggestion. See also Hills (2009) for a full discussion of the alleged importance of moral understanding.
[46] See Shafer-Landau (2003).

order to justify, e, doesn't entail that f is *what justifies* e, e.g., the structure of justification may be unclear to the subject.

Secondly, the fact that someone fails to give a good demonstrative justification for e, doesn't entail that they're not justified with respect to e, e.g., I might not be able to provide much if anything in the way of a justification for a fundamental arithmetical belief I have, e.g., $2 + 2 = 4$, or my belief that *the Law of Identity is true*. For example, in demonstratively justifying the belief in the Law of Identity, I might only be able to give circular justifications. Yet that needn't entail that my belief is unjustified.

Now apply these points to the emotional case under discussion: that subjects may end up engaging in circular justifications when attempting to provide demonstrative justification for their emotions would only be a problem for Sentimentalism if (i) demonstrative justification always tracked agential justification (since it would entail that subject's emotions are somehow justified by themselves), and/or, (ii) a failure to provide a good demonstrative justification always undermined agential justification (since engaging in dubious circular justification would undermine a subject's justification). But as I just argued, both of these claims are problematic.

Further, the emotional case is plausibly one where demonstrative justification doesn't track agential justification, and where failure to provide demonstrative justification doesn't undermine agential justification. Regarding both of these points recall that emotions are fundamental sources of evaluative justification. Emotions are justified by appropriate non-evaluative cognitive bases. Given this, a legitimate response to 'why does your having lied to your partner justify your guilt?' is (in a sense) 'it just does'. But the structure of justification may be unclear to subjects. Note also that, because emotions are fundamental sources of evaluative justification, it's unsurprising that, when challenged as to why features identified in the cognitive base justify the emotion, some subjects end up engaging in circular justification (compare with the Law of Identity case). Note of course that they might not, e.g., philosophically trained subjects may appeal to theories. However, Sentimentalists should claim that the emotion can confer justification for evaluative beliefs independently of such appeals.

That subjects may sometimes engage in dubious circular demonstrative justifications of emotions doesn't undermine Sentimentalism. In Section 5 I finally consider an objection to Sentimentalism which claims that the view is committed to the claim that emotions really do justify themselves, and thus ought to be rejected.

5. Self-Justification

Consider, finally, the Self-Justification Objection:

P1: If emotions can generate justification for reason-responsive mental phenomena, e.g., evaluative beliefs, then they could generate justification for themselves.

P2: Emotions cannot generate justification for themselves.

C: Emotions cannot generate justification for reason-responsive mental phenomena.

P1 says that, given the assumption that emotions can generate justification, and are themselves reason-responsive, an entailment is that emotions are capable of generating justification for themselves. P2 claims that 'self-justification' is illegitimate. Putting these two claims together we appear to be led to the conclusion that emotions cannot generate justification, i.e., they are not a fundamental source of justification for reason-responsive phenomena like evaluative beliefs. Put another way, the Self-Justification Objection appears to entail that the refined version of Sentimentalism—introduced to deal with the Epistemic Dependence Objection—is false.

There are two more specific versions of the Self-Justification Objection. On an Indirect version, P1 says that if emotions can generate justification for evaluative beliefs, then the evaluative belief could confer propositional justification for (and possibly constitute the base of) the emotion. P2 claims that this is illegitimate. On a Direct version, P1 says that simply by having a justification-conferring emotion, one gets a justificatory boost (in the propositional sense) for that very emotion. P2 claims that this is illegitimate.

Note that this worry is allegedly particular to emotions. It doesn't apply to beliefs, since although they are reason-responsive, apparently they can only *transmit* justification for propositions from other sources (e.g., perceptions) to other beliefs, rather than *generate* justification in the way that perception does. It doesn't apply to perceptions, since although they're capable of generating justification they're apparently not epistemically reason-responsive (but again see Section 2 for doubts about that view of perceptual experience).

How should Sentimentalists respond? Against the Indirect version, Sentimentalists should claim that the relevant evaluative beliefs can merely *preserve* the justification from the emotion. So the justification they confer for the content of the emotion is no more or less than the justification conferred by the emotion. Contra P1, subjects don't get an extra justification boost for the emotional content over and above that which they started with.[47]

Against the Direct version Sentimentalists should also deny P1. Although emotions can generate justification for believing their contents (regarding those contents as true) they cannot generate justification for themselves. They can preserve justification for their own contents, but they cannot provide an evidential boost for emotionally (re)presenting those contents.

This might seem ad hoc. I demur. Sentimentalists can point to cases where one entity has the authority to confer some status on another entity, but lacks the authority to do so upon themselves. For example, we might think that a judge in a just legal system will have the authority to hand down sentences to convicted citizens, but will at the same time lack the authority to pass a sentence upon themselves. Notice that it might not simply be a contingent matter that things are this way: instead it may be a constitutive part of being that sort of entity (a judge in a just legal system) that they can confer a normative status upon other entities, but not upon themselves. Or take another example: Catholic priests are able to administer confession—which, according to Catholicism, can lead to the forgiveness of sins by

---

[47] A more complex version of the Indirect Self-Justification objection would amount to a 'Bootstrapping' worry of the sort proposed by Vogel (2008). I address this in Cowan (2016). Let me simply note that this is an objection which can be brought against *any* theory which allows that experiences can generate justification for beliefs.

God—to laypersons and other members of the clergy. However, Catholic priests are not able to administer confession to themselves. That is arguably not because of some historical anomaly, but because of something about the nature of forgiveness and penance. So, if the nature of confession is bound up with the nature of forgiveness, then we might think that it is constitutive of being an entity that can administer confession to others that one cannot confer God's forgiveness on oneself.

Although these examples are by no means strict analogues of the emotional case, their purpose is to establish that we are already familiar with cases where claims that are analogous to P1 are false, i.e., it is false that *if a Catholic priest has the authority to administer confession to another person then they have the authority to administer it to themselves*. The thought then is that this should make it seem less ad hoc to deny P1 of the Self-Justification Objection. At least, it seems that the onus is on the proponent of P1 to provide some good reason for thinking that it could *not* be constitutive of a mental item—such as emotion—being a generator of epistemic justification, that it can only generate justification for other mental items, and not onto itself (even though that mental item is otherwise epistemically reason-responsive). Unless they do, Sentimentalism is not undermined.

6. Conclusion

Epistemic Sentimentalism can be defended against epistemic reason-responsiveness objections, whilst granting that emotions are epistemically reason-responsive. This puts Sentimentalists in a dialectically powerful position. However, perhaps emotions are not epistemically reason-responsive after all. Maybe we are confused into thinking this because we equivocate between different kinds of normative assessment, i.e., talk of the justification of emotion may be tracking a distinct set of norms—e.g., those essential to Neo-Sentimentalism—easily mistaken for epistemic justification. Considering that proposal is, however, the job for another paper.[48]

---

[48] Thanks to Michael Brady, Jennifer Corns, Michael Milona, and audiences at the 2015 Bled Philosophy Conference, and the 2016 British Society for Ethical Theory conference in Cardiff for very helpful feedback.

PART III
Evaluative Perception and Value Theory

12

Value Perception, Properties, and the Primary Bearers of Value

Graham Oddie

1. The Possibility of Value Knowledge

We make value claims about all manner of things. We attribute a variety of evaluative properties, relations, and magnitudes to an astonishing array of objects of just about every ontological type. There are the familiar thin evaluative attributes beloved of axiologists (*good, bad, better than*). In addition there is that vast storehouse of thick attributes that we draw on in our evaluations of persons, characters, actions, states of affairs, outcomes, dispositions, institutions, works of art, musical performances, artifacts, mathematical proofs, and the practitioners of all manner of trades, arts, and sciences. We evaluate people as *courageous, compassionate, callous, cruel, charming*, and *sexy*. We evaluate actions as *generous, vindictive, kind*, and *foolhardy*. We evaluate performances as *brilliant, elegant, clumsy, riveting, delightful*, and *poised*. We evaluate remarks as *tendentious, salacious, witty, craven, hurtful, sarcastic, biting*, and *helpful*. And so on. Some evaluative attributes appear to be applicable to different categories of entities. Agents as well as their actions can be described as *cruel* or *compassionate*. Proofs as well as performances can be described as *elegant* or *insightful*. Some of these attributes are evaluatively positive, others evaluatively negative, and for others their contribution to overall value may depend on the way they mesh with the other attributes with which they are combined.

That we make these value claims is undeniable. But whether we could know such claims, or whether we could be justified making them, is not quite as undeniable. Error theorists about value claim that this discourse is deeply defective—that there are no evaluative properties and hence there no truths about value available to be known. Value skeptics claim that even if there were such truths, there would be no plausible way for us to accumulate evidence concerning them. Others claim that such knowledge would be deeply mysterious because such knowledge would have to be intrinsically motivating in a way that knowledge could never be. But those are somewhat gloomy prognoses, and rather than embracing them, I will defend a more optimistic view. It is neither a pure value empiricism (according to which the justification for all value claims can be traced back to experiences of value) nor a pure value rationalism (according to which the justification for all value claims can be traced back to some a priori rational insight) but a kind of value fallibilism that accords to both reason and experience legitimate and complementary roles in the construction of a value theory, and explains how a certain kind of value knowledge could move us.

2. Value Appearances

Even an error theorist must concede, at least in her more generous moments, that things *seem* or *appear* to possess various value attributes. Pleasure seems better than pain; happiness seems better than misery; knowledge seems better than ignorance and error; gratuitous cruelty seems worse than gratuitous kindness; J. S. Bach's music seems better than Justin Bieber's; and so on. Not even an error theorist need deny the existence of these ubiquitous value appearances. They can concede that things appear valuable and go on to claim that such appearances constitute a gigantic and systematic (or perhaps rather messy) *illusion* of value. In our naïve unphilosophical state we take such appearances to be revelatory, and we mistakenly 'project' the properties and relations that they present to us onto an essentially value-free world.

This is a striking claim and—like analogous claims about the illusoriness of color, the illusoriness of the passage of time, the illusoriness of the physical world, and the illusoriness of the mind—it has to be backed up with some convincing arguments. There are arguments for the systematic illusoriness of value appearances, as there are for the illusoriness of other phenomena, and I cannot pretend to give any of them here the attention they deserve. But it is worth pointing out that, however *convincing* those arguments may seem, they all leave the illusion itself firmly in place. This is as true for the arguments that pertain to value as it is for the arguments that pertain to colors, temporal passage, material objects, and our mental life. When we pack up our philosophy books, get out the backgammon board, and turn on the stereo, the appearances of color, temporal flow, materiality, thought, and aesthetic value all come flooding back in. Some things just appear good, some things appear bad, some things appear better than other things, and no argument (no matter how good *that* might appear) can dislodge this stubborn phenomenological fact. Of course, particular value appearances may fluctuate—what seemed so good yesterday might lose its luster upon realization. And value appearances, like other appearances, are no doubt theory-laden. But even committed nihilists would be hard pressed to deny that things *appear* more or less good, even though they *judge* these appearances illusory.

This is just as well for the friend of value judgments, because without value appearances the prospects for justifying any substantive value judgments seem decidedly thin. It's true that there are a small number of truths about value that might be accessed by pure reason. For example, the structural properties of the relation of *better-than* (*irreflexivity*, *asymmetry*, and *transitivity*) all seem like good candidates for a priori value knowledge. There is a highly plausible principle of *universalizability* in the value domain that also seems to be a candidate for a priori knowledge: two things exactly alike as regards all their non-evaluative properties have to be exactly alike as regards all their evaluative properties (or, no difference in value without some difference in nature). Such principles as these can indeed be powerful tools in the derivation of value claims, since they place severe constraints on the kinds of value claims that can be consistently *combined*. I cannot consistently claim that my being in pain for two minutes is intrinsically bad, while your being in a qualitatively identical pain state is intrinsically good. I cannot consistently claim that my being in pain for two minutes is worse than my being in pain for one minute, and that my being in pain for one minute is worse than my not being in pain at all, but deny that my being in pain for two minutes is worse than my not being in pain at all. And I cannot affirm these claims while also affirming that my suffering pain for one minute is worse than your suffering pain for two minutes.

But one can only derive substantive value claims—such as that suffering pain is bad, and that more pain is worse than less pain—if one is supplied with some substantive value claims as inputs. Universalizability and the other formal properties of value, even when combined, leave open a vast range of substantive theories of value—including value nihilism. For example, one version of nihilism says that nothing is better than anything else. This satisfies universalizability—no difference in value without some difference in nature—simply by ensuring that there are no differences in value at all. It also ensures the irreflexivity, asymmetry, and transitivity of *better than*. And it seems that *all* purely a priori axiological principles will leave open a huge array of mutually incompatible value theories including, crucially, value nihilism. But then such principles, even when they are combined, cannot help us derive any substantive claims about value.

If value knowledge is to be possible we have to have a source of value *data*, a source that renders some substantive value claims more plausible than others. Value seemings could play this role. Fortunately, as already noted, such value seemings are ubiquitous. But what are these seemings of the value of things, and what things do they purport to present us as valuable?

Some take value seemings to be a certain kind of intellectual intuition.[1] Pleasure *seems* to me to be better than pain and 4 *seems* to me to be larger than 3. Perhaps these seemings have the same basic nature. Both seemings might constitute prima facie evidence for belief in the associated proposition. If *its seeming that pleasure is better than pain* were just the belief *that pleasure is better than pain* then it would be hard to see how the seeming could constitute independent evidence for the belief. Intellectual seemings must be distinct from beliefs but nevertheless provide evidence for them. But this is somewhat puzzling for it is not entirely clear how exactly an intellectual seeming differs from a belief.

An alternative hypothesis is that seemings are not belief-like, they are not purely cognitive. Rather they are perception-like. Consider the relation between visual perception and belief. One can be in a visual perceptual state in which, say, the rose seems pink, and being in that visual perceptual state provides one with prima facie or defeasible evidence for the belief that the rose is pink. But the perceptual state is clearly quite different from the belief for which it provides evidence. For a start the visual perception of the rose as pink is constituted in part by certain visual qualia— qualia that are distinctive of visual perception. The belief-state is not constituted by

---

[1] For the view that intellectual seemings are not beliefs, see Bealer (1998); Huemer (2005); Stratton-Lake (2016). Proponents of this view typically think that intellectual seemings about substantive and formal propositions are basically of the same kind.

visual qualia. The belief is widely thought not to be constituted or even accompanied by *any* distinctive qualia. But even if, contrary to the dominant tradition on these matters, there are distinctive 'cognitive qualia' then these are quite different from the qualia of visual perception. Further, one can clearly be in the visual perceptual state without having any tendency to adopt the corresponding belief, and one can have that belief without being in the perceptual state that would support it. So perceptual seemings should not be conflated with the beliefs about the world for which they supply defeasible evidence.

A purely intellectual seeming does not readily set itself apart from the belief it is supposed to support, or from associated belief-like states. There is some sense in which it seems to me that $7 + 5 = 12$. But I find it hard to set that kind of seeming apart from my unhesitating acceptance of $7 + 5 = 12$. And that unhesitating acceptance is, I think, just the belief that $7 + 5 = 12$. Now, one could just *stipulate* that intellectual seemings are not beliefs, that they are not at all belief-like, and that they thus provide evidence for the beliefs that share their propositional content. But I can't see what exactly sets them apart from beliefs. I can see how intellectual seemings might turn out to be a kind of *tentative* belief, a *weak* belief, or a *partial* belief, but these are all belief-like states, rather than perception-like states. Call such states *doxastic* seemings. A perceptual state is not a doxastic seeming. It need not be accompanied by any tentative, weak, or partial beliefs at all. One might be quite certain, as with the Müller-Lyer illusion, that one's perceptual state is totally illusory.

Whatever the case for purely doxastic value seemings, it is worth exploring the rival hypothesis that value seemings are non-doxastic seemings. That is to say, they are perception-like rather than belief-like. Note that by calling a state doxastic I do not mean simply that it is a *propositional attitude*. Beliefs are typically construed as propositional attitudes, but not all propositional attitudes need be beliefs or belief-like. There could well be propositional attitudes that are non-doxastic. For example, desires are often construed (rightly or wrongly) as propositional attitudes, and if that is right they are almost certainly non-doxastic propositional attitudes.[2]

What non-doxastic states might play the role of value seemings? A familiar typology divides the mental up into the cognitive, the conative, and the affective. Since the cognitive (in this sense) coincides with the doxastic, this suggests that there are two broad candidates for non-doxastic value seemings: conative states and affective states. But these terms are also quite heavily contested, so here I will go with simpler ones—namely, desires and emotions. I don't want to foreclose the possibility that both desires and emotions are value appearances, and in fact I think that this is indeed the case. Specifically I think a good case can be made for the thesis that desires are appearances of the thin evaluative attributes (goodness, badness, and betterness) whereas emotions are appearances of the thick evaluative attributes. Here I will focus on the former. What I call *the value appearance thesis* is simply that occurrent desires and felt preferences are appearances of the possession of goodness and betterness.

---

[2] I of course reject the view that desire for *P* just is the belief about the goodness of *P*. However, I reject Lewis's arguments that desires and beliefs about goodness must come apart. See Lewis (1988) and (1996a); Oddie (1994) and (2001).

This idea has an ancient pedigree. Augustine seems to be an adherent:

(In) the [pull] of the will and of love, appears the worth of everything to be sought or to be avoided, to be esteemed of greater or lesser value.[3]

And here is a very clear contemporary statement of the thesis:

The view I shall take is this: Desire is a kind of perception. One who wants it to be the case that P perceives something that makes it seem to that person as if it would be good were it to be the case that P, and seem so in a way that is characteristic of perception. To desire something is to be in a kind of perceptual state, in which that thing seems good[4]

This value appearance thesis has the following important features. There are appearances of value, and these appearances are perception-like rather than belief-like. (It is possible for something to appear good in the teeth of the contrary belief.) Value appearances are more or less accurate, their accuracy depending in part on the evaluative properties and relations possessed by the objects of those appearances. (As with sense perception more generally, accuracy may also depend in part on how the perceiver stands in relation to the objects of perception.) Finally, an occurrent desire for P is, or involves, an appearance of P *as good*.

The value appearance thesis has a number of virtues, but one in particular is worth highlighting here. Non-cognitivists about value have often argued that cognitivists cannot give a convincing account of the intrinsically motivational nature of valuing. Suppose (as cognitivists often claim) that to value something is to judge it valuable. And suppose (as Humeans claim) that desires play an essential role in motivation. Then cognitivists either have to abandon the Humean desire-motivation thesis; or deny that valuing is intrinsically motivating; or accept that value beliefs necessitate corresponding desires. None of these positions is entirely comfortable. The value appearance thesis provides the cognitivist with a couple of more attractive responses. She can plausibly maintain that valuing requires, in addition to value judgement, an experience of the valued object as good. Then, given the value appearance thesis, valuing becomes intrinsically motivational. But even without requiring such a tight link, if the data that informs and supports our value judgements is at bottom desiderative, then our reasons for making those judgements will be very closely connected to our reasons to act.[5]

3. Value Bearers

A theory of value has to address the question of what types of entity are potential value bearers.

In the value theory literature, three types of entity feature prominently: abstract states, concrete states, and concrete particulars.[6] A restrictive theory would allow just

---

[3] Augustine (1982), 109. Perhaps Augustine is here implying that both desires ('the pull of the will') and the emotions ('love') are appearances of value. Brentano (1889).

[4] Stampe (1987), 381. See also Oddie (2005). [5] See Oddie (2005), chs. 3 and 8.

[6] Zimmerman (2001), and Lemos (2005) argue that concrete states are the proper bearers of intrinsic value. Roderick Chisholm takes abstract states to be the value bearers in his (1968-9). Wlodek Rabinowicz

one type of entity to be the proper bearers of value. A liberal value theory would allow all three types to be proper value bearers. Let's consider views at the restrictive end of the spectrum.

On a *concrete state* view, the only proper bearers of value are *concrete* (or *actual*) states of affairs. Consider a concrete state of affairs—like Margaret's experiencing pleasure during some particular interval. Since this is an actual state, it is a candidate for possessing value, and it is typically assumed that it has positive value. On a restrictive concrete state view, a non-actual state incompatiblie with this, like *Margaret's being in pain*, has no value properties at all.

It would be odd for a concrete state theorist to embrace non-actual states as the relata of *dyadic* value attributes while denying *monadic* attributes to those same states. On the concrete state view, the relata of an obtaining value *relation* must also be actual states. It follows that two states of affairs that are *incompatible* cannot stand in the betterness relation, because at least one of them will not be actual. In particular, *Margaret's experiencing pleasure* cannot be better than *Margaret's being in pain*. The concrete state view is thus committed to what we can call *actualism*—that if a state of affairs S possesses a value attribute, or stands in a value relation, then S is an actual state of affairs. So if state S is better than state S^* then both S and S^* are actual states of affairs.

The concrete state view, while it seems to enjoy widespread support, appears to rule out many value claims—for example that Margaret's experiencing pleasure is better than Margaret's not experiencing pleasure. This might incline one to embrace one of the rivals to the concrete state view—namely, the *abstract state* view.[7] According to this, value bearers are *possible* states of affairs, or closely related entities like *propositions*. Consider these states: *Margaret's experiencing some pleasure, there existing happy egrets, Diana's wedding dress being precious*. These are all actual (or concrete)—and because of that they are also possible (or abstract). And of course they are plausible candidates for being good—each makes the world a better place than it would otherwise have been. Now consider the corresponding merely possible states: *Margaret's not experiencing any pleasure, there existing no happy egrets*, and *Diana's wedding dress being rather common*. While the former states are reasonable candidates for being bearers of positive value, their negations are presumably reasonable candidates for being bearers of negative (or perhaps neutral) value. So the former are candidates for bearing the better-than relation to their counterparts among the latter. The abstract state view can happily accommodate these judgments, whereas the concrete state view either has to repudiate them or find some non-literal way of making them acceptable.

---

and Tony Rønnow-Rasmussen appear to endorse a liberal (pluralist) account in their (2005), which is a reply to their own defense of a reduction of the value of persons and things to the value of abstract states of affairs in their (2000). There are at least two other possibilities. Jonas Olson argues that *tropes* (or particularized properties) are the fundamental bearers in his (2003). Tropes are, however, closely connected to states of affairs (wheter concrete or abstract). A minority view holds that it is universals, or *states of being*, that are the proper bearers of value. See Forrest (1988); Butchvarov (1989), and Oddie (1991).

[7] Chisholm (1968–9), 22.

States of affairs, even actual states, might strike those of a nominalist dispostion as not quite concrete enough to be genuine value bearers. Even more concrete, of course, are concrete *particulars*—like Mary, egrets, and wedding dresses. These strike some as quite natural bearers of value, and if states of affairs—whether actual or merely possible—possess value they may do so derivatively—in virtue of the valuable particulars which star prominently in them.

One could, of course, take a liberal rather than a restrictive view, deeming the particular that is *Diana's wedding dress* to be a genuine value bearer, as well as various states of affairs in which Diana's wedding dress stars—like the concrete state *Diana's wedding dress being precious* and perhaps even the abstract state, *Diana's wedding dress being common*—to be genuine bearers of value. Perhaps *being precious* is a thick value attribute that Diana's wedding dress bears; *being good* is a thin value that the concrete state *Diana's wedding dress being precious* bears non-derivatively; and finally, *being bad* is a thin value attribute that the non-actual, merely possible state, *Diana's wedding dress being rather common* bears. On this liberal view, concrete particulars, along with both concrete as well as abstract states of affairs, are all genuine bearers of value.

For ease of exposition I have been glossing over an important distinction here. Some types of entity may be the *fundamental* or *primary* value bearers, while other types do bear value, but do so only derivatively, in virtue of the values born by the primary value bearers. One could be either restrictive or liberal about the primary bearers of value. I don't know of any who explicitly hold the view that all these types of entities might be primary value bearers. Typically, one type of entity is deemed to be fundamental in this regard and others inherit their value attributes from those.

As I have tried to show elsewhere, a restrictive concretism (the view that the only value bearers are concrete particulars and/or concrete states) faces severe problems.[8] If I am right about that, we should embrace *abstract* states of affairs as value bearers too. But, as we will see, this is not the only alternative on offer. The abstract state view may be a limiting case of a somewhat different view—namely, that *states of being* are value bearers. And a very promising view is that states of being are the primary bearers of value, all other value bearers deriving their value attributes from the values of properties.

4. The Accuracy of Appearances and the Effects of Perspective

Suppose states of affairs are value bearers and bear value relations to other states, that there are appearances of the value of states, and that desires and preferences are just such appearances of value. At first blush it would seem that the desires and preferences of a *well-functioning* value perceiver should track the value facts reliably. So a well-functioning value perceiver will desire states just to the extent that they are good and prefer one state to another just to the extent that one is indeed better than the other. Her desires and preferences will thus be isomorphic to the value facts to which

---

[8] Oddie (2016).

she is responding. Furthermore, any two well-functioning valuers who are attending to the same portion of value reality will have desires and preferences that, since both are isomorphic to the facts, will be isomorphic to each other. But that seems quite a stretch. Surely there are situations in which different valuers can, quite legitimately, have conflicting desires and preferences, that one and the same state can be preferred by one and dispreferred by the other, even when those states possess their values independently of desires and preferences. Call this the *isomorphism problem* for value perception.

Is there an analogous isomorphism problem for regular perception? Suppose two objects A and B are exactly the same size. Dom is closer to A than to B while Eric is closer to B than to A. To Dom, A will appear larger than B, while to Eric, B will appear larger than A. But the differences in how these two things appear to them does not signal any defect in the perceptual apparatus of either perceiver. It is completely normal for objects to appear differently to the two observers, given the different relations the observers bear to the perceived objects. Perception is always perception of objects as they stand in relation to the perceiver. Visual appearance is always an appearance *from a certain point of view*, and as such the appearances may legitimately incorporate perspectival differences. The appearances for two differently situated perceivers should not in general be isomorphic to reality or to each other.

If there are genuine appearances of value—non-doxastic representations of value states—then there might well be value analogues of distance and perspective. If desires and preferences are value appearances then the appearances may not depend simply on perceiver-independent evaluative properties of states, but depend also on how the value perceiver stands in relation to those states. There could well be a perspectival element to value perception (desire) just as there is a perspectival element to visual perception. States that are distant from you in value space may not loom as large in your desires and preferences as states that are close to you, and justifiably so. Suppose we could make sense of this notion of the distance of valuers from loci of value. The weals and woes of those with whom you are closely connected, those for whom you care deeply, would be located closer to you in value space than the weals and woes of distant strangers.

Grant that pain is bad, and that qualitatively identical pains have the same disvalue whoever is the subject of that pain. I twist my ankle badly and I experience severe pain. I am very averse to the pain I am experiencing—on the value appearance thesis, this means that my pain appears bad to me, very bad. However, I remember twisting my ankle exactly the same way, twenty years ago, and I experienced a qualitatively very similar pain at that occasion. But that I experienced this kind of pain twenty years ago does not elicit such a strong aversion from me now as the state of pain that I am currently experiencing. Neither does the prospect of experiencing an exactly similar pain that I believe it is highly likely I will experience some time in the next twenty years. So I can have very different desiderative responses to various pain episodes all of which are, by assumption, qualitatively identical and hence equally bad. My current pain seems much worse to me at the moment than the qualitatively identical pain I experienced twenty years ago or any qualitatively identical pain I will likely experience some time in the next twenty years. These temporally distant pains are very distant from me now, and they are not just temporally distant. Their temporal distance from me now makes the locus of those values more distant from me in a space of value locations. Time can be thought of as a dimension in value space, one which should affect the perception of value states. The further away a state of affairs is in time, the less it looms in our experience of its value.

Suppose that a loved one very close to you, one of your 'nearest and dearest', is in extreme pain. But you are in a disaster zone and there are very limited medical supplies. There is a complete stranger not far away who is experiencing a qualitatively identical pain. The emergency paramedics have only one dose of morphine left and, because they judge these two sufferers to be in equivalent pain, they are going to toss a coin to see to whom to give the morphine. You do not find yourself completely indifferent as to where the pain relief will flow. In fact you strongly prefer that your beloved receive that last dose. When the medics announce the dose is going to go to your beloved you are happier than you would have been had it gone to the stranger. Are your preferences here defective? It seems to me entirely fitting for you to care more about the pain of people you love, and with whom you have deep connections, than about the pain of people with whom you have no connections at all. This is not to say that you would be entitled to *believe* that your beloved's pain is worse than the stranger's pain. You could not legitimately argue, for example, that the lottery shouldn't even take place, that the medics should give the morphine to your beloved, because your beloved's pain is just *worse* than its qualitative counterpart in the stranger. It is just to say that it is entirely fitting for you to *prefer* that your beloved be the recipient of this last dose of morphine than that she continue to suffer extreme pain while the stranger's pain is alleviated. If desires and preferences are non-doxastic appearances of value then this combination of belief (that the two pains are equally bad) and preference (your beloved's pain *seems* worse) are compatible and appropriate.[9]

One could argue that in this situation you are responding unfittingly, or incorrectly, to value. The value of things *should appear* to you just as they are, not skewed by your relations to them. Your beloved's pain and the stranger's pain, being qualitatively identical, should *appear* to you be equally bad. And so it should be a matter of indifference to you as to where the morphine flows. But that's implausible. As a being situated in a network of particular attachments, deep connections with particular others, with finite resources and a finite capacity to care, it would not only be impossible for you to respond in a totally detached way to all pain in the world wherever it happens to be located—the pain of total strangers as well as those you love deeply; pains past, present, and future; and pains actual as well as remotely possible—it would also be *bizarre* for you to do so. It would also be bizarre if you were obliged to randomly allocate your limited stock of care and resources regardless of your relationship to, or distance from, those who are suffering. So if a value which is located more closely to you *should* loom larger, and desires and aversions are appearances of value, then it is entirely fitting that desires and aversions should be sensitive not just to amount of value but to the distance of the valuing subject from the locus of that value.

---

[9] This combination of value distance and perspective was laid out and argued for in Oddie (2005).

Distance is not the only factor that affects value perception. A valuer's *orientation* to something of value may also affect perception. Take a variant of Nozick's famous case of past and future pain. You are to undergo an operation for which it would be dangerous to use analgesics. The surgeon tells you that on the first of the month you will go into hospital and on the afternoon of the second you will be administered a combination of drugs which will paralyze you during the operation, scheduled for that evening, and subsequently cause you to forget the experiences you will have during the operation, including all the dreadful pain. You wake up in hospital, and you don't know what day it is. If it is the third the operation was over twelve hours ago. If it is morning of the second, then you have yet to undergo the operation in twelve hours' time. So depending on which day it is, you are twelve hours temporal distance from the pain, either in the past or the future. And these two scenarios are equally likely given your information. So you are equidistant from these two painful possibilities in both temporal space and probability space. You are, however, much more averse to the 50-percent probability of the future, as yet unexperienced, pain to the 50-percent probability that the painful episode is now past. And this asymmetric response seems fitting. One is differently oriented towards past and future disvalues, and such an orientation can make a legitimate difference to how bad those disvalues should seem.

What about the *shape* of value, and the effect of shape, perhaps together with orientation, on value perception? Should the value of one and the same state of affairs be experienced by folk differently if they are differently oriented with respect to it?

Suppose that there is such a thing as desert. If there is, then sometimes those who inflict great harm and suffering on others deserve to suffer in some measure themselves. In The Girl with the Dragon Tattoo Lisbeth Salander devises a clever comeuppance for Nils Bjurman, her guardian abuser and rapist. What she proceeds to inflict on him (I will not spoil the story for those who have not read it) seems to me both proportionate and entirely just. The suffering inflicted on Nils Bjurman, I think, makes the world a better place than it would otherwise be, given what Bjurman did to Lisbeth. Consider three people differently related to Bjurman's receiving his just deserts—Lisbeth (the victim of Bjurman's crimes), some relatively uninvolved bystander (such as yourself), and Bjurman, the bad guy. It is certainly seems appropriate for Lisbeth to welcome the fact that her rapist is getting what he deserves. A neutral bystander may not feel as strongly about this as Lisbeth does, understandably, but provided he recognizes that Bjurman is getting his just deserts, he should prefer it to Bjurman's getting off scot-free. What about Bjurman himself? His punishment is, by assumption, a good thing, but Bjurman has to be averse to his suffering if it is to be any sort of punishment at all. The difference in the victim's and the bystander's degree of desire for the just deserts might be explained by their differing distances from the locus of the value. But the differing responses of the victim and the *wrongdoer* cannot be rationalized by distance alone. Desire and aversion pull in opposite directions. Unless Bjurman is averse to his suffering and humiliation at Lisbeth's hands (and I assure you he is) then he is simply not getting his just deserts. And if the victim has no desire at all for the wrongdoer to receive his just deserts, then his receiving them will not serve its function in restoring a measure of justice.

Whether or not this particular notion of desert makes sense (or whether it can be ultimately cashed out in a more consequentialist and less retributivist framework), value is one thing, and the appropriate response to it on the part of a peculiarly situated valuer is something else. A value fact may thus appropriately elicit different responses depending on how closely the value is located to a value perceiver, the shape of the value, and the orientation of the perceiver with respect to it. The thesis that desires and preferences are appearances of value, which are the product not just of the value born but also of the relation of a value perceiver to the value bearer, defuses what might otherwise be a powerful objection to subject-neutral value facts—that one's responses to value should not be at all sensitive to one's singular position in the complex network of relationships to the bearers of value.

This account seems a promising way to defuse the isomorphism objection, and something like it may have to be part of any reasonable defense of value perception. But it has to be conceded that its central notions are at least partially metaphorical and perhaps a little obscure. What I would like to show in the rest of the paper is that the opacity of this notion of distance and perspective can be substantially reduced by embracing a different account of both bearers of value and the objects of desire—properties, or states of being.

5. Properties as the Objects of Desire

For desires and preferences to be accurate appearances of value, the objects of desire and of preference also have to be bearers of value. The propositional/state account of value bearers thus sits happily with the traditional view of desire as a propositional attitude. But the propositional/state view, although it is widely held, sits somewhat unhappily with the, at least the surface, grammar of many typical desire claims. For example: *Harry wants a hokey-pokey ice cream*; *Garrison has a hankering for the Goldberg Variations*; *Oliver and Orlando both want to win the gold*; *Mary just wants to be happy*.

Now, *a hokey-pokey ice cream, the Goldberg Variations, winning the gold*, and *being happy* all appear to function here as objects of desire, and while they are related to various propositions and states of affairs they are not themselves propositions or states of affairs. So if the propositional view is correct, the surface grammar of many desire claims runs somewhat against the metaphysical grain.

We can, of course, recast these claims into something logically equivalent, with propositions or states of affairs as object. Whenever a desire seems to be for something other than a state of affairs—like *a hokey-pokey ice cream* or *the Goldberg Variations*—then it is reasonable to. What one *really* wants is a certain interaction with the entity at issue—to *lick* or *eat* the hokey-pokey ice cream, to *hear* the Goldberg Variations. Further, on the propositional view, Harry's wanting to lick an ice cream will have to be further parsed as Harry's wanting it to be the case *that Harry licks an ice cream*; what Oliver really wants is *that Oliver wins the gold*; what Mary desires is *the state of affairs consisting in Mary's being happy*.

There is, however, a rather natural rival to the propositional view. Suppose Orlando and Oliver are competing for Olympic gold in cross-country skiing. Oliver says *I really want to win the gold* and Orlando chips in *So do I!* The common object of their two desires is *to win the gold*. On the propositional view, they can only want the same thing if they want the very same state of affairs to obtain: but there is no state of affairs that is their common desire. But there is a single *state of being* rather than *state of affairs* that both want. They both want to have a certain *property*, the property of *winning the gold*. More generally what one desires is typically to possess or to have some property, what one prefers is the having of some property to the having some other property.[10] The property view can make literal sense of the claim that Oliver and Orlando want *the very same thing* (to have the property of winning the gold). If Orlando's desire is satisfied then Oliver's is frustrated, and vice versa.

In addition to her own happiness Mary wants *the war to be over*. Indeed the satisfaction of her desire for happiness turns on the satisfaction of her desire for the war to be over. But *the war's being over* seems to be a state of the world, not a property of Mary. So, at the very least, the property view has to be able to capture that class of desires that have as their apparent objects certain states of the world. Happily, there are quite natural property-surrogates for states of the world that can serve as the objects of these state-directed desires.

For each state of the world S there is exactly one state-property, ψ^S, characterized as follows: X has property ψ^S if and only if S obtains. ψ^S is the property of *being such that S obtains*.[11] Since X doesn't occur on the right-hand side of the definition, ψ^S is *global* in the sense that it is had by some individual if and only if it is had by all. Either every individual has it or none have it. The circumstances in which it is had by an individual are just those in which S obtains. So wanting to have the global property ψ^S is tantamount to wanting S itself to obtain. We can retrieve the class of propositional desires, or state desires (namely that X desires that S obtain) from desires the objects of which are these global properties (namely X desires to have ψ^S). When Mary and Martha both have the apparently state-directed desire *that the war be over* (**O**) the common object of their desires is to possess the global property ψ^O. Properties that are not global (which are most of them) we can call *local*. The characteristic feature of local properties is that one thing can have such without everything having such.

What does desire fulfillment consist in on this view? On the state or propositional view the desire that P is fulfilled if and only if the object of the desire, the proposition P, is true. But properties do not bear truth values. Whereas the extension of a proposition at a world is its truth value at that world, the extension of a property at a world is a class (the class of objects that have the property in that world) rather than a truth value. Further, on the property view, Orlando and Oliver share the *very same* desire—*to win the gold*. But how can those be *one and the same* desire if the

---

[10] Lewis (1979). Note that one does not have to buy into the more baroque aspects of Lewisian metaphysics to find the property view of desire plausible. Indeed, the view is probably more plausible if worlds are abstract ways that things can be, rather than large, causally isolated hunks of junk. Nor does one have to buy into Lewis's companion thesis that the objects of belief are also properties, though that view sits happily enough with what I am endorsing here.

[11] This is not how Lewis (1979) characterizes the property view but his characterization is dependent on his own idiosyncratic view of individuals and worlds—in particular the global denial of any trans-world identity.

fulfillment of Oliver's desire would constitute the frustration of Orlando's? That's a violation of Leibniz's principle.

These two puzzles are easily dissolved. Take the latter puzzle. *Desire* suffers the usual state/object ambiguity. *Oliver's desire* can pick out either Oliver's mental state of desiring, or the object of Oliver's desiring. Oliver and Orlando have the same desire in the latter object sense, but different desires in the former state sense. The object of their desiring is one and the same, even if there are two distinct desirings at issue, one on the part of Oliver, the other on the part of Orlando. If fulfillment were a property of the object desired then of course the argument from Leibniz's principle would set their objects apart too. But if fulfillment is a property of the desire state rather than the object of the desire then the argument from Leibniz's principle is unsound.

What is desire fulfillment? On neither the propositional view nor the property view is desire fulfillment a property of the object of desire. On the propositional view it is not the *object* of the desire, the proposition itself, that is said to be fulfilled. What is fulfilled is the *desire that P*, not *P* itself. A propositional desire is fulfilled if the object of that desiring episode, the proposition itself, is *true*. It is not the object of the mental state that is fulfilled. Rather it is the mental state itself, the state of desire, that is either fulfilled or not. So desire fulfillment is a relation between the desiring state, the desired object, and the world. Similarly, on the property view desire fulfillment is not a property of the object of desire (the property desired). For Oliver's desire to win the gold to be fulfilled, Oliver (rather than Orlando, or anyone else) must actually end up in the extension of the object he desires. Desire fulfillment on the property view is thus also a relation between a desiring state, the object of desire, and the world.

6. Properties as Value Bearers

Winning the election, eating a hokey pokey ice cream, hearing the Goldberg Variations performed, being happy, and the war's coming to an end, are not just objects of desire—they are also apt subjects of value attributions. Plausibly, these properties are all good. So, on the property view it is plausible that the objects of desire are also bearers of value.

Even if properties are value bearers, it would be absurd to claim that only properties are value bearers. We attribute value to many entities that seem to be neither properties nor states of affairs (ice creams, keepsakes, frying pans, wedding dresses, cities, paintings, works of music, landscapes, ecosystems, to list a few). But even if many different kinds of things are value bearers, it could still be that the *primary* value bearers are properties, and that everything else has value only in virtue of the value possessed by the primary value-bearing properties, and the relations that various objects bear to those properties.

Mary's being happy, Martha's being happy, and Marley's being happy are all good states (or so we may suppose for the sake of an example). But are these distinct *fundamental* value facts? If states of affairs are the fundamental value bearers then that has to be the upshot. But it seems odd that we should have to countenance, for each and every particular *X*, a distinct *fundamental* value fact: *X*'s being happy is good.

Suppose, instead, that *happiness*—the property of *being happy* itself—is good. That sounds fine. After all, we do say *happiness is good* and *it's a good thing to be happy*. That happiness is a good property can make *Mary's being happy*, *Martha's being happy*, and *Marley's being happy* good states of affairs. We need postulate only one fundamental value fact—that *happiness* is good—and this will explain a vast multitude of derivative value facts—all these states of affairs that consist in some one particular or other having the property of happiness at some particular time. All these distinct states of affairs are valuable *because* they all involve the instantiation of a single valuable state of being. I think it is far more natural to think that the value of these different states of affairs is rooted in a single fundamental value fact—the goodness of happiness—than that there are innumerable distinct fundamental value facts that collectively undergird, explain, and add up to one derivative value fact, that happiness is good.

Recently Panayot Butchvarov and Peter Forrest have explicitly defended the view that properties are the fundamental value bearers. Butchvarov writes:

> Let us say that facts of the form expressed by '*x is happy*' have in common the property of involving happiness in a cetain specific way. Surely they are good only because they have that property. And why then would we want to deny that that property itself is good?... It would be... mysterious that being a happy life should entail being at least partially a good life if happiness were not itself good.[12]

This passage is compatible with the modest thesis that properties are value bearers. But in the following passage he hints at the stronger thesis, that properties are the fundamental value bearers and states of affairs bear value derivatively:

> I suggest that a person's life can be said to be good on the grounds that it is happy only if happiness itself can be said to be good, and in general a concrete entity can be said to be good only on the grounds that it has some... property or properties that themselves have the property of being good.[13]

Here Butchvarov makes it explicit that there is a higher-order property, *Goodness*, that first-order properties have or lack, and that states of affairs and individuals have a related value property of *goodness* that derives from the Goodness of the properties they instantiate.

Even more explicitly Peter Forrest writes:

> Let us therefore think of intrinsic goodness as a property of the object's nature. Here, by a nature I mean the naturalistic nature, composed of the object's naturalistic properties. Intrinsic goodness is not, then, a property of the object but of its nature. To bring this out we may say that an object is intrinsically good because it has an intrinsically good nature. (Notice that this sounds quite familiar.) Now consider two objects with the same naturalistic properties and hence the same nature. If one has an intrinsically good nature, so must the other. For their natures are identical. This explains the supervenience of the object's being intrinsically good on its naturalistic properties.[14]

---

[12] Butchvarov (1989), 14–15. [13] Butchvarov (1989), 14. [14] Forrest (1988), 2.

It is really quite extraordinary how even very good value theorists simply glide over the property view without even noticing it is there. Take Chisholm for example:

> The *terms* we use in making up lists [of intrinsically good and bad things] are abstract—'pleasure', 'displeasure', 'love', 'hate'... And so on. What these terms refer to are not individual or concrete things or substances. They are rather propositional entities, or states of affairs:... there being individuals experiencing pleasure, or there being individuals experiencing displeasure.[15]

Or again:

> In saying, for example that *knowledge* is intrinsically good we mean, more exactly, that that state of affairs which is someone knowing something is intrinsically good.[16]

Of course 'pleasure' and 'knowledge' patently do *not* refer to state of affairs, and because of this obvious fact, Chisholm immediately has to go off in search of surrogate states to be the value bearers. But the value of pleasure or knowledge does not attach to one particular privileged state of affairs that involves some knowledge or pleasure. And it is not clear which state Chisholm intends to pick out. *Someone knowing something* is ambiguous. It might be an attempt to collectively gather up all the instances of the relation *X knows that P* for particular *X* and particular *P*, or it might just be what it purports to be—a single state that obtains if one existentially generalizes on X and P: that *someone is such that there is some proposition that he* knows. But even if this particular state is valuable (presumably barely minimally so) that is hardly what one means by claiming *that knowledge is valuable.*

It is much more natural to hold that the properties of experiencing pleasure, or of being knowledgeable, are what are fundamentally good, and that it is the value of experiencing pleasure and being knowledgeable as such that makes some individual's involving experiencing a particular pleasure, or knowing some particular thing, good.

7. The Isormorphism Objection Revisited

The shift from states of affairs to states of being as the fundamental bearers of value is a promising step in solving the isomorphism problem. This is because local properties (unlike states of affairs and global properties) have their own built-in *perspective* or *point of view*. A local property of individuals does not characterize a state of the world. Rather, it characterizes a *way of being in the world*. Let S_1 and S_2 be two distinct distributions of properties over Oliver and Orlando, except that Oliver and Orlando swap places. S_1 and S_2 are isomorphic and hence (by universalizability) they are equally valuable states. But the value of properties that Oliver has in one such state might be very different from the value of the properties that he has in the other.

Consider the property of *winning the gold*. Oliver and Orlando both want to win the gold. Both prefer winning the gold (**Win**) to losing (**Lose**). That's how the relative values of these properties *appear* to both of them. Let $>_X$ be the relation of felt

---

[15] Chisholm (1968-9), 22.   [16] Chisholm (1968-9), 22.

preference on the part of X and let $>_{\text{Value}}$ be the relation of *betterness*. Then we have that **Win** $>_{\text{Oliver}}$ **Lose** and **Win** $>_{\text{Orlando}}$ **Lose**. Suppose, as seems plausible, that the relative values of these two properties is just as they appear to the two competitors: **Win** $>_{\text{Value}}$ **Lose**. Now consider the following states of affairs.

T_1 **Win** (Oliver) & **Lose** (Orlando)
T_2 **Lose** (Oliver) & **Win** (Orlando)
T_3 **Lose** (Orlando) & **Lose** (Oliver).

Since Oliver prefers winning to losing, he will prefer T_1 (in which he wins) to both T_2 and T_3 (in which he loses). Similarly, Orlando will prefer T_2 (in both of which he wins) to both T_1 and T_3 (in both of which he loses). Oliver may well be indifferent between T_2 and T_3 or he may prefer one to the other. If Orlando is his special rival then he might prefer that Orlando lose to someone or other. If Orlando is his friend and teammate then he might prefer to lose to Orlando than to lose some stranger. Let **Rival** (X, Y) be the relation that consists in X and Y being each other's special rivals. (This is of course a symmetric relation.) We can consider the following properties: **Win**$_1$ and **Win**$_2$ are determinates of **Win**, while **Lose**$_1$ and **Lose**$_2$ are determinates of **Lose**:

Win$_1$ **Win**(X) & $(\exists Y)(\text{\bf Lose}(Y)$ & **Rival**$(X,Y))$ *wins by beating special rival*
Win$_2$ **Win**(X) & $(\exists Y)(\text{\bf Lose}(Y)$ & ~**Rival**$(X,Y))$ *wins by beating non-rival*
Lose$_1$ **Lose**(X) & $(\exists Y)(\text{\bf Win}(Y)$ & **Rival**$(X,Y))$ *loses to special rival*
Lose$_2$ **Lose**(X) & $(\exists Y)(\text{\bf Win}(Y)$ & ~**Rival**$(X,Y))$ *loses to non-rival*

Suppose both Orlando and Oliver have the following eminently reasonable preferences:

Win$_1$ > **Win**$_2$ > **Lose**$_2$ > **Lose**$_1$.

Each of these local properties is a way of being in the world. And their specifications have a particular structure. First there is a specification of one's status as regards **Win/Lose**. Then there is a specification of one's relations to others whose status as regards **Win/Lose** and **Rival** is specified.[17] The preference ordering that both Oliver and Orlando share also seems like the objective value ranking on these properties—or so we may assume.

Now consider the following states of affairs:

S_1 **Win** (Orlando) & **Lose** (Oliver) & **Rival** (Orlando,Oliver)
S_2 **Win** (Orlando) & **Lose** (Oliver) & ~**Rival** (Oliver,Orlando)
S_3 **Win** (Oliver) & **Lose** (Orlando) & **Rival** (Oliver,Orlando)
S_4 **Win** (Oliver) & **Lose** (Orlando) & ~**Rival** (Orlando,Oliver)

S_1 and S_3 are isomorphic, as are S_2 and S_4, and so—granting the highly-plausible a priori principle of universalizabiltity for value—those pairs are value equivalent. Let's

---

[17] These properties are a (simplified) subset of Hintikka's so-called *attributive constituents*, which in turn are generalizations of Carnap's *Q-predicates*. Attributive constituents yield the set of mutually exclusive and jointly exhaustive properties that can be specified relative to a set of basic properties and relations (here **Win** and **Rival**) and a certain degree of quantificational depth (here, depth-1, or one layer of quantifiers). See Hintikka (1963). For an informal presentation see Oddie (1986), ch. 4.

suppose that, other things being equal, a close competition between special rivals is better than a competition without rivals. It follows that S_1 is better than S_2 and S_3 is better than S_4. Then we have the following value ranking on these states:

$S_1 \approx_{Value} S_3 >_{Value} S_2 \approx_{Value} S_4.$

Note that this is also the value ranking we would get by considering those global properties that specify the distribution of properties without specifying which individuals have which properties. That is, consider the following global properties (or states of affairs) obtained by existentially generalizing on the local properties: Win_1, Win_2, Lose_1, Lose_2.

G_1 $(\exists X)\text{Win}_1(X) \approx (\exists X)(\text{Win}(X) \& (\exists Y)(\text{Lose}(Y) \& \text{Rival}(X,Y)))$
Someone *wins by beating his special rival.*

G_2 $(\exists X)\text{Win}_2(X) \approx (\exists X)(\text{Win}(X) \& (\exists Y)(\text{Lose}(Y) \& {\sim}\text{Rival}(X,Y)))$
Someone *wins by beating a non-rival.*

G_3 $(\exists X)\text{Lose}_1(X) \approx (\exists X)(\text{Lose}(X) \& (\exists Y)(\text{Win}(Y) \& \text{Rival}(X,Y)))$
Someone *loses by being beaten by a non-rival.*

G_4 $(\exists X)\text{Lose}_2(X) \approx (\exists X)(\text{Lose}(X) \& (\exists Y)(\text{Win}(Y) \& {\sim}\text{Rival}(X,Y)))$
Someone *loses by being beaten by his special rival.*

Since **Lose** is equivalent to ~**Win**, it's clear that G_1 is logically equivalent to G_3 and G_2 is equivalent to G_4. So these pairs of global properties are not just *value* equivalent, they are necessarily coextensive (or logically equivalent, given the logical/analytic connections between **Win** and **Lose**).

So we certainly have:

$G_1 \approx_{Value} G_3 >_{Value} G_2 \approx_{Value} G_4.$

The value ranking over these global properties and the corresponding states of affairs ($S_1 \approx_{Value} S_3 >_{Value} \approx_{Value} S_4$) will clearly not match Oliver's and Orlando's preference rankings over states of being:

$\text{Win}_1 >_{\text{Oliver/Orlando}} \text{Win}_2 >_{\text{Oliver/Orlando}} \text{Lose}_2 >_{\text{Oliver/Orlando}} \text{Lose}_1.$

The values of the states of affairs will not *strike* Oliver and Orlando in a way that matches the value rankings of the local properties. (They might strike some third party, like God, in this way, but then God will not be a bearer of any of the local properties at issue in these states of affairs.) So if Oliver strives for consistency in his preferences he is either going to have to align his preferences with the value of states of being or with the value of states of affairs. The same goes for Orlando. But what mandates that they should give priority to the value of states of affairs over the value of states of being? Why should they project the values of states of affairs *up* onto the properties that they will have in those states, rather than project the values of properties *down* onto the states that will obtain if they have those properties?

Should Oliver, for example, follow this line of reasoning?:

It seems to me much better to win than to lose. (I much prefer the former to the latter.) But whether or not I win or the other guy wins makes absolutely no difference to the value of the state of the world. These states of affairs have the same value. So I am totally indifferent as to which of these outcomes occurs.

That seems odd to me. Oliver and Orlando both want to win the gold despite the fact that, from a purely agent-neutral god's-eye view, whether one or the other wins is of no consequence. They wouldn't have devoted years of training, sweat, and effort to this goal if they hadn't *wanted* to win. Winning seems good—*very good*—to both of them. So what, exactly, is wrong with this quite different line of reasoning that Oliver might well take?

Whether or not I win or the other guy wins makes absolutely no difference to the value of the state of the world. But there is a huge difference in value between winning and losing. It is much better to win Olympic gold than to lose. So I much prefer to win than to lose. And as a consequence I prefer that state of affairs in which I win to the state of affairs in which Orlando wins.

If Oliver brings his preferences for states of affairs into line with his preferences for states of being, then his preferences for states of being will be isomorphic to the objective values of states of being, while his preferences for state of affairs will not be isomorphic to the objective value of states of affairs. So his preferences are more accurate as presentations of the value of states of being and less accurate as presentations of the value of states of affairs. Had Oliver gone the other way, bringing his preferences over states of being into line with the value of the states of affairs in which he enjoys those states of being, then his preferences would be a more accurate presentation of the value states of affairs and a less accurate presentation of the value of states of being.

If Oliver and Orlando take properties to be the primary bearers of value, and align their preferences over states of affairs with their preferences over states of being, their preferences over states of being will both align perfectly, while their preferences over states of affairs will be diametrically opposed. However, since they occupy entirely different niches within those states this is entirely consistent with the value appearance thesis.

State	Property distribution	Orlando's preferences	Oliver's preferences	Betterness relation
S_1	Win_1 (Orlando) $Lose_2$ (Oliver)	1	4	1=
S_2	Win_2 (Orlando) $Lose_2$ (Oliver)	2	3	2=
S_3	$Lose_1$ (Orlando) Win_3 (Oliver)	3	2	2=
S_4	$Lose_2$ (Orlando) Win_1 (Oliver)	4	1	1=

Thus by switching from states of affairs to states of being as the primary bearers of value we can explain many of the perspectival effects of value appearances (as regards the value appearances of states of affairs) without recourse to the metaphor of distance of a valuer from the bearers of value. The agent-neutrality of the fundamental values (that is, the values of states of being) is no longer at odds with the value appearances.

8. Conclusion

I have argued that there are value seemings and that these can serve as evidence for evaluative beliefs and judgments. I have also argued that such value seemings are better construed as perception-like rather than belief-life. Occurrent desires and felt preferences are just such value seemings, or appearances of value. The occurrent desire that P is an appearance of P as good, while the felt preference for P over Q is an appearance of P as better than Q. States are the common bearers of value and the objects of desire. An isomorphism problem arises for the view that these bearers of value and objects of desire are states of affairs. To accommodate what appear to be legitimate conflicts in preferences, the state-of-affairs theorist may invoke analogues of distance and perspective in value perception. But this defense makes appeal to a metaphor that it would be better to be able to cash out. If one switches to the view that the value bearers and the objects of desire are states of being, then the perspectival nature of value is built right into the value bearers which are the objects of value perception.

13
Moral Perception, Thick Concepts, and Perspectivalism

Anna Bergqvist

1. Introduction

Thick evaluative concepts include ethical concepts such as CRUEL, COWARD, GENEROUS.[1] Such concepts are often seen as 'first-order' evaluative concepts, which, if we want to say so, pick out evaluative properties and determine thin deontic properties such as rightness and wrongness. As is well known, G. E. Moore held that the thin moral property of intrinsic goodness is neither reducible to, nor constituted by, natural properties, but that it supervenes or is determined by natural properties, and that we know which things are intrinsically good by means of intuition. To many philosophers, R. M. Hare and Bernard Williams included (who both hold that thin evaluative concepts are not 'world-guided'[2]), this is too extravagant. They find it doubtful whether any scientifically respectable view of the world can allow properties other than natural ones. Hare sought to make progress with the familiar qualms about Moore's non-naturalism about thin evaluative concepts by drawing a distinction between descriptive and evaluative predicates such that the content of judgements involving thin moral terms is found, not in their extension (which is held to be empty), but in the functional role they play in expressing our belief about the desirability of doing certain actions and not others. Philippa Foot, by contrast, sought to make progress by reversing the order of explanation or analysis between general

---

[1] Aspects of the discussion in this section on the turn to thick concepts in the history of moral philosophy during the twenty-first century draw on Bergqvist (2015).

[2] Bernard Williams maintains that thick evaluative concepts are 'world-guided', in as much as the thoughts and judgements expressed by utterances involving terms such as 'elegant', 'garish', 'integrity' are candidates for truth and falsity. At the same time thick evaluative concepts are also held to be 'action-guiding', in the sense that, as Williams puts it, 'they are characteristically related to reasons for action. If a concept of this kind applies, this often provides someone with a reason for action' (Williams (1979), 140). Williams's caveat about the action-guidance or practicality of thick evaluative concepts is arguably due to his reasons internalism: S has a reason to only if there is a 'sound deliberative route' from S's 'actual motivational set' *M* to (intention to) do the action. On this reading, thick evaluative concepts provide reasons only for those who endorse it (the value it may be used to ascribe) as part of one's 'insider' evaluative outlook.

and specific value-terms.[3] Foot argues that thin evaluative concepts should be understood in terms of substantive value-terms, the thick ones, where the latter are seen as inherently evaluative concepts that, if we want to say so, pick out 'first-order' moral properties.

In her remarkable 1956 symposium piece 'Vision and Choice in Morality',[4] Iris Murdoch questions the very terms upon which the argument between Hare and Foot have been premised in a way that calls forth another category that is precluded by the traditional dichotomy between fact and value, between objective and subjective. With a focus on Hare, Murdoch aims to elucidate just why the disputants have gone wrong, which is so much more satisfying than the simple demonstration that they are wrong. Her central claim is that moral disagreement can stem from a difference in *world view*, questioning the very conceptual foundations of a given moral outlook, a vision of the actual world that shapes precisely what one takes to be salient and not in moral disagreement. Crucially, world views are *comprehensive* outlooks on reality, an unruly mix of evaluative and non-evaluative claims in complex interaction as a whole.

Hare's disagreement with neo-Aristotelianism is complex but the feature that Murdoch singles out as the most fundamental is Hare's position that a 'conceptual apparatus' is something that one adopts, and that adopting such an apparatus is distinguishable in principle from adopting a moral view, thus construed as a system of moral principles.[5] Hare's view of morality involves a Kantian-like notion of universalizability applied to some prescriptive standard that we hold in a way that allows the speaker to *choose* her own standards, so long as we are prepared to hold it for everyone in principle.[6] Such universalized standards serve as a basis for prescriptive statements of the form 'x is good' (translated as 'do or choose x'). Foot's attack on Hare is that a judgement cannot be identified as a moral judgement simply on the basis of formal characteristics such as universalizability and prescriptivity.[7] Instead, she holds goodness to be tied to human flourishing; what is common to moral evaluations is simply that all good things are 'of the kind to perform their function well'.[8]

Using Murdoch's conception of ethical vision as (all-encompassing) *world view*, we can explain the difficulty as follows. Because fundamental moral disagreements may be more a matter of differences in structure of competing visions, one party cannot even see how the other 'goes on' to apply the term in question to new cases, or what might be the point of doing so.

In his recent work on the relationship between Iris Murdoch and Nietzsche, Paul Katsafanas argues that understanding value experience as conceptually structured in

---

[3] It does not matter for the purposes of introduction what is the precise relationship between predicates and concepts: I will use 'term' to stay neutral on this metaphysical issue for the moment.
[4] Murdoch (1956).   [5] Hare (1965).
[6] Hare's use of the practical syllogism differs from that of Kant because, unlike Kant's Categorical Imperative, we are not constrained by what abstract reason allows in selecting our standards on Hare's analysis. For further discussion see e.g. Beardsmore (1969).
[7] See Foot (1959) and (1961).
[8] Foot (1961), 58–9. In Foot (1972), moral evaluations are 'hypothetical' in the sense that they serve an end (human flourishing) and will not be considered as reason-giving by those who do not share this end.

perspectival and parochial ways implies a form of value constitutivism. Katsafanas describes the sought view thus:

> Perception doesn't just attune us to important features of the environment, but *constitutes* the perceived environment in importantly different ways.[9]

On this view, value is determined by an individual's perspective—determined by the particular cultural-historical 'life-world' and other contingencies of the cognitive background conditions that continually structure our way of seeing the world. As such, the concepts that are said to structure our experience must be assessed *genealogically* from within an engaged parochial viewpoint. In contrast, Murdoch's account of moral value is that moral discernment is a matter of seeing things aright; as she puts it, goodness is 'a refined and honest perception of what is really the case, a patient and just discernment and exploration of what confronts one, which is the result not simply of opening one's eyes but of a certain perfectly familiar kind of moral discipline'.[10]

Scepticism about Murdoch's distinctive conception of value experience as a form of discernment of 'what is there anyway' is often motivated by worries that directly connect with the concerns with G. E. Moore's position with which we started, most famously articulated in John Mackie's[11] and Christine Korsgaard's[12] respective arguments to the effect that the only *real* moral realist there ever was in the history of philosophy is Plato (since Plato is allegedly the only metaethicist who has ever understood what moral realism would have to be like for it to discharge its explanatory obligations). Platonist moral realism postulates a structure of the world that is non-perspectival and inherently evaluative:

(a) It is non-perspectival in that it is not particularly attuned to our human perspective and its peculiarities.
(b) It is inherently evaluative in that cognitive contact with that reality is inherently motivational for a fully rational agent. (Note that this also partly explains the ancient conception of virtue *as* knowledge.)

While Nietzsche is sometimes said to be a nihilist, I will assume that it can be agreed on all hands that scepticism about absolute, non-perspectival, value representations *need not* imply a global form of value scepticism: it can instead be relativized to some of our inherited ideas, notably the kinds of commitment that Platonism exemplifies. That leaves the door open for a positive account of other values that do not depend, directly, on a *Platonic* form of vindication. One popular such strategy in contemporary metaethics is neo-Aristotelianism, notably John McDowell's dispositional account of value on a par with a dispositional account of secondary qualities.[13] Other positive 'subjective realist' accounts of value worth mentioning at this juncture are Bernard Williams's internal realism,[14] which fuels much of the recent turn to thick concepts in metatethics, and David Wiggin's conceptual realism.[15]

---

[9] Katsafanas (forthcoming). See also Katsafanas (2013).   [10] Murdoch (1997), 330.
[11] Mackie (1977).   [12] Korsgaard (1983).
[13] McDowell (1979). See also McDowell (1996).   [14] Williams (1979), *passim*.
[15] Wiggins (1989).

Williams sought to make progress with Moore's non-naturalism about thin concepts, such as intrinsic goodness, by distinguishing two conceptions of 'the world'. The first conception is of the world *absolutely* conceived as 'what is there anyway', the world of scientifically discoverable primary qualities (roughly). The second is the human world, the world of commitments that form part of human agents' 'subjective motivational set'—desires, attitudes, and needs. Thick evaluative concepts occupy centre stage in metaethics due to what has been claimed to follow from them in the wake of the work of Bernard Williams who argues that

(1) Thick evaluative concepts are 'world-guided'; the thoughts and judgements expressed by utterances involving terms such as 'cruel', 'generous', 'integrity' are candidates for truth and falsity.
(2) Thick evaluative concepts are 'action-guiding'; they are '*characteristically* related to reasons for action. If a concept of this kind applies, this *often* provides someone with a reason for action' (my emphasis).[16]

Williams's strategy is to distinguish between two conceptions of 'the world', one of the world *absolutely* conceived as 'what is there anyway'; the other of the world conceived as the meaningful life-world of situated historical human agents. Now consider his characterization of the overall theoretical vision in his later essay on moral intuitionism:

Nevertheless, the nature of the shared practice shows that it is the world guided, and explanation will hope to show how that can be. What the explanation exactly may be, is to be seen: but we know that a vital part of it will lie in the desires, attitudes, and needs that we and they have differently acquired from our different ways of being brought into a social world. The explanation will show how, in relation to those differences, the world can indeed guide our and their reactions. 'The world' in that explanation will assuredly not be characterized merely in terms of primary qualities; the account of it will need to mention, no doubt, both primary and secondary qualities and straightforwardly psychological items.[17]

As I read him, Williams holds that the idea that concepts such as *cruel* and *kind* are 'world-guided' is in fact not based on some appeal to emergence or supervenience or anything like that: Williams's position is precisely not a new non-naturalism parallel to Moore's initial account of how all and only things that are intrinsically good form the extension of the predicate 'is intrinsically good'.[18] Williams's notion of thick concepts as 'world-guided' instead turns on considerations about competence with thick concepts within a shared social practice. Many authors engaged in the contemporary debate about the thick have seized on this aspect of Williams's account

---

[16] Williams (1979), 140. Williams's caveat about the action-guidance or practicality of thick evaluative concepts is arguably due to his reasons internalism: S has a reason to only if there is a 'sound deliberative route' from S's 'actual motivational set' *M* to (intention to) do the action. On this reading, thick evaluative concepts provide reasons only for those who endorse it (the value it may be used to ascribe) as part of one's 'insider' evaluative outlook.
[17] Williams (1995), 186.
[18] For further discussion and defence of this claim, see Harcourt and Thomas (2013).

and further hold the view that thick evaluative concepts are *shapeless* and *exhaustive* with respect to the non-evaluative features that ground them:

> *Shapelessness of thick concepts*: For any thick evaluative concept, there need not be any corresponding non-evaluative categorization or kind that unifies all and only the things that fall under that concept from one case of application to the next. What unifies all and only the instances of the concept (namely, kind), or what constitutes the real similarity shared by all its instances, is evaluative.
>
> *Outrunning ('insiders'/outsiders')*: The nature of the quality picked out by some thick evaluative concept is not determinable without using the concept in question; it is not independently discernible.[19]

What thus emerges is a conception of thick moral concepts as playing a dual role in our moral thinking: Thick moral concepts trace out moral patterns in a nonetheless objective reality and at once guide action in a way that is bound up with appropriately developed ethical sensibilities.[20] On contemporary non-reductive moral realist versions of this claim beyond Williams's internal realism, the 'new' non-naturalism, as it were, thick evaluative concepts are (non-Platonically) *inherently evaluative*.

A common view, shared by the otherwise diverse positions of moral constructivism, versions of subjective and internal realism, and Nietzschean constitutivism,[21] assumes that understanding value experience as conceptually structured in perspectival and parochial ways implies that value itself is constituted by the contingent conceptual commitments of one's perspective.[22] Thus, much contemporary work on thick concepts in the wake of the work of authors such as John McDowell and Bernard Williams in metaethics often culminates in the claim that the meaning or sense of the intentional object of evaluative thought is anthropocentric ('subjective'). In contrast, what we find in Murdoch is the robust realist claim that the salient concepts of an individual's life-world can be *revelatory* of value.

2. The Way Ahead

My overall aim in this essay is to make good the robust realist claim that the salient concepts of an individual's life-world can be *revelatory* of value without appeal either to Platonism or value constitutivism. Drawing on Iris Murdoch's model of value experience and moral vision as implying the notion of an all-encompassing 'world view', my central positive thesis is the claim that the relevant notion that value is always value *for us* be understood as a transcendental condition for experience itself

---

[19] I borrow the term 'outrunning' from Väyrynen (2013), see esp. 193 ff.

[20] Bergqvist (2013).

[21] 'Constitutivism' is often used to refer to the view that the nature of value is fixed by the constitutive aim of action. But if I am reading Katsafanas correctly, he does not take constitutivism to imply anything about action having a constitutive aim. (I thank Michael Milona for this observation.) I should also note that Nietzsche's own position is usually referred to as 'perspectivism'. My use of the distinctive notion of 'perspectivalism' throughout this paper is partly motivated by this usage; it does not involve commitment to Nietzschean *perspectivism*.

[22] See Setiya (2013); Katsafanas (2013) and (forthcoming); Lovibond (2009); Thomas (2006) and (2012).

rather than a determinant of the representational content of such experience. Along the way, I draw out the implications of this view for the possibility of a value objectivism and what is sometimes called the 'absolute conception', which is implicit in many contemporary debates about thick evaluative concepts. What the resulting view brings to the table is a conceptual framework that allows us reconsider the evaluative/non-evaluative distinction concerning the way that we think about the significance of the first-person perspective in ethics and the nature of thick concepts as *practical concepts* beyond the polarized dichotomies (between the evaluative and non-evaluative, the subjective and objective) that drive many of the objections to robust non-reductive moral realism with which we started.

I begin (Section 3) by examining Murdoch's account of moral perception in relation to the general thesis of cognitive penetrability in the philosophy of perception, the claim that the character of perceptual experience can be affected by another mental state of the perceiving subject. As we shall see, what we find in Murdoch's distinctive account of evaluative appraisal in terms of what she sometimes refers to as 'just and loving perception' is not only the idea of being attuned to one's environment thanks to cognitive penetration through the *concepts* that we deploy, but also the claim that one's *conceptions* of these concepts decisively influence what we see. According to Murdoch's notion of moral vision, when people disagree about moral questions, their disagreements do not partition cleanly into evaluative and non-evaluative categories; it is rather that the disputants' different *world views* generate conflicting narratives about the situation.

The upshot of this discussion (Section 3) raises the explanatory desiderata for Section 4: how to understand Murdoch's difficult claim that agents with dissimilar world views 'see different worlds'. What assumptions do we need to add to the presence, or possibility, of variation in narratives and world views to make the slide from moral vision to value constitutivism seem *tempting*? I diagnose this as a problem concerning the relation between moral vision and non-perspectival value. I distinguish between two readings of the concept of 'non-perspectival value': an epistemic reading and a non-epistemic one. I argue that commitment to the thesis that value is in some sense always *value for us* does not as such rule out value being non-perspectival in the sense of existing independently of any actual worldviews or perspectives in the non-epistemic sense.

In Section 5 I address the relationship between the parochial and the perspectival. I argue that use of the notion '*variation in perspective*' masks an ambiguity that betrays a deeper confusion between concepts and conceptions in Nietzsche's perspectivism. On my reading, although Nietzsche and Murdoch both hold that there may be irreconcilable differences in competing *moral visions* (thus understood as conceptual schemes) this does not yet show that both authors hold that there is therefore no guarantee that we will arrive at a fully adequate, unproblematic set of *concepts*: the general non-Platonist claim that evaluative claims are 'perspectival' is ambiguous between a number of readings that we should be careful to distinguish.

In developing my positive account of value experience as revelatory of value, I invoke the notion of transcendental narrative structure in moral experience (thus understood as implying an all-encompassing moral vision). I use the idea of narrative structure as an *object of comparison* with the aim of defending the further claim that the emphasis placed on context that is present in both Katsafanas's and Murdoch's accounts of value experience as always already structured by the concepts and parochial sensibilities is best understood as the claim that content-involving (and so rationality-involving) phenomena in human life is inseparable from point or purpose.

In Section 6, I consider the possible objection to the resulting account as to how to account for the notion of structure and unity of moral thought: are there any limits as to what might plausibly be counted as 'value *for us*'? As we shall see, this question is especially pressing if we follow through on the argument from Sections 3–5 and take the central target notion of *world view* to be an unruly holistic admixture of evaluative and non-evaluative concepts.

3. Murdoch on Rich Description

In philosophy of perception the general idea of perceptual experience itself being evaluative has sometimes been discussed in terms of 'cognitive penetration', the claim that the character of perceptual experience can be affected by another mental state of the perceiving subject: the cognitive states and characters of perceptual agents can alter how they perceive the world. It also relates to the more general idea that the character of perceptual states is *theory-laden*, in as much as the experiences we have are structured by our conceptual capacities and cognitive background knowledge. Potential cognitive penetrators include moods, beliefs, hypotheses, knowledge, desires, and traits. Thus, to borrow an example from Susanna Siegel,

> it is sometimes said that in depression, everything looks grey. If this is true, then mood can influence the character of perceptual experience: depending only on whether a viewer is depressed or not, how a scene looks to that viewer can differ even if all other conditions stay the same.[23]

In some cases, cognitive penetration can be epistemically beneficial. This claim has recently been defended by Siegel. She writes:

> If an x-ray looks different to a radiologist from the way it looks to someone lacking radiological expertise, then the radiologist gets more information about the world from her experience (such as whether there's a tumor) than the non-expert does from looking at the same x-ray.[24]

Moreover, if cognitive penetrability by personal traits is possible we may also elucidate the intuitively plausible idea that having the right kind of traits typically makes a subject more sensitive to relevant features of her environment. Philosophically, the intuitive idea that can be traced back to the ancient moral philosophical dictum that 'virtue is knowledge', which has been the focus of more recent contributions to the literature on moral perception in the wake of Iris Murdoch's and John McDowell's respective work. As Siegel puts it:

> If Iris Murdoch and John McDowell are correct in thinking that having the right sort of character lets you see more moral facts than someone lacking that character sees when faced

---

[23] S. Siegel (2012).   [24] S. Siegel (2012), 201.

with the same situation, then there too, your perceptual experience becomes epistemically better, thanks to its being penetrated by your character.[25]

According to this view, a rash person will not perceive the danger in a situation where a courageous person would.

Like Siegel, I find it helpful to think of Murdoch's notion of 'moral vision' in terms of cognitive penetrability. I also agree that the epistemic claim that cognitive penetrability by personal traits (of the right kind) typically makes a subject more sensitive to relevant features of her environment is a good way of understanding Murdoch's commitment to the claim that 'virtue is knowledge'. While this aspect of Murdoch's position, that adequate moral 'vision' may itself be conditional upon virtue, has been much discussed in the literature, I want to explore a rather different and, to my mind, more significant way in which perception can be ethically relevant. What we find in Murdoch's distinctive account of evaluative appraisal in terms of what she sometimes refers to as 'just and loving perception' is not only the idea of being attuned to one's environment thanks to cognitive penetration through the *concepts* that we deploy, but also the claim that one's *conceptions* of these concepts decisively influence what we see. While R. M. Hare and others present morality as primarily a matter of *choice*, and treat moral *disagreement* as a matter of difference in the ways in which people 'choose' among alternatives, Murdoch advocates a shift in focus from the concept of 'choice' to the concept of 'vision': a person's conception of salient concepts may restrict, or enlarge (and may focus in one way or another) the range of *options* that she is in a position to recognize as available for her to choose from. Thus, Murdoch wants to deny that the person 'chooses his reasons in terms of, and after surveying, the ordinary facts which lie open to everyone'.[26] Difference, then, for Murdoch, is not just a difference in application of shared concepts, but in the *repertoire* of concepts that different people understand and employ. The key claim is that adequate moral deliberation is conditional upon first getting your initial *descriptions* of the practical moral situation right. Thus, to borrow an example from Elijah Millgram, if you take someone to be distant and aloof, you may be rather 'standoffish' yourself, but 'once you come to see his manners as shy, it will be more natural to be more open towards him'.[27]

As intimated in Section 1, part of the problem of finding the right description in Murdoch is the idea that moral conflicts, e.g., doing the brave thing or the honest thing, can be *resolved* by successful redescription (maybe the honest thing *is* the brave thing). The more controversial thesis is that getting the description right is itself an 'evaluative' matter for which you are morally responsible, unlike the case of merely 'factual' descriptions (like representing the wood anemones in the vase before you as being thus and so).

Murdoch argues for this conclusion at length by her well-known example of a mother who comes to see her daughter-in-law in a new light as 'refreshingly spontaneous' (rather than juvenile and vulgar) through an active and conscientious effort to *attend* to the girl and see her 'as she really is'.[28] Let us set aside the issue

---

[25] S. Siegel (2012), 201.   [26] Murdoch (1997), 327.   [27] Millgram (2005), 175.
[28] Murdoch herself is a Platonist Realist, but these remarks can be made consistent with a whole variety of views. Perhaps most obviously, the emphasis on activity, conceptual framework, and practical interests

whether Murdoch is right in assuming that such reassessments are themselves expressions of 'just' and 'loving' moral perceptivity or if having the relevant vision is itself conditional upon virtue.[29] The important point for present purposes is the assumption that the mother-in-law's conscientious effort to view the girl afresh in a way that also enables her to relate to her in a more sympathetic way points toward a moral *improvement* of some sort. What we have here is not just the reminder of the importance of keeping one's mind open so that one does not overlook some interesting *alternative* ways of representing the circumstances. The claim is rather that you are morally required to adopt a critical stance because you could otherwise miss those morally salient aspects that could actually make a difference to the appropriateness of one's practical response. Thus, as Justin Broackes emphasizes, Murdoch's interest 'is not just in the phenomenon of *changing one's mind* about a particular case, but also in the processes of *revision*, of development and "deepening" of moral vocabulary and conceptual scheme ([1964] IP 29/322, 31-33/324-326) and particularly, and most remarkably, in a kind of *privacy* of understanding ([1964] IP 25-9/319-22)'[30]—where the very subject matter of ethics is claimed to be *all-encompassing* rather than limited to overtly 'moral' concepts (such as 'duty', 'permissible', or other evaluative standards for right conduct). As Murdoch expresses it in her 1967 Leslie Stephen Lecture (published in 1970 as part of *The Sovereignty of Good*): 'The area of morals, and ergo of moral philosophy, can ... be seen ... as covering *the whole of our mode of living* and the *quality of our relations with the world.*'[31]

On the face of it, Murdoch's emphasis on thick description and, more importantly, *redescription* of moral scenarios in perception bears striking similarities with Nietzsche's account of the continuous process of *revaluation*. Revaluation consists in examining the *practical* considerations of a value commitment or concept in terms of whether it contributes to a project that is life-enhancing (the value is vindicated), or life-denying (the value is discarded). How should we understand this? Drawing on Max Weber's[32] reflections on the predicament of us moderns, Katsafanas argues that Nietzsche's practical orientation culminates in a nihilistic diagnosis that fails to take any existing values as worthwhile ends in themselves. He writes:

> To put it in Nietzschean terms: our current perspective, with its commitments to an ideal of efficiency, continually structures our ways of viewing the world and our habits of thinking, such that reflections on the possibility of non-instrumental value can be, for most individuals, only difficult reminders that are not put into everyday practice.[33]

There seems to be a conflation here between value and the subjective conditions for valuation. It is one thing to say that value-sensitive creatures set themselves ends or

---

lies at the very heart of various pragmatist or 'constructivist' positions. But such ideas are equally central (though in a different way) with certain forms of realism and, in particular, the 'anti-representationalist' lessons that McDowell has urged on the back of his take on Sellars and Wittgenstein's respective critical remarks about the mythical Given (which again yield internally different accounts).

[29] Murdoch (1970), 17–19. For a similar idea that adequate moral 'vision' is itself conditional upon virtue, see Nancy Sherman's discussion of moral perception, in Sherman (1989), esp. 28–44. See also McDowell's (*passim*) vast and influential work on moral motivation and 'silencing'.

[30] Broackes (2012), 'Introduction', 12–13.   [31] Murdoch (1970), 97.
[32] Weber (1930/2002).   [33] Katsafanas (forthcoming), 20.

purposes. It is quite another thing to say that how agents set values as their ends or goals in the course of deliberation about what to do determines what *makes* something a value. The conflation, as Alan Thomas[34] notes, and as Christine Korsgaard[35] pointed out before him, is to run together two separate distinctions: value 'for its own sake' versus 'instrumental' value; and 'intrinsic' versus 'extrinsic' value. The intrinsic/extrinsic distinction applies to values and what *makes* something a value; the latter applies to how agents set values as their ends or goals in the course of deliberation about what to do. If this is right, we may follow Thomas and be open to *complementing* Nietzsche's account of how the free spirits are supposed to revalue the old values and set themselves ends or purposes in ways compatible with Murdoch's moral realism.[36] We have already the comparison with versions of subjective realism. In what follows I focus on an alternative strategy based on the notion of situated representation (of a certain sort).

4. Concepts and Conceptions

According to Murdoch's notion of moral vision, when people disagree about moral questions, their disagreements do not partition cleanly into evaluative and non-evaluative categories; it is rather that the disputants' different *world views* generate conflicting narratives about the situation. Moreover, our occurrent experiences and judgements, particularly about value, are informed by our background concepts and conceptions of those concepts (akin to what the aforementioned thesis of cognitive penetrability predicts). Moral vision arises out of a total world view. A narrative like the one we find in Murdoch's rich descriptions of M (the mother in the story) frames the objects of evaluative appraisal, where the framing is a result of selection, prioritization, and organization on behalf of not only the author but also the participating reader. For example, on one narrative, an individual is described as shy; but on another, as aloof. Because so many different narratives are often possible, some philosophers naturally worry that the narratives are never *revealing* moral reality but only *constructing* it. It is however a mistake to think that radical subjectivism is entailed by the fact of different narratives because these are *conceptions* of the object of inquiry, not the object itself. There is no implication, or so I claim, for the meaning or nature of the object of evaluative appraisal from the fact of different narratives.

One is easily led to suspicion of narrative explanation as a genuine form of explanation by exaggerating the role of interpretation. Taking a leaf from Peter Goldie's work on historical and autobiographical narratives, part of the problem is that the suspicion that putative supporting documents for any such particular narrative are 'just more text, multiply open to interpretation' motivates the

---

[34] Thomas (2012), 134.   [35] Korsgaard (1983).

[36] Indeed, as Thomas notes, we may develop a further account of the 'subject' end of Nietzsche's critique of slave morality: 'we might, as a culture, not fail to find values but, rather, fail to find any values worth setting as our goals or ends. In explaining the latter claim evaluative realism is not repudiated but, again, rather *presupposed*. However, it is a subjective realism in which conditions on the subject are allowed to enter into an account of the nature of value in a non-reductive way' (Thomas (2012), 134).

assimilation of narratives and what they are about.[37] Transposed to the present case, the exaggeration about interpretation is the simple point that all these salient features pointed to in making good some particular appraisal are themselves open to radically open-ended interpretation in line with the individual viewer's experience and, so the constructivist argument would continue, 'meaning-making' propensities.

The idea of narrative as *revelatory* of significance can be brought into sharper focus by comparison with Wittgenstein's idea of a 'perspicuous representation' as being a key aspect of the task of philosophy as he sees it: offering a model of comparison that 'earmarks the form of account we give, the way we look at things' in order to achieve a 'clear view' of that which is troubling us.[38] However this does not mean that there is some single philosophical method through which this is achieved. On the contrary, Wittgenstein presents the philosopher with an *open-ended* range of conceptual tools and techniques that can be used in a variety of different ways including (but not limited to): offering 'objects of comparison' and presenting 'alternative pictures'; pointing out particular 'family resemblances' and 'neglected aspects' of our language; grammatical analysis of our use of language in practice. The real task at hand is to discern which method available to one is the most *pointful* in each context of critical appraisal for attaining clarity and reveal meaning—to which *'whatever it takes'* would be the only answer to give in the abstract.[39]

Now, in terms of what we may think of how Murdoch's and Wittgenstein's methods look in practice, one is reminded of Frank Sibley's notion of 'perceptual proof' in aesthetic evaluations.[40] The focus of Sibley's discussion in his 'General Criteria and Reasons in Aesthetics'[41] is Michael Scriven's scepticism about what he calls the 'independence requirement' on aesthetic evaluation.[42] The independence requirement is a demand on rational (aesthetic) thought that 'we must be able to know the reason or reasons for a conclusion without first having to know the conclusion; otherwise we can never get the reason as a means to the conclusion'.[43] In its strongest form, the independence requirement demands that reasons must be *logically prior* to aesthetic verdicts (as opposed to temporally prior in perception). Like Wittgenstein before him, Sibley does not attempt a refutation of the sceptic by way of showing the independence requirement could be met. Instead he effectively uses the strategy of offering a 'perspicuous representation' of art criticism by pointing

---

[37] Goldie (2012), 153–4.   [38] Wittgenstein (1963), §§122, 133.

[39] The meaning of the notion a 'perspicuous representation' is controversial within Wittgenstein scholarship. Read and Hutchinson argue that the notion of a perspicuous representation is not to be understood as a way of seeing things and there cannot be multiple perspicuous ways of seeing the rules of 'our grammar'; any difference we might perceive between multiple perspicuous representations of an area of our grammar is merely a difference in how they are selected and arranged, something that *can* vary depending on the purpose of the investigation. Whether or not this is the best representation of Wittgenstein's position falls beyond the scope of this paper. I am inclined to agree with Currie (1993) (who in turn follows John McDowell) that a *representation* (as used in ordinary contexts) that transcends any point of view seems incoherent, but I cannot argue for this claim here. For further discussion see e.g. A. W. Moore (1997); Baker (2006); Read and Hutchinson (2008).

[40] Sibley first introduced the notion of a 'perceptual proof' in his seminal article 'Aesthetic Concepts', n. 23. Sibley (1959/2001).

[41] Sibley (1983/2001).   [42] Scriven (1966).   [43] Sibley (1983/2001).

to the way it is actually practised to show that aesthetic evaluations stand in no need for external validation. He writes:

> How a critic manages by what he says and does to bring people to see aesthetic qualities they have missed has frequently puzzled writers. But there is no real reason for mystification. [...] What mainly is required is a detailed description of the sorts of thing critics in fact do and say, for this is what succeeds if anything does; the critic may make similes and comparisons, describe the work in appropriate metaphors, gesticulate aptly and so on. Almost anything he may do, verbal or non-verbal, can on occasion prove successful. To go on to ask how these methods can possibly succeed is to begin to ask how people can ever be brought to see aesthetic (and Gestalt and other similar) properties at all.[44]

Thus, for Sibley and Wittgenstein, there is no *one* method of how we ought to do philosophy, but rather we employ a range of different tools that fit the task at hand; *whatever it takes*. As mentioned earlier (Section 1), a central feature of Murdoch's account of moral vision, in turn, is that the recognition that moral philosophers, when presenting themselves as studying specific issues in moral philosophy, are in fact always relying on background beliefs about the world that are, themselves, *contestable*.[45]

But what is the analogue conception of *value* that this new way of seeing the matter of meaning brings with it?

What needs explaining is a way in which agents could, as Murdoch puts it, '*see different worlds*'. What assumptions do we need to add to the presence, or possibility, of variation in narratives and world views to make the slide from moral vision to value constitutivism seem tempting? A crucial constraint here is that the commitment to Murdoch's idea of a difference in comprehensive world view, and not just mere variation in individual moral belief and preference, should play an important role in tempting us. Recall Murdoch's objection to Hare's presentation as primarily a matter of *choice* that we discussed in Section 3, where Hare thinks of moral *disagreement* as a matter of difference in the ways in which people 'choose' among alternatives (and not as a disagreement in competing visions implied by to the concept of 'world view'). Here is a different way to ask the same basic question.[46] Why might value constitutivism seem *less* tempting on the view that accepts variation but denies moral vision?

Recall Thomas's (2012) remarks to the effect that those who slide from moral vision to value constitutivism tend to conflate 'value and the subjective conditions of valuation' (see Section 3). I argue that Kastafanas's use of the notion of '*variation in perspective*' masks a similar ambiguity that betrays a deeper confusion between concepts and conceptions in Nietzsche's perspectivism. On the one hand there is the familiar variation in *subjective conditions of valuation*: people set themselves different goals and live their lives in accordance with such decisions. On the other

---

[44] Sibley (1965/2001), 38.
[45] For further discussion of this issue, see e.g. Wiggins (1989) and Väyrynen (2014b).
[46] Suppose that we reject Murdoch's idea of moral vision. This might be because we go in for a picture of moral concepts, thought, and experience more in line with R. M. Hare or G. E. Moore. I thank Michael Milona for raising this concern.

hand, there is a putative variation in the concepts themselves. In sum, Katsafanas's Nietzschean constitutivism adopts a Kantian story about concepts structuring experience, but rejects the claim that these concepts are fixed and uniform for all rational agents; instead, they change over time. Moreover, he claims that although conceptual schemes can be ranked as better and worse, there is no one best or correct set of concepts.[47]

The last claim is a departure from Hegel who, like Nietzsche, but unlike Kant, argues that the conceptual schemes through which we experience the world, the schemes that on the account *structure* our most basic understandings of ourselves and our relations to the world, are historically fluid. Katsafanas gives us the example of imagining a creature that cognizes things without seeing them as causally conditioned; or, imagine an agent that reasons practically while lacking any understanding of perfect and imperfect duty. These agents would, on the account, have experiences sufficiently dissimilar to us that it would make sense to speak of them as 'seeing different worlds'.[48]

Hegel, as Dancy notes, combines this claim that contingencies of the parochial may enter into our model of objectivity with a vindicatory story about conceptual change: he proposes a method of *stepping back* from the human standpoint in a way such that our conceptual schemes are progressively more adequate.[49] As Dancy explains this Hegelian notion of objectivity, 'nothing is 'left behind' in this process; rather, each succeeding view is retained (if perhaps somewhat altered)'.[50] Nietzsche, by contrast, dispenses with this Hegelian story of moral progress, opening us to the possibility that later conceptual schemes might be regressive and impoverished rather than more 'refined', as per Murdoch's account (recall the idea of moral vision as 'just and loving' that was outlined in Section 1).[51]

It is worth pausing to note that, on my reading, although Nietzsche and Murdoch both hold that there may be irreconcilable differences in competing *world views* (thus understood as conceptual schemes) this does not yet show that both authors hold that there is therefore no guarantee that we will arrive at a fully adequate, unproblematic set of *concepts*. Katsafanas, by contrast, moves from the claim that the fact that there may irreconcilable differences in our conceptual scheme to the additional claim that value itself is perspectival, that there *are no genuine evaluative concepts* (thus understood in cognitivist terms as picking out genuine properties of things).

Now, recall Nietzsche's distinctive account of the continuous process of *revaluation*. The central motivation for Nietzsche's account of revaluation consists in examining the distinctly *practical* considerations of a value or commitment or concept in terms of whether it contributes to a project that is life-affirming, or life-denying. How should we understand this idea of practical agency in relation to the property of *being attuned to our human perspective*, which also motivates Murdoch's claim of world views being revelatory of value?

---

[47] Katsafanas (forthcoming).   [48] Katsafanas (forthcoming).
[49] Dancy (1993), 144–65.   [50] Dancy (1993), 147.
[51] For further discussion of Hegel's method as applied to evaluative thought and judgement, see A. W. Moore (1997); Dancy (1993).

In what follows I will speak of narrative structure in moral experience as making certain reasons available to the agent, where the concept of 'narrative' is to be understood as something fundamentally perspectival. I will use this non-committal formulation deliberately in order to avoid more theoretically loaded models of the relationship between the normative content of ethics and practical agency, and the general notion of deliberating 'from a personal point of view'. A familiar representative theoretical model of the relation between the moral agent and ethical values uses the idea of agent-neutral reasons for action. This is a standard way of understanding the idea that a reason stands in a special relation to a particular agent or class of agents (see Scheffler,[52] Kagan,[53] and Nagel[54]). However, understanding *point of view* as a determinant of a special class of agent-relative reasons or values that contrasts with another class of values or reasons determined by the impartial perspective is entirely optional, and not something that I myself endorse. Instead, we may think of point of view as an agent's standpoint on an independent reality (evaluative or otherwise) such that the concept of a world view identifies something that makes value available *to* an agent's judgement rather than being a determinant of value itself.[55]

A second feature of my use of the notion of moral vision is that the relevant sense of 'narrative' be treated as a transcendental condition in understanding the significance of the first-person perspective, as opposed to a feature of the object of critical evaluation itself. More specifically, in suggesting that value is in some sense always value *for us*, my claim is that perspectivalism be seen as transcendental condition for experience itself rather than a determinant of the representational content of such experience. Here I side with Goldie and Solomon, who warn against confusing the notion of autographical narrative with its intentional object.[56]

According to my thesis about moral vision and the target concept of 'point of view', subjectivity is not a dissociable aspect of our mental lives as embodied agents, but a transcendental precondition for all conscious experience. By contrast, other authors[57] reserve the phrase 'sense of agency' to refer to what Bayne and Pacherie,[58] in a different context, call 'agentive judgements'. Bayne and Pacherie draw a distinction between agential *experience* and agentive *judgement* in what they refer to as the 'architecture of agentive self-awareness', which suggests a potential rapprochement between the top-down narrative construction and other low-level 'vehicles' for agentive self-awareness. On this approach, while the top-down narrative module

---

[52] Scheffler (1982).   [53] Kagan, (1989).   [54] Nagel (1986).

[55] It could further be argued that agent-neutral value is incompatible with an independently attractive account of the nature of practical reasoning as reasoning that terminates in action as its conclusion. That will not be my focus here, but I will explore a different route to essentially the same claim in defending my position that discernment is a form of practical rationality expressive of first-personal thinking. See Thomas (2005); Dancy (1993).

[56] See Goldie (2012); Solomon (2015). Goldie expresses the point thus: 'it is sometimes suggested that life, or parts of life, such as an illness or a process of grieving *is* a narrative. This is a simple mistake that, I think, often leads to the worry that real life narratives are fundamentally no different from fictional narratives [...]. There can be such a thing as a narrative *of* a life or *of* an illness or *of* a grieving, but to say that a life or an illness or a grieving *is* a narrative is to run together what is represented with the representation' (Goldie (2012), 153–4).

[57] Stephens and Graham (2000).   [58] Bayne and Pacherie (2007).

has a role to play in explaining agentive judgements, there is a second dimension to the 'mode' of agentive awareness located in the very machinery of action production. They write:

> Think of what it is like to push a door open. One might judge that one is the agent of this action, but this judgment is not the only way in which one's own agency is manifested to oneself; indeed, it is arguably not even the primary way in which one's own agency is manifested to oneself. Instead, one *experiences* oneself as the agent of this action. Such states are no more judgments than are visual experiences of the scene in front of one or proprioceptive experiences of the current position of one's limbs.[59]

Theorists disagree as to whether such pre-reflexive (and maybe also prelinguistic) experiences are themselves part of agentive self-hood, sometimes referred to as 'the minimal self'. Gallagher's[60] formulation of the minimal model is premised upon a phenomenological account of self-awareness that involves a commitment to what is sometimes referred to as the 'self-reflexivity thesis'. According to this thesis, consciousness always already implies a tacit form of *self*-awareness; Stephens and Graham reserve the phrase 'sense of agency' to refer to agentive judgements.[61] To forestall possible confusion, because nothing in this paper hangs on the plausibility of the stronger reading of minimal self-awareness as implying the reflexivity thesis, I follow Bayne and Pacherie in using the term 'agentive awareness' to cover both readings.

What matters for present purposes in relation to Bayne and Pacherie's work on the interplay of top-down and bottom-up effects in the so-called architecture of agential awareness is a potential integration of the top-down narrative construction of selfhood and the minimal approach at one point: it suggests that (resistant) evaluative experience are best seen against the background of agency of *whole persons*. Katsafanas's model of 'value/meaning-making', by contrast, opens the door to something more: to the prospect that we can see value content as *determined* by independently specifiable conceptual frameworks, patterns of attention, or on a larger scale, generic sociopolitical cultural narratives that are discernible in public discourse. This seems to me to be the central upshot of Nietzschean constitutivism. In so far as the promises of a reappraisal of Murdoch's account lies in such a reduction of meaning and value to a perspective, it is a new paradigm I think we should resist. And the reason is that we should distinguish conditions on the valuing subject from conditions on the associated value.

5. The Parochial and the Perspectival

So far I have sought to show that we can make sense of Murdoch's claim that world views can reveal value without committing ourselves either to Platonism or Nietzschean constitutivism. The suggestion was that moral vision puts pressure on us to have a conception of value according to which what is valuable is not valuable

---

[59] Bayne and Pacherie (2007), 476. [60] Gallagher (2000).
[61] Stephens and Graham (2000).

from the point of view of the universe but valuable *for us*. Although moral vision on its own is largely neutral to the question of the nature of value, my position is that Murdoch's notion of the concept ultimately fits best with a conception of value that is in some sense perspectival (although not in the radical sense entailed by constitutivism) rather than Platonic. This raises a number of questions concerning the relation between moral vision and the notion of non-perspectival value with which we started.

On my account, the property of being attuned to a human perspective has to do with the nature of value rather than the nature of evaluative thought or experience. It is worth pausing to note the difference between this reading of Murdoch's claim that world views can reveal value and an alternative epistemic construal whereby the perspectivalness of value thesis is defined as a feature of Murdochian moral vision. If the central notion of perspective were understood as epistemic in this way, the resulting account of moral vision would trivially rule out Platonism (since moral vision and Platonism would just be defined in incompatible ways).[62] By contrast, my impression is that some value is non-perspectival just in case it does not depend on human perspectives and world views for its existence. To illustrate, if value were non-perspectival, then vision of value would be analogous to vision of objects such as, say, pine trees (e.g., a Scots pine). Pine trees don't depend on human perspectives or world views for their existence, although our human sensibilities are capable of perceiving them.

Now, on the face of it, if I am right that the notion of non-perspectival value is better understood in metaphysical terms, does it not follow that the concept of *perspectival* value is value that *does* metaphysically depend on human perspectives and world views for its existence? No. We can talk of perspectival value in different ways. It might mean that value is fixed by our *actual* perspectives and world views, whatever those happen to be. This would lead to a highly subjectivist picture. But there is space for an alternative view. The alternative says that value would not exist but for creatures with perspectives and world views, but *actual* perspectives and world views can be mistaken. Such perspectival value is *for us*, and we can be better or worse at detecting it. To see this, it is helpful to turn to more theoretically loaded models of the relationship between the normative content of ethics and practical agency, and the general notion of deliberating 'from a perspective', in the debate over partiality and impartiality in ethics.

Suppose that all values are eudaemonistic and constitutively connected to human flourishing: there are no values that do not stand in a constitutive relation to a mental subject. One option is to say that content and human-involving interests are interdependent: neither can be understood except in connection with the other. As Alan Thomas puts it, 'we respond to value and yet everything relevant to our subjective [human] perspective can bear on the process of evaluation and hence what those eudaimonistic values mean *for* us'.[63] Thomas maintains that the correct way to conceive of this value is, indeed, presuppositionally. It does not enter into the truth conditions of an evaluative claim that such claims are relativized to the human

---

[62] I thank Michael Milona for this observation.   [63] Thomas (2012), 150.

standpoint.[64] Secondly, even within subjective realism, there is still an ambiguity in understanding the relationship between us and these facts. Suppose we appropriately respond to something:

(i) Do we react as we do *because the world* is such as to merit the reaction? This suggests robust realism.
(ii) Is the world such as to merit the reaction *because we react* in these ways? This suggests projectivism or quasi-realism.

John McDowell denies both directions of explanation for the class of eudaemonistic values. He says that neither our reactions nor the facts we are reacting to can be understood apart from each other: they are both basic, and *fit* one another. He calls this the No Priority View: we respond to value and yet everything relevant to our (human) perspective can bear on the process of valuing and hence what those eudaemonistic values mean *for* us. As McDowell puts: 'If there is no comprehending the right sentiments independently of the concepts of the relevant [evaluative] features, a no-priority view is surely indicated.'[65] This brings me to a related distinction between value and evaluation, which bears directly on Katsafanas's discussion of genealogy that I discussed earlier (see Sections 1 and 4).

Rather than holding that the conceptual schemes through which we experience the world literally structure the intentional object of human thought and judgement in a way that implies that agents with dissimilar world views see different *worlds* (because the schemes that shape our basic understanding of ourselves and our relations to the world are historically fluid), I suggest that we may think of conceptual frameworks as *models of comparison*, deployed in the interests of uncovering meaning and value in a way that is perhaps analogous to the very activity of philosophy itself. Maybe the question of what exactly is to be understood in the continuous task of setting oneself goals and living one's life in accordance with those decisions is itself an ill-posed question, and it is this 'dislodging' of ideas that aspects of Murdoch's difficult work endeavour to illuminate.[66] If we may think of ethical and aesthetic vindication as taking on this task (as Wittgenstein does with philosophy), we can also preserve a critical perspective in favour of a purely sociological or autobiographical one.

Such reorientation of focus makes available a distinctive mode of criticism, in which claims to 'objective' meaning *in* conceptual frameworks are criticized not as false per se, but as failing to yield the insight about the problem of objective meaning it was the point of those claims to provide. The conceptual framework of one's 'life-world' can reveal (or obfuscate) the object's meaning—but it does not determine the object's meaning. To think otherwise would be to conflate what is represented with the representation.

---

[64] Thomas gives the following example: 'Postboxes are not red for humans; postboxes are red. In the latter claim the perspectivalness of colour discourse as a *whole* is presupposed—and similarly for the notion of value relative to our human perspective' (Thomas (2012), 150).

[65] McDowell (1987/1998), 160.

[66] This seems to be Cora Diamond's reading of Murdoch, but it is difficult to be sure. See Diamond (1996).

To make good this claim we may follow the basic tactic of Adrian Moore's defence of 'absolute representations', representations that can be added without danger of conflicting points of view, and distinguish between the conditions of the production of a representation on the one hand and 'the role that the representation can play in such process as indirect integration' on the other.[67] The central claim would be that the perspectivalness of the *production* of a representation, expressive of an answerable stance upon the world that (at least in the evaluative case) includes the history of whatever conceptual apparatus that is used in it, has no effect on the stance-independence of the latter.[68]

Just how we should best understand the relation of the parochial to that of an absolute conception of the world is something that I leave open for future work. The claim here is simply that the 'producer' of an evaluative representation has a point of view *operative* in producing it; the context of the agent *betrays* a stance upon the world. This preserves a critical stance, in as much as we are now in a position to hold that the route to ethical truth will be stance-dependent, shaped by one's conceptions, and yet think of competing conceptual frameworks as offering different perspectives on the object of inquiry—without thereby reducing meaning and truth to a perspective.

In this section I have argued that the emphasis placed on context that is present in both Katsafanas's and Murdoch's accounts of value experience as always already structured by the concepts and parochial sensibilities at one's disposal effectively declares content-involving (and so rationality-involving) phenomena in human life to be inseparable from point or purpose. Katsafanas's Nietzschean value constitutivism was motivated by the thought that the emphasis on point or purpose must presuppose that facts about the valuer enter into the reflective explanation of the truth conditions of ethical claims in ways that render them radically perspectival. But this conclusion is premature: the general non-Platonist idea that evaluative claims are 'perspectival' is ambiguous between a number of readings that we should be careful to distinguish.

In Section 6, I consider the possible objection whether the present account can make sense of the notion of structure and unity of moral thought: are there any limits as to what might plausibly be counted as 'value *for us*'?

6. Thick Concepts and the Unity of Evaluative Thought

Murdochian moral vision, recall, says roughly that our experiences and beliefs about the world do not partition cleanly into evaluative and non-evaluative categories; and,

---

[67] A. W. Moore (1997), 89.

[68] Moore writes: 'One attractive feature of this tactic is that it leaves considerable room for concession whenever anyone insists on the parochial, conditioned, nay, perspectival character of any act of producing a representation. They are right to insist on this, if it is properly understood. Apart from anything else, any act of producing a representation in an *act*, and agency itself is impossible without some (evaluative) point of view giving sense to the question of what to do. But one possible thing to do is to represent the world from no point of view' (A. W. Moore (1997), 89).

moreover, our occurrent experiences and judgements, particularly about value, are informed by our background concepts and conceptions of those concepts. Moral vision arises out of a total world view.

Now consider the following concern. Intuitively, our world views give rise to perceptual experiences and beliefs about *ostensibly* non-perspectival objects, properties, and relations, such as pine trees, causal relations, chairs. The worry is whether my account of moral vision requires us to radically rethink, say, causation, construing it as in some sense *for us* in the same way that value is *for us*. This would be an unwelcome result. For the natural answer here is that this is implausible. For example, it seems as if there could be causation even if there were no comprehensive world views in my sense; this was the key motivation for resisting the epistemic construal of the target notion. Conversely, on my metaphysical approach according to which some value is non-perspectival just in case it does not depend on human perspectives and world views for its existence, if value were non-perspectival, then vision of value would be analogous to vision of objects such as flowers (e.g. a wood anemone). Wood anemones don't depend on human perspectives or world views for their existence, although our human sensibilities are (thankfully) capable of perceiving them.

So far, so good. The deeper issue is what, if anything, identifies any (thick) concept as a distinctly *evaluative* concept. The problem here is this. Even if Murdoch's idea that we cannot clearly separate evaluative and non-evaluative categories in the deployment of a world view is right, we still do seem to be able to identify some things as purely non-evaluative; causation, for instance. What, on the account, could justify such distinctions? Is there room for the very concept of the unity and structure of evaluative thought *as such*?

There are a number of options here. One possibility is to adopt a broadly pragmatist stance and say that a flattened moral landscape is no bad thing; maybe some version of the normative reading of Wittgenstein, such as that of Alice Crary, to the effect that linguistic competence is a *moral* or evaluative competence is true.[69] Another option is to work with the particularist notion of a 'default' moral reason and say that although there is nothing *intrinsic* about any feature that makes it a moral reason, this does not imply that we cannot distinguish the concept of a (moral) reason from that of context.[70] A third option is to think further about thick evaluative concepts.

In what follows I will focus on two recent trends in metaethics. One is the renewed interest in the non-reductive cognitivist conception of thick evaluative concepts such as *kind* or *cruel* as non-evaluatively shapeless with respect to the lower-level properties that ground them. The second is the preoccupation with arguments in the philosophy of language as applied to metaethics, notably the rule-following argument and debates over semantic contextualism. As we shall see, these two trends are not unconnected. What is distinctive about the contextualist version of non-reductive moral realism is a shift in focus from the orthodox view that CRUEL conceptually

---

[69] Crary (2007).
[70] For further discussion and defense of such an approach, see Dancy (1993), (2010), and (2013) *passim*; Bergqvist (2009) and (2010). For a different argument to a similar conclusion, see S. G. Chappell (2013).

entails good (inherent evaluation in meaning) to that of semantic underdetermination in evaluative property ascription.

The initial worry with the new version of non-reductive moral realism is that the general notion of linguistic competence, which also motivates the *outrunning* thesis that was mentioned in Section 1, does not seem to capture what, if anything, makes a (class of) thick concept evaluative. In response, defenders of the claim that thick concepts are *inherently evaluative*, and not evaluative in virtue of standing in an analytic or conceptual relation of entailment to some thin evaluative concept, can instead appeal to the claim that thick concepts require an 'evaluative eye', sensitivity to human practical concerns, to determine or recognize their instances.[71] Thus, for instance, Debbie Roberts's (2013) version[72] of the thesis that thick concepts are inherently evaluative is formulated as a claim about what makes a concept evaluative in terms of property *ascription*, where the notion of 'ascribing an evaluative property' in using thick concepts is distinguished from Eklund's notion of a concept being evaluative in virtue of *standing for* an evaluative property.[73] The distinction serves to highlight different ways of picking out the property in question: a direct, non-dependent way, and a parasitic one. Following Kit Fine,[74] Roberts further elucidates the notion of ascribing an evaluative property 'directly' in using thick concepts as a matter of latching onto one of its essential, rather than accidental, features given by the *real definition* for the kind in question which again brings us back to the shapelessness thesis, the thesis that what constitutes the real similarity shared by all instances of the concept in question, is evaluative—thus understood as a claim about the *semantic values* of thick concepts rather than their linguistic meaning: 'evaluation determines extension in the case of evaluative concepts, because evaluative concepts and properties are non-evaluatively shapeless'.[75]

The problem with this tactic as I see it is this. Even if formulated as a claim about the extension (semantic values) of thick concepts, and not just the meanings (or senses), the general notion of *shapelessness* does not seem to distinguish specifically evaluative concepts from other concepts ascribing emergent or metaphysically dependent properties. If all, or some, thick concepts really verify the thesis that thick concepts can be used as full evaluative judgements on their own and not indicate positive or negative thin evaluative judgement—and this cannot be explained as simply due to pragmatic factors—then one may question whether the relationship between thick concepts and evaluation is a *semantic* relationship.[76] Moreover, as noted above, if a broadly Wittgensteinian conception of linguistic competence as normative per se is right, maybe the shapelessness hypothesis is true of *all* 'higher-level' artefact and social kind terms and concepts.

In general, and here I side with Pekka Väyrynen:[77] *either* the relevant notion of shapelessness isn't characteristic of the evaluative in particular (maybe it holds for mental concepts and properties as well?), in which case it is not clear why the thesis should carry the sorts of distinctive metaethical implications that get attributed to it,

---

[71] Dancy (2013), 58.   [72] D. Roberts (2013).   [73] Eklund (2013).
[74] See Fine (1994) and (1995).   [75] D. Roberts (2013), 87.
[76] For further discussion and defense of this claim, see Väyrynen (2011); Bergqvist (2013).
[77] Väyrynen (2014).

or else the relevant notion of shapelessness (proper) is supposed to be characteristic of the evaluative in particular (*contra* Crary (2007), for instance), in which case it will be a problem for the inherent value thesis about thick concepts if shapelessness can be explained on the basis of more general factors that have nothing in particular to do with being evaluative.[78] The upshot from this seems to be that something stronger than conceptual competence or inquiry is required for the identification of thick evaluative concepts as such.[79] That also seems to the position of Jonathan Dancy, who argues that we instead understand competence with thick concepts as a *practical competence*. He writes:

> [Competence with thick concepts] will be practical competence, since it consists in knowledge of the sorts of [reason-providing] difference it can make that it is here instantiated. This sort of knowledge brings with it the ability to tell one case from another in this respect; *the competence is not just an ability to determine whether the concept is instantiated or not*, but also the ability to determine what difference this makes on the present occasion.[80]

The problem with this suggestion as an articulation of the thesis that thick evaluative concepts are (non-Platonically) *inherently* evaluative is that it seems possible for a non-evaluative concept to require the evaluative eye as well, in which case the evaluative nature of thick concepts is yet to be explained. Take Margaret Little's example of noticing a child alone in the crowd. As Dancy notes, 'while loneliness might be a thick concept, aloneness might not be, and one can imagine saying that it is a non-evaluative matter whether the child is accompanied or not'; yet, for all that, 'the ability to notice such a thing requires an understanding of human practical purposes'.[81] As noted by Siegel,[82] Bengson gives an example of this sort in an excellent discussion of similar phenomena,[83] where someone gives up their seat on the bus to someone else who is visibly tired (a pregnant or elderly person, for instance). Again, even if it is a wholly non-evaluative matter whether some person is visually tired or not, appreciating the *action-oriented* dimension of seeing someone in that state in one's close proximity requires, precisely, the 'evaluative' eye for human practical concerns.[84] So how should we understand this?

As we have seen, the revival of the non-reductive conception of thick concepts has gained fuel from arguments in the philosophy of language. There is a presentiment about, that the new version's reorientation promises to make non-reductive realism about moral properties a more viable metaethical position. While I am myself

---

[78] Väyrynen (2014), reference to Crary mine; see Crary (2007).

[79] Similarly Roberts claims that a property is evaluative if it is 'anthropocentric', where the relevant notion of 'anthropocentric' may further be elucidated in terms of (a) response-dependency or else (b) 'being intrinsically linked to human concerns and purposes in terms of importance or *mattering*' (D. Roberts (2013), 94).

[80] Dancy (2013), 58.   [81] Dancy (2013), 58.

[82] S. Siegel (2014).   [83] Bengson (2016).

[84] John Bengson (2016) distinguishes the idea of feeling that an action is simply pulled out of you by the situation (in something like the way a reflex might be), from the feeling that it is pulled out of you by the situation, because the situation mandated it. As noted by S. Siegel (2014), since Bengson wants to distinguish between actions, and reflexes aren't actions, ultimately he glosses his distinction in terms of different levels or kinds of understanding of the situation that elicits (Bengson says 'extorts') the action from the subject.

broadly sympathetic to the moral particularist contextualist position in metaethics, I argue that the recent semantic contextualist turn in the literature about thick evaluative concepts masks an ambiguity regarding the relation between competence with thick evaluative concepts and the fact that something is a moral property or reason, which I argue is helpfully elucidated further by clearly distinguishing the issue of what makes something an evaluative judgement and judgements concerning the applicability of given concepts. In my view, to determine whether some thick concept *applies* in a given context of evaluative appraisal is not to 'make an evaluation' as such (other than the sense in which, e.g., aesthetic concepts may be seen as 'taste concepts' such that judgement of taste is logically prior to, and therefore can be used to explain, *competence* with thick aesthetic terms). We need a separate argument that speaks to the *practicality* of thick moral concepts as action-guiding concepts (compare worries about competence above), and the notion of *action-oriented perception* more generally.[85]

In the context of moral philosophy, Maximilian De Gaynesford argues that reference to the first person—first-personal thought—in ethical thinking is of greatest importance in understanding the very notions of 'rational agency' (agency that involves responsiveness to reasons) and 'practical reasoning' (reasoning leading to action). As he puts it, '[u]nless some *situation* is *mine*, I am unable to recognise it as open to my agency or as relating me to various reason-giving facts. And unless some *reasons* are mine, I am unable to engage in reasoning that leads to action'.[86] What is the relation of agency that discloses objects of evaluative appraisal as 'open' to me as a responsible moral judge?

What I have tried to do in this section is to offer a new way of understanding the evaluative/non-evaluative distinction concerning the way that we think about the nature of thick concepts in terms all-encompassing world views. Such reorientation of focus makes available a novel conception of thick evaluative concepts, in which the emphasis on underdetermined evaluative meaning in metaethics is criticized not as false per se, but as failing to yield the insight about the problem of an occasion-insensitive semantics for the thick it was the point of that move to make in understanding moral properties.

7. Concluding Remarks

This essay has critically explored the implications of Murdoch's distinctive conception of value experience as conceptually structured in perspectival and parochial ways for the possibility of a value objectivism, with special emphasis on the so-called 'absolute conception' that is implicit in many contemporary debates about thick evaluative concepts. A popular moral cognitivist strand in the contemporary debate in the wake of the work of authors such as John McDowell and Bernard Williams is the non-reductive subjective realist position that evaluative thought and judgement deploying such concepts be understood as anthropocentric ('subjective'). What

---

[85] For further discussion of this issue in relation to the debate over the admissible contents of perceptual experience, see e.g. S. Siegel (2014); S. Kelly (2010); and, of course, J. J. Gibson (1977/1979).
[86] De Gaynesford (2010), 91.

I have sought to make good in this paper is the stronger robust realist claim that the salient concepts of an individual's life-world can be *revelatory* of value, without appeal to Platonism (or value constitutivism). Drawing on Iris Murdoch's model of value experience and moral vision as implying the notion of an all-encompassing 'world view', my central positive thesis is the claim that the relevant notion that value is always value *for us* be understood as a transcendental condition for experience itself rather than a determinant of the representational content of such experience.

This, in view of the familiar concerns with G. E. Moore's non-natural moral realism with which we started, raised a problem about the relation between moral vision and the notion of non-perspectival value. Against Katsafanas, I argued that commitment to the thesis that value is in some sense always *value for us* does not as such rule out value being non-perspectival in the sense of existing independently of any actual world views or perspectives. I have argued that the converse thesis is unsustainable due to the problems associated with the epistemic construal of perspectival and non-perspectival value, whereby the perspectivalness of value thesis is defined as a feature of Murdochian moral vision. And the reason is that we can still distinguish conditions on the valuing subject from conditions on the associated value.

In developing my positive account of value experience as revelatory of value, I then went on to argue that we regard the salient notion of structure in moral experience, thus understood as implying an all-encompassing 'world view', as an object of comparison. I further made the claim that the emphasis placed on context that is present in both Katsafanas's and Murdoch's accounts of value experience as always already structured by the concepts and parochial sensibilities is best understood as the claim that content-involving (and so rationality-involving) phenomena in human life is inseparable from point or purpose.

This raised the objection about the structure and unity of moral thought and judgement as *evaluative* thought as such: are there any limits as to what might plausibly be counted as 'value for us'? This question is especially pressing once we follow Murdoch and take the central target notion of *world view* to be an unruly holistic admixture of evaluative and non-evaluative concepts.

I considered, and rejected, a recent contextualist version of the non-reductive moral realist view of thick concepts according to which evaluative concepts are (non-Platonically) *inherently evaluative*, and not evaluative in virtue of standing in an analytic or conceptual relation of entailment to some thin evaluative concept such as GOOD. Instead, I suggested that we reconsider the evaluative/non-evaluative distinction concerning the way that we think about the nature of thick concepts in terms of all-encompassing world views.

In my estimate, what is needed is a separate argument that speaks to the *practicality* of thick moral concepts as action-guiding concepts, and the notion of *action-oriented perception* more generally. Such reorientation of focus makes available a novel conception of thick concepts, in which the emphasis on underdetermined evaluative meaning in metaethics is criticized not as false per se, but as failing to yield the insight about the problem of an occasion-insensitive semantics for the thick it was the point of that move to make in understanding moral properties.

Where does this leave us? If I am right, the general notion of *shapelessness* does not seem to distinguish specifically evaluative concepts from other concepts ascribing emergent or metaphysically dependent properties. But does that mean that we should reject the semantic contextualist inherent value thesis of thick concepts in favour of a broadly pragmatist one, or try to assimilate the two? Well, in one respect this is academic—it does not matter what name we give to the resulting theory. Having said this, it is still illuminating to see how putting pressure on polarized dichotomies (between the evaluative and non-evaluative, the subjective and objective) opens up new possibilities in understanding the significance of the notion of 'point of view' in value philosophy. The resulting options are either to think that a flattened evaluative landscape is no bad thing, or to develop something akin to the model of thick concepts as both situated and action-oriented that I have here begun to sketch.[87]

---

[87] I am grateful to Robert Cowan, Michael Milona, and Philip Mallaband for their written comments and suggestions. I have also benefited from discussions of the core themes of this paper with Paul Katsafanas, Susanna Siegel, Kate Manne, Jonathan Dancy, Pekka Väyrynen, Alan Thomas, James Lenman, Simon Kirchin, Michael Brady, Ben Colburn, James Lenman, Fiona Macpherson, Simon Robertson, Sophie Grace Chappell, David Hunter, and Constantine Sandis. Earlier versions of this paper were presented at conferences at Harvard University, University of Southampton, University of Sussex, University of Warwick, University of Colorado Boulder, University College Dublin, and as keynote addresses at the 2016 Moralism conference at the University of Essex and the 2016 Deep Disagreement conference at the University of Freiburg. I am grateful to the audiences present on those occasions for their questions and feedback. Special thanks are also owed to Bob Cooke for his wonderful kindness that has helped me complete this work.

14
The Primacy of the Passions

James Lenman

1

This afternoon I rather fancy going for a walk. So I'm going for a walk. If my friend Septimus fancies coming along he may very well do so. As well as going for walks Septimus is quite partial to watching old westerns on TV with his friend Olivia. Happily it's a partiality Olivia shares and so that is what they will be doing this very evening.

Perhaps I shouldn't. Perhaps Septimus shouldn't. Perhaps Olivia shouldn't. Perhaps I am supposed to be teaching all afternoon. Perhaps Septimus promised his wife he would stop seeing Olivia. Perhaps Olivia promised her probation officer she would stop seeing Septimus.

But perhaps no such defeating conditions obtain. What more then do I, do Septimus and Olivia need to do, as responsible autonomous agents, to justify acting as we do, going for a walk, watching *The Man Who Shot Liberty Valance*? Not, surely, a whole lot. It's natural to think that if I want to go for a walk or watch a western that normally just about suffices, absent defeaters, to make it a good idea to do so.

'Normally' is important. One way things might fail to be normal is if certain general considerations of coherence fail to obtain.[1] Often, though certainly not always, a desire to do something is linked to a belief that, when I do it, I will like doing it.[2] If such a belief turns out false there is normally a problem. I watch a TV show about skiing and think, *That looks fun. I want to do that*, so I book myself a skiing holiday and can't wait to go. Then I do go and, it turns out, I hate it. It's cold. It's frightening. The food is awful. The people ghastly. I made a mistake. Skiing is not for me. That is familiar enough. We all make those sort of mistakes in life.

Something odder, rather less normal, would be if I didn't entertain the false belief that I would enjoy skiing. I confidently expect to hate it. Puzzled you press me, *So why do you want to go?* Perhaps for some instrumental reason as I subject myself to other disagreeable experiences—visits to the dentist, say—for instrumental reasons? *No*, I say, *I just want to*. Then my desire looks odd, fetishistic, arbitrary, like a random desire to turn on a radio, not for the sake of the music and the pleasure of hearing it, just for the sake of turning it on.[3]

---

[1] For more detailed thoughts about the coherence and stability of pleasure and desire, see Lenman (2011).
[2] See Lenman (2011), 146.   [3] Quinn (1993).

On a good day our desires are reasonably stable over time. At six I want to listen to *Just a Minute* on the radio at half six. At six-fifteen I still want to do this. Tuning in at half past I still want to do this. And now, at six-forty-five, listening away, this is still what I want to be doing. Of course when we've got hold of the desired thing talk of desire may become a little strained. We most often speak of desiring things we *lack*. Once we see the desired state of affairs has come into being we speak of liking it or welcoming it rather than desiring it. But I think it's harmless enough to abstract a little. We say I want to go for a walk and then I like going for a walk. Or we can say I'm all for going for a walk before I go and, when it lives up to expectations, still all for it when it is under way. Going for my walk, I am doing what I want to be doing.[4]

There's certainly a pro-attitude, a desire broadly construed (and I will for the most part be construing 'desire' very broadly to cover all the passions in our soul), that's stably present across this process at those times when things go well. I want now to have then what I expect still to want then and thenceforth. This is a basic kind of coherence deriving from the interest I take at any time in how it is with me at other times. If my six o'clock self cares about my six-forty-five self, then he's ordinarily unlikely to desire something for himself that he will then hate. If he doesn't care, it would be odd if he bothered forming desires about what radio shows six-forty-five me shall or shall not listen to. Unless perhaps my six o'clock self has some spiteful desire that my six-forty-five self have an unpleasant time. That would be rather an odd way for a human being to be. I don't much want to be like that.

More generally a desire I have at a given moment to do this or that can conflict with a more global desire to be a certain kind of person or live a certain kind of life. I wake up every morning with a desire to lounge around in bed till midday. And I truly expect to enjoy lounging around in bed till midday. But I don't want to be the sort of guy who is given to lounging around in bed till midday. So I make myself get up. (Well, on a good day.) But for such short-term, morally innocent desires as desires to take walks or watch westerns, such ideals of the person don't necessarily kick in.

Of course the mere fact that you want to do something is not much of a reason to do it. I have a lot of desires, many of them very weak or very transitory. I have desires from which I am more or less alienated and view with disapprobation and disgust. A desire needs to be of significant strength and reasonably durable to have much claim on my attention. And it needs to cohere with my values and ideals. Taking walks and watching westerns seems to be good stuff to be doing, for all sorts of reasons, better ways to pass the time than poisoning pigeons or watching porn. One might perhaps insist that desires should have no normative weight at all.[5] I want to read *Madame Bovary* and I should read it, not because I want to but because it is likely—as I have abundant testimony-based reason to believe—very good. Indeed it is for that reason I want it and it is that reason and not my wanting it that gives me reason to do it. This thought is certainly on to something. As we've seen I want my pro-attitudes to what I'm going to do to cohere with my pro-attitudes to what

---

[4] Cf. Oddie's (2005) discussion of the 'Platonic thesis', pp. 70–2.
[5] Cf. Parfit (2011), vol. 1, ch. 3.

I'm doing now and my pro-attitudes to what I've done. I ordinarily want the things I want to be things that, when they happen, I welcome or enjoy and that, after they happened, I don't regret. But when this stability and coherence is in place, it seems hard to deny some normative weight to what I firmly and stably desire. It is important to most of us that the world conform as much as can realistically be hoped to our pro-attitudes even if we resist the fallacy, popular with some economists, of thinking that is all that matters. If Lewis really wants, and has for some time really wanted, to climb Snowdon, then Lewis has a reason to climb Snowdon, *more* of a reason than Louise who has no such desire even though the inherent worthwhileness of climbing Snowdon may give them both *some* reason to do so. Climbing all the Munros is a wonderfully worthwhile project and many people want to do it for that reason. But it would be an odd project to undertake just for that reason if you have no desire to. Indeed, still using 'desire' broadly to cover any pro-attitude, an attitude with world-mind direction of fit, it would be quite odd to deny all such attitudes any measure of normative weight. If you love to cook but hate to clean and your spouse has the opposite attitudes to those, it's pretty obvious what domestic division of labour will make most sense for you both and why.

2

When we do epistemology we worry that justification is subject to a regress problem. As an epistemically responsible believer I might expect to be invited to justify my belief that Z and I might seek to justify it by invoking some other belief that Y that I take to warrant it. But why believe *that*? Well, maybe because X. But then...Of course there are three familiar ways to go now. One has it that this chain of justification stops somewhere, one that it goes on forever, and one that it goes round in a big circle. There are problems of course with all three of these possibilities and talking about them makes up quite a lot of epistemology.

One nice strategy is that sometimes at least the regress bottoms out with desires, mental states that do not aim to fit the world and so don't themselves call for epistemic justification. If the universe is to remain well behaved enough for inductive reasoning to make sense, then it makes sense to use it but we'll find ourselves in the soup if we don't. If it is not, we'll be in the soup whatever we do. We don't want to be in the soup. So let's use it. I have a lot more to gain, given my preferences, by believing God to exist should he do so than I have to lose by falsely so believing should he not. So, given my preferences, it makes sense to believe. Not believing you all have minds if you do would be a bigger disaster for me, again given my preferences, than believing you do if you don't. So it's rational to take that gamble.[6] But there's always a worry here that epistemic reasoning, the business we're in when we seek to justify beliefs, demands epistemic reasons, not the more pragmatic kind of rationale supplied by speaking to our desires or preferences. Indeed there can seem to be something a bit disreputable about such pragmatic reasons. We may insist we want *epistemic* reasons for beliefs, reasons that speak directly to the truth of the thing to be

---

[6] Pascal, B. (1670/1974), 355 ff.; Reichenbach (1938), ch. 5; Lenman (1994).

believed to think things are true. However, when we are concerned with the normative domain, with *practical* reason, this worry might seem less stark. Practical reason, especially on a roughly Humean picture of it, helps us to figure out how best to serve ends that our desires largely shape so what more natural place than desire for us to seek its ultimate ground?

3

Beliefs have two big problems. They turn out to be wrong, misrepresenting the world. And they conflict with each other. Epistemic reason is how we try to respond to and fix those problems. Desires have, to begin with, one big problem. They conflict. Practical reason is how we respond to that. Reflective critical normative thought of the kind that takes us beyond mere problem-solving intelligence has these two problems, conflict and error, as its parents. But with practical thought, plausibly, conflict is the more fundamental of the two.

In thinking about practical conflict, we turn naturally for inspiration to Frankfurt and his rich descriptions of the hierarchical character of desire.[7] There are the desires with which I identify, the desires which I disown, the things I want which I want to want, the things I want which I do not want to want or am indifferent to wanting. If I can cure my mild short-sightedness by taking a pill that will relieve me of my weakness for lemonade I will take the pill like a shot. If I can cure it by taking a pill that will relieve me of my love of the operas of Britten or of my friend Alice's company, I will abstain and continue to put up with wearing specs. I highly value being someone who loves *Billy Budd* and Alice's daft sense of humour. I'm not especially wedded to being a lemonade-drinker. There are features of my complex endowments of desires and aversions, loves and hates that I embrace, others I repudiate and disown. There are passions in my soul that I reflectively endorse, others I reflectively reject. Indeed it is natural to suppose that such reflective endorsement when it is decisively wholehearted and stable, is what valuing is.[8] That thought in turn invites an expressivist picture where what judgements of value express is just such states, stable higher-order desires and/or ground-floor desires ratified at the court of stable reflection.

Some are unimpressed by this picture. What, they demand to know, is so special about higher-order desires? What could endow them with any special authority? But this challenge, famously levelled by Gary Watson, seems to me one we can meet.[9] The thing to remember is where we began, with the problem of conflict. Pre-reflectively, my desires are a chaotic bloody mess. I want to stick in here and keep writing this paper. I want to go home and watch the snooker. I want to order all the dishes on the menu, stay slim, and save money. I want to be a rebellious free spirit. I want the contentment and security of stable bourgeois respectability. Post-reflectively, I'm sorry to inform you, I *still* want all these things. The ground floor of the structure that is my hierarchy of desires is irreparably disorderly and it is always going to be.

---

[7] Frankfurt (1988).   [8] Cf. e.g. Lewis (1989).   [9] Watson (1975).

So is yours. So is everybody's. It might be otherwise were we very different kinds of animals but we're not and it's not. That's human condition stuff. The higher stories, however, are, or at least can be made, more orderly. It's a humanly realistic aspiration to arrive at a pattern of reflectively sanctioned, wholehearted desires, at what we might call an evaluative sensibility, that is at least tolerably coherent. *That's* what's special about the higher order.[10]

But even when I stably and wholeheartedly endorse some wanting or liking of mine, there is a possibility that that stability might break down in the light of further, or better, reflection ('better' here taken as expressive of my evaluative sensibility as a whole). Were I more like the kind of person I am disposed, stably under reflection, to want to emulate and admire, a person, that is, who is, by my lights, virtuous, I might not value what I now value. The valuings I am most confident about are those I am most confident will pass this test. The worry that some of my evaluations might fail it is readily to be understood as the worry that they might be wrong or, as we might say, false. And so begins the familiar transition from old-school Stevensonian expressivism to quasi-realism. Normative facts and properties enter the scene at this point; truth and error. Desires speak or fail to speak to desires. Values serve or fail to serve values. *Standards* kick in and with them the kind of systematic normative discipline that permits evaluative utterances to behave, syntactically and logically, like assertions. When all this happens, a space of desire comes to determine a space of reasons, of considerations that speak to the desires we endorse and embrace.

On the Humean view I defend,[11] a space of reasons is a space of desires where the latter are the desires of a creature with a reasonably stable affective psychology that engages in reflection and deliberation in an effort to resolve the problem presented to it by the fact of conflict. And that creature, or one of those creatures, has got to be me. From a detached third-personal perspective, there is nothing more going on than the unfolding of prosaically descriptive psychological facts. Normativity enters the picture when these psychological facts are facts about me, when I am myself the creature—or one of the creatures—who inhabits this psychology and seeks to direct his action wisely enough to shape a life that will bear his survey. Reasons are desires seen from inside, desires that, from their bearers' perspective, are apt to confer importance on their objects, not least when they express deep features of our natures such as our instinct for self-preservation and our sociability. Only as the subject of a space of desires does one feel the volitional pull, the magnetism that Humeans take to lie at the heart of normativity.

Once we are in this business, desire moves, in large measure into the background of deliberation[12] and it is reason, not desire, that structures our thought. Now evaluation and desire can diverge in ways that allow us to distinguish deliberative normative weight from motivational strength. The unwilling addict's[13] reflective endorsement of his desire for health and clean living assigns it a priority over his

---

[10] I think this thought—or something very close to it—is at work in Bratman's very rich discussions of Frankfurt and Watson. See Bratman (2007), esp. essay 3 and essay 10 (esp. sect. 7).
[11] See further Lenman (2009a), (2009b), and (2010).
[12] Cf. Pettit and Smith (1990).   [13] Frankfurt (1988), essay 2.

desire for narcotics despite the latter being too strong to resist.[14] The backgrounding of desire also makes way for objectivity. Normative and evaluative thought pursued over years and generations endows us with complex normative and evaluative sensibilities that respect the kind of objectivity that insists that, while judgements of value may express desires, desires nonetheless do not determine values. My evaluative sensibility is constituted by a complex, aspiringly coherent set of reflectively endorsed desires. In having it I take certain things to be important and take their importance not to depend on my so taking them.[15] So that my sensibility, while constituted by desires, may or may not accord desires as such any normative significance. Chances are it will accord a good deal to some, but none at all to others.

4

Now an imaginary reader might object that in saying what I just said I have gone back on what I said at the beginning. All that stuff in Section 1 about wanting to do something as a reason for doing it. All that stuff in Section 2 about desires as termini for justification. Didn't I just, in the last paragraph, take it all back?

No. I stand by Section 1. Absent all kinds of things that might act as defeating conditions, morally innocent, short-term desires like the desire to go for a walk or watch a western, can give us reasons to act on them. That's a very weak, very modest claim. It's not the claim that reasons talk reduces to talk of desires or talk of what would satisfy desires. That claim is a species of reductive naturalism that I just rejected. It is a view that is widely argued against on the grounds that (a) it analyses normative claims in ways that strip away their normativity and (b) it has repellent substantive consequences about what reasons people might have or might lack, for example that someone who is indifferent to future agony would have no reason to avoid it.[16] My expressivist view has no such consequences. As I stressed in Section 3, it contrasts with any reduction of normative and evaluative talk to prosaically descriptive third-person talk about our psychology precisely in capturing the dynamic, practical significance so plausibly essential to the former. And it has little or nothing by way of substantive normative consequences, repellent or otherwise. If I think you have reason to avoid the future agony to which you are indifferent, the fact of your indifference does not make me wrong to think that.

However the claim about the normative significance of desire in Section 1 is a substantive claim *internal* to normative talk. It is not a claim that attributes some kind of Archimedean significance to desire. It's not a claim that is part of or that is implied by the metaethical position articulated in Section 3. And yet I do want to claim, as I did in Section 3, that ultimately desire, the passions in our souls, is the source of normativity. And I do want to claim, as I did in Section 2, that desire is where justification, ultimately starts. How and in what sense? I'll address that question in Section 9 of this paper.

---

[14] A useful discussion of deliberative weight from an expressivist standpoint is Gibbard (2003), 188–91.
[15] See Blackburn (1984), 217–20.   [16] See e.g. Parfit (2011), vol. 1, chs. 3 and 24.

5

Do we perceive value? It is widely supposed that we do and in various ways. Desires.[17] Emotions.[18] Moral intuition.[19] Regular sensory perception.[20] All these have been proposed as ways this is meant to happen.[21]

Sensory perception might certainly do the trick if we were reductive naturalists about value. On that view, evaluative and normative questions are straightforwardly empirical questions to be addressed in the very same way as empirical questions of other kinds. And perhaps also if we are non-reductive naturalists about value.[22] Thus Richard Boyd famously asks: 'What plays in moral reasoning, the role played in science by observation?' and responds, 'I propose the answer: "Observation".'[23] But such empiricist views seem unpromising to me. In the light of a given substantive normative or moral perspective, certain moral questions may indeed reduce to empirical questions, *Which options best promote human welfare?* Or whatever. But it is much harder to envisage straightforwardly empirical ways of confirming or measuring the truth of the substantive perspectives such reductions inevitably presuppose, at least it is hard if our warrant for putting our trust in any test we apply is to be sufficiently independent of the very thing we are testing for the test to be at all meaningful.[24]

Moral intuition, as understood by the more robust species of realist, is readily viewed with some suspicion, a dubious appeal to a poorly understood and desperately underdescribed species of, in effect, extra-sensory perception whereby we somehow just 'see' that we can turn this lethally targeted trolley this way in this case but not in that case. As Gibbard writes, 'If this is what anyone seriously believes I simply want to debunk it. Nothing in a plausible, naturalistic picture of our place in the universe requires these non-natural facts and these powers of non-sensory apprehension.'[25] And while many philosophers do continue to accord intuition a central role in the methodology of normative ethical thought, this role has long been the target of considerable criticism and scepticism.[26] Yet, if we don't embrace the Harean optimism that the whole edifice of our normative and evaluative can be constructed on the slender basis of 'logic and the facts',[27] it can seem hard to see how we could hope simply to dispense with it.

I have myself defended a role in moral inquiry for intuitions where these are understood, along expressivist lines, as, in the first analysis,[28] desires rather than as

---

[17] Oddie (2005). [18] Döring (2003). [19] Huemer (2005).
[20] Boyd (1988); Audi (2013).
[21] The critical survey of these ideas that follows is very quick and dirty. For one that is slow and painstaking, see Cowan (2011) (his criticisms are not the same as mine).
[22] Boyd (1988); Brink (1989). The position defended by Oddie (2005) seems to me to be a kind of non-reductive naturalism.
[23] Boyd (1988), 124.
[24] For more detailed versions of this thought, see Zangwill (2008); Lenman (2013).
[25] Gibbard (1990), 154. Cf. e.g. Williams (1985), 94.
[26] See e.g. Hare (1971), 117–35; Brandt (1979); Posner (1999); Singer (2005); Appiah (2008), ch. 3; T. Kelly and S. McGrath (2010). I discuss some of these critics in Lenman (2007), (2015a), (2015b).
[27] Hare (1981), 6, 101 ff.
[28] Only in the first analysis as (a) with expressivism there is always a quasi-realist second analysis in the offing and (b) a certain kind of finessing is likely to be needed to evade the wrong kind of reason worries: not just any old unwillingness for any old reason will do.

beliefs or as quasi-perceptual seemings. More precisely, I have defended a conception of moral intuitions as attitudes of unwillingness. So when I say I have a strong intuition that killing children for fun is wrong I express an unwillingness to accept or conform to any set of rules for the regulation of my community that permits members of that community to kill children for fun. This unwillingness is important to me and it is affirmed wholeheartedly. It resounds, as Frankfurt would say, through the higher orders.[29] This is a good theory because it demystifies intuition. It doesn't regard intuition as a mysterious species of extra-sensory perception that puts us in touch with a domain of values constituted prior to and independently of our engagement with it. Indeed it doesn't regard intuition as a species of perception at all. It is also a good theory because it helps us to see why intuition is important in moral inquiry. Moral inquiry is, most centrally, the practice in which we deliberate together about how to live with one another in moral community. When we arrive at the table of codeliberation sharing confident intuitions, they can be, as it were, banked, as considerations that will shape and constrain further reflection, not ordinarily to be supposed open to revision. Less confident intuitions are nearer the periphery of the web and may be more readily up for revision but will still have a shaping and constraining role to play. When I arrive at the table with an intuition you don't share, that's something, if our project of moral community is to succeed, that you need to respect and engage with, seek to reason me out of, be open to reason yourself into, accommodate, work around, in any case, not disregard. The foregoing picture of moral epistemology is of course a highly moralized one but that should neither surprise nor concern us. Moral epistemology need not and should not aspire to moral neutrality.[30]

That leaves the passions in our souls, emotions and desires.[31] These certainly frequently respond appropriately to the value we encounter in our lives. The smell of curry flooding the street as I pass the restaurant brings on a craving to eat some. I respond to your kindness with love and, much later perhaps, having come to love you, respond to your death with grief. That said, they *very* frequently do *not* so respond. The teenage palate doesn't see anything to like in the taste of Bruichladdich. We see plenty. The crowds who line the street cheering the tyrant think they are looking at moral greatness. They are not. A good deal of emotion and desire *misperceives* value. Sometimes they do match up nicely but they only do so reliably and pervasively if one is a perfect *phronimos* and none of us, alas, can claim to be one of those. Sense perception, by contrast, is normally reliable enough and only goes wrong in special circumstances as when we are drunk or mad or the light is playing tricks on us. But our desires are constantly going off in wrong directions, forever in need of policing by reflective scrutiny.

Moreover a great many desires and emotions are not *responses* to their objects at all. My desire to go for a walk is not and cannot be a response to the walk I have yet to go on, even if my subsequent enjoyment of it is. *Some day, he'll come along, the man I love*, thinks Bridget yearningly, after Gershwin. But her yearning is not very readily supposed to be caused, in anything like the manner of a perception, by its object. The

---

[29] Frankfurt (1988), 21, 167.   [30] Cf. Lenman (2015a).
[31] Construing 'desire' broadly as I do here, I don't sharply distinguish these. Cf. Oddie's remarks in his (2005), 74–8.

loved man in question, alas, has, ex hypothesi, failed, as yet, to materialize and is thus in no position to cause anything where Bridget's feelings are concerned. Of course we are normally responding to *something* in our experience. I have come, over the years, to know all about walks, what they are like and how they can be nice, and that kind of general experiential knowledge shapes and directs the formation of my desires. But that kind of shaping over a history of experience seems much more analogous to a kind of induction than to the non-inferential immediacy we associate with perception.

If a robustly realist picture of intuition as perceptual or quasi-perceptual contact with independent evaluative or normative facts seems mysterious and poorly motivated, a similarly robustly realist understanding of emotion or desire as so placing us doesn't look like much of an improvement. It simply takes the same not very credible story and clips it onto a rather different bit of our evaluative phenomenology. When we move away from realism to some more idealist take on the evaluative things might get less mysterious but at the same time close analogies with perception will perhaps become rather less natural. Certainly on my own account our experience over our lives of emotion and desire can be expected to shape and inform our evaluative and normative sensibilities but this is more naturally unpacked as a process of self-constitution or self-interpretation than a perceptual engagement with an externally constituted evaluative reality.

6

Do we perceive value? It may still seem very natural to suppose we do. The passions in our souls light up (and sometimes darken) the world and we experience it so illuminated (and so darkened). The sunlight on the snows of the high peaks. The paintings in the gallery. The faces and bodies of loved others. The tastes and smells of the restaurant quarter. The rich experiential landscapes of nature and art are awash with beauty and wonder and the more we explore them the more we find.

And yet the idea that we perceive value quickly comes under strain. With moral value this is perhaps especially clear. Often enough good and evil look very much the same. A case of wilful murder, carefully observed, can look exactly the same as a case of conscientious professional care. Here is a doctor administering an injection to a patient. What we see is not, on its surface, a whit different whether he is a good doctor treating her or a wicked doctor murdering her. Justice is likewise elusive. Here is a judge pronouncing a sentence. Here is a woman writing a cheque. Perhaps an injustice is being done. Perhaps a fraud is being perpetrated. Just looking won't tell you unless you know a lot of other, offstage, facts.[32] But those too are still just facts. The vice escapes you as long as you consider the object.[33] Even with the hedonic and aesthetic cases emphasized above, it is plausibly the sentiment within the onlooker's breast by which the object is, by speaking to it, lit up. Warthogs, no doubt, sometimes look extremely sexy and alluring to other warthogs. To us they look, well, like warthogs. It's not that they can see something we can't—at least we have no reason to believe they can. They just like what they see in ways we don't.

[32] Cf. Broad (1944), 142–7.   [33] Hume (1740/2000), 3.1.1.26.

THE PRIMACY OF THE PASSIONS 291

There's a physical world out there, most of it not of our making. It's mostly constituted prior to and independent of our cognitive engagement with it. It's made of atoms. It was there before we came along and it will go on being there after we're gone. We know about it through perception, whereby it causally impacts on our receptive organs and surfaces. That's how we know to avoid the bits of it that we might bump into or that might eat us, how to find the bits that are useful or just nice. Nothing about it, considered by itself, tells us what to do. That only happens when we start to care about something. Eating. Not being eaten. Sex, money, friendship, shelter, love, beauty, truth. The things we want. The things we like. Of course our wants make themselves known to us through experience but not exactly through sensation: reflective, not original impressions.[34] Of course too our wants are not dumb, raw things. Nussbaum's 'neo-Stoic' view of emotions as judgements of value is plausibly an overcorrection of the view she opposes it to that sees them as 'unthinking energies that simply push the person around, without being hooked up to the ways in which she perceives or thinks about the world'[35] but the latter is certainly a view that cries out for some correction. Our passions are, or can be, intelligent things, things that inform themselves by our engaging cognitively with the world in all the myriad ways we know of engaging with the world: perception, induction, testimony, imagination (and of course that engagement with the imaginations of others that is literature and the other arts). Our passions shape and structure and inform our perceptual scrutiny of the world and it in turn shapes them.

7

It may help to consider the familiar order of explanation problem that philosophers sometimes raise about value and desire.[36] Are things valuable because we desire them or do we desire them because they are valuable? It is sometimes tempting to respond *Both* and urge that the dichotomy is a false one. Consider Zuleika. Zuleika is, notoriously, immensely, overwhelmingly attractive. But what makes her so? Plausibly the fact that she possesses many characteristics that many people are disposed, pervasively and stably, to find attractive. It is just our stable, pervasive, and patterned habits of attraction that make these characteristics attractive ones. It's just our liking them that makes them nice. Once people have stable, pervasive, and patterned habits of response and attitude, we can start to speak of things in the world as having the property of being such as to elicit such responses, the property in this case, so conspicuously possessed by Zuleika, of being attractive. But now that this property is up and running we can ask the question, *How are we to explain the fact that the Duke of Dorset, in particular, on this particular occasion, a dinner at Judas College, comes to be attracted to her*? And in response we can invoke, informatively and nontrivially, the significant fact about Zuleika that she is attractive. So she is attractive because folk are attracted to her. And folk are attracted to her because she is attractive.

---

[34] Hume (1740/2000), 1.1.2, 2.1.1.   [35] Nussbaum (2001), pp. 24–5.
[36] See e.g. Griffin (1986), ch. 2, sect. 3; Oddie (2015).

Only, you see, I cheated there. I made things too easy for myself. 'Attractive' is rather a weak kind of evaluative concept. It's a bit like 'funny' in the sense on which something is funny if it makes us laugh even if we wish it didn't, even if we ought not to. Notoriously, in his 'Proof' of the Principle of Utility Mill errs, or appears to err, in supposing 'desirable' is like that.[37] ('[T]he sole evidence it is possible to produce that anything is desirable is that people do actually desire it.') Being desirable is not just being disposed to elicit desire but being such as to *merit* desire. So we can't surely say, in the same way, that something is desirable because we desire it or because it is the sort of thing people desire.

If we are to moralize (or valorize) one of our explanatory relata, and if we are to avoid being pressured towards reductionism, we will plausibly want to moralize (or valorize) both. It's not that it is the sort of thing people desire but that it is the sort of thing *good* people desire. But is it desirable *because* it is the sort of thing good people desire? Well, no. It's desirable because of what it *is*, not because of how we (even if we are good) respond. It is, let's say, a long-sought peace treaty. And peace treaties are desirable. Peace treaties are desirable because they end war. And wars are undesirable because they are hugely costly in death and suffering and because they are extremely suboptimal ways of settling conflicts that are highly favourable to power and largely indifferent to justice. And justice is desirable because... And so the story goes on. Its desirability is a matter of its place in the whole Big Web of reasons and values, not the mere fact that it triggers some psychological response. So do good people desire it because it is desirable? Well, yes, of course they do. But we needn't understand that as a perceptual process where the good people 'see' its value, simply as one where they see it clearly for what it is and bring their evaluative sensibilities to bear on it. The Big Web is made of desires but it is not always very immediately interested in them. It is interested in justice and peace and the avoidance of suffering and a million other things. That's what pushes desire into the background amplifying the quasi-realist turn in favouring the realist side of the order of explanation question. Locally at least, we desire things because they are valuable but not vice versa.

8

The Big Web is *awfully* big. It's the space of reasons constituted by the whole of my moral sensibility. In fact it is really much bigger even than that. Evaluative and normative thought is not something we do on our own. Moral inquiry, particularly but by no means peculiarly, is dialogical. It's a conversation we have with the rest of our community about how that community should be ordered and what goods it should pursue. And that conversation does not start now, from here, but has been going on for as long as there have been people to conduct it. It is shaped by centuries of tradition that we have no hope, should we want to, of stepping outside and starting anew. Not least because it has 'thickened' our very conceptual repertoire, shaping the most basic verbal tools we have to reflect on justice, generosity, fidelity, integrity, nobility, and everything else that is important to us. Our sensibility is ineliminably

---

[37] Mill (1861/1998), ch. 4.

shaped by our communities and by our histories even when we bring it to bear on critical reflection on the often dubious practices of those very communities and the often ugly barbarities that often disfigure those very histories. That is why so much of the best work in contemporary metaethics emphasizes the central role in moral theorizing not of perception but of interpretation.[38] Such work often represents itself as hostile to the kind of Humean picture I offer here but it needn't be. The two are not opposed. Understanding the evaluative as intimately linked to and ultimately expressive of the passions in our soul should not lead us into what we might call the Existentialist Fallacy that the process of normative self-constitution is something to be undertaken ex nihilo right now from a standing start. It isn't and cannot be like that. It's a project we inherit and pass on.

9

By the Big Web then I mean human evaluative sensibility, or at least human evaluative sensibility at its best. It is, as I have said, awfully big. Almost all the time we are inside it, engaging with the space of reason with desire in the background. Why is justice good? Because I like it? No, silly. Justice is good because we are social animals and it allows us to live together in orderly, peaceable communities sharing the benefits of cooperation on terms acceptable to us all. Or whatever. And so on. Inside the space of reasons, the currency is reasons. It's a space animated by the passions in our souls but so unobtrusively we barely notice and the practice of normative inquiry is almost exactly as the most robust of realists would say it should be. Our passions furnish the very fabric of our thought but it is not *about* our passions or at least not about them in particular.

But we may distinguish global and local questions. The local questions are the ones we ask and seek to answer *inside* the Big Web inhabiting the complex evaluative sensibilities we bring to bear on them. We ask them all the time every day, big questions and small. What is a just society? What shall I do this weekend? Here, inside the web, the epistemology is coherentist as we seek to shape and order our thoughts towards something like reflective equilibrium. Then there is the global question, not about any part of the Big Web but about the whole damn thing. Looking at the Whole Thing in its totality, we want to ask, What justifies *that*? This, it seems to me, is the point where desire comes out of the background and even the quasi-realist has to qualify their line on mind-independence. This is where we say, You know what: it's just us.[39] It's just what we wholeheartedly want, drawing its authority simply from our willingness to embrace and endorse it. And that's us all right, for from this supremely comprehensive perspective what we want is who we are: Just us humans in all our stark contingency and the best moral sense we can make of our world given the kind of beasts we are and the kind of stuff we care about. It's just us but we, at our best, we suppose, by our own lights, are not so bad. We can be, we often enough are, quite horrible, but taken at our best, we find, or hope to find,

---

[38] See e.g. Hurley (1989); Dworkin (2011).
[39] *Pace*, of course, Nagel (1999).

ourselves able to embrace being who we are. Inside the Big Web the epistemology is coherentist but there is a foundational story to tell about the whole thing that comes to an end with the brute contingency of what we care about, comprehensively considered and our basic willingness to embrace and affirm our being that way.[40] Locally we desire things because they are valuable but globally, in the last analysis, they are indeed valuable because we (at our best) desire them. Here the role of desire is grounding and global but it is still not *Archimedean*: it is not a matter of raw, brute desire but of evaluation informed by all the substantive ideals from which the web itself is woven. Even when we tell our foundational story we remain inside the web. Outside it there is normatively speaking nothing to say. The passions in our souls light up the world and we find on reflection that, so lit, it is not a bad place to be and we will be sorry to leave it. Or let's hope we do. If we don't we have a problem philosophy cannot solve.[41]

---

[40] Even Dworkin comes close to recognizing this: 'External scepticism should disappear from the philosophical landscape. We should not regret its disappearance. We have enough to worry about without it. We want to live well and to behave decently, we want our communities to be fair and good and our laws to be wise and just' (Dworkin (2011), 68).

[41] Conversations with Anna Bergqvist and Luca Barlassina have helped me immensely. So have comments by Chris Bennett, Robert Cowan, and Valerie Tiberius.

15
Sexual Objectification, Objectifying Images, and 'Mind-Insensitive Seeing-As'

Kathleen Stock

1. Existing Accounts of Objectification

Objectification, broadly speaking, involves relating to other people as if they were objects. There is more than one way to do this, and Martha Nussbaum lists several. Her aim is to treat 'objectification' as

a relatively loose cluster-term, for whose application we sometimes treat any one of these features as sufficient, though more often a plurality of features is present when the term is applied.[1]

According to her, an objectifier perceives or treats the objectified as some or all of the following: as an instrument; as lacking in autonomy; as inert or lacking in agency; as fungible; as violable; as capable of being owned; or as lacking in subjectivity, in that the objectified person's experiences and feelings are irrelevant.[2] To this list, Rae Langton,[3] building on Nussbaum's theory, proposes to add: as reduced to her body, or body parts; as reduced to appearances; or as silent and lacking the capacity to speak.

Nussbaum treats *sexual* objectification, broadly speaking, as involved in cases 'where a human being is regarded as, or treated as an object' (that is, in one or more of the ways she lists) 'in the context of a sexual relationship'.[4]

Meanwhile, Sandra Bartky gives sexual objectification a narrower emphasis: on her view, it refers to disproportionately focusing on a person's sexual parts or sexual function:

A person is sexually objectified when her sexual parts or sexual functions are separated out from the rest of her personality and reduced to the status of mere instruments or else regarded as if they were capable of representing her.[5]

Examples involve staring at a woman's breasts as she is being interviewed, or catcalling a woman in the street. This looks potentially different to, for instance, a person being treated as violable in the course of a sexual relationship, something that would also count as sexual objectification by Nussbaum's lights.

---

[1] Nussbaum (1995), 258. [2] Nussbaum (1995), 275. [3] Langton (2009), 228–30.
[4] Nussbaum (1995). [5] Bartky (2005), 108.

On a third view, sexual objectification is characterized in a way that is tied to a theory of gender. According to Catherine MacKinnon, one's gender is identified in virtue of one's place in a social hierarchy, and whether one falls into one of two groups, one with far more power than the other. The social role of 'men' is necessarily to forcibly instrumentalize 'women' in order to fulfil their sexual and other interests; the role of 'women', to be forcibly subordinated in this way. A woman is socially defined, as such, as a thing to be used by men, sexually and in other ways. On this account, objectification counts as 'sexual' on two counts: first, because it involves women being used for men's sexual interests, among others;[6] and second, in the sense that masculine dominance and feminine submission are eroticized, both by men and women.[7] Explicitly building on MacKinnon's account, Sally Haslanger adds that in sexual objectification, women are falsely believed by men to have a nature which makes them sexually subordinate, rather than it being recognized that they have been forcibly made to be as they are via social construction.[8] Since this is an intrinsic feature of objectification as she intends it, according to Haslanger, it follows that objectification in that sense isn't only necessarily morally but also necessarily epistemically objectionable.[9]

Occasionally, pseudo-disputes are identified between such accounts.[10] For instance, it is an implication of the MacKinnon and Haslanger view that, since objectification essentially involves autonomy-violation, there is no possible world where objectification (as they intend it) isn't harmful. Yet Nussbaum criticizes MacKinnon for not recognizing that certain forms of objectification can be morally neutral or even 'wonderful' in the course of a sexual relationship.[11] Such an observation would only be problematic for MacKinnon had she set out to characterize the whole of (sexual) objectification, rather than some particular form of it in a patriarchal context. Instead, her aim, I assume, is to name and describe some *particular* context in which one group gets treated as objects by another group. It is true that the rather general language used by both MacKinnon[12] and Haslanger[13] is not particularly helpful. But since neither could be reasonably denying that there are many ways and contexts in which to treat another human as an object, it is charitable to take their pronouncements on objectification as implicitly qualified in the way I've just indicated. Moreover, they clearly intend—in advance—to focus on a form of objectification that involves autonomy-violation. It follows that, as such, it could never count as morally neutral. But this is not to say that other forms of objectification might not count as such, in certain contexts.

2. What Might a Theory of Objectification Be Looking For?

Like Nussbaum and Langton, and unlike Bartky, MacKinnon, and Haslanger, my focus in what follows will be objectification generally: objectification understood

---

[6] MacKinnon (1989a), 327.   [7] MacKinnon (1989b), 113–14.   [8] Haslanger (2012), 67.
[9] For discussion, see Langton (1993).   [10] Stock (2015).
[11] Nussbaum (1995), 250. See also Papadaki (2010).   [12] e.g. MacKinnon (1989a), 327.
[13] Haslanger (2012), 66.

broadly and not specifically as a sexual or eroticized activity. Also like Nussbaum, I will be concerned with forms of objectification which, though undoubtedly usually harmful to those on the receiving end given the sexist and racist contexts in which they tend to occur, need not always be that way. They may well have morally benign forms, on occasion.

What work might a theory of objectification usefully do? One aim might be to offer a list of the forms that objectification takes: this is what Nussbaum does, fairly comprehensively, with the later help of Langton. A different more empirically informed aim might be to try to identify particular causal factors behind objectifying behaviour. For instance: can we identify any common psychological factors behind objectifying behaviour? And if so: can we identify any cultural practices which enable those psychological factors, in particular, to flourish?

In this paper I shall try to do both of these latter things. Working backwards, I shall start by examining certain objectifying *images*, organizing those images into groups, and then arguing that it is by the use of such images that objectification often gets a foothold. This will not seem particular startling to most, since it is often suggested that there is a connection between uses of media imagery and objectifying attitudes towards women. My next move will be more controversial: to posit a psychological factor that mediates between the viewing of objectifying imagery and objectifying practices. This is what I'll call 'mind-insensitive seeing as', a kind of seeing-as encouraged, I'll argue, by the use of objectifying imagery in the media. I'll identify three prevalent varieties of it. I'll then suggest that 'mind-insensitive seeing-as', in its various guises, should be taken seriously as an explanatory factor in practices of objectification: it results in particular attentional and cognitive habits towards members of objectified groups, which in turn contribute to further pernicious differences in treatment. I will finish by exploring several further consequences of my view.

3. Objectifying Images

It's often said that images 'objectify'. Indeed, this is a primary context in which objectification is discussed, outside of academia. When academic feminists discuss objectifying images, they often focus on pornography. However, many images plausibly 'objectify' without being pornographic.

When we look at non-pornographic 'objectifying' media depictions, we find several significant tendencies, which I'll now describe. It should be understood in what follows that I'm concerned with ways of representing which could in theory be used towards groups other than women. Contingently, however, given the patriarchal context of media imagery, it is women that tend most often to be represented in these ways, and so my focus will be on that.

Most obviously: images can focus upon the bodily parts of women: that is, we might say, they can represent women-as-bodies. As I write, the clothing company American Apparel produces adverts that exemplify this tendency. In some of their images, mere bits of female bodies are framed, with the head out of shot. In others, women lie with their legs spread and their crotches in the centre of the shot; or on their stomachs, contorting their heads round to stare blankly at the camera. The fashion industry is rife with images which draw elaborate attention to women's bodies: just pick up a high fashion women's magazine for evidence. Women in sport are also often represented as bodies: for instance, apparently the only way to represent a female beach volleyball player in a newspaper sports report is to take a partial body shot of her from behind. Even images which focus on a person's face can still represent that person as a body: for instance, where the face is conventionally beautiful, deliberately blank and expressionless, and the implication of the image is that we are to treat that face as an aesthetic object. The clear meaning of such images generally is that the physical aspect of the person in the image is to be focused upon as her most salient feature.

A second trope used in media imagery of women represents women-as-animals. This is used more sparingly than the ubiquitous 'woman-as-body'; however, it is still sometimes present in fashion magazines. For instance, women are represented as big cats or other 'wild animals', snarling, crawling, and dressed in animal print; or placed alongside real animals whilst dressed in a way designed to highlight some sort of resemblance. This is a manner of representation most frequently used where the pictures are of women of colour.[14] In another related sort of case, a woman can be depicted as 'meat', as in an advert for People for the Ethical Treatment of Animals (PETA) featuring Pamela Anderson, with the butcher's grid of meat cuts superimposed on her body.[15]

A third tendency in media imagery is to represent women-as-duplicates: that is, as 'fungible' or, in Nussbaum's terms, 'interchangeable with objects of the same type'.[16] This is not just the same as presenting a woman who as a matter of fact is, as far as the viewer can tell, fungible with other women, relative to a given purpose: to some extent all media representations which don't rely on well-known celebrities do this, since usually any person in an advertising image of a certain 'look' might easily have been exchanged for some other person with the same 'look', for the same end. It is rather that the woman's fungibility is built into the meaning of the image in an identifiable way. For instance, this is so where a range of similar-looking women, dressed (or undressed) alike, are presented in a group shot in a way which de-emphasizes individual personality and other mental differences between them, in order to emphasize appearance or bodily characteristics they all have in common. To enhance the impression of fungibility, often women in this context are depicted with only limited facial expressions. For an example, see Wade,[17] or consider a style of *Vanity Fair* cover which ranges several actresses in a line in different poses, yet all dressed in the same or similar shades.

These latter three sorts of images—of women-as-bodies, women-as-animals, and women-as-duplicates—and the concomitant ways of seeing encouraged by each, are those I will focus on in later sections. However, I also note two other related tendencies of representation. The first is the rather common trope of representing women-as-children. This is achieved via their pose: e.g. a shy expression, finger-biting, sitting with knees together and feet splayed; and props: knee socks, bubblegum, pigtails, etc. (For examples, again see most women's fashion magazines.) The second

---

[14] See Wade (2009b), accessed 6 October 2014.   [15] Adams (2010).
[16] Nussbaum (1995), 227.   [17] Wade (2011), acessed 6 October 2014.

is rather more infrequent: women who are represented in ways deliberately suggestive of an insensate object. Sometimes a women's body and a material object being advertised are 'merged': for instance, in an advert for Tom Ford for Men aftershave (2007) the bottle is placed between a naked women's legs. Very occasionally, women are represented as receptacles for other objects: e.g. plates or tables, as in a feature by *Details* magazine.[18]

4. 'Mind-Suppressing' Images

On the face of it at least, taken together, all these images look like quite a diverse class. Can we find a general category covering this diversity, and explain why it is all objectifying, in a way that doesn't simply echo a Nussbaum-style inventory of relatively diverse-looking behaviours? The particular emphasis of Bartky, on 'reducing' a person to body parts and/or appearance, applies well to images which focus on the body, but not so well on those which represent women-as-animals, or women-as-duplicates, or women-as-children, for instance. Meanwhile, the MacKinnon-Haslanger theory, which focuses on women being non-autonomously instrumentalized, doesn't seem to cover any of the cases, since arguably all represent women acting autonomously, and furthermore many don't always focus on a sexual aspect. (Of course, this isn't to say that the *models* were acting autonomously or happily; only that the represented subjects in the images are—see below).[19]

Here then is a claim: images which depict women-as-bodies, women-as-animals, women-as-duplicates, women-as-children, and women-as-insensate objects are objectifying, in that they are all to a greater or lesser extent 'mind-suppressing'. One way to produce a mind-suppressing image of a woman is to represent her in a way that almost exclusively emphasizes her physical appearance, at the expense of attention to her inner mental life. Another method is to have her crawl along the ground, dressed in animal prints, mimicking the emotions and behaviour of an animal (e.g. snarling, fleeing). Another is to deliberately pose her in a range of similar-looking women, so as to minimize any impression of her individual personality. Another is to have her pose or dress like a child. An extreme way of 'suppressing the mind' of a represented woman in an image, in my sense, is to represent her as an insensate object for resting things on. Such strategies of representation are often enhanced by posing and shooting the subject so that her facial expression is highly limited, and no complex emotion or thought is expressed or suggested.

To be clear: I'm not just claiming such images give limited information about the real mental states of the model at the time of the making of the image, though they generally do. My claim is rather that to some extent, such images 'suppress the mind' of the *represented subject*. A snapshot taken by mistake, which shows only a subject's

---

[18] Wade (2009a), accessed 13 October 2014.

[19] It's true that occasionally media images count as objectifying in a sense close to theirs—that is, they are images depicting women as forcibly mistreated for the sexual ends of men. For instance, both Calvin Klein (2010) and Dolce & Gabbana (2007) have run advertising campaigns depicting gang rape. However, these sorts of images, whilst frequent in pornography, are still relatively rare in media imagery, presumably because of their limited commercial value.

feet, gives no information about the real mental states of the person it is of, but does not 'suppress the mind' of a represented subject: arguably, because there is no represented subject in that image. Meanwhile, images representing a subject as highly animate and expressive, in a way suggestive of some particular complex mental state, may limit information about the mind of the actual model in a different way, since the model may be acting; but the *represented subject*'s mind would not count as suppressed in my sense.

To say the mind of the represented subject of an image is suppressed is to make a claim about the image's meaning. This meaning is conveyed by a conjunction of various factors, possible here only to sketch inadequately: the posing of the model and her clothes; her requested facial expression; the composition of the shot; the style of the image; the context in which the image appears; and so on. For an instructive case of a deliberately mind-suppressing image, see the 11 July 2014 cover of *Science* magazine, which depicts the legs and lower halves of two transgender sex workers.[20] Mind-suppression may also be conveyed by more subliminal features: for instance, across a wide range of images, men's faces tend to be represented as proportionately larger than that of women, with consequences for viewer's relative ratings of intelligence of the represented subjects.[21]

In the goal of being mind-suppressing, the medium of the static photographic image is a positive boon. First, a static image makes it easier for the eye to linger for sustained periods on any bodily or appearance features, and thus often facilitates distraction from what evidence there is of the subject's mental life. Second, what evidence there is can be intentionally limited in virtue of features of the medium: e.g. the static nature of the imagery allows the photographer to maximally control pose and facial expression of the model. Finally, the typical limitations of single images in conveying any complex narrative makes them poor vehicles for the representation of their subject's mental life in any detailed way.

Presenting mind-suppressing images of women is clearly of commercial value in advertising. Among other things, it allows the female purchaser to identify more easily with the represented subject—the fewer the individualizing details of that subject, the easier the identification for a large number of presumably quite different viewers. This presumably increases sales. However such images can have other, more sinister effects too, as we will later see.

5. Seeing X as Y

My next claim is that 'mind-suppressing' images encourage a particular way of *seeing* women: both the women in the images and more generally. Namely, such images encourage what I will call 'mind-insensitive seeing-as'.

But first: what is 'seeing-as', generally? As I shall be concerned with it, seeing-as involves two relata—an object X in one's visual field, which one sees, and some further object or property Y, which may or may not be an accurate description of X.

---

[20] Waldman (2014), accessed 12 October 2014.   [21] Archer et al. (1983).

I will assume: where one sees X as Y, one has to see X (seeing X is factive).[22] However, one can see X as Y where X is not in fact Y (e.g. seeing the shadow as a burglar); equally one can see X as Y, where X is in fact Y (e.g. seeing the chair as a Chippendale).[23] Where one sees X as Y, there has to be a possibility that one might not have seen X that way, but rather in some other way.[24]

Seeing X as Y, as I am using the notion, is more than *thinking of* X as a Y. It is *at least* thinking, of X, that it is Y: either believing this, or something less committed, as when one knowingly sees a cloud as an elephant but does not believe it is identical to an elephant.[25] But it is more than this: there is a relevant gestalt: a form, over and above the visual parts which make it up, and not reducible to those parts. Phenomenologically speaking, it is (somewhat) as if a Y is also perceptually present. For instance, where one sees a cloud as an elephant, it is somewhat as if one sees an elephant, as well as a cloud. This is not to say that it is *exactly like* a Y being present. But there's more than simply an X which one thinks of as a Y. To put the point in terms conducive to the philosophy of perception, seeing X as Y has a different phenomenal character from seeing X as X or as some other thing. Relatedly, possible variables for Y only include things that can be seen or detected via visual experience. I can't see X as *perfumed*, or as *loud*, or as *born on a Tuesday*, though I can think of X in those ways.[26]

6. Images and Seeing-As

Generally speaking, it is well established that still images can promote seeing-as of various kinds. We can further understand how still images can promote types of mind-insensitive seeing-as by a helpful analogy with the way certain caricatures work. A famous caricature depicts Winston Churchill as a bulldog. That is, it promotes seeing Churchill as a bulldog; it supplies basic visual material (i.e. a representation which, roughly, is experienced both as of Churchill and as of a bulldog) making this kind of seeing-as possible, with respect to Churchill-in-the-image. The phenomenology of seeing-as is, naturally enough, hard to describe, but there is some sort of transformative identification of Churchill and a bulldog.

This isn't just a matter of *thinking* of Churchill as a bulldog—it's perceptual. However it's a kind of perception with relatively deep cognitive effects. For seeing Churchill as a bulldog in the image can mould the viewer's visual attention and thought patterns in the future. For one, it can lead her to visually attend to bulldog-like features of (representations of) Churchill in future. Equally it can influence her

---

[22] There is a complication here with 'seeing' people in photos or pictures, where (*pace* Walton 1994) one does not literally see them; I shall ignore this for present purposes.
[23] Wilkerson (1973); Kvart (1993).   [24] Annalisa (2012), 130.
[25] One possible candidate for the mental state here is *imagining* that one sees an elephant, though this is controversial.
[26] It is true that the seeing-as I am identifying is not identical in every feature to 'seeing-as' as discussed, most famously, by Wittgenstein, though this would not seem to delegitimize talk of seeing-as altogether. For one, there need be no 'aspect-dawning' or 'aspect-switch', as in the famous case of the duck-rabbit figure—one simply sees Churchill as a bulldog. For another, there is also no obvious 'subjectivity to the will' (Wittgenstein (1998), §899), though in any case, it is moot to what extent seeing-as has the latter, even in classical instances (Avner (2000), 109).

cognitions, in that, for instance, it can cause her in future to focus on the ways in which Churchill is like a bulldog, and ignore ways in which he isn't. It can encourages her to explore ways in which Churchill resembles the stereotype of a bulldog generally: e.g. in term of pugnaciousness, courage, and 'Britishness'. Moreover, the fact that seeing-as occurs in relation to the caricature relatively passively and spontaneously looks partly responsible for the power of the image to shape future responses to (representations of) Churchill in other contexts. (I will return to a related point in what follows.)

7. Varieties of Mind-Insensitive Seeing-As

I suggest that, just as a caricature of Churchill as a bulldog might encourage us to see Churchill as a bulldog, and so in future to visually attend to Churchill's bulldog-like aspects, and/or to think of him as a bulldog, so too objectifying images encourage us to *see women as* bodies/animals/duplicates/children/insensate objects, and so to relate to them in that way more generally. Seeing women as bodies/animals/duplicates/children/insensate objects all count as 'mind-insensitive' ways of seeing them. Each of these varieties of seeing-as, when applied to humans, are ways of seeing a person which are insensitive to some aspect of their mind, to a greater or lesser extent. They each involve a phenomenal experience that de-emphasizes or ignores minded aspects of a person.[27] Moreover, I suggest, this seeing-as is likely to have effects on future visual attention patterns and thought, in certain ways. People repeatedly exposed to images of women-as-bodies are likely to later see women as bodies. People repeatedly exposed to images of women-as-animals are likely to later see women as animals.[28] And so on.

I will now further describe three varieties of mind-insensitive seeing-as in particular, using extracts from literary sources to give a flavour of what I have in mind.

7.1. Seeing-as-a-body

In literature, there are many descriptions which apparently identify something like seeing a person as a body and give us a sense of what it is like to relate to another human in that way. Predominantly, there is an exclusive focus on physical characteristics. For instance:

Her belly was tanned and her arms were thin and her prominent buttocks were round and firm and her slender legs were strongly muscled and her breasts were substantial for someone not much more than five feet tall. She had the curvaceous lusciousness of a Varga Girl in the old 1940s magazine illustrations, but a miniaturized, childlike Varga Girl.[29]

---

[27] In arguing thus, I am assuming that features of one's mental life (e.g. emotion, mood, humour, human intelligence) are detectable to others via facial expression and observable bodily gesture. However, it should be noted that my position does not depend on the assumption that these features can be *directly* seen rather than indirectly detected via evidence. If the former, mind-insensitive seeing-as inhibits one's ability to see such things. If the latter, it inhibits one's ability to detect the evidence for them.

[28] A caricature of Churchill-as-a-bulldog encourages us in the future to see him and think of him as a bulldog, but not to see men this way *generally*.

[29] Roth (2007), 132.

Seeing-as-a-body, as the example suggests, involves seeing a person in a way which prioritizes their body whilst de-emphasizing attention from their inner mental life. As such, it doesn't have to be sexual, though it usually is: a doctor could see a patient as a body, for instance. It does not even have to be about the body, understood as something distinct from the face: the face and head can be seen in this way too.

Now she looked him full in the face and smiled. Her teeth were white in her brown face and her skin and her eyes were the same golden tawny brown. She had high cheekbones, merry eyes and a straight mouth with full lips. Her hair was the golden brown of a grain field that has been burned dark in the sun but it was cut short all over her head so that it was but little longer than the fur on a beaver pelt.[30]

Images which represent women-as-bodies encourage us to see women more generally as bodies. One sees a person as a body in these images in a way analogous to the way one sees Churchill in the caricature as a bulldog. The viewer's perceptual experience is phenomenologically transformed, so that one sees a body that is also, somehow, a woman. By this, I mean something different from the familiar experience of seeing a woman *who has a body*. The experience has a different gestalt. Inevitably, phenomenology is hard to capture in words: but perhaps seeing-as-a-body might equally involve the seeing of 'colourless bodily movements', as some behaviourists used to falsely characterize our experience generally; rather than the seeing of people doing things like 'running from danger, telling us their woes, nursing painful bruises, grimacing, frowning in disapproval, and so on'.[31]

I am effectively claiming that there is such a thing as seeing-a-person-as-a-body, and that this simultaneously involves (a) attention towards bodily and other physical characteristics and (b) attention away from 'minded features'. One's attention is heavily focused upon bodily features, understood in terms of such properties as colour, shape, texture, line, weight, and aesthetic qualities; and not at all, or in a relatively reduced way, on evidence of mental life or personality.

There is some limited empirical evidence to back this thought up. For instance, there is evidence that isolated attention to body parts spontaneously occurs when looking at certain images of partly nude women but not images of partly nude men.[32] Arguably this is due to our repeated exposure to images of women's bodies but not men's. In a similarly suggestive vein, Gervais et al. find that unlike with men, 'women's sexual body parts presented in isolation were recognized similarly to and in some cases better than women's sexual body parts presented in the context of the entire body'.[33] Moreover, there is evidence that when attention to the bodies and appearances of women in images is *artificially* induced in study participants, there is an accompanying decrease in their attention to certain minded features. Loughnan et al.[34] suggest that images of women's torsos and images of partly clothed women, as well as images of partly clothed men, are accompanied by decreased 'mind attribution' and attribution of moral status.[35]

---

[30] Hemingway (1976), 27.   [31] Cook (1969), 127.   [32] Bernard et al. (2012), 469.
[33] Gervais, Vescio, Maas et al. (2012).   [34] Loughnan et al. (2010).
[35] See also Heflick and Goldenburg (2009), (2014); Heflick (2011).

Meanwhile, Gray et al.[36] present evidence that focusing on partly clothed images of both women and men cause both female and male perceivers to diminish attention to the represented subjects' capacity for complex mental attributes like 'self-control', 'acting morally', 'planning', 'communication', 'memory', and 'thought', but increase attention to their capacity for experiences such as 'pleasure', 'hunger', 'desire', 'fear', and 'rage'. This still potentially counts as mind-insensitive seeing-as, since there is a significant sense in which attention to complex mentality is decreased (mind-insensitivity is a matter of degree). There is also evidence that 'hostile sexist' men—that is, men who believe 'women seek to control men and use sexuality or feminist ideology as a means to achieving status'—perceive the agency of partly clothed women represented in advertising images in a diminished way.[37]

7.2. Seeing-as-an-animal

Seeing a person as an animal is not just thinking of a woman as like an animal in some respects. One *sees* her as a cat, or as a fox, or as a lion. It is as if she is somehow both a woman and an animal. Seeing-as-an-animal does not imply a lack of attention to mind altogether, since many animals have minds; however, since the stereotype of an animal associates only relatively basic mental features to animals, seeing-as-an-animal still causes a decrease in attention to more complex mental life, and so counts as mind-insensitive, to some degree.

Turning again to literature, we again find many descriptions of what looks like seeing-women-as-animals:

All at once the angry squirrel-like expression on the princess's pretty little face changed to a moving and piteous look of fear. Her beautiful eyes gave a sidelong glance at her husband and her face assumed the timid, deprecating expression of a dog when it rapidly but feebly wags its drooping tail.[38]

she didn't make a face and run off laughing at him but took it with an agreeable little catlike smile that could easily have been accompanied by a purr.[39]

he passed a heavy-set, big, blue-eyed woman, with bleached-blonde hair showing under her old man's felt hat, hurrying across the road, her eyes red from crying. Look at that big ox, he thought. What do you suppose a woman like that thinks about?[40]

Again, some empirical evidence appears to support my claims here indirectly, albeit in a limited way. There is strong evidence of people likening other 'out'-groups—often, those in other racial groups—to animals.[41] There is also evidence that in-group members will be more likely to associate their in-group with 'human' as opposed to 'animal' words in comparison with some out-group.[42] In relation to women, Vaes, Paladino, and Puvia[43] report evidence that 'sexually objectified' (that is, women represented in sexualized ways) tend to be associated with less human and more animal concepts. Meanwhile, the likening of other groups to animals, generally, is thought to be accompanied by a de-emphasis of supposedly 'uniquely human'

---

[36] Gray et al. (2011). [37] Cikara, Eberhardt, and Fiske (2011). [38] Tolstoy (1978), 30.
[39] Roth (2007), 133. [40] Hemingway (1972), 130. [41] Haslam (2006).
[42] Viki et al. (2006). [43] Vaes, Paladino, and Puvia (2011).

characteristics such as 'civility, moral sensibility, and higher cognition'.[44] Rudman and Mescher[45] also report that men who, via automatic association between images of women and certain words, implicitly think of women in terms of either animals or objects, are more likely to report negative attitudes towards rape victims, as well as display sexual aggression.

7.3. Seeing-as-duplicate

I finish with seeing-a-person-as-duplicate.[46] As I intend it, this involves seeing her in relation to others, as a member of a series, with a resulting decrease in attention to mental individuality. A characteristic context for seeing another as duplicate is where she is perceptibly in a group of similar individuals (as one looks, for instance, at a group of soldiers on parade, or a group of schoolboys in the street). However, being in a group isn't necessary to be seen-as-duplicate: seeing a person as a member of a series of others can occur even where those others are perceptually absent (as when one sees a person *as a member of a particular family* even though no other family members are present).

It should be noted that any resulting mind-insensitivity attached to this form of seeing-as could in theory be mild, especially relative to other forms of mind-insensitive-seeing-as already discussed. What is principally suppressed here, in terms of a viewer's attention and thought, is information about *individualizing* differences in facial expression, emotion, and other visible features of mental life on the face or via bodily gestures. However, this is consistent with attention being paid to visible features of a subject's mental life, *as long as they are not individualizing*. In theory, an image of a group of people ranged in a row, laughing at a joke but with exactly the same posture, could encourage us to see them as having certain minded features—e.g. intelligence and humour. However, if so, it presumably would not do so in a way which individualized the subjects in the image from one another. That is, attention to any individual personality traits or thoughts expressible through appearance and gesture would still be minimized, and to this extent the resulting way of seeing the subjects would still count as mind-suppressing, to some degree.

As with the other varieties of seeing-as which I have posited, there is no essential connection between seeing-as-duplicates, and women being the objects of such seeing. Nonetheless, I suggest, women are often seen this way, and particularly women from racial groups other than one's own. For a flavour of what I have in mind, consider the following literary example (vaguely suggestive of a comparison with animals for good measure):

Here, discordantly, in Eights Week, came a rabble of womankind, some hundreds strong, twittering and fluttering over the cobbles and up the steps.[47]

---

[44] Haslam (2006), 257; Haslam and Loughman (2014).   [45] Rudman and Mescher (2012).
[46] I have not discussed seeing-women-as-children or seeing-women-as-insensate-objects. I know of no psychological literature which specifically supports the claim that women tend to be seen and related to as children, in a way accompanied by de-emphasis of minded features. There is some psychological literature which supports the fact that out-groups (usually racial) tend to be perceived as feeling less pain (Trawalter, Hoffman, and Waytz 2012) and that such biases occur 'automatically' (Mathur et al. 2014). There is also historical evidence that nineteenth-century surgeons did not recognize the pain of slaves (see Briggs 2000).
[47] Waugh (1962), 23.

Or consider this more complex example from Graham Greene, in which his character Scobie seems to see, or have seen, a young girl as fungible under two descriptions—'black' and 'physically beautiful':

> The girl waited patiently for his decision. They had an infinite capacity for patience when patience was required—just as their impatience knew no bound of propriety when they had anything to gain by it. They would sit quietly all day in a white man's backyard in order to beg for something he hadn't the power to grant, or they would shriek and fight and abuse to get served in a store before their neighbor. He thought: how beautiful she is. It was strange to think that fifteen years ago he would not have noticed her beauty—the small high breasts, the tiny wrists, the thrust of the young buttock, she would have been indistinguishable from her fellows—a black.[48]

With respect to seeing-as-duplicate, there is a small amount of indirect evidence for the thought that members of certain groups are sometimes seen-as-duplicates. There is some evidence that

> women with ideal bodies, women with average bodies, and men with ideal bodies were more fungible (perceivers made more body–face pairing errors) than men with average bodies. Furthermore, it appears that when people are fungible they are interchangeable with people with similar body types.[49]

This is established via the use of still imagery of women and men respectively (clothed). Meanwhile, well-publicized research documents that we are less able to distinguish the faces of those in other racial or 'out-groups';[50] this may well also be relevant.

8. Possible Objection Considered

In this section, I briefly consider an objection to the possibility of mind-insensitive seeing-as, generally. One might object: in order to grant the possibility of mind-insensitive-seeing-as towards a person X, don't we equally require a positive account of what it would be to see-as 'mind-sensitively'? That is, isn't it required that there be something like 'seeing-X-as-a-minded-being', where this too has a distinctive gestalt? And if we cannot give an account of this sort of seeing-as, doesn't that in turn leave the notion of mind-insensitive-seeing-as in doubt?

In short, I don't think so. What is required for the relevant contrast, perhaps, is that there be a way of seeing X which does not detract any attention or thought from X's minded features. But this doesn't have to involve positively seeing-X-as-a-minded-being, where this is supposed to have a distinctive gestalt. In fact, it doesn't have to involve seeing-as at all. Rather it might simply involve seeing X, and thereby paying full attention to minded features as expressed through facial expression and gesture. As long as this is possible, then we have enough of a contrast with

---

[48] Greene (1971), 21.   [49] Gervais, Vescio, and Allen (2012), 499.
[50] Bernstein, Young, and Hugenberg (2007).

seeing-as-a-body, seeing-as-an-animal, and so on—where attention to such features is, I claim, less than full—for my claims to get a grip.

9. Consequences

What might follow, should we take seriously seeing-as of the kinds I have identified? I shall conclude by describing five potential consequences.

First, it looks as if mind-insensitive seeing-as might be potentially identified as causally prior in many cases to several of the varieties of objectification of women identified by Nussbaum and supplemented by Langton. For instance, seeing-as-a-body plausibly looks potentially causally prior to: treating another as lacking in autonomy/agency; or reduced to body parts; or reduced to appearances. Seeing-as-an-animal plausibly looks potentially causally prior to: treating another as lacking in autonomy; or as lacking in subjectivity; or as capable of being owned; or as violable. Seeing-as-duplicate plausibly looks potentially causally prior to treating another as fungible; or as (somewhat) lacking in subjectivity. In other words, it seems that we have a candidate causal explanation of many instances of objectification.

Second, my view also allows us, potentially, to reach some interesting reflections on the connections between objectifying practices and moral harm. On my view, mind-insensitive seeing-as isn't necessarily harmful; in the context of doctor's surgeries, football pitches, or, I dare say, within otherwise healthy sexual relationships, it can harmlessly occur. It does not involve any forcible violation of autonomy. It is primarily a way of perceiving rather than a way of treating.[51] However, it seems clear that in many cases, mind-insensitive seeing-as does lead to morally criticizable forms of treatment of women. For instance, many of the harms discussed by psychologists under the heading of 'objectification' might be attributed to mind-insensitive seeing-as in particular, or the anticipation of it. Frederickson and Roberts[52] detail the wealth of psychological harms done to women via the widespread tendency to value them in terms of their bodies. Calogero reports that 'anticipating a male gaze' (which we might interpret as the anticipation of being seen-as in mind-insensitive ways) 'produced significantly greater body shame and social physique anxiety than anticipating a female gaze'.[53] Gay and Castano[54] suggest women take on increased cognitive load as a result of anticipating 'the male gaze', making it more likely they will perform poorly on tasks; possibly because cognitive resources are being used on self-monitoring. Rudman and Mescher[55] report that men who, via automatic association between images of women and certain words, implicitly think of women in terms of either animals or objects, are more likely to report negative attitudes towards rape victims, as well as display sexual aggression. And so on.

---

[51] MacKinnon makes clear she is primarily interested in forms of treatment: 'Objectification is different from stereotyping, which acts as though it's all in the head...the problem goes a great deal deeper than illusion or delusion', MacKinnon (1987), 118.
[52] Fredrickson and Roberts (1997). [53] Calogero (2004).
[54] Gay and Castano (2010), 701. [55] Rudman and Mescher (2012).

To this we might speculatively add: it's well documented that men's looking at women is often accompanied by sexually evaluative and derogatory commentary.[56] It's reasonable to ask why such commentary can so casually be made within earshot, given social norms of interaction generally, and even a well-established human tendency to anthropomorphize the inanimate.[57] One reason is perhaps that female targets are believed to be powerless, relative to the commentator, so that their feelings are judged to be irrelevant. But another might be that the woman is being seen mind-insensitively. Equally, the oft-reported experience of women's voices being ignored in business meetings might also be partly explained.

So, since my account posits a causal factor behind much objectification, and since objectification tends to cause harm, we also have a potential causal explanation of some of the harm done by objectification. Yet, at the same time, the tendency to mind-insensitive seeing-as looks relatively passive, spontaneous, and non-deliberate. It is partly brought on, I suggest, by exposure to objectifying images in a way that, given their saturating presence in the media, a viewer can hardly escape. If I'm right, then objectifying images sets up habits of attention and thought that are not deliberately acquired, and which are presumably quite hard to eradicate. Hence personal responsibility for such habits and thoughts, and so for any subsequent objectifying behaviour, looks more reduced than one might have first thought. In short: if we want objectification of women to stop, as a culture perhaps we should focus on stopping producing those objectifying images of women which bring about mind-insensitive seeing-as, rather than on exclusively focusing on trying to control behaviour further down the line.

Third, my view underlines the fact that objectification, understood generally, need not be only directed towards women, but other groups as well. Men can be seen-as-bodies too (though they rarely are). Women of colour tend to be represented-as-animals in imagery more often than Caucasian women.[58] My literary examples of seeing-as-duplicates focused on racial cases as well as gendered ones. And so on. In other words, this view apparently provides a tool to bring together discussion of objectification across sexual and racial contexts, and perhaps others.

Fourth, countenancing the category of mind-insensitive seeing-as also allows us to reconfigure certain discussions in social psychology. For instance, occasionally psychologists have treated objectification as differentiated from the practice of perceiving or treating people as animals.[59] If mind-insensitive seeing-as is countenanced, it becomes clear how, in at least one coherent sense, seeing people as animals counts as an instance of the same practice as seeing people as (fungible, insensate) objects.

Fifth and finally: we have gained along the way a unified account of how still non-pornographic images, which show no autonomy-violation or coercion or violence, can nonetheless 'objectify' their represented subjects and by extension the associated group: namely, by being 'mind-suppressing' and promoting mind-insensitive seeing-as.

---

[56] Frederickson and Roberts (1997), 176.
[57] Epley, Schroeder, and Waytz (2013). [58] Wade (2009b).
[59] Heflick and Goldenburg (2014), 225.

In short, I think we should take mind-insensitive seeing-as seriously, as a possible tool in understanding objectification, its causes, and its consequences. I have suggested that empirical evidence indirectly supports at least some of it: further more targeted work is needed to solidify the hunch. But at the very least, we have a promising-looking idea for future research.[60]

---

[60] The material here is drawn from talks given at the 2013 Evaluative Perception conference, University of Glasgow; the Philosophy Departments of UC Irvine, the Open University, Manchester, and Nottingham Trent; the British Society of Aesthetics Cambridge Lecture Series; and the Edinburgh Women in Philosophy Workshop on Objectification. Thanks very much to audiences for their helpful questions and comments.

Bibliography

Adams, C. (2010), *The Sexual Politics of Meat: 20th Anniversary Edition* (London: Continuum).
Alston, W. P. (2002), 'Sellars and the "Myth of the Given"', *Philosophy and Phenomenological Research*, 65/1: 69–86.
Annalisa, C. (2012), 'Human Diagrammatic Reasoning and Seeing-As', *Synthese*, 186: 121–48.
Appiah, K. A. (2008), *Experiments in Ethics* (Cambridge, MA: Harvard University Press).
Archer, D., Iritani, B., Kimes, D. D., and Barrios, M. (1983), 'Face-ism: Five Studies of Sex Differences in Facial Prominence', *Journal of Personality and Social Psychology*, 45/4: 725–35.
Armstrong, D. M. (1968), *A Materialist Theory of Mind* (London: Routledge and Kegan Paul).
Armstrong, D. M. (1973), *Belief, Truth and Knowledge* (London: Routledge and Kegan Paul).
Athanassios, A. (2009), *Cognition and Perception: How Do Psychology and Neural Science Inform Philosophy?* (Cambridge, MA: MIT Press).
Audi, R. (1998), *Epistemology* (London and New York: Routledge).
Audi, R. (2004), *The Good in the Right: A Theory of Intuition and Intrinsic Value* (Princeton: Princeton University Press).
Audi, R. (2006), *Practical Reasoning and Ethical Decision* (London and New York: Routledge).
Audi, R. (2010a), 'Moral Perception and Moral Knowledge', *Proceedings of the Aristotelian Society*, suppl. vol. 84: 79–97.
Audi, R. (2010b), *Epistemology: A Contemporary Introduction to the Theory of Knowledge* (London and New York: Routledge).
Audi, R. (2013), *Moral Perception* (Princeton: Princeton University Press).
Audi, R. (2014), 'Normative Generality in Ethics and Aesthetics', *Journal of Ethics*, 18: 373–90.
Audi, R. (2015), 'Perceptual Intuitionism', *Philosophy and Phenomenological Research*, 90/1: 164–93.
Augustine (1982), *The Literal Meaning of Genesis*, vol. 1, bks. 1–6, trans. J. H. Taylor SJ: no. 42 of J. Quasten, W. J. Burghardt, and T. C. Lawler (eds.), *Ancient Christian Writers* (New York: Paulist Press, 1982).
Aune, B. (1972), 'Remarks on an Argument by Chisholm', *Philosophical Studies*, 23/5: 327–34.
Avner, B. 'What's the Point in Seeing Aspects?', *Philosophical Investigations*, 23/2 (2000): 109.
Bain, D. (2013), 'What Makes Pains Unpleasant?', *Philosophical Studies*, 166/1: 69–89.
Baker, G. (2006), *Wittgenstein's Method: Neglected Aspects* (London: Blackwell).
Balog, K. (1999), 'Conceivability, Possibility and the Mind-Body Problem', *Philosophical Review*, 108/4: 497–528.
Bar, M. (2009), 'Predictions: A Universal Principle in the Operation of the Human Brain', *Philosophical Transactions of the Royal Society of London B: Biological Sciences*, 364/1521: 1181–2.
Barnes, E. (2012), 'Emergence and Fundamentality', *Mind*, 121/484: 873–901.
Bartky, S. L. (2005), 'On Psychological Oppression', in A. Cudd and R. Andreason (eds.), *Feminist Theory: A Philosophical Anthology* (Oxford: Blackwell), 105–14.
Bayne, T. (2009), 'Perception and the Reach of Phenomenal Content', *Philosophical Quarterly*, 59/236: 285–404.
Bayne, T., and Montague, M. (2011a), 'Cognitive Phenomenology: An Introduction', in Bayne and Montague (eds.), *Cognitive Phenomenology* (New York and Oxford: Oxford University Press), 1–34.

Bayne, T., and Montague, M. (2011b), *Cognitive Phenomenology* (New York and Oxford: Oxford University Press).
Bayne, T., and Pacherie, E. (2007), 'Narrators and Comparators: The Architecture of Agentive Self-Awareness', *Synthese*, 159: 475–91.
Bealer, G. (1998), 'Intuition and the Autonomy of Philosophy', in M. DePaul and W. Ramsey (eds.), *Rethinking Intuition: The Psychology of Intuition and Its Role in Philosophical Inquiry* (Lanham, MD: Rowman and Littlefield), 201–40.
Beardsmore, R. M. (1969), *Moral Reasoning* (London: Routledge and Kegan Paul).
Bengson, J. (2016), 'Practical Perception', *Philosophical Issues*, 26/1: 25–58.
Bergmann, M. (2006), *Justification Without Awareness* (Oxford: Oxford University Press).
Bergmann, M. (2013), 'Phenomenal Conservatism and the Dilemma for Internalism', in C. Tucker (ed.), *Seemings and Justification* (Oxford: Oxford University Press), 154–78.
Bergqvist, A. (2009), 'Semantic Particularism and Linguistic Competence', *Logique et analyse*, 52 (208), 343–61.
Bergqvist, A. (2010), 'Why Sibley is Not a Generalist After All', *British Journal of Aesthetics*, 50/1: 1–14.
Bergqvist, A. (2013), 'Thick Concepts and Context Dependence', *Southwest Philosophy Review*, 29/1, 221–32.
Bergqvist, A. (2015), 'Thick Description Revisited: Tanner on Thick Concepts and Perspectivalism in Value Philosophy', *Methods in Ethics*, virtual issue no. 3, guest ed. B. Colburn (*Proceedings of the Aristotelian Society*), 202–17.
Bergqvist, A. (forthcoming), 'Thick Aesthetic Concepts: Giving Sibley His Due'.
Bernard, P., Gervais, S., Allen, J., Campomizzi, S., and Klein, O. (2012), 'Integrating Sexual Objectification With Object Versus Person Recognition', *Psychological Science*, 23/5: 469–71.
Bernstein, M. J., Young, S. G., and Hugenberg, K. (2007), 'The Cross-Category Effect Mere Social Categorization Is Sufficient to Elicit an Own-Group Bias in Face Recognition', *Psychological Science*, 18/8: 706–12.
Biederman, I., and Shiffrar, M. M. (1987), 'Sexing Day-Old Chicks: A Case Study and Expert Systems Analysis of a Difficult Perceptual-Learning Task', *Journal of Experimental Psychology: Learning, Memory and Cognition*, 13/4: 640–5.
Blackburn, S. (1984), *Spreading the Word: Groundings in the Philosophy of Language*, (New York: Oxford University Press).
Blackburn, S. (1988), 'How to Be an Ethical Antirealist', *Midwest Studies in Philosophy*, 12: 364–5.
Blackburn, S. (2006), 'Antirealist Expressivism and Quasi-Realism', in D. Copp (ed.), *The Oxford Handbook of Ethical Theory* (Oxford: Oxford University Press), 146–62.
Blackburn, S. (2013), 'Deflationism, Pluralism, Expressivism, Pragmatism', in N. J. Lee, L. Pedersen, and C. D. Wright (eds.), *Truth and Pluralism: Current Debates* (Oxford: University Press), 263–77.
Block, N. (1983), 'Mental Pictures and Cognitive Science', *Philosophical Review*, 92: 499–541.
Blum, L. (1994), *Moral Perception and Particularity* (Cambridge: Cambridge University Press).
Boghossian, P. (1996), 'Analyticity Reconsidered', *Noûs*, 30: 360–91.
BonJour, L. (1978), 'Can Empirical Knowledge Have a Foundation?', *American Philosophical Quarterly*, 15: 1–14.
BonJour, L. (2003), *Epistemic Justification* (Oxford: Blackwell).
Boyd, R. (1988), 'How To Be a Moral Realist', in G. Sayre-McCord (ed.), *Essays on Moral Realism* (Ithaca, NY: Cornell University Press), 181–228.
Brady, M. (2009), 'The Irrationality of Recalcitrant Emotions', *Philosophical Studies*, 145/3: 413–30.

Brady, M. (2013), *Emotional Insight: The Epistemic Role of Emotional Experience* (Oxford: Oxford University Press).
Brandt, R. (1979), *A Theory of the Good and the Right* (Oxford: Clarendon Press).
Bratman, M. (2007), *Structures of Agency: Essays* (New York: Oxford University Press).
Brentano, F. (1889), *Vom Ursprung sittlicher Erkenntnis* (Leipzig: Duncker & Humblot).
Brewer, B. (1999), *Perception and Reason* (Oxford: Oxford University Press).
Briggs, L. (2000), 'The Race of Hysteria: "Overcivilization" and the "Savage" in Late Nineteenth-Century Obstetrics and Gynecology', *American Quarterly*, 52/2: 246–73.
Brink, D. O. (1989), *Moral Realism and the Foundations of Ethics* (Cambridge: Cambridge University Press).
Broackes, J. (2012), 'Introduction', in Broackes (ed.), *Iris Murdoch, Philosopher* (Oxford, Oxford University Press), 1–92.
Broad, C. D. (1944), 'Reflections on the Moral Sense Theory in Ethics', *Proceedings of the Aristotelian Society*, 45: 131–66.
Brogaard, B. (2013), 'Do We Perceive Natural Kind Properties?', *Philosophical Studies*, 162: 35–42.
Brogaard, B. (2014), 'Phenomenal Seemings and Sensible Dogmatism', in C. Tucker (ed.), *Seemings and Justification* (Oxford: Oxford University Press), 270–89.
Bruner, J. S., and Goodman, C. C. (1947), 'Value and Need as Organizing Factors in Perception', *Journal of Abnormal and Social Psychology*, 42: 33–44.
Bruner, J. S., and Postman, L. (1948), 'Symbolic Value as an Organizing Factor in Perception', *Journal of Social Psychology*, 27: 203–8.
Bubic A. et al. (2009), 'Violation of Expectation: Neural Correlates Reflect Bases of Prediction', *Journal of Cognitive Neuroscience*, 21/1: 155–68.
Budd, M. (1992), 'On Looking at a Picture', in J. Hopkins and A. Savile (eds.), *Psychoanalysis, Mind and Art: Perspectives on Richard Wollheim* (Oxford: Blackwell), 259–80.
Budd, M. (1995), *Values of Art* (Harmondsworth: Penguin Books).
Burge, T. (2010), *Origins of Objectivity* (Oxford: Oxford University Press).
Butchvarov, P. (1989), *Skepticism in Ethics* (Bloomington, IN: Indiana University Press).
Byrne, A. (2009), 'Experience and Content', *Philosophical Quarterly*, 59: 429–51.
Calogero, R. M. (2004), 'A Test of Objectification Theory: The Effect of the Male Gaze on Appearance Concerns in College Women', *Psychology of Women Quarterly*, 28/1: 16–21.
Carruthers, P. (2006), *The Architecture of the Mind: Massive Modularity and the Flexibility of Thought* (Oxford: Clarendon Press).
Chalmers, D. (2004), 'The Representational Character of Experience', in B. Leiter (ed.), *The Future for Philosophy* (Oxford: Oxford University Press), 153–81.
Chalmers, D. (2006), 'Perception and the Fall from Eden', in T. S. Gendler and J. Hawthorne (eds.), *Perceptual Experience* (Oxford: Oxford University Press), 49–125.
Chappell, S. G. (2013), 'There Are No Thin Concepts', in S. Kirchin (ed.), *Thick Concepts* (Oxford: Oxford University Press), 182–96.
Chappell, T. (2008), 'Moral Perception', *Philosophy*, 83: 421–37.
Chase, W., and Simon, H. (1973), 'Perception in Chess', *Cognitive Psychology*, 4: 55–81.
Chasid, A. (2016), 'Imaginatively-Colored Perception: Walton on Pictorial Experience', *Southern Journal of Philosophy*, 54/1: 27–47.
Chisholm, R. (1968–9), 'Objectives and Intrinsic Value', *Proceedings and Addresses of the American Philosophical Association*, 42: 21–38.
Chisholm, R. M. (1989), *Theory of Knowledge* (3rd edn., Engleworth Cliffs, NJ: Prentice Hall).
Chudnoff, E. (2013), *Intuition* (Oxford: Oxford University Press).
Church, J. (2010), 'Seeing Reasons', *Philosophy and Phenomenological Research*, 85/3: 638–70.
Church, J. (2013), *Possibilities of Perception* (Oxford: Oxford University Press).

Churchland, P. (1988), 'Perceptual Plasticity and Theoretical Neutrality: A Reply to Jerry Fodor', *Philosophy of Science*, 55: 167–87.
Cikara, M., Eberhardt, J. L., and Fiske, S. T. (2011), 'From Agents to Objects: Sexist Attitudes and Neural Responses to Sexualized Targets', *Journal of Cognitive Neuroscience*, 23/3: 540–51.
Clark, A. (2000), *A Theory of Sentience* (New York: Oxford University Press).
Clark, A. (2015), *Surfing Uncertainty: Prediction, Action, and the Embodied Mind* (Oxford: Oxford University Press).
Cohen, T. (1973), 'Aesthetics/Non-Aesthetics and the Concept of Taste', *Theoria*, 39: 113–52.
Conee, E. (2014), 'Seeming Evidence', in C. Tucker (ed.), *Seemings and Justification* (Oxford: Oxford University Press), 52–68.
Conee, E., and Feldman, R. (1995), *Evidentialism* (Oxford: Oxford University Press).
Cook, J. W. (1969), 'Human Beings', *Studies in the Philosophy of Wittgenstein* (London: Routledge), 117–51.
Corns, J. (2014), 'Unpleasantness, Motivational Oomph, and Painfulness', *Mind and Language*, 29/2: 238–54.
Corns, J. (forthcoming), 'Hedonic Rationality', in D. Bain, M. Brady, and J. Corns (eds.), *The Philosophy of Suffering: Metaphysics, Value, and Normativity* (London: Routledge).
Cowan, R. (2011), 'Intuition, Perception and Emotion: A Critical Study of the Prospects for Contemporary Ethical Intuitionism', PhD Thesis, University of Glasgow.
Cowan, R. (2014), 'Review: Robert Audi, *Moral Perception*', *Mind*, 123/492: 1167–71.
Cowan, R. (2015a), 'Perceptual Intuitionism', *Philosophy and Phenomenological Research*, 90/1: 164–93.
Cowan, R. (2015b), 'Cognitive Penetrability and Ethical Perception', *Review of Philosophy and Psychology*, 6/4: 665–82.
Cowan, R. (2016), 'Epistemic Perceptualsim and Neo-Sentimentalist Objections', *Canadian Journal of Philosophy*, 46/1: 59–81.
Cowan, R. (2017), 'Rossian Conceptual Intuitionism', *Ethics*, 127/4: 821–51.
Crary, A. (2007), *Beyond Moral Judgement* (Cambridge, MA: Harvard University Press).
Cullison, A. (2010), 'Moral Perception', *European Journal of Philosophy*, 18: 159–75.
Cuneo, T. (2003), 'Reidian Moral Perception', *Canadian Journal of Philosophy*, 33: 229–58.
Cuneo, T. (2014), Commentary on *Moral Perception*, Pacific Division of the American Philosophical Association, 2014, MS.
Cuneo, T., and Shafer-Landau, R. (2014), 'The Moral Fixed Points: New Directions for Moral Nonnaturalism', *Philosophical Studies*, 171/3: 399–443.
Currie, G. (1993), 'Interpretation and Objectivity', *Mind*, 102: 413–28.
Currie, G. (1995), *Image and Mind: Film, Philosophy, and Cognitive Science* (Cambridge: Cambridge University Press).
Dancy, J. (1993), *Moral Reasons* (Oxford: Blackwell).
Dancy, J. (2010), 'Moral Perception and Moral Knowledge', *Proceedings of the Aristotelian Society*, suppl. vol, 84: 99–118.
Dancy, J. (2013), 'Practical Concepts', in S. Kirchin, *Thick Concepts* (Oxford: Oxford University Press), 44–59.
Danto, A. C. (1979), 'Moving Pictures', *Quarterly Review of Film Studies*, 4: 1–21.
Davidson, D. (1970), 'Mental Events', in L. Foster and J. Swanson (eds.), *Experience and Theory* (New York: Humanities Press).
De Gaynesford, M. (2010), 'The Bishop, the Chambermaid, the Wife and the Ass: What Difference Does It Make If Something Is Mine?', in J. Cottingham, P. Stratton-Lake, and B. Feltham (eds.), *Partiality and Impartiality: Morality, Special Obligations and the Wider World* (Oxford: Oxford University Press), 84–97.
De Neys, W. (2012), 'Bias and Conflict: A Case for Logical Intuitions', *Perspectives on Psychological Science*, 7: 28–38.

Delk, J. L., and Fillenbaum, S. (1965), 'Differences in Perceived Colour as a Function of Characteristic Colour', *American Journal of Psychology*, 78/2: 290–3.
Dennett, D. C. (1988), 'Quining Qualia', in A. Marcel and E. Bisiach (eds.), *Consciousness in Modern Science* (Oxford: Oxford University Press).
Dennett, D. C. (1991), *Consciousness Explained* (London: Allen Lane).
Deonna, J., and Teroni, F. (2012), *The Emotions: A Philosophical Introduction* (London: Routledge).
DePaul, M. (1993), *Balance and Refinement* (London: Routledge).
Diamond, C. (1996), '"We Are Perpetually Moralists": Iris Murdoch, Fact, and Value', in M. Antonaccio and W. Schweiker (eds.), *Iris Murdoch and the Search for Human Goodness* (Chicago: University of Chicago Press), 79–109.
Doggett, T., and Egan, A. (2012), 'How We Feel About Terrible, Non-Existent Mafiosi', *Philosophy and Phenomenological Research*, 84/2: 277–306.
Döring, S. A. (2003), 'Explaining Action By Emotion', *Philosophical Quarterly*, 53/211: 214–30.
Döring, S. A. (2007), 'Seeing What to Do: Affective Perception and Rational Motivation', *dialectica*, 61/3: 363–94.
Döring, S. A. (2015), 'What's Wrong with Recalcitrant Emotions? From Irrationality to Challenge of Agential Identity', *dialectica*, 69/3: 381–402.
Doring, S. A., and Lutz, A. (2015), 'Beyond Perceptualism: Introduction to the Special Issue', *dialectica*, 69/3: 259–70.
Dretske, F. (1969), *Seeing and Knowing* (London: Routledge and Kegan Paul).
Dretske, F. (1981), *Knowledge and the Flow of Information* (Cambridge, MA: MIT Press).
Dretske, F. (1993), 'Conscious Experience', *Mind*, 102/406: 263–83.
Dretske, F. (1995), *Naturalizing the Mind* (Cambridge, MA: MIT Press).
Dretske, F. (2003), 'Experience as Representation', *Philosophical Issues*, 13: 67–82.
Dretske, F. (2004), 'Change Blindness', *Philosophical Studies*, 120: 1–18.
Drier, J. (2004), 'Metaethics and the Problem of Creeping Minimalism', *Philosophical Perspectives*, 18/1: 23–44.
Dworkin, R. (2011), *Justice for Hedgehogs* (Cambridge, MA: Harvard University Press).
Eklund, M. (2013), 'Evaluative Language and Evaluative Reality', in S. Kirchin (ed.), *Thick Concepts* (Oxford: Oxford University Press), 161–81.
Enoch, D. (2011), *Taking Morality Seriously: A Defense of Robust Realism* (New York: Oxford University Press).
Epley, N., Schroeder, J., and Waytz, A. (2013), 'Motivated Mind Perception: Treating Pets as People and People as Animals', in S. J. Gervais (ed.), *Objectification and (De)Humanization* (New York: Springer, 2013), 127–52.
Evans, J. (2003), 'In Two Minds: Dual-Process Accounts of Reasoning', *Trends in Cognitive Sciences*, 7: 454–9.
Faraci, D. (2015), 'A Hard Look at Moral Perception', *Philosophical Studies*, 172: 2055–72.
Farennikova, A. (2013), 'Seeing Absence', *Philosophical Studies*, 166/3: 429–54.
Farennikova, A. (2014), 'Perception of Absence and Penetration from Expectation', *Review of Philosophy and Psychology*, 6/4: 621–40.
Fine, K. (1994), 'Essence and Modality', *Philosophical Perspectives*, 8: 1–16.
Fine, K. (1995), 'Ontological Dependence', *Proceedings of the Aristotelian Society*, 95: 269–90.
Fiocco, M. O. (2007), 'Conceivability, Imagination, and Modal Knowledge', *Philosophy and Phenomenological Research*, 74/2 (2007), 364–80.
Firestone, C., and Scholl, B. J. (2014), '"Top-Down" Effects Where None Should Be Found: The El Greco Fallacy in Perception Research', *Psychological Science*, 25/1: 38–46.
Fischhoff, B. (1975), 'Hindsight Is Not Equal to Foresight: The Effect of Outcome Knowledge on Judgment Under Uncertainty', *Journal of Experimental Psychology: Human Perception and Performance*, 1/3: 288–99.

Fish, W. (2009), *Perception, Hallucination and Illusion* (Oxford: Oxford University Press).
Flanagan, O. (1991), *The Science of the Mind* (2nd edn., Cambridge, MA: MIT Press).
Fodor, J. A. (1983), *Modularity of Mind* (Cambridge, MA: MIT Press).
Fodor, J. A. (1988), 'A Reply to Churchland's "Perceptual Plasticity and Theoretical Neutrality"', *Philosophy of Science*, 55: 188–98.
Fodor, J. A. (2000), *The Mind Doesn't Work That Way: The Scope and Limits of Computational Psychology* (Cambridge, MA: MIT Press).
Foley, R. (1987), *The Theory of Epistemic Rationality* (Cambridge, MA: Harvard University Press).
Foot, P. (1959), 'Moral Beliefs', *Proceedings of the Aristotelian Society*, 59: 83–104.
Foot, P. (1961), 'Goodness and Choice', *Aristotelian Society*, suppl. vol. 35: 45–60.
Foot, P. (1972), 'Morality as a System of Hypothetical Imperatives', *Philosophical Review*, 81/3: 305–16.
Forrest, P. (1988), 'Supervenience: The Grand-Property Hypothesis', *Australasian Journal of Philosophy*, 66: 1–12.
Frankfurt, H. G. (1988), *The Importance of What We Care About: Philosophical Essays* (Cambridge: Cambridge University Press).
Fredrickson, B. L., and Roberts, T.-A. (1997), 'Objectification Theory: Toward Understanding Women's Lived Experiences and Mental Health Risks', *Psychology of Women Quarterly*, 21: 173–206.
Friston, K., and Kiebel, S. (2009), 'Predictive Coding Under the Free-Energy Principle', *Philosophical Transactions of the Royal Society of London B: Biological Sciences* 364/1521: 1211–21.
Gallagher, S. (2000), 'Self-Reference and Schizophrenia: A Cognitive Model of Immunity to Error Through Misidentification', in D. Zahavi (ed.), *Exploring the Self: Philosophical and Psychopathological Perspectives on Self-Experience* (Amsterdam: John Benjamins Press), 203–39.
Gasking, D. (1962), 'Avowals', in R. J. Butler (ed.), *Analytical Philosophy* (Oxford: Basil Blackwell), 154–69.
Gay, R., and Castano, E. (2010), 'My Body or My Mind: The Impact of State and Trait Objectification on Women's Cognitive Resources', *European Journal of Social Psychology*, 40/5: 695–703.
Gazzaley, A., and Nobre, A. (2012), 'Top-Down Modulation: Bridging Selective Attention and Working Memory', *Trends in Cognitive Science*, 16: 129–35.
Gervais, S. J., Vescio, T. K., Maass, A., Förster, J., and Suitner, C. (2012), 'Seeing Women as Objects: The Sexual Body Part Recognition Bias', *European Journal of Social Psychology*, 42: 743–53.
Gervais, S., Vescio, T., and Allen, J. (2012), 'When Are People Interchangeable Sexual Objects? The Effect of Gender and Body Type on Sexual Fungibility', *British Journal of Social Psychology*, 51/4: 499–513.
Gibbard, A. (1990), *Wise Choices, Apt Feelings: A Theory of Normative Judgment* (Oxford: Oxford University Press).
Gibbard, A. (2003), *Thinking How to Live* (Cambridge, MA: Harvard University Press).
Gibson, E. J. (1969), *Principles of Perceptual Learning and Development* (New York: Appleton-Century-Crofts).
Gibson, J. J. (1966), *The Senses Considered As Perceptual Systems* (London: George Allen and Unwin).
Gibson, J. J. (1977/1979), 'The Theory of Affordances', in R. Shaw and J. Bransford (eds.), *Perceiving, Acting, and Knowing* (Hillsdale, NJ: Laurence Erlbaum, 1977), 67–82; repr. in

Gibson, *The Ecological Approach to Visual Perception* (Boston: Houghton Mifflin, 1979), 27–37.
Gibson, J. J., and Gibson, E. J. (1955), 'Perceptual Learning: Differentiation or Enrichment?', *Psychological Review*, 62: 32–41.
Gilovich, T., Griffin, D., and Kahneman, D. (2002) (eds.), *Heuristics and Biases: The Psychology of Intuitive Judgment* (Cambridge: Cambridge University Press).
Goldie, P. (2000), *The Emotions: A Philosophical Exploration* (Oxford: Oxford University Press).
Goldie, P. (2012), *The Mess Inside* (Oxford: Oxford University Press).
Goldstone, R. L. (1988), 'Perceptual Learning', *Annual Review of Psychology*, 49: 585–612.
Gombrich, E. H. (2002), *Art and Illusion: A Study in the Psychology of Pictorial Representation* (6th edn., London: Phaidon Press Ltd).
Goodman, N. (1976), *Languages of Art* (Indianapolis: Hackett Publishing Company, Inc.).
Gray, K., Knobe, J., Sheskin, M., Bloom, P., Barrett, L., and Judd, C. M. (2011), 'More Than a Body: Mind Perception and the Nature of Objectification', *Journal of Personality and Social Psychology*, 101/6: 1207–20.
Greco, J. (2000), *Putting Skeptics in Their Place: The Nature of Skeptical Arguments and Their Role in Philosophical Inquiry* (New York: Cambridge University Press).
Green, M. (2010), 'Perceiving Emotions', *Proceedings of the Aristotelian Society*, suppl. vol. 84: 45–62.
Greene, G. (1971), *The Heart of the Matter* (Harmondsworth: Penguin).
Gregory, D. (2010), 'Imagery, the Imagination and Experience', *Philosophical Quarterly*, 60/241: 735–53.
Gregory, R. L. (1970), *The Intelligent Eye* (London: Weidenfeld & Nicolson).
Griffin, J. (1986), *Well-Being: Its Meaning, Measurement and Moral Importance* (Oxford: Oxford University Press).
Hampshire, S. (1967), 'Logic and Appreciation', in W. Elton (ed.), *Aesthetics and Language* (Oxford: Oxford University Press), 161–9.
Hansen, T., Olkonnen, M., Walter, S., and Gegenfurtner, K. R. (2006), 'Memory Modulates Color Appearance', *Nature Neuroscience*, 9: 1367–8.
Hanson, N. R. (1958), *Patterns of Discovery* (Cambridge: Cambridge University Press).
Hanson, N. R. (1969), *Perception and Discovery: An Introduction to Scientific Inquiry* (San Francisco: Freeman and Cooper).
Harcourt, E., and Thomas, A. (2013), 'Thick Concepts, Analysis and Reduction', in S. Kirchin (ed.), *Thick Concepts* (Oxford: Oxford University Press), 20–43.
Hare, R. M. (1965), *Freedom and Reason* (Oxford: Oxford University Press).
Hare, R. M. (1971), 'The Argument from Received Opinion', in Hare, *Essays on Philosophical Method* (London: Macmillan), 117–35.
Hare, R. M. (1981), *Moral Thinking: Its Levels, Method and Point* (Oxford: Clarendon Press).
Harman, G. (1977), *The Nature of Morality* (Oxford: Oxford University Press).
Haslam, N. (2006), 'Dehumanization: An Integrative Review', *Personality and Social Psychology Review*, 10/3: 252–64.
Haslam, N., and Loughman, S. (2014), 'Dehumanization and Infrahumanization', *Annual Review of Psychology*, 65: 399–423.
Haslanger, S. (2012), *Resisting Reality: Social Construction and Social Critique*, Oxford: Oxford University Press.
Hawkins, J. (2008), 'Desiring the Bad under the Guise of the Good', *Philosophical Quarterly*, 58/231: 244–64.
Hawley, K., and Macpherson, F. (2011) (eds.), *The Admissible Contents of Experience* (Malden, MA: Wiley-Blackwell).

Heflick, N. (2011), 'From Women to Objects: Appearance Focus, Target Gender, and Perceptions of Warmth, Morality and Competence', *Journal of Experimental Social Psychology*, 47: 572–81.
Heflick, N., and Goldenburg, J. (2009), 'Objectifying Sarah Palin: Evidence that Objectification Causes Women to be Perceived as Less Competent and Less Fully Human', *Journal of Experimental Social Psychology*, 45: 598–601.
Heflick, N., and Goldenburg, J. (2014), 'Seeing Eye to Body: The Literal Objectification of Women', *Current Directions in Psychological Science*, 23/3: 225–9.
Hemingway, E. (1972), *To Have and Have Not* (London: Grafton).
Hemingway, E. (1976), *For Whom The Bell Tolls* (London: Grafton).
Hill, C. (2009), *Consciousness* (Cambridge: Cambridge University Press).
Hills, A. (2009), 'Moral Testimony and Moral Epistemology', *Ethics*, 120/1: 94–127.
Hintikka, J. (1963), 'Distributive Normal Forms in First-Order Logic', in J. N. Crossley and M. A. E. Dummett (eds.), *Formal Systems and Recursive Functions* (Proceedings of the Eighth Logic Colloquium) (Amsterdam: North-Holland), 47–90.
Hohwy, J. (2013), *The Predictive Mind* (Oxford: Oxford University Press).
Hopkins, R. (1998), *Picture, Image and Experience: A Philosophical Inquiry* (Cambridge: Cambridge University Press).
Hopkins, R. (2003), 'What Makes Representational Painting Truly Visual?', *Proceedings of the Aristotelian Society*, suppl. vol. 77/1: 149–67.
Hopkins, R. (2006), 'Critical Reasoning and Critical Perception', in D. Lopes and M. Kieran (eds.), *Knowing Art* (The Hague: Springer), 137–53.
Hopkins, R. (2011), 'How to Be a Pessimist About Aesthetic Testimony', *Journal of Philosophy*, 108/3: 138–57.
Horgan, T., and Tienson, J. (2002), 'The Intentionality of Phenomenology and the Phenomenology of Intentionality', in D. J. Chalmers (ed.), *Philosophy of Mind: Classical and Contemporary Readings* (Oxford: Oxford University Press), 520–32.
Horgan, T., and Timmons, M. (2008), 'What Does Moral Phenomenology Tell Us about Moral Objectivity?', *Social Philosophy and Policy*, 25: 267–300.
Huang, Y., and Rao, R. P. (2011), 'Predictive Coding', *Wiley Interdisciplinary Reviews: Cognitive Science*, 2/5: 580–93.
Huemer, M. (2001), *Skepticism and the Veil of Perception* (Lanham, MD: Rowman and Littlefield).
Huemer, M. (2005), *Ethical Intuitionism* (Basingstoke: Palgrave Macmillan).
Huemer, M. (2007), 'Compassionate Phenomenal Conservatism', *Philosophy and Phenomenological Research*, 74/1: 30–55.
Huemer, M. (2013), 'Phenomenal Conservatism Uber Alles', in C. Tucker (ed.), *Seemings and Justification* (Oxford: Oxford University Press), 328–50.
Huemer, M. (2016), 'Inferential Appearances', in B. Coppenger and M. Bergmann (eds.), *Intellectual Assurance: Essays on Traditional Epistemic Internalism* (Oxford: Oxford University Press), 144–60.
Hume, D. (1739/1975), *A Treatise of Human Nature*, (1739), with introduction and analytic index by L. A. Selby Bigge, 2nd edn. with text revised and notes by P. N. Nidditch (Oxford: Oxford University Press, 1975).
Hume, D. (1740/2000), *A Treatise of Human Nature* (1740), ed. Norton and Norton (Oxford: Oxford University Press, 2000).
Hume, D. (1748/1975), *Enquiries* (1748), ed. L. A. Selby-Bigge and P. H. Nidditch (Oxford: Clarendon Press, 1975).
Hume, D. (1757/1874–5), 'Of the Standard of Taste' (1757), in *The Philosophical Works of David Hume*, ed. T. H. Green and T. H. Grose (London: Longman, Green, 1874–5), vol. 1.

Hurley, S. (1989), *Natural Reasons: Personality and Polity* (Oxford: Oxford University Press).
Hutcheson, F. (1728/1991), *An Essay on the Nature and Conduct of the Passions and Affections: With Illustrations on the Moral Sense* (1728), in D. D. Raphael (ed.), *British Moralists 1650-1800* (Indianapolis: Hackett Publishing, 1991), 300-21.
Hyman, J. (2006), *The Objective Eye: Color, Form and Reality in the Theory of Art* (Chicago: University of Chicago Press).
Isenberg, A. (1967), 'Critical Communication', in W. Elton (ed.), *Aesthetics and Language* (Oxford: Oxford University Press), 131-46.
Johnston, M. (2001), 'The Authority of Affect', *Philosophy and Phenomenological Research*, 61/1: 181-214.
Johnston, M. (2011), 'On a Neglected Epistemic Virtue', *Philosophical Issues*, 21/1: 165-218.
Kagan, S. (1989), *The Limits of Morality* (Oxford: Oxford University Press).
Kagan, S. (2001), 'Thinking About Cases', *Social Philosophy and Policy*, 18/2: 44-63.
Kahneman, D. (2011), *Thinking, Fast and Slow* (New York: Farrar, Straus and Giroux).
Katsafanas, P. (2013), *Agency and the Foundations of Ethics: Nietzschean Constitutivism* (Oxford: Oxford University Press).
Katsafanas, P. (forthcoming), 'Nietzsche and Murdoch on the Moral Significance of Perceptual Experience', *European Journal of Philosophy*.
Kauppinen, A. (2013), 'Review of Robert Audi's Moral Perception', *Notre Dame Philosophical Reviews 2013.06.29* (https://ndpr.nd.edu/news/40724-moral-perception/).
Kelly, S. (2010), 'The Normative Nature of Perceptual Experience', in B. Nanay (ed.), *Perceiving the World* (Oxford: Oxford University Press), 146-59.
Kelly, T., and McGrath, S. (2010), 'Is Reflective Equilibrium Enough?', *Philosophical Perspectives* 24: 325-59.
Kim, J. (2005), *Physicalism, or Something Near Enough* (Princeton: Princeton University Press).
Kivy, P. (1975), 'What Makes "Aesthetic" Terms Aesthetic?', *Philosophy and Phenomenological Research*, 36: 197-211.
Kornblith, H. (1982), 'The Psychological Turn', *Australasian Journal of Philosophy*, 60/3: 238-53.
Korsgaard, C. (1983), 'Two Distinctions in Goodness', *Philosophical Review*, 92/2: 169-95.
Korsgaard, C. (1986), 'Skepticism about Practical Reason', *Journal of Philosophy*, 83/1: 5-25.
Kriegel, U. (2009), *Subjective Consciousness* (Oxford: Oxford University Press).
Kuhn, T. (1962), *The Structure of Scientific Revolutions* (Chicago: University of Chicago Press).
Kulvicki, J. (2009), 'Heavenly Sight and the Nature of Seeing-In', *Journal of Aesthetics and Art Criticism*, 67: 387-97.
Kvart, I. (1993), 'Seeing That and Seeing As', *Noûs*, 27/3: 279-302.
Langton, R. (1993), 'Beyond a Pragmatic Critique of Reason', *Australasian Journal of Philosophy*, 71/4: 365-84.
Langton, R. (2009), *Sexual Solipsism: Philosophical Essays on Pornography and Objectification* (Oxford: Oxford University Press).
Lemos, N. (2005), 'The Bearers of Intrinsic Value', in T. Rønnow-Rasmussen and M. J. Zimmerman (eds.), *Recent Work on Intrinsic Value* (Dordrecht: Springer), 181-90.
Lenman, J. (1994), 'Beliefs about Other Minds: A Pragmatic Justification', *American Philosophical Quarterly*, 31: 223-34.
Lenman, J. (2007), 'What is Moral Inquiry?', *Proceedings of the Aristotelian Society*, suppl. vol. 81: 63-81.
Lenman, J. (2009a), 'Naturalism without Tears', *Ratio* 22: 1-18.
Lenman, J. (2009b), 'The Politics of the Self: Stability, Normativity and the Lives We Can Live with Living', in L. Bortolotti (ed.), *Philosophy and Happiness* (Houndmills: Palgrave Macmillan), 183-99.

Lenman, J. (2010), 'Humean Constructivism in Moral Theory', in R. Shafer-Landau (ed.), *Oxford Studies in Metaethics*, vol. 5 (Oxford: Oxford University Press), 175–93.
Lenman, J. (2011), 'Pleasure, Desire and Practical Reason', *Ethical Theory and Moral Practice*, 14: 143–9.
Lenman, J. (2013), 'Science, Ethics and Observation', in H. Carel and D. Meacham (eds.), *Royal Institute of Philosophy Supplement*, 72. *Phenomenology and Naturalism* (Cambridge: Cambridge University Press), 261–74.
Lenman, J. (2015a), 'Moral Inquiry and Mob Psychology', in C. Daly (ed.), *The Palgrave Handbook of Philosophical Methods* (Houndmills: Palgrave MacMillan), 637–51.
Lenman, J. (2015b), 'Scepticism about Intuition', in S. G. Chappell (ed.), *Intuition, Theory and Anti-Theory in Ethics* (Oxford: Oxford University Press), 24–39.
Le Poidevin, R. (2007), *The Images of Time: An Essay on Temporal Representation* (Oxford: Oxford University Press).
Leslie, A. (2005), 'Developmental Parallels in Understanding Minds and Bodies', *Trends in Cognitive Sciences*, 9: 459–62.
Levinson, J. (1984), 'Aesthetic Supervenience', *Southern Journal of Philosophy*, 22: 93–110.
Levinson, J. (1994), 'Being Realistic About Aesthetic Properties', *Journal of Aesthetics and Art Criticism*, 52: 351–4.
Lewis, D. (1979), 'Attitudes *De Dicto* and *De Se*', *Philosophical Review*, 88: 513–43.
Lewis, D. (1988), 'Desire as Belief', *Mind*, 97/418: 323–32.
Lewis, D. (1989), 'Dispositional Theories of Value', *Proceedings of the Aristotelian Society*, 63: 113–37.
Lewis, D. (1996a), 'Desire as Belief II', *Mind*, 105/418: 303–13.
Lewis, D. (1996b/1999), 'Elusive Knowledge', *Australasian Journal of Philosophy*, 74 (1996): 549–67, repr. in Lewis *Papers in Metaphysics and Epistemology* (Cambridge: Cambridge University Press, 1999).
Livingston, P. (2003), 'On an Apparent Truism in Aesthetics', *British Society of Aesthetics*, 43/3: 260–78.
Loar, B. (2003), 'Phenomenal Intentionality as the Basis of Mental Content', in M. Hahn and B. Ramberg (eds.), *Reflections and Replies: Essays on Tyler Burge* (Cambridge, MA: MIT Press), 229–58.
Logue, H. (2013), 'Visual Experience of Natural Kind Properties: Is There Any Fact of the Matter?', *Philosophical Studies*, 162: 1–12.
Logue, H. (2014), 'Disjunctivism', in M. Matthen (ed.), *Oxford Handbook of the Philosophy of Perception* (Oxford: Oxford University Press), 198–216.
Lopes, D. (1996), *Understanding Pictures* (Oxford: Oxford University Press).
Lopes, D. (2005), *Sight and Sensibility: Evaluating Pictures* (Oxford: Oxford University Press).
Loughnan, S., Haslam, N., Murnane, T., Vaes, J., Reynolds, C., and Suitner, C. (2010), 'Objectification Leads to Depersonalization: The Denial of Mind and Moral Concern to Objectified Others', *European Journal of Social Psychology*, 40: 709–17.
Lovibond, S. (2009), *Ethical Formation* (Oxford: Oxford University Press).
Lyons, J. (2005a), 'Perceptual Belief and Nonexperiential Looks', *Philosophical Perspectives*, 19: 237–56.
Lyons, J. (2005b), 'Clades, Capgras, and Perceptual Kinds', *Philosophical Topics*, 33: 185–206.
Lyons, J. (2009), *Perception and Basic Beliefs: Zombies, Modules, and the Problem of the External World* (New York: Oxford University Press).
Lyons, J. (2011), 'Circularity, Reliability, and the Cognitive Penetrability of Perception', *Philosophical Issues*, 21: 289–311.
Lyons, J. (2014), 'The Epistemological Import of Morphological Content', *Philosophical Studies*, 169: 537–47.

Lyons, J. (2015a), 'Critical Notice: *Seemings and Justification*, ed. Chris Tucker', *Analysis*, 75: 153–64.
Lyons, J. (2015b), 'Unencapsulated Modules and Perceptual Judgment', in A. Raftopoulos and J. Zeimbekis (eds.), *Cognitive Penetrability* (Oxford: Oxford University Press), 103–22.
Lyons, J. (2016), 'Inferentialism and Cognitive Penetration of Perception', *Episteme*, 13: 1–28.
McBrayer, J. P. (2010a), 'A Limited Defense of Moral Perception', *Philosophical Studies*, 149: 305–20.
McBrayer, J. (2010b), 'Moral Perception and the Causal Objection', *Ratio*, 23/3: 291–307.
McDowell, J. (1979), 'Virtue and Reason', *The Monist*, 62: 331–50.
McDowell, J. (1982), 'Criteria, Defeasibility, and Knowledge', *Proceedings of the British Academy*, 68: 455–79.
McDowell, J. (1985/1998), 'Values and Secondary Qualities', in T. Honderich (ed.), *Morality and Objectivity* (London: Routledge and Kegan Paul, 1985), 110–29; repr. in McDowell, *Mind, Value, and Reality* (Cambridge, MA: Harvard University Press, 1998), 131–50.
McDowell, J. (1987/1998), 'Projection and Truth in Ethics' (1987), repr. in McDowell *Mind, Value, and Reality* (Cambridge, MA: Harvard University Press, 1998), 151–66.
McDowell, J. (1996), *Mind and World* (Cambridge, MA: Harvard University Press).
McDowell, J. (1998), *Mind, Value and Reality* (Cambridge, MA: Harvard University Press).
McDowell, J. (2009), 'Avoiding the Myth of the Given', in McDowell, *Having the World in View* (Cambridge, MA: Harvard University Press), 256–72.
McGinn, C. (1983), *The Subjective View* (Oxford: Oxford University Press).
McGinn, C. (2004), *Mindsight: Image, Dream, Meaning* (Cambridge, MA: Harvard University Press).
McGrath, M. (2013), 'Phenomenal Conservatism and Cognitive Penetration: The Bad Basis Counterexamples', in C. Tucker (ed.), *Seemings and Justification* (Oxford: Oxford University Press), 225–47.
McGrath, S. (2004), 'Moral Knowledge by Perception', *Philosophical Perspectives*, 18: 209–28.
McGrath, S. (2011), 'Moral Knowledge and Experience', in R. Shafer-Landau, *Oxford Studies in Metaethics*, vol. 6 (New York: Oxford University Press), 107–27.
McGrath, S. (unpublished), 'Moral Knowledge' (MS).
Mackie, J. L. (1977), *Ethics: Inventing Right and Wrong* (London: Penguin Books).
MacKinnon, C. A. (1987), *Feminism Unmodified: Discourses on Life and Law* (Cambridge, MA: Harvard University Press).
MacKinnon, C. A. (1989a), 'Sexuality, Pornography, and Method: Pleasure under Patriarchy', *Ethics*, 99/2: 314–46.
MacKinnon, C. A. (1989b), *Towards a Feminist Theory of the State* (Cambridge, MA: Harvard University Press).
McNaughton, D. (1988), *Moral Vision* (Oxford: Blackwell).
MacNell, L., Driscoll, A., and Hunt, A. N. (2015), 'What's in a Name: Exposing Gender Bias in Student Ratings of Teaching', *Innovative Higher Education*, 40/4: 291–303.
Macpherson, F. (2006), 'Ambiguous Figures and the Content of Experience', *Noûs*, 40: 82–117.
Macpherson, F. (2012), 'Cognitive Penetration of Colour Experience: Rethinking the Issue in Light of an Indirect Mechanism', *Philosophy and Phenomenological Research*, 84/1: 24–62.
Mandelbaum, Maurice (1955), *The Phenomenology of Moral Experience* (Glencoe, IL: The Free Press).
Markie, P. (2006), 'Epistemically Appropriate Perceptual Belief', *Noûs*, 40: 118–42.
Martin, J. R., and Dokic, J. (2013), 'Seeing Absence or Absence of Seeing?', *Thought: A Journal of Philosophy*, 2/2: 117–25.
Martin, M. G. F. (2004), 'The Limits of Self-Awareness', *Philosophical Studies*, 120: 37–89.

Martin, M. G. F. (2006), 'On Being Alienated', in T. Szabo Gendler and J. Hawthorne (eds.), *Perceptual Experience* (Oxford: Oxford University Press), 354–410.
Martin, M. G. F. (2010), 'What's in a Look?', in B. Nanay (ed.), *Perceiving the World* (Oxford: Oxford University Press), 160–225.
Masrour, F. (2011), 'Is Perceptual Phenomenology Thin?', *Philosophy and Phenomenological Research*, 83/2: 366–97.
Mathur, V. A., Richeson, J. A., Paice, J. A., Muzyka, M., and Chiao, J. Y. (2014), 'Racial Bias in Pain Perception and Response: Experimental Examination of Automatic and Deliberate Processes', *Journal of Pain: Official Journal of the American Pain Society*, 15/5: 476–84.
Mill, J. S. (1861/1998), *Utilitarianism* (Oxford: Oxford University Press).
Millar, A. (1991), *Reasons and Experience* (Oxford: Oxford University Press).
Millar, A. (2000), 'The Scope of Perceptual Knowledge', *Philosophy*, 75/291: 73–88.
Millar, A. (2011), 'How Visual Perception Yields Reasons for Belief', *Philosophical Issues*, 21: 332–51.
Millar, B. (2013), 'Colour Constancy and Fregean Representationalism', *Philosophical Studies*, 164: 219–31.
Millgram, E. (2005), 'Murdoch, Practical Reasoning and Particularism', in Millgram, *Ethics Done Right: Practical Reasoning as a Foundation for Moral Theory* (Cambridge, Cambridge University Press), 168–97.
Milona, M. (2016), 'Taking the Perceptual Analogy Seriously', *Ethical Theory and Moral Practice*.19/4: 897–901.
Milona, M. (2017), 'Intellect vs. Affect: Finding Leverage in an Old Debate', *Philosophical Studies* 174/9: 2251–76.
Mole, C. (2015), 'Attention and Cognitive Penetration', in A. Raftopoulos and J. Zeimbekis (eds.), *Cognitive Penetrability* (Oxford: Oxford University Press), 218–36.
Moore, A. W. (1997), *Points of View* (Oxford: Oxford University Press).
Moore, G. E. (1903), *Principia Ethica* (Cambridge: Cambridge University Press).
Moores, E., Laiti, L., and Chelazzi, L. (2003), 'Associative Knowledge Controls Deployment of Visual Selective Attention', *Nature Neuroscience*, 6: 182–9.
Moss, J. (2012), *Aristotle on the Apparent Good: Perception,* Phantasia, *Thought, and Desire* (New York: Oxford University Press).
Mothersill, M. (1984), *Beauty Restored* (Oxford: Oxford University Press).
Murdoch, I. (1956), 'Vision and Choice in Morality', *Proceedings of the Aristotelian Society*, suppl. vol. 30: 32–58.
Murdoch, I. (1970), *Sovereignty of Good* (London: Routledge).
Murdoch, I. (1997), *Existentialists and Mystics: Writings on Philosophy and Literature*, ed. Peter Conradi (New York: Penguin).
Nagel, T. (1986), *The View From Nowhere* (Oxford, Oxford University Press).
Nagel, T. (1999), *The Last Word* (New York: Oxford University Press).
Nanay, B. (2010), 'Perception and Imagination: Amodal Perception as Mental Imagery', *Philosophical Studies*, 150: 239–54.
Nanay, B. (2011), 'Do We See Apples as Edible?', *Pacific Philosophical Quarterly*, 92: 305–22.
Nanay, B. (2012), 'Action-Oriented Perception', *European Journal of Philosophy*, 20: 430–46.
Newall, M. (2011), *What Is a Picture?* (New York: Palgrave Macmillan).
Newall, M. (2015), 'Is Seeing-In a Transparency Effect?', *British Journal of Aesthetics*, 55/2: 131–56.
Nichols, S. (2004), *Sentimental Rules; On the Natural Foundations of Moral Judgment* (New York: Oxford University Press).
Noë, A. (2009), 'Conscious Reference', *Philosophical Quarterly*, 59/236: 470–82.

Noordhof, P. (1997), 'Making the Change: The Functionalist's Way', *British Journal for the Philosophy of Science*, 48: 233-50.
Noordhof, P. (1999), 'Moral Requirements Are Still Not Rational Requirements', *Analysis*, 59/3: 127-36.
Noordhof, P. (2008), 'Expressive Perception as Projective Imagining', *Mind and Language*, 23/3: 329-58.
Noordhof, P. (forthcoming), 'Imaginative Content', in Fabian Dorsch and Fiona Macpherson (eds.), *Perceptual Memory and Perceptual Imagination* (Oxford, Oxford University Press).
Nussbaum, M. (1995), 'Objectification', *Philosophy and Public Affairs*, 24/4: 249-91.
Nussbaum, M. C. (2001), *Upheavals of Thought: The Intelligence of Emotions* (Cambridge: Cambridge University Press).
Oddie, G. (1986), *Likeness to Truth* (Dordrecht: Reidel).
Oddie, G. (1991), 'Supervenience, Goodness, and Higher-Order Universals', *Australasian Journal of Philosophy*, 69/1: 20-4.
Oddie, G. (1994), Harmony, Purity, Truth', *Mind*, 103/412: 451-72.
Oddie, G. (2001), 'Hume, the BAD Paradox, and Value Realism', *Philo*, 4/2: 109-22.
Oddie, G. (2005), *Value, Reality, and Desire* (Oxford: Clarendon Press).
Oddie, G. (2015), 'Value and Desires', in I. Hirose and J. Olson (eds.), *The Oxford Handbook of Value Theory* (Oxford: Oxford University Press), 60-79.
Oddie, Graham (2016), 'Fitting Attitudes, Finkish Goods, and Value Appearances', in R. Shafer-Landau (ed.), *Oxford Studies in Metaethics*, vol. 11 (Oxford: Oxford University Press), 74-101.
Olkkonen, M., Hansen, T., and Gegenfurtner, K. R. (2008), 'Colour Appearance of Familiar Objects: Effects of Object Shape, Texture and Illumination Changes', *Journal of Vision*, 8: 1-16.
Olson, J. (2003), 'Revisiting the Tropic of Value: Reply to Rabinowicz and Rønnow-Rasmussen', *Philosophy and Phenomenological Research*, 67/2: 412-22.
O'Shaughnessy, B. (2000), *Consciousness and the World* (Oxford: Oxford University Press).
Papadaki, L. (2010), 'What Is Objectification?', *Journal of Moral Philosophy*, 7: 16-36.
Parfit, D. (2011), *On What Matters*, vols. 1 and 2 (Oxford: Oxford University Press).
Pascal, B. (1670/1974), *Pensées* (Paris: Mercure de France).
Payne, B. K. (2001), 'Prejudice and Perception: The Role of Automatic and Controlled Processes in Misperceiving a Weapon', *Journal of Personality and Social Psychology*, 81: 181-92.
Peacocke, C. (1983), *Sense and Content: Experience, Thought, and Their Relation* (Oxford: Oxford University Press).
Peacocke, C. (1987), 'Depiction', *Philosophical Review*, 96: 383-410.
Pelser, A. C. (2014), 'Emotion, Evaluative Perception, and Epistemic Justification', in S. Roeser and C. Todd (eds.), *Emotion and Value* (Oxford: Oxford University Press), 107-23.
Perruchet, P., and Pacton, S. (2006), 'Implicit Learning and Statistical Learning: One Phenomenon, Two Approaches', *Trends in Cognitive Sciences*, 10/5: 233-8.
Pettersson, M. (2011), 'Seeing What Is Not There: Pictorial Experience, Imagination, and Non-localization', *British Journal of Aesthetics*, 51/3: 279-94.
Pettit, P., and Smith, M. (1990), 'Backgrounding Desire', *Philosophical Review*, 99: 565-92.
Pollock, J. L. (1986), *Contemporary Theories of Knowledge* (Savage, MD: Rowman & Littlefield).
Pollock, J. L., and Cruz, J. (1999), *Contemporary Theories of Knowledge* (Lanham, MD: Rowman and Littlefield).
Posner, R. (1999), *The Problematics of Moral and Legal Theory* (Cambridge, MA: Harvard University Press).

Price, R. (2009), 'Aspect-Switching and Visual Phenomenal Character', *Philosophical Quarterly*, 59: 516.
Prinz, J. J. (2006), 'Is the Mind Really Modular?', in Robert J. Stainton (ed.), *Contemporary Debates in Cognitive Science* (Malden, MA: Blackwell), 22–36.
Prinz, J. J. (2007), 'Can Moral Obligations Be Empirically Discovered?', *Midwest Studies in Philosophy*, 31: 271–91.
Prinz, J. J. (2008), *The Emotional Construction of Morals* (New York: Oxford University Press).
Pryor, J. (2000), 'The Skeptic and the Dogmatist', *Noûs*, 34/4: 517–49.
Pryor, J. (2005), 'There is Immediate Justification', in M. Steup and E. Sosa (eds.), *Contemporary Debates in Epistemology* (Oxford: Blackwell), 181–202.
Pylyshyn, Z. (2003), *Seeing and Visualizing: It's Not What You Think* (Cambridge, MA: MIT Press).
Quinn, W. (1993), 'Putting Rationality in Its Place', in R. Frey and C. Morris, *Value, Welfare, and Morality* (Cambridge: Cambridge University Press, 1993), 26–50; repr. in Quinn, *Morality and Action* (Cambridge: Cambridge University Press, 1993), 228–55.
Rabinowicz, W., and Rønnow-Rasmussen, T. (2000), 'A Distinction in Value: Intrinsic and For Its Own Sake', *Proceedings of the Aristotelian Society*, 100/1: 33–51.
Rabinowicz, W., and Rønnow-Rasmussen, T. (2005), 'Tropic of Value', *Philosophy and Phenomenological Research*, 66: 389–403.
Raftopoulos, A., and Zeimbekis, J. (2015) (eds.), *Cognitive Penetrability* (Oxford: Oxford University Press).
Read, R., and Hutchinson, P. (2008), 'Toward a Perspicuous Presentation of "Perspicuous Presentation"', *Philosophical Investigations*, 31/2: 141–60.
Reb, J., Greguras, G., Luan, S., and Daniels, M. A. (2013), 'Performance Appraisals as Heuristic Judgments under Uncertainty', in S. Highhouse, R. S. Dalal, and E. Salas (eds.), *Judgment and Decision Making at Work* (New York: Routledge), 13–36.
Reichenbach, H. (1938), *Experience and Prediction* (Chicago: University of Chicago Press).
Reiland, I. (2014), 'On Experiencing High-Level Properties', *American Philosophical Quarterly*, 51/3: 177–87.
Reiland, I. (2015), 'Experience, Seemings, and Evidence', *Pacific Philosophical Quarterly*, 96/4: 510–53.
Richardson, L. (2009), 'Seeing Empty Space', *European Journal of Philosophy*, 18/2: 227–43.
Roberts, D. (2013), 'It's Evaluation, Only Thicker', in S. Kirchin (ed.), *Thick Concepts* (Oxford, Oxford University Press), 78–96.
Roberts, R. C. (2003), *Emotions: An Essay in Aid of Moral Psychology* (Cambridge: Cambridge University Press).
Roberts, R. C. (2013), *Emotions in the Moral Life* (New York: Cambridge University Press).
Rock, I. (1983), *The Logic of Perception* (Cambridge, MA: MIT Press).
Ross, W. D. (1930), *The Right and the Good* (Oxford: Oxford University Press).
Roth, P. (2007), *Everyman* (New York: Vintage).
Rudman, L., and Mescher, K. (2012), 'Of Animals and Objects', *Personality and Social Psychology Bulletin*, 38/6: 734–46.
Saffran, J. R., Aslin, R. N., and Newport, E. L. (1996a), 'Statistical Learning by 8-Month-Old Infants', *Science*, NS 274/5294: 1926–8.
Saffran, J. R., Aslin, R. N., and Newport, E. L. (1996b), 'Word Segmentation: The Role of Distributional Cues', *Journal of Memory and Language*, 35: 606–21.
Sainsbury, R. M. (1996), 'Crispin Wright: Truth and Objectivity', *Philosophy and Phenomenological Research*, 56/4: 899–904.
Salmela, M. (2011), 'Can Emotion be Modelled on Perception?', *dialectica*, 65/1: 1–29.

Scheffler, S. (1982), 'Ethics, Personal Identity and Ideals of the Person', *Canadian Journal of Philosophy*, 12/2: 229–46.
Schellenberg, S. (2013), 'Experience and Evidence', *Mind*, 122: 699–747.
Schier, F. (1986), *Deeper Into Pictures: An Essay on Pictorial Representation* (Cambridge: Cambridge University Press).
Schnall, S., Haidt, J., Clore, G., and Jordan, A. (2008), 'Disgust as Embodied Moral Judgment', *Personality & Social Psychology Bulletin*, 34: 1096–109.
Schwitzgebel, E. (2006), 'Do Things Look Flat?', *Philosophy and Phenomenological Research*, 72/3 (2006), 589–99.
Scriven, M. (1966), *Primary Philosophy* (New York: McGraw Hill).
Seth, A. K., Suzuki, Keisuke, and Critchley, Hugo D. (2011), 'An Interoceptive Predictive Coding Model of Conscious Presence', *Frontiers in Psychology*, 2: 395.
Setiya, K. (2012), *Knowing Right From Wrong* (Oxford: Oxford University Press).
Setiya, K. (2013), 'Murdoch on the Sovereignty of Good', *Philosopher's Imprint*, 13/9: 1–21.
Shafer-Landau, R. (2003), *Moral Realism* (Oxford: Oxford University Press).
Shefrin, H. (2007), 'Behavioral Finance: Biases, Mean-Variance Returns, and Risk Premiums', *CFA Institute Publications*, 24/2: 4–12.
Sherman, N. (1989), *The Fabric of Character: Aristotle's Theory of Virtue* (Oxford: Oxford University Press).
Shoemaker, S. (1980), 'Causality and Properties', in Peter Van Inwagen (ed.), *Time and Change* (Dordrecht: D. Reidel Publishing Co.), 109–35.
Shoemaker, S. (1984/2003), *Identity, Cause and Mind* (Cambridge: Cambridge University Press, 1984); repr. and extended in Shoemaker, *Identity, Cause and Mind* (Oxford, Oxford University Press, 2003).
Shoemaker, S. (1994), 'Self-Knowledge and "Inner Sense"-Lecture III: The Phenomenal Character of Experience', *Philosophy and Phenomenological Research*, 54: 291–314.
Sibley, F. (1959/2001), 'Aesthetic Concepts', *Philosophical Review*, 68 (1959): 421–50; repr. in Sibley, *Approach to Aesthetics: Collected Papers on Philosophical Aesthetics by Frank Sibley*, ed. J. Benson, B. Redfern, and J. Roxbee Cox (Oxford: Clarendon Press, 2001), 1–23.
Sibley, F. (1965/2001), 'Aesthetic and the Non-Aesthetic', *Philosophical Review*, 74 (1965): 135–59; repr. in Sibley, *Approach to Aesthetics: Collected Papers on Philosophical Aesthetics by Frank Sibley*, ed. J. Benson, B. Redfern, and J. Roxbee Cox (Oxford: Clarendon Press, 2001), 33–51.
Sibley, F. N. (1983/2001), 'General Criteria and Reasons in Aesthetics', in J. Fisher (ed.), *Essays on Aesthetics: Perspectives on the Work on Monroe C. Beardsley* (Philadelphia: Temple University Press, 1983), 3–20; repr. in, Sibley, *Approach to Aesthetics: Collected Papers on Philosophical Aesthetics by Frank Sibley*, ed. J. Benson, B. Redfern, and J. Roxbee Cox (Oxford: Clarendon Press, 2001), 104–18.
Sibley, F. N. (2001), 'Particularity, Art, and Evaluation', in Sibley, *Approach to Aesthetics: Collected Papers on Philosophical Aesthetics by Frank Sibley*, ed. J. Benson, B. Redfern, and J. Roxbee Cox (Oxford: Clarendon Press, 2001), 88–103.
Sibley, F., and Tanner, M. (1968), 'Symposium Objectivity and Aesthetics', *Proceedings of the Aristotelian Society*, suppl. vol. 42: 31–72.
Siegel, M. H. (2014), 'Review: Robert Audi, *Moral Perception*', *Ratio*, ns 57: 238–44.
Siegel, S. (2006), 'Which Properties Are Represented in Perception?', in T. S. Gendler and J. Hawthorne (ed.), *Perceptual Experience* (Oxford: Oxford University Press), 481–503.
Siegel, S. (2009), 'The Visual Experience of Causation', *Philosophical Quarterly*, 59: 519–40.
Siegel, S. (2010a), *The Contents of Visual Experience* (Oxford: Oxford University Press).
Siegel, S. (2010b), 'The Contents of Perception', *The Stanford Encyclopedia of Philosophy*, http://plato.stanford.edu/archives/win2014/entries/perception-contents/.

Siegel, S. (2012), 'Cognitive Penetrability and Perceptual Justification', Noûs, 46/2: 201–22.
Siegel, S. (2013), 'The Epistemic Impact of the Etiology of Belief', Philosophical Studies, 162: 697–722.
Siegel, S. (2014), 'Affordances and the Contents of Perception', in B. Brogaard (ed.), Does Perception Have Content? (Oxford: Oxford University Press), 51–75.
Siewert, C. (1998), The Significance of Consciousness (Princeton: Princeton University Press).
Siewert C. (2012), 'Respecting Appearances', in D. Zahavi, The Oxford Handbook of Contemporary Phenomenology (Oxford: Oxford University Press).
Silins, N. (2013), 'The Significance of High Level Content', Philosophical Studies, 162: 13–33.
Singer, P. (2005), 'Ethics and Intuitions', Journal of Ethics, 9: 331–52.
Solomon, M. (2015), Making Medical Knowledge (Oxford: Oxford University Press).
Sorensen, R. (2008), Seeing Dark Things: The Philosophy of Shadows (Oxford: Oxford University Press).
Sosa, E. (1999), 'How to Defeat Opposition to Moore', Philosophical Perspectives, 13: 137–49.
Sosa, E. (2007), Virtue Epistemology (New York: Oxford University Press).
Sosa, E. (2015), Judgment and Agency (Oxford: Oxford University Press).
Smith, M. (1988), 'Reason and Desire', Proceedings of the Aristotelian Society, 88: 243–58.
Smith, M. (1994), The Moral Problem (Malden, MA: Blackwell).
Smithies, S. (2011), 'Attention is Rational-Access Consciousness', in C. Mole, D. Smithies, and W. Wu (eds.), Attention (Oxford: Oxford University Press), 247–73.
Stampe, D. (1987), 'The Authority of Desire', Philosophical Review 96/3: 335–81.
Stanovich, K., and West, R. (2000), 'Individual Differences in Reasoning: Implications for the Rationality Debate', Behavioral and Brain Sciences, 39: 645–726.
Stephens, G. L., and Graham, G. (2000), When Self-Consciousness Breaks: Alien Voices and Inserted Thoughts (Cambridge, MA: MIT Press).
Stock, K. (2015), 'Sexual Objectification', Analysis 75/2: 191–5.
Stokes, D. (2012), 'Perceiving and Desiring: A New Look at the Cognitive Penetrability of Experience', Philosophical Studies, 158: 479–92.
Stokes, D. (2013), 'The Cognitive Penetrability of Perception', Philosophy Compass, 8: 646–63.
Stokes, D. (2014), 'Cognitive Penetration and the Perception of Art', dialectica, 68: 1–34.
Stokes, D. (2015), 'Towards a Consequentialist Understanding of Cognitive Penetration', in A. Raftopoulos and J. Zeimbekis (eds.), The Cognitive Penetrability of Perception (Oxford: Oxford University Press), 76–99.
Stokes, D. (forthcoming), 'Attention and the Cognitive Penetrability of Perception', Australasian Journal of Philosophy, 1–16.
Stokes, M. G., Atherton, K., Patai, E. Z., and Nobre, A. C. (2012), 'Long-Term Memory Prepares Neural Activity for Perception', Proceedings of the National Academy of the Sciences, 109: 360–7.
Stratton-Lake, P. (2016), 'Intuition, Self-Evidence, and Understanding', in R. Shafer-Landau (ed.), Oxford Studies in Metaethics, vol. 11 (Oxford: Oxford University Press), 28-44.
Strawson, P. F. (1966), 'Aesthetic Appraisal and Works of Art', in Strawson, Freedom and Resentment (London: Methuen), 196–207.
Sturgeon, N. (2002), 'Ethical Intuitionism and Ethical Naturalism', in P. Stratton-Lake (ed.), Ethical Intuitionism: Re-Evaluations (Oxford: Clarendon Press), 184–211.
Summerfield, C., and Egner, T. (2009), 'Expectation (and Attention) in Visual Cognition', Trends in Cognitive Sciences, 13/9: 403–11.
Swinburne, R. (2015), 'Necessary Moral Principles', Journal of the American Philosophical Association, 1/4: 620.
Tappolet, C. (2011), 'Values and Emotions: Neo-Sentimentalism's Prospects', in C. Bagnoli (ed.), Morality and the Emotions (Oxford: Oxford University Press), 117–34.

Tappolet, C. (2012), 'Emotions, Perceptions, and Emotional Illusions', in C. Clotilde (ed.), *Perceptual Illusions: Philosophical and Psychological Essays* (Houndmills: Palgrave Macmillan), 207–24.
Tenenbaum, S. (2007), *Appearances of the Good: An Essay on the Nature of Practical Reason* (New York: Cambridge University Press).
Thomas, A. (2005), 'Reasonable Partiality and the Personal Point of View', *Ethical Theory and Moral Practice*, 8: 25–43.
Thomas, A. (2006), *Value and Context* (Oxford: Oxford University Press).
Thomas, A. (2012), 'Nietzsche and Moral Fictionalism', in C. Janaway and S. Robertson (eds.), *Nietzsche, Naturalism and Normativity* (Oxford: Oxford University Press), 133–59.
Thompson, B. J. (2009), 'Senses for Senses', *Australasian Journal of Philosophy*, 87: 99–117.
Thoreau, H. D. (1897), *Walden*, vol. 1 (Boston and New York: Houghton, Mifflin & Company).
Tolstoy, L. (1978), *War and Peace*, trans. Rosemary Edmonds (London: Penguin Classics).
Trawalter, S., Hoffman, K. M., and Waytz, A. (2012), 'Racial Bias in Perceptions of Others' Pain', *PLoS ONE* 7/11: e48546. doi:10.1371/journal.pone.0048546.
Tucker, C. (2013) (ed.), *Seemings and Justification* (Oxford: Oxford University Press).
Tucker, T. (2010), 'Why Open-Minded People Should Endorse Dogmatism', *Philosophical Perspectives*, 24: 529–45.
Turnbull, O. H., Evans, C. E., Bunce, A., Carzolio, B., and O'Connor, J. (2005), 'Emotion-Based Learning and Central Executive Resources: An Investigation of Intuition and the Iowa Gambling Task', *Brain and Cognition*, 57: 244–7.
Tversky, A., and Kahneman, D. (1974), 'Judgment Under Uncertainty: Heuristics and Biases', *Science*, 185: 1124–31.
Tye, M. (1995), *Ten Problems of Consciousness: A Representational Theory of the Phenomenal Mind* (Cambridge, MA: MIT Press).
Tye, M. (2000), *Consciousness, Color, and Content* (Cambridge, MA: MIT Press).
Vaes, J., Paladino, P., and Puvia, E. (2011), 'Are Sexualized Women Complete Human Beings? Why Men and Women Dehumanize Sexually Objectified Women', *European Journal of Social Psychology*, 41: 774–85.
Vance, J. (2014), 'Emotion and the New Epistemic Challenge from Cognitive Penetrability', *Philosophical Studies*, 169: 257–83.
Van Gulick, R. (1994), 'Deficit Studies and the Function of Phenomenal Consciousness', in Van Gulick, *Philosophical Psychopathology* (Cambridge, MA: MIT Press), 25–49.
van Ulzen, N. R., Semin, G. R., Oudejans, R., and Beek, P. (2008), 'Affective Stimulus Properties Influence Size Perception and the Ebbinghaus Illusion', *Psychological Research*, 72: 304–10.
Väyrynen, P. (2008a), 'Some Good and Bad News for Ethical Intuitionism', *Philosophical Quarterly*, 58/232: 489–511.
Väyrynen, P. (2008b), 'Usable Moral Principles', in M. Norris Lance, M. Potrč, and V. Strahovnik (eds.), *Challenging Moral Particularism* (London: Routledge), 75–106.
Väyrynen, P. (2009), Commentary on 'Moral Perception and Moral Knowledge', *Pacific Division of the American Philosophical Association*, MS.
Väyrynen, P. (2011), 'Thick Concepts and Variability', *Philosopher's Imprint* 11/1: 1–17.
Väyrynen, P. (2013), *The Lewd, the Rude and the Nasty: A Study of Thick Concepts in Ethics* (New York: Oxford University Press).
Väyrynen, P. (2014a), 'Shapelessness in Context', *Noûs*, 48: 573–93.
Väyrynen, P. (2014b), 'Essential Contestability and Evaluation', *Australasian Journal of Philosophy*, 92/3: 471–88.
Velleman, J. D. (1992), 'The Guise of the Good', *Noûs*, 26/1: 3–26.

Viki, G. T., Winchester, L., Titshall, L., Chisango, T., Pina, A., and Russell, R. (2006), 'Beyond Secondary Emotions: The Infrahumanization of Outgroups Using Human-Related and Animal-Related Words', *Social Cognition*, 24: 753–75.

Vogel, J. (2008), 'Epistemic Bootstrapping', *Journal of Philosophy*, 105/9: 518–39.

Vogt, S., and Magnussen, S. (2007), 'Expertise in Pictorial Perception: Eye-Movement Patterns and Visual Memory in Artists and Laymen', *Perception*, 36/1: 91–100.

Wade, L. (2009a), 'Women as Items for Conspicuous Consumption', *Sociological Images*, 6 April, http://thesocietypages.org/socimages/2009/04/06/women-as-items-for-conspicuous-consumption/.

Wade, L. (2009b), 'Black Woman Posed as and among Animals (NSFW)', *Sociological Images*, 19 August, http://thesocietypages.org/socimages/2009/08/19/another-photoshoot-places-a-black-woman-among-animals/.

Wade, L. (2011), 'Line 'Em Up: A Visual Trope', *Sociological Images*, 28 October, http://thesocietypages.org/socimages/2011/10/28/line-em-up-a-visual-trope/.

Waldman, K. (2014), 'Science Has a Gender Problem: *Science* Just Made It Much Worse', *Slate* magazine, 17 July, http://www.slate.com/blogs/xx_factor/2014/07/17/science_cover_the_magazine_s_aids_and_hiv_issue_is_sexist_and_transphobic.html.

Walton, K. L. (1970), 'Categories of Art', *Philosophical Review* 79/3: 334–67.

Walton, K. L. (1978), 'Fearing Fictions', *Journal of Philosophy*, 75: 5–27.

Walton, K. L. (1984), 'Transparent Pictures: On the Nature of Photographic Realism', *Critical Inquiry*, 11: 246–77.

Walton, K. L. (1990), *Mimesis as Make-Believe: On the Foundations of the Representational Arts* (Cambridge, MA: Harvard University Press).

Walton, K. L. (2008), 'Seeing-In and Seeing Fictionally', in Walton, *Marvelous Images: On Value and the Arts* (Oxford: Oxford University Press), 133–42.

Watkins, M., and Jolley, K. D. (2002), 'Pollyanna Realism: Moral Perception and Moral Properties', *Australasian Journal of Philosophy*, 80: 75–85.

Watson, G. (1975), 'Free Agency', *Journal of Philosophy*, 72/8: 205–20.

Waugh, E. (1962), *Brideshead Revisited*, (Harmondsworth: Penguin).

Weber, M. (1930/2002), *Protestant Ethic and the Spirit of Capitalism*, trans. Peter Baer and Gordon C. Wells (London: Penguin Books).

Werner, P. (2016), 'Moral Perception and the Contents of Experience', *Journal of Moral Philosophy*, 13/3: 294–317.

Wiggins, D. (1989), *Needs, Values and Truth: Essays in the Philosophy of Value* (3rd edn., Oxford: Clarendon Press).

Williams, B. (1979), *Ethics and the Limits of Philosophy* (London, Penguin).

Williams, B. (1985), *Ethics and the Limits of Philosophy* (London: Fontana).

Williams, B. (1995), 'What Does Intuitionism Imply?', in Williams, *Making Sense of Humanity* (Cambridge: Cambridge University Press), 182–91.

Williamson, T. (2000), *Knowledge and Its Limits* (Oxford: Oxford University Press).

Wilkerson, T. E. (1973), 'Seeing-As', *Mind*, 82/328: 481–96.

Wittgenstein, L. (1953/2009), *Philosophical Investigations*, trans. G. E. M. Anscombe, 4th edn., ed. P. M. S. Hacker and J. Schulte (London: Wiley-Blackwell, 2009).

Wittgenstein, L. (1963), *Philosophical Investigations*, trans. G. E. M. Anscombe (2nd edn., Oxford: Blackwell Publishers) [paperback 3rd edn., 1968].

Wittgenstein, L. (1998), *Remarks on the Philosophy of Psychology*, ed. G. E. M. Anscombe, G. H. von Wright and Michael Biggs; trans. G. E. M. Anscombe (reissued 1st edn., Oxford: Blackwell).

Witzel, C., Valkova, H., Hansen, T., and Gegenfurtner, K. (2011), 'Object Knowledge Modulates Colour Appearance', *i-Perception*, 2: 13–49.

Wollheim, R. (1980a), *Art and Its Objects* (Cambridge: Cambridge University Press).
Wollheim, R. (1980b), 'Seeing-As, Seeing-In, and Pictorial Representation', in Wollheim, *Art and Its Objects* (2nd edn., Cambridge: Cambridge University Press, 1980), 205–26.
Wollheim, R. (1987), *Painting as an Art* (London: Thames and Hudson).
Wollheim, R. (1991), 'A Note on *Mimesis as Make-Believe*', *Philosophy and Phenomenological Research*, 51/2: 401–6.
Wollheim, R. (1998), 'On Pictorial Representation', *Journal of Aesthetics and Art Criticism*, 56/3: 217–26.
Wright, J. (2007), 'The Role of Perception in Mature Moral Agency', in J. J. Wisnewski (ed.), *Moral Perception* (Newcastle: Cambridge Scholars Publishing), 1–24.
Wu, W. (2013), 'Visual Spatial Constancy and Modularity: Does Intention Penetrate Vision?', *Philosophical Studies*, 165: 647–69.
Yablo, S. (1993), 'Is Conceivability a Guide to Possibility?', *Philosophy and Phenomenological Research*, 53: 1–42.
Zagzebski, L. T. (1996), *Virtues of the Mind* (Cambridge: Cambridge University Press).
Zangwill, N. (2008), 'Science and Ethics: Demarcation, Holism and Logical Consequences', *European Journal of Philosophy*, 18: 126–38.
Zimmerman, M. (2001), *The Nature of Intrinsic Value* (Lanham, MD: Rowman and Littlefield).

Index

absences 11, 129, 143–51, 147n7, 149n10, 151, 154n23, 155–7
affordance 11, 137n40, 143
a priori 61n4, 65, 68, 75, 77, 96, 100, 168, 195, 201n6, 240–1, 254
Aristotelian/ism 66, 259–60
Aristotle 2, 218n71
Audi, Robert 3, 5, 8, 8n35, 8n36, 10, 12, 12n47, 58n1, 61n4, 70, 71n19, 71n20, 73, 74n27, 83, 83n7, 84, 84n10, 93n35, 109n1, 109n4, 112n13, 113n17, 114n18, 115n23, 120, 161n1, 178n28, 179, 200n1, 200n3, 204, 204n22, 205, 205n23, 205n24, 205n25, 205n26, 205n28, 206, 206n30, 206n31, 206n32, 206n33, 207, 207n35, 207n36, 207n38, 207n39, 211, 211n52, 211n53, 212, 214, 214n61, 215n63, 288n20

Bergqvist, Anna 2n8, 2n12, 4, 7, 9, 14, 15, 41n44, 46n22, 108n66, 128n63, 199n38, 218n72, 258n1, 262n20, 276n70, 277n76, 294n41

cognitive penetration 9, 10, 13–14, 29n24, 37, 38n36, 39, 39n40, 40, 73–5, 94, 111, 111n7, 111n8, 111n9, 114, 114n20, 118, 119, 121, 122n45, 122n46, 123, 125n54, 126, 137n38, 139n42, 141n51, 142, 149n10, 154, 189, 196–8, 224–5, 263–5
cognitivism 59n2, 243, 270, 276, 279
constitutivism 14, 260, 262, 262n21, 263, 269–70, 272
Contrast Argument 6–7, 7n32, 7n34, 24–30, 36, 44–8, 115–18, 122n46, 123, 127–8, 205n25
Cowan, Robert 3, 3n22, 5, 9, 9n38, 13, 14n52, 41n44, 65n11, 73n24, 77n28, 77n29, 81n2, 108n66, 109n1, 110n5, 114n20, 114n21, 115n23, 118n32, 119n34, 120n41, 121n44, 122n45, 122n47, 125n54, 127n61, 128n63, 182n34, 199n38, 200n3, 203n15, 204n19, 206n31, 207n37, 218n72, 219n1, 219n2, 220n7, 231n43, 235n47, 281n87, 288n21, 294n41

desire 3, 5, 9, 11–15, 44, 73–4, 100, 103–6, 111, 122–3, 147–52, 148n8, 148n9, 154–6, 189, 197, 203, 207n38, 215, 218, 220n5, 225, 242–51, 242n2, 243n3, 250n10, 257, 261, 264, 282–94, 282n1, 289n31, 304

emotion 2, 3, 5, 8n35, 9, 10, 12–15, 45–6, 46n19, 48n27, 59, 63, 67–9, 73, 79, 98, 103–5, 112–14, 113n14, 114n20, 116–17, 116n28, 119, 119n34, 119n37, 121, 122n46, 123, 125–7, 128n62, 145–6, 151n12, 157–8, 194n30, 198, 200, 204n21, 206, 207n38, 208n44, 209–12, 212n55, 212n57, 218, 219–24, 220n4, 220n5, 220n9, 221n13, 226–36, 227n33, 228n35, 229n36, 231n42, 231n43, 242, 243n3, 288–91, 299, 302n27, 305
empty, empty space 10, 129–42, 132n19, 135n27, 136n32, 136n35, 141n49, 145, 150–1
error theory/ist/ism 4, 178, 239–40
expressivism/st 15, 285–8, 287n14, 288n28

Farennikova, Anya 3, 10, 11, 146n5, 149n10, 150n11, 154n23

gestalt 7, 15, 23, 26n18, 28–30, 28n22, 34–6, 40–1, 269, 301, 303, 306

high-level content/properties 2, 6–8, 20, 22n3, 24, 26–8, 30, 32–4, 42–4, 42n2, 49–50, 50n34, 56–7, 65, 74, 76, 106, 111, 114–16, 119n34, 121–2, 171–2, 175–6, 188, 188n12, 190–1, 194–5, 196n33, 197, 200–1, 200n3, 200n4, 203–4, 204n18, 204n20, 204n21, 204n22, 205n25, 205n26, 205n29, 206n31, 207–11, 207n38, 208n44, 209n47, 209n48, 213–18, 213n58, 213n59, 214n61, 216n67
Hume, David 2, 19, 21n2, 80n1, 194, 194n28, 194n29, 194n30, 195, 290n33, 291n34
Humean 243, 285–6, 293

imagination/imaginative episode 10, 46, 71, 87, 98, 102, 106, 121, 131, 135–6, 135n27, 136n33, 138, 139, 142, 207n39, 208n42, 209n47, 211n51, 207–14, 216, 228–9, 291
inference 4, 7, 22, 24, 64n7, 69–71, 71n20, 72, 77, 79, 104, 112, 113n15, 118–20, 119n36, 122, 123n49, 127n60, 145, 162–7, 163n6, 169, 169n13, 170n17, 176–9, 180n31, 187, 190, 190n17, 195–6, 225–6, 230
inferential 4, 11, 67, 70–1, 75, 77, 162–8, 168n7, 169, 169n13, 176–7, 179–81, 180n31, 186, 189–90, 192–3, 196, 226, 229–30
intentionalism/ist 4n23, 26n18, 27n19, 43, 55

intuition 12, 21, 40, 45, 48n29, 49, 73, 79, 87, 115, 117n31, 206, 206n33, 211, 212, 215, 220, 225, 229, 241, 258, 288–90

Kant, Immanuel 19, 270
Kantian 259

Lenman, James 4, 15, 281n87, 282n1, 282n2, 284n6, 286n11, 288n24, 288n26, 289n30
Logue, Heather 3, 6, 7, 7n34, 8, 9, 11, 45n17, 49n32, 55n41, 56n44, 108n66, 115n24, 115n26, 127n60, 128n63
Lyons, Jack 3, 4n25, 5, 8, 9, 12, 13, 48n26, 87n18, 88n25, 186n7, 187n8, 188n12, 189n14, 189n15, 190n17, 190n18, 190n19, 192n23, 192n24, 192n25, 193n27, 196n35, 224n24

Macpherson, Fiona 3n18, 10n41, 26n16, 26n18, 37n34, 55n40, 73n24, 139n42, 149n10, 189n15, 199n38, 218n72, 281n87
McDowell, John 2, 2n10, 42n5, 83, 83n5, 110n6, 178n28, 260, 260n13, 262, 264, 266n28, 266n29, 268n39, 274, 274n65, 279
McGrath, Sarah 3, 11, 12, 84, 84n9, 109n1, 111n10, 113n15, 114n21, 161n1, 181n33, 207n40, 208n46, 215n61, 288n26
metaphysical naturalism/st 15, 76, 220, 287–8, 288n22
metaphysical non-naturalism/st 258, 261–2, 280
Milona, Michael 3, 5, 12, 12n47, 13, 203n14, 203n16, 207n37, 236n48, 262n21, 269n46, 273n62, 281n87
Moore, G. E. 258, 260–1, 269n46, 280
Murdoch, Iris 2, 2n11, 2n12, 14, 15, 109n1, 110n6, 112n12, 259, 259n4, 260, 260n10, 262–5, 265n26, 265n28, 266, 266n29, 266n31, 267, 268, 269, 269n46, 270, 272–4, 274n66, 275, 276, 279–80

Naïve Realism 43, 75
natural kind properties 21, 27n21, 30, 31, 33, 33n30, 34, 36, 40, 42n2, 70, 84–5, 111, 205n25, 214
natural properties 59, 76–7, 202
non-cognitivism/t 59, 76, 243
non-inferential 4–6, 11–14, 63, 69–71, 75–7, 163, 176, 178, 180, 191, 209, 223n20, 290
non-natural properties 76, 288
Noordhof, Paul 3, 5, 6, 8, 8n36, 9, 9n37, 12, 13, 81n3, 87n21, 98n49, 100n56, 105n63, 107n64, 107n65

Oddie, Graham 3n19, 4, 5, 5n26, 14, 200n1, 200n5, 215n62, 218n71, 220n5, 242n2, 243n4, 243n5, 244n6, 245n8, 247n9, 254n17, 283n4, 288n17, 288n22, 289n31, 291n36

pain 3, 5, 9, 9n37, 10, 12, 53–4, 64, 81, 84, 98–103, 105, 107, 161, 164–5, 172, 209, 240–1, 244, 246–8, 251, 305n46
painting 19–20, 23–4, 31, 53, 58, 62, 75, 98, 129–30, 135–6, 136n32, 139–41, 141n49, 142, 144, 171, 171n19, 173, 175, 251, 290
perspectival 14, 246, 257, 260, 262–3, 270–3, 275, 275n68, 279–80
Pettersson, Mikael 2n15, 3, 9, 10
Platonism/ic 14, 55, 56, 260, 262, 265n28, 272–3, 280, 283n4
Projectivism 151n12, 157, 240, 274

Quasi-Realism/st 15, 274, 286, 288n28, 292–3

Rationalism 76–7, 239
Realism/st 15, 76, 106, 184, 199, 260, 262, 265n28, 280, 288, 290, 293
Relationalism/ist 4n23, 82, 93
Representationalism/ist 4n23, 20, 27n19, 88, 96, 111
response-dependence 7, 9, 49n30, 54, 81, 95–9, 106, 157–8

seeing-as 15, 25–7, 27n20, 28n22, 30–1, 36–41, 39n40, 67, 133n21, 297, 300–9, 301n26, 302n27, 305n46
seeing-in 2, 10, 129–36, 131n10, 131n16, 132n17, 132n19, 133n21, 135n27, 138, 140–2
seeing-that 4, 6, 10, 11, 43, 66, 72, 94, 133n19, 134, 135, 135n27, 136, 138, 204
seemings 5, 5n29, 8, 12, 45n18, 66–7, 72–3, 87–8, 95, 186–7, 188n12, 190–3, 190n19, 192n23, 192n25, 199, 224n23, 225–6, 226n32, 229–30, 241–2, 241n1, 257, 289
sensory 3, 5, 8–9, 19, 21, 23n8, 24, 26–7, 29–30, 34, 34n31, 36–40, 43, 59, 62, 64, 72, 74, 81, 83–95, 98, 107, 114, 132, 143, 145, 147n7, 149, 153–4, 185, 197, 208, 208n42, 209n47, 216–17, 219, 224, 226, 229, 231, 288
Sentimentalism/st (concepts and properties) 3, 13, 14, 80, 151n12, 157, 220
Sentimentalism (epistemic) 219–24, 220n4, 220n8, 221n13, 229, 231n43, 232, 234–6
Sibley, Frank 1, 1n5, 2, 19, 19n1, 21n2, 22n4, 47n24, 47n25, 49n30, 268, 268n40, 268n41, 268n43
Siegel, Susanna 2n17, 3n18, 6, 6n31, 22n3, 23n8, 24, 24n10, 25, 27n19, 28n22, 31n28, 37n34, 41, 41n43, 42n2, 42n3, 43, 43n8, 44, 44n13, 44n14, 45, 45n18, 73n24, 82, 82n4, 84, 85, 85n11, 85n12, 86n15, 86n16, 94n37, 110n6, 111n7, 111n8, 111n9, 115n26, 118n33, 127n61, 178, 188n11, 188n12, 188n13, 203n17, 204n20, 205n25, 205n26, 218n72, 225n27, 264, 264n23, 264n24, 265, 265n25, 278, 278n82, 278n84, 279n85, 281n87
Stock, Kathleen 4, 15, 296n10

Stokes, Dustin 3, 5, 6, 7, 9, 9n40, 13, 24n12, 29n24, 37n34, 38n36, 46n20, 74n25, 74n26, 111n7, 123n50, 139n42, 141n51, 189n15, 199n38
sui generis 2–3, 5, 7, 10, 12, 42n1, 42n6, 43, 46n21, 131, 227

taste 2, 20, 21n2, 42, 47, 120, 120n40, 146, 279, 289–90

Väyrynen, Pekka 2n16, 3, 5, 6, 7, 7n33, 7n34, 8n35, 9, 12n47, 13, 70, 70n17, 70n18, 109n2, 113n15, 120n39, 163n6, 180n31, 182n34, 201n6, 204n22, 218n72, 262n19, 269n45, 277, 277n76, 277n77, 278n78, 278n78

vision 2, 6, 8, 21, 22n3, 24, 28, 31, 34–6, 43, 50–2, 59, 65, 71, 73, 90, 130, 148n9, 184, 204, 207, 259, 261–3, 265–7, 266n29, 269–73, 269n46, 275–6, 280

Wittgenstein, Ludwig 25, 25n13, 38, 38n35, 266n28, 268, 268n38, 268n39, 269, 274, 276–7, 301n26
Wollheim, Richard 2, 2n14, 129n1, 130, 130n3, 130n4, 130n5, 130n7, 130n8, 130n9, 131, 131n10, 131n13, 133, 133n20, 133n21, 133n22, 134, 134n23, 135, 135n28, 135n29, 135n30, 138, 208n41